DATE DUE

AP2-99			

BURN THIS HOUSE

BURN THIS HOUSE

The Making and Unmaking of Yugoslavia

Jasminka Udovički & James Ridgeway, editors

DUKE UNIVERSITY PRESS *Durham & London 1997*

© 1997 Duke University Press   All rights reserved
Printed in the United States of America on acid-free paper ⊗
Typeset in Trump Mediaeval by Tseng Information Systems, Inc.
Library of Congress Cataloging-in-Publication Data appear on
the last printed page of this book.
Portions of this book were previously published in *Yugoslavia's
Ethnic Nightmare: The Inside Story of Europe's Unfolding Ordeal,*
edited by Jasminka Udovički and James Ridgeway (New York:
Lawrence Hill Books, 1995). All of the material previously published
has been revised and updated for this volume.

For D, D, D, and K. And for Jovan Divjak.

For D, D, D, and K. And for Jovan Divjak.

CONTENTS

PREFACE

This book grew out of a reporting trip Jasminka Udovički and I made with *Village Voice* photographer Sylvia Plachy to former Yugoslavia in 1992. Like *Yugoslavia's Ethnic Nightmare: The Inside Story of Europe's Unfolding Ordeal*, which we published in 1995, the present book—incorporating aspects of the previous work—discusses the history of the Yugoslavs and the roots of the 1991–95 war from the point of view of journalists, historians, and former diplomats still living in the region.

The understanding of the war among the Western public was shaped by the pronouncements of Western politicians and the writing of Western journalists—of whom far too many stubbornly stuck to their claim that at the root of the war lay ancient Balkan hatreds. With this kind of interpretation, the term *Balkanization* was reintroduced into the vernacular, implying incessant feuding and fragmentation.

The authors of this book argue differently. Providing a historical analysis of a broad range of subjects—cultural, political, and economic—the contributors project an infinitely more complex picture of the ethnic dynamics in the region and, ultimately, of the causes of war.

The book begins with the sixth century, when the South Slavs settled the Balkan peninsula, and follows the origins, development, and fall of their medieval states, from the ninth century to the fourteenth. The partition of the Balkans between the Ottomans and the Hapsburgs that followed divided its population—peoples of the same language and origin—forcing them to fight against each other in the armies of their conquerors. Yet in the nineteenth century, despite the divisions imposed by the foreign powers, the movement for the unification of all South Slavs emerged, laying the ground for the twentieth-century creation of Yugoslavia.

The writers in this volume see the roots of ultranationalism that destroyed Yugoslavia not in some insidious historical pattern of ethnic hatreds and conflagration, but rather in the quite specific set of circumstances that crystallized following the death of Marshal Tito in 1980. Among those, three were of utmost importance: the leadership vacuum; the deep economic crisis; and the absence of liberal political traditions, which had much to do with the preceding waves of foreign conquest. To explain the particular character of the Yugoslavian crisis, the authors discuss Tito's legacy and the experience the Yugoslavs had with socialism. Particular attention is paid to the 1980–90 decade of political and moral disillusionment and economic downfall. At the end of that period, Slobodan Milošević and Franjo Tudjman, relying heavily on the use of television, carried out their fatal nationalistic programs, deeply destabilizing the ethnic balance and destroying the Titoist pledge to uphold "brotherhood and unity."

In the approaching war, the Yugoslav People's Army played a significant part. Its role is examined in a separate chapter. The authors argue that the wars in Croatia and Bosnia, presented in detail, did not start out as ethnic wars, and that the extreme brutality witnessed by the world was not inherent in the Balkan—or the Serbian—national character. On the contrary, the assumption of some unfathomable ethnic conflict surfacing of its own momentum provided the rationale for the international community to stay on the outside while attempting to manage the crisis.

Finally, this book offers valuable insight into the activity since 1991 of the forces of the non-nationalist opposition and the independent media in Serbia and Croatia—an aspect of the war years that remained largely unreported in the United States. Without the commitment and the moral integrity of non-nationalist journalists working for the independent media in Split, Belgrade, Zagreb, and Sarajevo—journalists whose eyewitness reports and analysis supply a wealth of hard data for the story of Yugoslavia's ruin—a good part of this book could not have been written.

James Ridgeway

Introduction

Jasminka Udovički

The fall of Yugoslavia was brought about by brutal military force, but the energy needed to utterly dismantle the country was supplied by political ethno-kitsch. Beginning in 1987, and throughout the prewar years, ethno-kitsch was everywhere in Serbia: at seemingly spontaneous yet officially orchestrated mass rallies; in the new "turbo-folk" rock flooding the airwaves; in the slogans chanted by fans of the favorite national football club, Crvena Zvezda; in public statements by some well-known writers, lawyers, actors, painters, generals, academicians, and journalists; even in the TV ads of the up-and-coming, privately owned bank of the Karić Brothers.

At the root of the new wave of ethno-kitsch was a gradually growing perception that Serbian people have been wronged and were hated—entirely undeservedly—by other ethnic groups in former Yugoslavia; that their unsparing sacrifice for the common good of all South Slavs—in the Balkan Wars of 1912–13, in World War I, and again in World War II—met with little recognition and less appreciation; that instead of respect, they encountered hostility. "We do not hate them—*they* hate us!" was a comment one heard on the streets and in cafés, expressed with vehemence, dismay, and self-righteousness.

A xenophobic sense of isolation grew steadily following the emergence, in 1987, of Slobodan Milošević on the national scene. The television and print media that Milošević took over soon after his ascent to power encouraged the conviction that through no fault of their own Serbs had been reduced to the status of "the Jews of the Balkans." Patriotic charge, resulting from the feeling of a deep national grievance, found its expression in the newspeak, drawn from an anachronistic reservoir of archetypal national vernacular. Its focus was the victimization of Serbian people, not hatred of others. Its claims were for justice and fairness. It warned of an uncertain, haunting future.[1]

Former Yugoslavia. Courtesy of Harvard College Library.

Soon rhymed verse, expressing in condensed, quotable form the pre-vailing grievances and fears, invaded public space. The verse imitated traditional folk poetry, which inevitably fictionalized the content of mes-sages.[2] One might have expected that fictionalization would have weak-ened the content, lending it the echo of myth. Instead, nationalistic pathos soared. In 1987, Serbs were no longer talking about the ongoing emigration of Serb peasants from Kosovo as a displacement or even as exodus; that emigration was now "genocide" against the Serbian people. New journals controlled by the regime juxtaposed to the alleged genocide the heroic struggle of the Serb nation against the Turks throughout the five hundred years of their domination. Gypsy bands, playing around din-ner tables at restaurants, sounded old nostalgic patriotic songs. Officially sponsored public events often featured old symbols, rituals, uniforms, and folk costumes from previous eras. Favorite actors read medieval epic poetry on television. And in the center of Belgrade, on the hill above the Slavija Square, the largest Orthodox basilica was under construction, its cupola visible from miles away.

All this was aimed at placing the cult of the Serbian people at center stage.[3] Eventually and imperceptibly, the new Volk mythology merged the arcane notion of "people's spirit" (*duh naroda*) with the particular interests of the advocates of war.

In Croatia an attempt to rally the masses around alleged national grievances began in early 1970. Matica Hrvatska, the leading institution for the advancement of Croatian culture, backed a movement comprised largely of students and intellectuals, as well as some party leaders, decrying the republic's economic and cultural exploitation by the federation.[4] Their outcry—that Belgrade export firms drained Croatian revenue, that Serbs had penetrated the Croatian hotel industry, and that an effort was under way to Serbianize the Croatian language—convinced many people not only that they were "being exploited, but exploited as Croats."[5] To buttress their appeal, Croats, like Serbs, reached deep into their past and mythologized their political discourse. But they avoided folkloric woe. Summoning an aristocratic mythos, Croats evoked their early medieval kings—Tomislav from the tenth century, Krešimir and Zvonimir from the eleventh—as paleo-emblems of Croatian statehood. Some eighteen years later, in the late 1980s, as if the archaic past were somehow a part of the everyday present, the myth of "a thousand-year dream of independence" gripped the Croatian imagination.

Indeed, we had altogether too much past.[6]

In a culture with a solid public realm independent of the state, the mass culture of ethno-kitsch—one hopes—would have encountered a resilient web of democratic institutions. That web did not exist in the former Yugoslavia. Western lifestyle, by contrast, did. It was evident in the streets of all larger cities and in the habits, ambitions, and tastes of the middle class. During the early and mid-eighties a liberal spirit, discouraged in its genuine expression during Tito's period—yet even so, much more resonant in Yugoslavia than anywhere in Eastern Europe—had a chance at last to flourish, particularly in Belgrade, which had always been the center of dissident activity, and in Ljubljana as well.

Still, in the 1980s as before, the broad masses viewed politics not as a culture of democratic debate but, above all, as force and as power. During Tito's period, the concept of human rights, while encoded in the constitution, was officially treated as a vehicle for disloyalty, something suspect and contrary to the progressive spirit of socialism. Authorities viewed those who insisted on the protection of human rights with mistrust and often accused them of the "abuse of human rights."[7]

This practice served to blur the distinction between the state and society, to discredit the civil sphere, to preserve the pattern of political paternalism, and to uphold the figure of the leader as a protector of the people and the "father of the nation."

In the late 1980s, the mass culture of ethno-kitsch was particularly aggressive in promoting the image of Slobodan Milošević as that kind of national leader.[8] Paradoxically, by advancing a theory of historical Serbian victimhood to explain the current economic and social crisis, some leading Serbian intellectuals participated in the same anti-intellectual, reactionary anti-Yugoslavism that permeated ethno-kitsch.[9]

The late-twentieth-century primitive anti-Yugoslavism contrasted sharply with the refined pan-Slavism, also called Yugoslavism, of the nineteenth century.[10] Ljudevit Gaj, the Croat who launched the pan-Slavic Illyrian movement in the 1830s, studied in Buda and Graz, and was supported by Janko Drašković, an educated member of Croatian high nobility. The formidable Josip Juraj Strossmayer, at the age of thirty-four the bishop of Djakovo's ancient see, was an aesthete who collected Italian paintings and spoke French, Italian, and German in addition to his native Croatian—yet maintained he could express himself best, most clearly, in Latin.[11] Strossmayer devoted most of his life and almost all his sizable fortune to bringing to life the idea of South Slav unification. Other intellectuals of the time favoring the South Slav unification—including not only the Croatian historian Franjo Rački but also the Serbian linguist Vuk Stefanovic Karadžić and his disciple, the young philologist and grammarian Djuro Daničić, among others—all benefited from Strossmayer's generosity, which afforded them leisure time for intellectual work. Yugoslavism of the nineteenth century appealed to the noble impulse for the community of peoples with a common origin and speaking the dialects of the same language, and it carried within itself the seeds of enlightened liberalism.

Still, the affair with liberalism in South Slav history remained semi-platonic and fugitive. The concrete historical circumstances of the nineteenth-century Balkans demanded that progressive political energies focus on overthrowing Turkish and Austro-Hungarian domination. Within the framework of national liberation, pan-Slavism offered a common purpose and a basis for political cohesion.[12] Yet precisely because the bottom-line issue in the Balkans was foreign domination—and not the overthrow, as in Western Europe, of the arbitrary authority of the state and church in favor of a free and independent individual—the nineteenth-century struggle in the Balkans remained, in geopolitical terms, a premodern struggle.

Its results were not negligible. Serbia contributed significantly to the collapse of the Ottoman Empire and, together with the Allied powers, to the subsequent collapse of the dual monarchy. But the society that emerged after the centuries-long foreign hegemony had been overthrown lacked a public sphere of autonomous citizens free from the state and constitutionally protected as sovereign. Serbia was indeed the military Piedmont of the Balkans and had paid a disproportionately higher price for the freedom from foreign rule than had any other South Slav nation. Yet, despite the work of enlightened socialists and social democrats—Svetozar Marković, Dimitrije Tucović, Jovan Cvijić, Jovan Skerlić, Stojan Novaković, Slobodan Jovanović—Serbia never became a civilizational precursor.[13]

The legacy of the past, the isolation under the Ottomans for almost five hundred years from the currents that had shaped modern Europe—the Renaissance, the Reformation, the Enlightenment, the industrial revolution—weighed heavily on Serbia's future and the future of South Slavs in general. The Serbian Radical Party, which dominated political life between 1903 and 1914, remained deeply tied to the anti-individualist traditions of a paternalistic, predominantly agrarian society, mistrustful of the West, unwilling to contemplate political pluralism, and committed not to economic and political modernization, but to an isolationist nationalistic agenda with pronounced territorial ambitions.[14]

The Kingdom of Serbs, Croats, and Slovenes that came into being on the first day of December 1918 offered a new chance at modernization and democratization. But again the emergence of a civil society was prevented. The time had been too short to give rise to the genuinely democratic currents. Belgrade was determined to play the dominant role in the new union. The rudimentary, politically timid middle class was unprepared to demand universal rights as a guarantee, among other things, of the autonomy of its business.[15]

Tito's anti-Stalinism failed to bring about a genuine democratic transformation, even though as early as the 1960s the borders were completely opened, free travel allowed, and the influx of Western mass and high culture taken for granted. Marx was studied at the Belgrade Department of Philosophy from which I graduated, but so were Max Weber, Talcott Parsons, and Alvin W. Gouldner. This made all the difference—and no difference at all. Rather than encouraging the emergence of a robust public sphere, Titoism encouraged civic privatism. Politics remained the business of the politicians, committees, and secretariats. Their clumsy official titles, a mouthful to pronounce, alienated the common citizen. Collective political actions were organized from above, and the tradition of open public debate, independent political clubs, associations, ad hoc groups, and the free and fearless press never took hold.

In the late 1980s, nationalism prevailed in the former Yugoslavia, not because of internecine ethnic strife—the claims about age-old ethnic hatreds contradict and falsify historical reality—but because of the fragility of the civil society. The Yugoslav body politic did not recognize the tide of nationalism for what it was: a pernicious assault on the most basic norms of democratic life and a populist subterfuge engineered from above as a prelude to war. The public instead identified nationalism with patriotism. It dismissed the antiwar groups and their leaders as being indifferent to the national plight and national interest.[16] These groups, on the other hand, were inexperienced in building public trust and following, in organizing wider-scale dissident political activity, and in conducting day-to-day dissent. Their inexperience was a crucial factor in their failure to win over in greater numbers the silent opponents of nationalism and war. When in the winter of 1996–97 hundreds of thousands in Belgrade joined anti-Milošević demonstrations, the protesters were as astonished as the rest of the world at their capacity to fill the streets and to keep the high-energy but peaceful protest going for 113 days.

Throughout the war years, many in the European and the U.S. media and politics adopted the mythology of ethnic hatreds endemic to the Balkans, thereby echoing the claims of the ultranationalists.[17] But ethnic conflict in itself would not have destroyed Yugoslavia, as it will not destroy Belgium or Canada. What Yugoslavia, in contrast to the other two, lacked, are the institutions of civic and political life compatible with *conflict tolerance*, and able to effectively exercise it in time of crisis. Bosnians of all three ethnic groups, but particularly the Muslims, as well as the civilians of all other nationalities of former Yugoslavia, are the innocent victims of such mythology. This book advances the view that the war did not start as a people's war and that the passions that drove it were neither spontaneous nor imminent.

Jim Ridgeway and I met most of the contributors to this book, journalists and intellectuals, when we were sent on assignment to former Yugoslavia in 1992. Paradoxically perhaps, it was under the most extreme wartime circumstances that highly professional alternative free presses, working under dismal conditions and continuous threats, emerged in Serbia and in Croatia. Their circulation remained limited. Yet the weekly *Vreme*, the daily *Borba* (as of 1995 *Naša Borba*), and the monthly *Republika* in Serbia, as well as the weekly *Feral Tribune* in Croatia, have functioned all along not only as reliable sources of information but also as strong voices of moral conscience in times that literally tried the soul.

The journalists represented here, Milan Milošević, Ejub Štitkovac, Stipe Sikavica, and Ivan Torov—a Serb, a Muslim, a Croat, and a Macedonian—are joined by two Americans, Susan L. Woodward, Brookings Institution Senior Fellow in Foreign Policy Studies, and James Ridgeway, the Washington, D.C., correspondent for the *Village Voice*; a former foreign minister of Yugoslavia, Mirko Tepavac, who is of mixed Croatian-Serbian origin; the historian Branka Prpa-Jovanović and the writer Sven Balas, who are both Croats; and myself, a Serb. We were fortunate to have had a sharp critic in a person as knowledgeable about former Yugoslavia as Professor Sabrina Ramet. This book owes a great deal to her energetic commentary, her superb suggestions, and her hawk's eye for the minutest detail.

The book spans the history from the arrival of the South Slavs in the Balkans in the sixth century to the present day. Our intention was not to cover this history wall-to-wall. Rather, we tried to outline patterns that lay cradled in the confusing intersection of unfolding events and fates of six different peoples, living, for much of their history, not simply under different rulers but in different worlds, as it were—Europe and Asia. Their unification in the twentieth century carried the possibility of a national rebirth. Tracing the causes of the union's tragic collapse in the fury of an unimaginably cruel war occupies the major body of the book. The authors point to the deep economic crisis in the 1980s as the general background against which the Serbian and consequently Croatian political hierarchies played out their tightly controlled, strident, and shameless media campaigns, and, subsequently, the campaigns to clandestinely arm the civilian population for "self-defense." Nationalism, the contributors argue, functioned very effectively as an instrument for blocking progressive social and political change in former Yugoslavia at the crucial point of the breakdown of Communism in Europe.

Hatred surfaced much later—a consequence of the engineered turmoil, not its cause. In bringing about the war and sustaining its momentum, Slobodan Milošević and Franjo Tudjman were engaged almost from the beginning in a dance of perfect enemies. Through that uncanny partnership, the worst criminals, irregular combatants, and political and ethnic fanatics were enfranchised in the actions of the official armies. The communities where people had lived together as friends for generations were brought to the edge of utter inhumanity, and then pushed beyond the edge. Their future is now in their country's ruins.

NOTES

1   At the regional workshop The Balkans: Nationalism and Ethnicity (Hamilton College, Clinton, N.Y., 9 April 1994), Chris Gagnon argued that the important feature of the rhetoric of injustice was that it referred to the events that allegedly happened to the Serbs living outside Serbia proper—the Serbs "out there," whether in Kosovo, Croatia, or Bosnia. The claims were thus beyond the direct personal experience of the audience to whom the propaganda was primarily directed.

2   Because the claims were not intended to be verified through personal experience, they allowed for excessive hyperbole, half-truths, and outright fabrications. To enhance the rhymed message of victimhood and injustice, medieval historical figures, kings, and leaders were addressed as though they were present: "Obiliću, zmaju ljuti, Srbi su ti potisnuti" [Obilić, you ferocious hero, the Serbs, your kin, are being repressed]; "Sini jarko sunce sa Kosova, Ne damo te, zemljo Dušanova" [Kosovo sun, shine on us, we won't let down Dušan's land]; "Teku suze sa Kosova, To su deca Lazarova" [Tears roll from Kosovo, the tears of Lazar's children] (quoted in Ivan Čolović, *Bordel ratnika* [Beograd: Biblioteka XX vek, 1993], pp. 31–32).

3   The folk ethnologist Ivan Čolović argues that most messages used "the people" as the key word. Reference to the people served to lend authenticity to the messages. Above all, the people were the essential focus of each message—for example: "The people make the best judge"; "The people will take no more injustice"; "Do not be deaf to the voice of the people"; "You can't silence the people"; "The people have spoken, listen"; "Even the deaf hear the voice of the people" (Čolović, p. 26). For the analysis of war-propaganda folklorism see Čolović's monograph *Fudbal, huligani i rat* published in the Ogledi Edition of the Belgrade journal, *Republika* (June 1995).

4   The most comprehensive analysis of the Croatian movement can be found in Ante Čuvalo, *The Croatian National Movement, 1966–1972* (Boulder, Colo.: East Euro-

pean Monographs; distributed by Columbia University Press, 1990). A more condensed but sharp analysis is Sabrina Ramet, *Nationalism and Federalism in Yugoslavia, 1962–1991* (Bloomington: Indiana University Press, 1992).

5 Ramet, p. 98.

6 See Ranko Bugarski, *Govor skrivenih namera,* Ogledi Edition, *Republika* (June 1995), p. xii. See also Bugarski's *Jezik od rata do mira* (Beograd: Beogradski krug, 1994).

7 Vojin Dimitrijević suggests that Yugoslavia, in regard to human rights, was quite similar to other East European regimes. Those who used the constitutionally guaranteed right to petition state organs, for example, were marked, harassed, and scornfully called petitionists (see "Upotreba ljudskih prava," in *Raspad Jugoslavije, produžetak ili kraj agonije,* ed. Radmila Nakarada, Lidija Basta-Posavec, and Slobodan Samardžić [Beograd: Institut za Evropske studije, 1991], pp. 77, 79; see also Dimitrijević, "Medjunarodno zaštićéna ljudska prava u Jugoslaviji," *Anali pravnog fakulteta u Beogradu* [1987]: 715–27).

8 The songs dedicated to that purpose had a particularly naive, semiliterate, folkloric tone, reflecting open cultism: "Na nas, tvoju braću, sestre, ne prestaje hajka. Pomozi nam Slobo, brate, ti si nam i otac i majka" [The outcry against us, your brothers and sisters, does not cease. Help us, Slobo, brother, you are our father and our mother] (cited in Čolović, p. 33).

9 For a detailed analysis of the role of the intellectuals in construction of Serb nationalism see two monographs published in the Ogledi Edition of *Republika:* Drinka Gojković, *Trauma bez katarze* (June 1995), and Olivera Milosavljević, *Upotreba autoriteta nauke* (July 1995).

10 See Aleksa Djilas, "Krvavo pero: Savremeno antijugoslovenstvo i njegovi izvori," in Nakarada, Basta-Posavec, and Samardžić, pp. 102, 103. Djilas argues that the anti-Yugoslavism of Serbian intellectuals was not based on some new historical discoveries that would justify the egregious national grievances of the Serbs but on entirely unfounded fatalistic claims. "Anti-Yugoslavism seems to be antithetical to high aesthetic standards and incapable of expressing itself in any other form but through kitsch," says Djilas.

11 In 1884 Strossmayer donated three hundred paintings from his collection to the Southern Slav Academy in Zagreb, which he financed, hoping it would lend a common impulse to the intellectual unification movement among the Bulgars, Serbs, and Croats.

12 It must be noted that Yugoslavism was more popular among the Croatian intellectual elite than among the Serbs. Charles Jelavich argues that in the Serbia of the late nineteenth century the government, the church, the middle class, the political parties, the peasantry, and the army were united around the primary goal of resurrecting the Serbian state as it had been before the onslaught of the Ottoman Empire, and that Yugoslavism appeared to many to run at cross-purposes with that essential objective ("Serbian Nationalism and the Question of Union with Croatia in the Nineteenth Century," *Balkan Studies* 3 [1962]: 3).

13 See Branko Petranović, in Dragan Mojović, "Izolacija je smrt na duže staze," *Borba,* 24–25 April 1993, p. x.

14 Olga Popović-Obradović argues that the Radical Party—which in 1904 split into the old Radicals and Independent Radicals and, under the leadership of Nikola Pašić, led the country into war in 1912, 1913, and 1914—construed a "golden age" myth of its rule as the first democratic period of Serbian history. The author refutes the myth in "Zablude o 'zlatnom dobu,'" *Republika* (May 1995): 14–16.

15 Jürgen Habermas sees a strong link between the imperative independence of capitalist enterprise in the modern period and the emergence first of the reading public and then the political public—the civil public sphere—in eighteenth- and nineteenth-century Europe (*Strukturwandel der Öffentlichkeit* [Darmstadt und Neuwied: Herman Luchterhand Verlag GmbH, 1978], pp. 217–78).

16 Vesna Pešić, the chair of the Civic Association (the most outspoken antiwar group in Belgrade) and one of the leaders of the 1996–97 Zajedno coalition, identified the inability to acknowledge that others also had legitimate interests as the most insidious obstacle in her communication with nationalists (interview of Pěsic by author [summer 1992]).

17 Robert J. Donia and John V. A. Fine have argued that there was no basis to the claim of "collective ignorance" in the United States about former Yugoslavia. They note that Yugoslavia was open to foreign scholars, that some of the best studies in Yugoslav and Bosnian history were written in English, and that many Yugoslavs studied and taught at American universities, all amounting to a substantial amount of available information on former Yugoslavia (*Bosnia and Hercegovina: A Tradition Betrayed* [New York: Columbia University Press, 1994] pp. 2–3).

The Bonds and the Fault Lines
Jasminka Udovički

It took almost a century, from the emergence of the South Slavic unification movement in the early nineteenth century to the end of World War I, to create Yugoslavia. It took only a few years to destroy it. Visions of national liberation and modernization brought the South Slavs—the Yugo-Sloveni—excluding only the Bulgarians, together at last in 1919. Seventy years later, a retrograde, mythical, antimodern vision tore them apart.

At the heart of their history lay the experience of plural ethnic communities fought over for hundreds of years by competing foreign rulers: Roman popes, Venetian potentates, Byzantine emperors, Hungarian and Hapsburg kings, and Ottoman sultans. Their separate histories under domination from outside divided the South Slavs at the same time as it united them through a shared desire to rid themselves of their overlords.[1] After World War I the Yugoslav state was created on the basis of six Slavic peoples: Slovenes, Croats, Serbs, Montenegrins, Macedonians, and Muslims (although the latter three groups were at that time effectively counted as Serbs). The country's population also included two large non-Slav minorities: Albanians and Hungarians. The foundation of Yugoslavia followed the long, slow collapse of the decadent empires, resulting from the work of intellectuals and political leaders throughout the nineteenth century and the first two decades of the twentieth. The best of these leaders hoped the bonds of a common Slav origin and close linguistic ties would prove stronger than differences in habits of heart and mind and ways of life imposed under foreign influence. The unification of the South Slavs into a single state, according to nineteenth-century advocates, offered the only way to overcome the alien powers and to secure the survival of small and economically disadvantaged nations in a harsh environment ruled by the great powers.

Today, separated from each other since 1991 by almost five years of terror and massacre, these nations seem even smaller, their environment
even harsher and more unjust. The chaos of evil unleashed in Croatia in
1991 and subsequently in Bosnia seems to have drowned, perhaps forever,
the vision of a common future that so profoundly marked the previous
century of their history.

Their knotted existence together, and apart, involved always two parallel historical realities—the Slavic identity and the sub-Slavic particulari-
ties within the Slavic "race" of Slovenes, Croats, Bosnians, Serbs, Montenegrins, and Macedonians. The same resilience and pride that helped each
group endure half a millennium or more of foreign domination turned
out, however, to be the most formidable obstacle to the eventual lasting
Pan-Slavic unification.

Each national group built its own sense of enduring identity around the
same core: the period of medieval prosperity and statehood preceding the
centuries of foreign hegemony. For different groups those periods differed,
but the memories of long-past independence and glory, preserved in the
national folk songs, myths, and legends, came to constitute the heart of
national consciousness. Slovenia—formed in 623 in the Eastern Alps as
the independent duchy of Karantania—found any possibility of a medieval political identity erased after 745 by the Frankish invasions.[2] Croatia was constitutionally absorbed into the Hungarian realm four hundred years later. Serbia, which contended with Bulgaria for Macedonia,
was overwhelmed in the fifteenth century by the Turks, who conquered
Bosnia soon after.

Only two South Slavic entities remained semi-independent. On the
Adriatic, Dubrovnik, also known as Ragusa, maintained itself as a trading city-state under the remote and light-handed suzerainty of Venetians,
Hungarians, and Turks, and flourished in its curious isolation. Montenegro, touching on the Dubrovnik Republic along the Adriatic coast, remained free until 1699 and then finally fell to the Turks. But even so, it
remained almost impenetrable. Its "black" mountains covered with dark
forests that gave the land its name were too high to reach and too hard
to govern. They also offered no revenue to exploit. And so the shepherds
and free peasants of Montenegro retained throughout the times of Turkish occupation considerable self-rule—the source of the remarkable local
tradition of independence and honor.[3]

For the other groups, the dream of the eventual resurrection of their

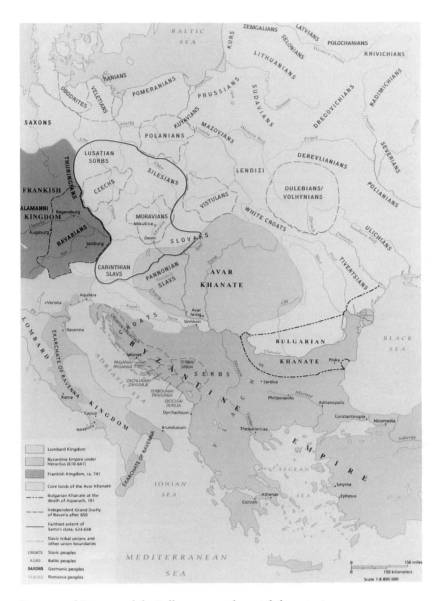

East central Europe and the Balkans: seventh to eighth centuries.
Courtesy of University of Washington Press.

states offered the only basis for resistance, endurance, and hope. In the late 1980s, in a development utterly at odds with the times, the schemes for the resurrection of former statehood were reborn along the fault lines that separated the ethnic territories. Few of those fault lines were of local making. Most had formed over time as a result of the actions of outside powers, whose intersecting interests fragmented the fabric of indigenous life in a pattern contradicting the vital needs of the South Slavic nations.

The fault line separating Croats and Serbs was set in place even before their arrival in the region, with the division of the Roman Empire in A.D. 395 between West and East, along a vector leading from Belgrade, the ancient Roman city of Singidunum placed on the Danube in the north, to the now Albanian town of Scodra, or Shkodâr, in the south.[4] In the sixth and seventh centuries the Croats (Chrobati, or Chorvati) settled, and formed their early states, north and west of the dividing line, the Serbs south and east. At the end of the eighth century, however, Croatia fell first to the advancing Franks led by Charlemagne, then to Byzantium. When in 925 it was granted autonomy under King Tomislav, who received his royal crown from the pope, Croatia encompassed not only modern Croatia and Slavonia but also northern and western Bosnia, and a good portion of the Dalmatian coast. Those three regions made up the "triune kingdom," a Croatian state that remains at the heart of the Croat national consciousness to this day.

Supported by the pope, Croatia became a significant force on the Adriatic. Still, at the end of the eleventh century it fell to the Hungarians—the descendants of the former nomadic Magyar tribe that invaded the Balkans at the end of the ninth and in the tenth century—and remained occupied by them for the next eight hundred years. In 1102, Hungarian king Koloman signed with Croatian notables a famed agreement, Pacta conventa, which gave him overlordship in Croatia, without integrating the Hungarian and the Croatian states. In exchange for electing Koloman their king, Croatian aristocracy—the great landowners, lesser nobles, clergy, and the delegates from the towns—kept their privileges. Above all, the Croatian Diet (Sabor) remained intact. The nobles retained control over internal administration, courts, and land policies. But the official language changed as Latin clergy assumed high positions on the Croatian court and Latin was accepted in the church and the judiciary. All Croatian documents, royal letters, charters, and land grants from that and

East central Europe and the Balkan peninsula: ca. 1250.
Courtesy of University of Washington Press.

later times were written in Latin. Rome had banned the use of Slav books in the churches even before the Hungarians had established their rule. Priests who continued to perform service in their native language found themselves stripped of their priesthood, subjected to public whipping, even marked on the forehead with hot iron, and sometimes imprisoned for life. For much of the Slav clergy the only way to survive was to retreat into remote small villages.[5]

The tensions between the western, Latin and the eastern, Slav culture, one backed by Rome, the other by Byzantium, were further deepened with the creation in 1578 of the Military Frontier, or Vojna Krajina, a zone extending in a wide arc from the Adriatic district of Lika in Dalmatia, north and east through Slavonia and Hungary, to the Iron Gates of the Danube. The frontier, which remained in effect until 1881, was established by Ferdinand, the Holy Roman Emperor, who was elected king of Croatia, and by Maximilian II, Ferdinand's successor, as a defense zone to protect Europe from further Turkish incursions.

The idea of the frontier was brilliant. Instead of having to raise armies to protect themselves from Ottoman attacks, Ferdinand would use local Christian colonists to inhabit and defend the Balkan buffer zone—a gateway to Europe.[6] With the establishment of the Military Frontier, Croatia was divided into Civil Croatia, governed by the local ecclesiastical and aristocratic elite, and Military Croatia, ruled from Vienna. This event deeply marked the subsequent history of the Balkans.

By the time the Military Frontier was set up, the terrain had been devastated and largely depopulated by the wars with the Turks. Croatian nobles who owned much of the land protested the formation of a separate frontier zone, claiming that it violated "Croatian state right guaranteed by Pacta conventa."[7] The enduring political traditions of the triune kingdom were preserved through the ancient Croatian institutions, that of the Ban (the Viceroy), and that of the Sabor, an assembly of notables that embodied the autonomy of the Croatian elite.[8] By the time the Hapsburgs came to dominate Croatia in 1524, they had to deal with a native nobility used to a strong tradition of rights the Sabor stood to defend. After the creation of Vojna Krajina, for the first time in its history the Sabor lost jurisdiction over a vast area of the Croatian land. Croatia could hardly imagine a greater insult.

The desolation of the Krajina was advantageous for Ferdinand's project. Krajina's fertile northern soil proved a strong incentive to the Serbs driven out from their own native land. The Serbs, it was thought, would make up a tenacious border force. In exchange for their service to the king, they were freed from the obligation to pay any taxes and granted title to the land, local autonomy, and freedom to practice the Orthodox faith.[9]

The offer was hard to refuse. Free land was a privilege otherwise unimaginable for the newcomers. The threat of war, however, was constant, and Serb men found themselves under arms most of the time. Gradually, a rigid military mentality developed among them, encouraged and fostered by the imperial authorities. Inevitably, this provoked ire among the Croats, laying the basis for centuries of conflict between the two groups.

Yet conflict was not universal. Around the town of Varaždin, the headquarters of one of the two Krajina "generalities," one-third of the population in the sixteenth and the seventeenth centuries remained Catholic, thus subject to taxation. In 1642 Serbs condemned the taxation placed on the Varaždin Croats by the Zagreb bishop, saying: "You know well, your highness, that we are one brotherhood [*jedna braća*], they can't live without us, we without them."[10] This solidarity characterized many other parts of the Krajina at the time.

Every *granitschar*, or frontiersman, eighteen years of age was obliged to perform military service and to bear arms at all times against the invader.[11] Considering themselves warriors, the Serbs felt responsible to the emperor alone and acted defiantly toward Croatian authorities. This outraged the Croatian elite, whose land had been awarded to the Serbs without proper compensation.[12]

But distrust of the newcomers was not limited to the gentry, to whom the Serbs' status as free peasants was a permanent irritant. Distrust grew everywhere. The Catholic Church regarded Orthodox Serbs as schismatics. The Sabor passed laws prohibiting them from permanently residing or purchasing property in the towns. Even some landless Croatian serfs resented the Serbs, who came to enjoy privileges denied to Croat commoners.

Yet their privileges failed to bring prosperity to the Serbian community. The southern part of Krajina in particular was by the end of the eighteenth century still by far the poorest region of Croatia, one-third of its population living in desolate small hamlets in a deforested, limestone terrain. Their poverty—which the Serbs shared with the Croatian serfs living in the same area—played a distinct role in forming the perception of Serbs as a backward and inferior race.

For Catholic Croats, prideful of their efficiency, law, and order, and considering themselves, with some reason, to be more culturally developed, the Serbs were primitive semi-Orientals. The gentry of central Croatia emulated the splendor of the Hungarian and Austrian courts, while the Croatian priests and writers in Venetian-ruled Dalmatia and Ottoman Bosnia, continuing long-established traditions, excelled in poetry, philosophy, and science.[13] They were at home in Latin as well as in Croatian

Krajina, the military frontier district (diagonally shaded crescent capping Bosnia), protecting the Hapsburg Empire and Western Europe from the Ottoman Empire: seventeenth to eighteenth centuries. Courtesy of University of Washington Press.

and in the Croatian "recension" of Old Church Slavonic. Literacy was more widespread in Croatia than in Serbia, and the birthrate lower. In the fifteenth century already, Dalmatian scholars studied in Padua and Budapest. By the late nineteenth century, the sons and often the daughters of the landowning families, even those of moderate means, took piano lessons and were sent to the University of Vienna and beyond.

By contrast, in Serbia land was customarily divided among the offspring after a father's death, becoming fragmented into smaller and smaller plots.[14] More important still, the golden period of Serbian prosperity was over when the Ottomans wiped out Serbian nobility and crushed the Serbian state at its zenith under the Emperor Dušan (1331–55). Dušan not only greatly enlarged the territory of Serbia but also promoted the economic life, and particularly mining and trade. He invited experienced Hungarian miners to help in the extraction of ore, gold, copper, lead, and above all, silver. Trade flourished and new coins were minted, replacing the Byzantine and Roman currency. Dušan gave special rights and protections to the merchants of the free Dubrovnik Republic trading with Venice on Serbia's behalf. They were also reimbursed by the emperor for all losses stemming from damage or theft. Serbia exported leather, wool, honey, fur, and lumber, as well as silver, copper, and lead, and imported cloth, precious stones, rare furs, china, spices, and southern fruit. For the peasants—who lost their freedom through capture, indebtedness, or simply by putting themselves under the protection of a lord, and who lived simply and poorly as did serfs across Europe at the time—the state imported salt, salted fish, oil, and cheap jewelry.

In 1349 the summit of the notables of Skopje adopted Dušan's law code (Dušanov Zakonik), a historic document aimed at strengthening the power of the lords while limiting personal whim of the ruling order. After Dušan's death, however, feuds over land weakened centralized power just as the aggressive and strong military Ottoman state was being established on the Gallipoli Peninsula. The Black Plague, which decimated the European population, played into the Ottoman military designs. So did the indifference of Germany and the involvement of Britain and France in the Hundred Years' War (1338–1453). Venice and Genoa, poised against each other, were equally unwilling to engage the Ottomans. Serbian prince Lazar was on his own in 1389, when his army confronted Sultan Murad I and his son Bayezid I on the legendary Field of the Blackbirds (polje Kosovo). Lazar requested help from the Bosnian king Tvrtko I, himself a descendant of the Serbian Nemanjića dynasty. Tvrtko sent his army, but Lazar still lost his kingdom—the event that marked the point of precipitous downfall for Serbia. Skopje (today the capital of Macedonia and at the time the site of Dušan's coronation in southern Serbia) was reduced to a Turkish military base. Serbia became a vassal state of the Ottoman Empire.

Subsequent Turkish raids toward Hungary left much of the land plundered, razed, and torched. Males over fourteen were often killed, women and children taken into slavery. The Serbian feudal class was destroyed, the Serbian Patriarchate temporarily extinguished, and a series of historic mass migrations of Serbian population to the north were triggered. Late-fifteenth-century documents suggest that from 1473 to 1483 up to two hundred thousand Serbs left their homes to settle in the southern Hungarian provinces of Banat, Bačka, and Srem. The migrations continued into the next two centuries. Much of Serbia was left uncultivated and unpopulated.[15] Over time, central Serbia, in particular, turned vacant, much of it swallowed up by a wilderness of forest and brush. Few roads wound through the thick woodland.

"Like American frontiersmen," wrote one traveler, "the Serbian peasants regarded the surrounding forests as a nuisance to be rid of as soon as possible. They set fire to vast strands in order to scatter corn seed between the charred stumps. Also, the manner of everyday life in the Morava Valley closely resembled that in the Ohio Valley—the same log cabins, homemade furniture, plain food but plenty of it, plum brandy in place of rum—and an abundance of malaria and other diseases which were treated with a combination of home remedies, barbers, and quacks."[16]

In Croatia the wealth of the local nobility, although limited, added luster to the way of life to which Croatians aspired, even if the peasants lived in a manner that was far from cultured and comfortable. No such luster existed in Serbia. To the Croats everything to the east of the Drina River appeared tainted by the lawlessness, corruption, and poor hygiene characteristic of "Asia." And the Krajina Serbs seemed to have brought that mentality into Croatia, along with the arms they brazenly displayed.

These tensions had a profound effect on the historical relations between the Croats and Serbs. The resentment of all strata of the Croatian population and acceptance by none strengthened over time the internal cohesion and militancy of the Krajina Serbs. Also strengthened was their belief that their real home was in Serbia. Nostalgia for the original homeland persisted well into the twentieth century, even though by then the Serbs were largely assimilated into Croatian society and the Military Frontier had ceased to exist.[17] What was left, however, was a dream that somehow the Serbs—divided between the semiautonomous Serbian principality (where one-third lived) and the Ottomans and Hapsburgs—could be reunited in the same state. In the nineteenth century the Krajina Serbs began to press for special rights, which they hoped would strengthen them against Hungarian and Catholic pressure.[18]

Had the Krajina never been used as a human shield keeping Europe out of reach for the Ottomans, the history of Croatia-Serbian relations could have turned out rather differently. Still, until World War II, despite tensions emanating from the role assigned to each group in the designs of the great powers, no armed conflict of any sort broke out between the Serbian and Croatian communities. Instead, in the nineteenth century, about fifty years before Krajina was dissolved, a strong Illyrian movement in favor of Serb-Croat unification took root in Croatia, under the leadership of the most enlightened minds of the time.[19] The authorities in Vienna and Pest were alarmed, banning even the use of the Illyrian name in the press, schools, and in public debate in 1844. Trying to uproot any sign of national sentiment, the Hungarian Diet declared that within six years Magyar was to become the official language in Croatia. In 1909 a famous trial of fifty-eight Serbs, all accused of treason, took place in Zagreb. The indicted were the archpriest of Glina, two other priests and a curate, seven schoolteachers, and a country doctor, as well as a number of well-to-do merchants. The purpose of the Hungarian authorities was to portray the Serbs as a disloyal element and plant distrust between Serbs and Croats.[20] Distrust and historical rivalries between Serbs and Croats in the Krajina, encouraged by the foreign powers, defined the social character of the region, and had their delayed effects in the events of 1991–95.

In Bosnia-Hercegovina, a part of whose territory also belonged to the Military Frontier at the time, the affairs were further complicated by the existence of not only Serbian and Croatian communities but also strong Muslim culture, and a powerful Muslim political and landowning elite. Within its borders—more stable than those of either Serbia or Croatia—the Bosnian territorial state developed and preserved a strong identity all of its own.[21] Beginning in the 1180s, its ruler, Ban Kulin, wrought a certain independence from both Croatian and Serbian states by accepting Bogomilism in 1199.[22] The Hungarians, who retained suzerainty over Bosnia in the twelfth and the thirteenth centuries, tried to assert tighter control by accusing Bosnia of deviating from Catholicism and convincing the pope in Rome to subordinate it to the Hungarian archbishop. Bosnians responded by adhering to their own "Bosnian church," whose members were frequently called Bogomils and were condemned as heretics by both the Catholic order and Orthodox powers.[23]

The Turkish conquest in 1463 profoundly changed life in Bosnia.[24] Before the fall, in the first half of the fourteenth century, Bosnia had expanded to the southwest, reaching the Adriatic coast. Trade was established down the Neretva River valley with Dubrovnik, Zadar, and Šibenik, the thriving Dalmatian cities. Inland, mines were opened, including Kičevo, Fojnica, Zvornik, and above all Srebrenica (silver vessel), famous for its silver mines. King Tvrtko I (1353–91) centralized royal power and expanded his state at the expense of Hungary and Serbia, much weakened by continuous Turkish invasions.

By the end of Tvrtko's rule, however, the Ottomans were crossing the Drina River from the Serbian side into Bosnia. The assaults of the crusades, the Hungarian raids, and the warring between the local lords caused the weakening of the Bosnian state. From the end of the fifteenth century, the Turks were launching their attacks on Croatia from Bosnian territory, which they by that time considered their own. Still, Bosnia was recognized as a coherent unit, and from 1554 to 1878 was granted the status of a separate vilayet.

Sarajevo—originally a humble settlement of no more than thirty houses—became the seat of the Bosnian Sandžak, numbering in 1516 about twenty thousand inhabitants. By 1561 the Mosque of Ali Pasha, the endowment of the Bosnian governor Gazi Ali Pasha and a masterpiece of Turkish architecture, was constructed in the town's center. Novi Pazar, Zenica, Banja Luka, Foča, Čajniče, Zvornik, and Mostar were expanding around their own mosques, clock towers, and *hamams* (public baths).

Islam became the dominant religion and thousands converted. It has long been held that the conversion took place en masse, primarily by the adherents of the Bosnian Church, to reinforce their difference from their Catholic and Orthodox neighbors. But as Donia and Fine argue, Islam was a "dynamic, well preached religion," attracting members of all three Bosnian denominations.[25] Anyone aspiring to state service—scribes, paid soldiers, officers, judges—had a pragmatic reason to accept Islam. So did the many merchants, who wanted to feel safe in the transporting of their wares and needed greater freedom of movement.[26] The military hierarchy was also Muslim, maintained through the Janissari and later the devsirme system, whereby boys from Christian villages were taken to Istanbul for military training, converted to Islam, and swore loyalty to the Sultan. The training was aimed not only at making them into first-rate officers of a military state but also at changing their sense of identity: most returned to the lands of their origin feeling they were, above all, Turks.

Islamization, while not imposed on the population, brought with it significant social advantages and rewards. The serfs willing to convert were granted freedom; feudal landowners refusing to convert ran the risk of losing first their privileges and then the land itself. Finally, Christians and Jews were taxed more heavily than Muslims.[27] All these were logical incentives for conversion, which eventually generated a specific, Muslim-dominated social hierarchy, with the landowning and administrative classes overwhelmingly Muslim.[28] Yet irrespective of religion, Bosnians continued to observe the same religious holidays up to the most recent time. The ranks of Islam as the dominant religious order were open to all ethnic groups. Ethnicity played no part in the social hierarchy, as Ottomans stratified their populations according to the creed, not ethnic origin.[29] As in Croatia, in Bosnia ethnic conflict never erupted until World

War II, and then only because Bosnia was pushed into collaborating with the pro-Hitler state of Croatia, and not because of ethnic hatreds on the ground. Before that point in the twentieth century, tolerance always outweighed tensions, and the local *raja* (common folk, originally flock, herd) —the poorest in the Ottoman Empire, whether Orthodox, Catholic, or Muslim—felt bound by class rather than separated by ethnicity.[30]

As the Ottoman Empire began its long decline through the eighteenth and nineteenth centuries, the *agas* and *begs*, or Muslim landlords—comprising less than 1 percent of the total Bosnian population but enjoying absolute power—levied ever heavier taxes on the empire's *kmet* (serf, overwhelmingly Serb) population. Brought to despair, *kmets* rose six times between 1834 and 1862, and were ruthlessly suppressed every time. Many Serbian peasants began to view all Muslims, and not only the agas and begs, as their *dušmanin* (killers of the soul). In 1875 a massive uprising broke out in Hercegovina. With one-third of its population living in Bosnia, Serbia supported the uprising and the rise of national consciousness among the Bosnian Orthodox population. A considerable part of the Serbian political elite at the end of the nineteenth century held Bosnia to be Serbian land, with a Serbian majority. In addition, they claimed, Hercegovina, the southeastern part of the country, was the home of the Serbian dialect, considered by the founder of modern Serbian language and grammar, the linguist Vuk Stefanović Karadžić, to be its purest dialect.

Vuk, as Karadžić became known among the people, was the first and only person to travel to the most remote Serbian-speaking areas to record dialects, compile a dictionary, and collect folk stories, poems, and proverbs.[31] He reformed the Cyrillic alphabet to adapt it to Serbian usage and created a singularly simple, logical spelling system. "Write the way you speak," Vuk was known to say, insisting that each sound be represented by a single letter. His *Serbian Lexicon* remains a classic, unsurpassed work. Seeking to replace prior standards that were based on the ancient Slavonic —the language of the church, which was alien to native speech and an obstacle to literacy—Vuk elevated the idiom of the Serb masses in Hercegovina to the status of a national literary language. Having found the "purest Serbian," as he called it, in Hercegovina, he unwittingly encouraged the ambitions of some Serb nationalist politicians to claim Hercegovina—the land awaiting liberation from the Ottomans—as Serbian land.

The intoxicating idea of liberation from the Ottoman yoke penetrated the discontented Bosnian peasantry, as it did the peasantry in Bulgaria, Macedonia, and other Ottoman provinces. Bosnian Muslims and Jews also rebelled against the Ottoman power. Many (and not just Serbs) spoke of the unification of Bosnia with "free, Slavic" Serbia. And so the idea of national freedom came to be linked, for certain influential politicians, with the idea of expanding Serbia into Bosnia. The Hapsburg Empire, which bordered on Bosnia and Serbia, had its own interests in Bosnia and was also eager to exploit the discontent by adding Bosnia to Croatia.

To a very great extent, Serbia had already been freed of Ottoman rule. The First Serbian uprising in 1804 under a remarkable figure known as Black George or Karadjordje, a pig trader from the Serbian heartland, and the Second Uprising in 1814, led by the Serbian ruler, Miloš Obrenović, forced the sultan in the 1830s to issue a *firman*, or ruling, granting Serbia significant freedom under Russian protection, although it remained officially a Turkish possession. By 1804, three years after the beginning of the extraordinarily brutal mistreatment of Serbian peasants by four Turkish Dahis, or Janissaries, Karadjordje had thirty thousand peasants under his command. The troops captured the fortress of Smederevo in 1805, and Belgrade in 1806. In 1815 the sultan's firman established Serbia as an autonomous state under his suzerainty.

The slow advance of the Serbian national cause, aided by the Russian czars, led to the concept of a Greater Serbia that would unite all the Serb lands—Serbia proper, within its late-nineteenth-century borders, along with Montenegro, long considered a Serb territory; old Serbia, as Kosovo to the south was known; Vojvodina to the north; the Serbian-inhabited Krajina in Croatia; and finally Bosnia. Macedonia, then called South Serbia, was eventually added to the scheme.

The national rebirth of Serbia excited tremendous hopes within Serbia, and without. Yet the rhetoric of liberation of the "historic Serb lands" inevitably implied not only defeating the Ottomans but also expanding at the expense of others: Bosnians, Bulgarians, and Albanians. In the nineteenth century, however, this level of political consciousness was rare in western Europe as well as in the Balkans, although, most notably, the Serbian political writer Svetozar Marković, a member of the Socialist International, warned of the pitfalls of the Great Serbian dream.

Along with Bulgaria and Greece, Serbia found itself at the forefront of the Balkan movement to overthrow the Ottomans. Greece, which had attained full national independence, was its closest ally; Bulgaria, although Slavic speaking and still struggling against the Turks as late as 1878, was Serbia's rival for support from Russia. Together, Serbia and Greece began planning the division of Macedonia and Albania once the Turks were expelled.

In the 1876–78 war against the Ottoman Empire, Bulgaria gained its freedom and seized much of Macedonia and a part of Albania. Serbia, which had started the war, believed that as a reward, Bosnia would be united to Serbia. But the central and western European powers—Germany, Austria-Hungary, Britain, and France—had their own stakes in the emerging geopolitical arrangement. The Ottoman Empire, the Sick Man of Europe, could collapse at any time, bringing down with it the existing balance of forces in Europe, and thoroughly destabilizing the political, economic, and military situation on the continent as a whole. The point, then, was to assure a gradual and painless disintegration of the empire over time though diplomatic means, maintaining the status quo as much as possible by annulling the achievements of the liberation movements.

One of the veritable feats of the German chancellor Bismarck's diplomatic craft was to have preserved the stability in Europe around the negotiating table in Berlin, despite the sea change under way, triggered by the gradual demise of the Ottoman Empire. Bismarck's diplomatic success, however, owed much to the further balkanization of the Balkans as the means of preserving European territorial and political stability at the dusk of Ottoman power.

In the sixteenth century, at the dawn of the Ottoman conquests, the creation of the Krajina had served an analogous purpose. The military frontier slashed through the Balkan territory, fragmenting it politically, ethnically, and religiously, in complete disregard of the will or the needs of the local populations. The Congress of Berlin, almost three centuries later, recast once again the map of the Balkans, to prevent the Russian czar from dominating the Bosporus and thus from controlling access to the Black Sea, the Mediterranean, and the gateway to the Middle East.[32] The stability of Europe was preserved, but at a cost of setting in motion a long process of fermentation of mutual resentments and rivalries in the Balkans. The arrangements made by the European powers as the nineteenth century was drawing to a close came to haunt the world, and above all the Balkans at the end of the twentieth century.

It took not one diplomatic congress but two of them to end the Russo-Turkish War. The first congress, dictated by Russia, ended with the Treaty of San Stefano, which allowed Bulgaria to greatly expand its size by keeping all of Macedonia and a large section of Thrace. Montenegro also tripled in size. Serbia, by contrast, received a very small reward of only about 150 square miles. The outcome alarmed the European powers, particularly Austria-Hungary, Britain, and France, because they saw Bulgaria as Russia's puppet, which would have facilitated Russian expansion at the expense of the Ottoman Empire. The second, the Berlin congress, convened before the ink had fully dried on the first one. It ended with what was billed "a compromise," a deal that shrank Bulgaria by returning the territories it had won to Turkey, divided Bulgaria in two, and allowed Austria-Hungary (which coveted Bosnia as a route to Dalmatian coast), not Serbia, to gain control over Bosnia. In addition, a portion of southeastern Bosnia, the Sandžak of Novi Pazar, was simply sliced off and placed under Turkish control. Immediately following the congress, 268,000 troops, made up of Krajina Serbs and Croats, marched into Bosnia. It took them three months to subdue local protests. The migration that followed, as many Moslems and Turks left for Constantinople, accounts in great part for the subsequent preponderance of Serbs in Bosnia. For the Berlin compromise to look more like a compromise, Serbia and Montenegro were granted full independence.[33]

The partition of Bulgaria curbed Russian ambitions but created the Macedonian question, which remains unsettled to this day. The annexation of Bosnia to Austria-Hungary in turn augmented Serbian nationalism. It also provoked a growing conflict between Serbia and Croatia, whose many politicians rejoiced that Bosnia was not given to Serbia. The restoration of Sandžak of Novi Pazar, the easternmost pocket of Bosnia, to Turkey, capriciously separated a portion of the Bosnian population from its homeland. Equally capriciously, that portion was later annexed to Serbia. For the time being, however, Sandžak of Novi Pazar separated Serbia from Montenegro, while the new western border with Austria-Hungary confounded Serbia economically and cut off its economic routes.[34]

Meanwhile, the dissolution of the Military Frontier that began in 1873 and was completed in 1881 prompted the Hungarian Financial Directorate to impose even higher taxes, provoking a surge of the already existing bitter peasant discontent. The 1882 revolt of hungry Serbian peasants in Hercegovina was suppressed by a Hapsburg unit made up of Croatian troops.

Finally, in 1908 Bosnia was legally absorbed into Austria-Hungary, which deepened the growing antagonism between Austria and Serbia. The sentiment against Austria surged in 1906, after the monarchy had imposed the hog and cattle tariff war on Serbia, crippling its economy. The monarchy's rural policy in Bosnia represented another strong affront. Land remained in the hands of the begs, 90 percent of whom were Muslim, while eighty thousand out of ninety thousand Serb peasants remained landless as late as 1911. The tensions between Serbia and Croatia were also raised to a new level because of the prospect that eventually the western part of Bosnia would be joined to Croatia. Those factors—hardly of local making—had their profound delayed effects, catalyzing a number of significant twentieth-century developments.[35]

The Serbian desire to have Bosnia joined to Serbia implied a confrontation with Austria-Hungary.[36] The trend toward such a conflict was heightened when, in 1903, the dynasty ruling in Serbia, the Obrenovići—long considered pawns of the Hapsburgs—were brutally overthrown by Serb military officers and replaced by the Karadjordjevići family. Still, Serbia was not prepared to contemplate outright conflict with the dual monarchy—not in 1908 and not in 1914, when a Serbian youth from Bosnia, Gavrilo Princip, fired a shot at the Hapsburg crown prince Franz Ferdinand and his princess in Sarajevo. Many Hapsburg and other historians interpret Ferdinand's assassination as an act masterminded and directed by the secret Black Hand society stationed in Belgrade. Historical evidence does not bear this out, however. Princip's Young Bosnia organization consisted not only of Bosnian Serb youth, but also of Croatian and Muslim members. They claimed a right to assassination "for all ills that our people are forced to suffer under Austria." At the trial Gavrilo Princip was above all concerned that the peasants who had helped Young Bosnians be spared. "The peasant is impoverished, they have totally ruined him," Princip said at the trial. "I am a son of a peasant; I know peasant life." Another defendant stated: "I was not inspired by Serbia, only by Bosnia." Fuzzy as the idea of Yugoslavism was among the Young Bosnians, Gavrilo Princip invoked Yugoslavism, and not any sort of Serbian nationalism, when he said to the judge: "I am a Yugoslav nationalist, wishing for the unification of all Yugoslavs into whatever form of state, but it must be free of Austria."[37]

Vienna accused Princip of acting as the instrument of Belgrade. Yet Belgrade was not at all eager to provoke the monarchy, knowing that if it did, it would be taking on too much.

But shots had been fired and Serbia was pushed into war. Austria-Hungary made demands; Serbia, backed by Russia, rejected them. Armies mobilized on both sides of all borders. For the first time in their history, Serbia and Croatia found themselves fighting each other, the former as one of the Allied powers, the latter as part of the Hapsburg empire. This also meant that many Croatian Serbs, conscripted with the Croats in the army of the monarchy, turned their guns against their kin in Serbia. In the war, Serbia was devastated, its armies decimated, and one-quarter of its civil population killed.[38] But the war had been won, and the South Slavs were free to unite. The Serbs, who had indeed borne the brunt of the war, gave themselves credit for it.

Two decades later, World War II brought Serbs and Croats into bloody confrontation again. The genocide of Serbs in Croatia—which exceeded by far that of Jews, communists, or Romanies—was, however, less an expression of grassroots hatreds than of a foreign, imported ideology embraced by the Croatian regime in power.[39] This history, also involving in eastern Hercegovina particularly Muslim ss divisions, left deep scars in the collective memory of the Serbs and served as stock for the engineering of Serbian nationalism in the late 1980s.

Three days before the Berlin congress was to open in June 1878, the League of Prizren, the first Albanian national organization, formed in 1877 by both Muslim and Christian Albanian notables, addressed Bismarck, asking the congress to grant Albania autonomy within the Ottoman Empire.

Albanians—the largest non-Slavic ethnic group in the Balkans to predate the Slavic invasions of the Balkans—most likely originate from the Illyrians, the oldest known Balkan tribe.[40] Following the Slav immigration, Albanians withdrew to the high ground of the Kosovo mountain rim and descended into the plain only in the fifteenth and sixteenth centuries, following the Ottoman conquest. The Ottomans considered the Albanians, who converted to Islam in greater numbers than any other Balkan population, to be Turks and employed them as governors or soldiers.[41]

The medieval Serbian kingdom, with Kosovo at its center, had not excluded the Albanians. They were invited into Emperor Dušan's state administration and drafted into his army. Albanian historians argue that many Albanians fought with the Serbs against the Turks in the battle of Kosovo of 1389, the event that was to change the course of history for Serbs and Albanians alike. Epic songs of the battle exist in Albanian and were traditionally sung by Albanian folk poets as well as by Serbs.[42]

During the centuries of Turkish rule, Albanian family clans helped protect and preserve treasured Orthodox churches and monasteries dotting the Kosovo landscape. Many Serbian historians deny these arguments, insisting that Albanians held high administrative posts in the Ottoman Empire, served as soldiers for the sultans, and were as responsible as the Turks for the mayhem that led to the mass migrations of Serbs northward, to Austria-Hungary, in 1690, and again in 1734. In the 1878 Russo-Turkish War, which they viewed as the all-Christian uprising against the Turks, the Serbs tried to regain their old Kosovo homeland. In the minds of Serb soldiers, the liberation of Kosovo was something that had been foretold in dreams and inexplicable natural events. In their advances, the Serb troops reached the town of Prizren itself, resting in the heart of Kosovo. It was perhaps understandable, then, that Albanians, who needed the protection of a stronger power, would seek, in their request to Bismarck in 1878, limited autonomy under the sultan, not full independence. The Serbian leadership, whose goal was not just autonomy under Ottoman suzerainty but the expulsion of the Turks, declared Albanian calls for autonomy to be anti-Serb. Bismarck, for his part, did not believe there was such a thing as an "Albanian nation" and found no grounds for autonomy. But the congress assigned Kosovo to Turkey, not to Serbia, and Dervish Pasha, a Turkish governor, took control of it in 1881. Serbs in Kosovo paid a high and brutal price in blood, and this made Serbian-Albanian relations even more bitter.

The next transfer of power, however, thirty-two years later, when finally Albanians won the desired autonomy, passed in peace. Albanians launched no reprisals against Serbian civilians. At the end of 1912, however, in the First Balkan War — launched by the Balkan League of Bulgaria, Greece, Serbia, and Montenegro to complete the destruction of what was then called Turkey-in-Europe — the Serbs and Montenegrins captured Kosovo and drove deep into northern Albania proper, aiming for the town of Shkodâr and the Albanian Adriatic coastline. Montenegro had borne the brunt of the anti-Turkish struggle for long years, always with the ideal of a free Serbian nation at heart. In 1912, while Greece attacked Albania from the south, the Montenegrins captured Shkodâr, at the cost of ten thousand Montenegrin lives.

In the process of establishing what they considered a Christian birthright, the commanders of the Serb forces ordered looting and massacres of Albanians, including the sick and wounded, women and children, many of them Christian themselves although speaking Albanian rather than Serbian. Five thousand were executed in and around Prizren alone; a total of twelve thousand to fifteen thousand perished. Any settlement where an Albanian weapon was fired was ordered destroyed. Thousands of Albanians, as well as Turks, fled to Turkey. Leon Trotsky, then working as a war correspondent for the Russian liberal press, sent home fiery dispatches describing and denouncing the atrocities. In one, he declared, "An individual, a group, a party or a class that is capable of 'objectively' picking its nose while it watches men drunk with blood, and incited from above, massacring defenseless people is condemned by history to rot and become worm-eaten while it is still alive."[43]

Alarmed at the Serbo-Montenegrin advance, Austria-Hungary meddled in the conflict, inciting the Albanians. In response, during the fall of 1913, Serbian troops further razed Albanian villages, an action Dimitrije Tucović, a leading Serbian socialist of the time, described as the Third Balkan War.[44] The Serbian socialists bitterly opposed their government's military policies. They also offered a solution: the unification of the Balkan countries with full political and cultural autonomy for all the constituent nations. They pointed out the deep gulf between Serbian war propaganda, which rapturously proclaimed the glory of Kosovo's redemption, and the low morale of the Serbian forces in Albania. Although there continued to be atrocities, few of the ordinary soldiers, or their officers for that matter, were avid for the occupation of what, according to Tucović, was clearly a foreign land. The Serbian troops were starving and poorly dressed, toes sticking out of their torn shoes. Their enthusiasm, as they slowly made their way to the Adriatic coast, was so lacking that the decision to order a battalion into battle would be made, it was said, by a throw of dice the night before. In 1913, at the London conference, Britain, France, and Russia (belonging since 1878 to an alliance called the Triple Entente) assigned Kosovo to Serbia. This had nothing to do with Serbian dreams of the redemption of their ancestral lands. The point was to keep Albania, an Austrian client state, from gaining strength.

In 1919, at the end of World War I, the Serbian socialists argued that the newly formed Kingdom of Serbs, Croats, and Slovenes, which included Kosovo, should support the maintenance of the Albanian state—whose independence had in any case been recognized by the great powers—and work toward friendly relations with it. This was not done, but worse, in Kosovo itself the improvement of relations was not even attempted. The Kosovar Albanians again fought back, but an uprising was quelled in blood. After that, a popular Albanian guerrilla movement, known as the *kacaks* and led by a handsome young couple, Azem Bejta and his wife, Shota Galica—who in the highly patriarchal Albanian society was compelled to take a man's name, Querim, and disguise herself as a man while fighting—pursued insurgency for five more years.[45] Kacaks attacked Serbian officials, bombed government buildings, sabotaged trains, and stole cattle. They urged Albanians not to pay taxes or serve in the state army so long as the Serbian authorities violated their rights. Bejta had under his command two thousand active fighters and about one hundred thousand adherents.[46] He was killed by the gendarmes in 1924 and the kacak resistance was stifled.

In 1941 the monarchist Kingdom of Yugoslavia, in existence since 1929, collapsed under Axis aggression; fascist Italy, which had already conquered Albania in 1939, secured the unification of Kosovo and western Macedonia with Albania proper. It was small wonder that Kosovar Albanians viewed this action as a liberation. Italy permitted schooling in Albanian, the use of Albanian in the state administration, the display of the Albanian flag, and the carrying of arms. A blind eye was also turned to the actions of Albanians against Serbian and Montenegrin civilians. During World War II, although many within Albania proper joined the Communist partisans, few Kosovo Albanians did, even after the Germans took over direct control of the region.

Restless nationalism remained an abiding feature of Kosovo Albanians' twentieth-century history. Slobodan Milošević brought the tensions in Kosovo to a high pitch in 1987 and has sustained them on that level for the last ten years. This has only strengthened the resolve of the Albanians and compelled some of them to seek an alliance with Albanians living in Macedonia, across the Šar Planina (Mountain Shar) to the south.

In 1878 at the Berlin congress Bismarck disappointed both Serbia and Bulgaria by restoring Macedonia, like Kosovo, to Turkey. Despite the radical change of the war's outcome in Berlin, however, the Treaty of San Stefano remained for Bulgaria the point of reference regarding Macedonia. This, of course, made Bulgaria an enemy of Serbia as well as Greece, and Macedonia the object of designs of all three. They all saw the control of Macedonia's Vardar valley as the key to control of the Balkans as a whole. From 1878 to the end of the century, an exceptionally strong, radical nationalist movement emerged in Macedonia, with factions subsidized by Serbia, Bulgaria, and Greece. In 1912, Serbia, Montenegro, Bulgaria, and Greece united to correct Bismarck's decision of 1878.

In 1908, a modernizing revolution had broken out in Turkey. That movement stimulated the Macedonians, Albanians, Armenians, and other restive nationalities under Turkish rule to further action. The Serbian faction in Macedonia declared Macedonia to be South Serbia; the Bulgarians called it West Bulgaria; the Greeks harked back to the Hellenic culture of the Macedon that produced Alexander the Great. The large Sephardic Jewish and Macedonian Muslim communities in the country were caught in the cross fire, but many of them also supported the various national revolutionary efforts.[47]

In the Middle Ages, Macedonia, although linguistically closest to the Bulgars, fluctuated between their rule and domination by the Serbs, beginning in the ninth and continuing through the thirteenth and fourteenth centuries.[48] The population converted to the Orthodox faith. In 1331, in the Macedonian town of Skopje, the greatest of all Serbian kings, Czar Stefan Dušan, was crowned emperor. After the 1371 battle of Maritsa however, all of Macedonia became a military stronghold, a base for Ottoman scouting missions and military expeditions south into Greece, west into Albania, and north into Serbia and Bosnia. Part of the Macedonian population was enslaved, another part dispersed. The rich, hilly pastures were settled by Turkish herdsmen from Asia Minor and by Albanians, although a considerable Slav population remained in place. Turkish mosques and hamams sprang up in the midst of the Christian landscape. Like elsewhere in the Balkans where the Ottomans ruled, the need to protect life and property compelled many to convert to Islam. The 1515–19 census reflected twice as many Muslim houses as Orthodox ones in Skopje. The rest, a small number, were houses of the Spanish Jewish refugees who had migrated to this region in the fifteenth century. They were gladly accepted by Turks, who appreciated their trade connections with the West and their expert knowledge in making weapons.

Nevertheless, the Orthodox archiepiscopate, the most vital religious institution of the Serbs and Macedonians alike during the five hundred years of Turkish rule, was permitted to remain in the Macedonian town of Ohrid, by a splendid lake, to acquire land, and thrive. The archiepiscopate represented a deep link between the Serbs and Macedonians. During the Turkish invasions at the end of the sixteenth century (1593–1606) and again in the eighteenth century, when Macedonia and large portions of Serbia were thoroughly devastated, Serbs and some Macedonians and Albanians fled together into southern Hungary. A new war between Turkey, Austria, and Russia two hundred years later (1787–92) brought new raids, plunder, arson, and massacres. Desperate, Macedonians abandoned their villages, towns, and fields, again fleeing northward. In Macedonia "all life and trade died out," a French traveler through the wasted land wrote at the time, "and the sultan's laws were disregarded."[49]

In 1878, after the Congress of Berlin, Macedonia was again plunged into despair. Unchecked by foreign powers, Turkey levied excessive taxes on the exhausted population. Those unable to pay were locked up, beaten, and tortured. Wanton violence descended on the land. Captured men had their eyes gouged and ears cut off. Women and girls were raped. Never having known the good life, Macedonians accepted their brutal history, and poverty, with the fatalism of the doomed. Still, a remarkable capacity to take delight in small pleasures and to give their subdued sufferings a deeply sensual, nostalgic expression through their exceptional folk songs survived.

The Ottoman Empire continued to weaken, and the first Macedonian uprising broke out in 1881. The Turks suppressed it with extraordinary brutality. In 1893, the Internal Macedonian Revolutionary Organization (known internationally as IMRO and in Macedonian as VMRO) was formed, led by the young schoolteacher Goce Delčev, a former Bulgarian military cadet. Goce, a wise and broad-minded insurgent leader, called for the "elimination of chauvinist propaganda and nationalist dissentions that divide and weaken the population of Macedonia . . . in its struggle against the Ottoman foe."[50] His name is still honored by street signs and the plaques of cultural societies across Macedonia as well as in Bulgaria and Serbia.

In May 1903 Goce Delčev was gunned down by the Turks at the age of thirty-one. Three months later, on Ilinden, St. Elias's Day (August 21), a splinter VMRO group launched a desperate uprising that lasted for two months, against the exploitation of peasants and the abuses by Albanian and Muslim warlords. In retaliation, more than forty-five hundred civilians and a thousand anti-Ottoman guerrilla fighters were killed by Turks, and one hundred fifty villages around the town of Bitola burned. Thirty thousand Macedonians sought refuge in Bulgaria.[51]

The liberation of Macedonia by Bulgaria, Greece, Serbia, and Montenegro in the First Balkan War of 1912 marked an incomparably larger event: the virtual dissolution of the Ottoman Empire, which was completed with the close of World War I. The victory of 1912 was celebrated in Serbia and hailed in Dalmatia, Croatia, and Slovenia as a Serbian triumph following a long campaign to end the Turkish presence in Europe. But rather than bringing autonomy to Macedonia, the victory provoked a further bloody scramble over the Macedonian lands between the erstwhile war allies. Their conflicting appetites in Macedonia precipitated the Second Balkan War of 1913, with the Serbs and Greeks successfully joined against Bulgaria by an ally, Romania, which had designs on other parts of Bulgaria. After Bulgaria was defeated, Macedonia was partitioned anew: Greece grabbed more than half of the region's total territory, known as Aegean Macedonia and including the coveted jewel of Salonika, a rich port city that until the late nineteenth century had a population consisting of a Sephardic Jewish majority; Serbia received Vardar Macedonia, named after a major river and its valley; Bulgaria had to settle for the smallest part, Pirin Macedonia.

Following the brutality of the Balkan Wars, in all respects matching Turkish brutality of the previous centuries, VMRO—which sought an independent Macedonia where all nations would enjoy equal rights—became a terrorist organization. After World War I, with the division of Macedonia reaffirmed, VMRO continued its terrorist activities in Vardar and Pirin Macedonia alike. For their part, the Serbian authorities tried to repress every trace of the Macedonian nationalist sentiment and undertook widespread Serbianization of Macedonian names and the planned settlement of Serbian colonists on Macedonian territory. In 1923 VMRO massacred thirty colonists, to send a message to future settlers.[52] VMRO remained active against the Kingdom of Serbs, Croats, and Slovenes, in which Macedonia was included but without being granted any autonomy at all. The kingdom persecuted the Macedonian nationalists, seeing in them, primarily, an anti-Serbian force.

VMRO split between a rightist wing that insisted on Macedonian independence and a leftist, Soviet-oriented faction that called for the old socialist ideal of a Balkan federation. The former group formed an alliance with the Croatian ultranationalist Ustashe, who were bankrolled by Italian and Hungarian fascists. In 1934, a Bulgarian member of VMRO, Vlado Chernozemski, known as Vlado the Chauffeur, with support from the Ustashe, assassinated the Yugoslav king Aleksandar in France.

VMRO ceased to function in Titoist Yugoslavia when for the first time in its history Macedonia was granted the status of a separate republic. With the breakup of Yugoslavia, beginning in 1990, VMRO reappeared as the nationalist VMRO-DPMNE, attracting many Slavic Macedonians. In the meantime, the Albanian community living in western Macedonia also organized politically. It demanded and gained a share of power. Tensions between Albanians and Slavic Macedonians persisted. In a destabilized Balkan region, Macedonia faces internal instability; in case of another war, it could again find itself up for grabs—a prey to its neighbors.

Centuries-long experience of cultural, political, and economic submission, which profoundly affected the local culture's moral life, turned the Balkan peninsula into a complex environment of deep national ambiguities. Like organisms in a petri dish, the ambiguities have waxed over time, later to cure or kill. Yet until World War II no ethnically motivated armed conflicts ever erupted. And for fifty years after that war, the cherished komšiluk—one's neighborhood—was infinitely more important to most Yugoslavs than ethnicity. For ethnicity to become paramount, four long years of systematic, insidious, ruthless and tightly controlled media campaign—appealing to the sense that at stake was biological survival, and playing on existential fears—were necessary.

In the summer 1991, the world one thought one knew suddenly swung wildly out of control, incinerating, damning everything in its path.

NOTES

1   In 1911 R. W. Seton-Watson wrote of the intolerable situation: "We find that Croatia-Slavonia forms an autonomous kingdom under the crown of Hungary; Dalmatia and Istria are two provinces of the Austrian Empire, each within its separate Diet and administration; the town of Fiume forms a unit of its own, under a Governor appointed direct from Budapest; close upon 500,000 Serbs inhabit the three most southerly countries of Hungary proper; Bosnia and Hercegovina are administered jointly by Austria and Hungary with a provincial government and Diet in Sarajevo; Servia and Montenegro form two independent kingdoms, while Old Servia is the most northerly vilayet of European Turkey" (*The Southern Slav Question and the Habsburg Monarchy* [London: Constable, 1911], p. 336).

2   Among the states created after the Slavs had settled in the Balkans, the Slovenian principality of Karantania was the first, and the shortest lived. It covered, in addition to its current territories, the Austrian provinces Carinthia and Styria, as well as the Istrian Adriatic peninsula south of Trieste, now belonging to Croatia. The Salzburg archdiocese carried out the conversion of Slovenes to Catholicism as early as the eighth century. The Slovenes lived under German/Austrian rule from 874 to 1918. Immediately after the takeover in the eighth and the ninth century, the Frankish kings stamped their seals on land titles they dished out to Frankish feudal lords. By the twelfth century, a solid stratum of German nobility controlled the Slovenian Alpine fringe. The Slovenian lords, in turn, adopted Frankish feudal rights and changed their names. Among the nobility, Slovenian names all but disappeared.

By the thirteenth century, foreign nobility had solidly established their dynastic territories in Slovenia. One of the dynasties were the Hapsburgs, whose history in the Balkans starts in the year 1247. In the fifteenth century the towns swelled with German merchants, artisans, bankers, and clergy, as well as many Slovenian peasants looking for employment. Silver and ore mines, and smelting plants, boosted their production.

In the sixteenth century, the Hapsburgs united all their Slovenian lands within Austria and ruled it until 1918. For the Hapsburgs the Slovenian territory was an important link with Italy and the Adriatic coast. Until World War I most Slovenes thought their best future was with Austria (see Anto Babić et al., eds., *Istorija naroda Jugoslavije*, vol. 2 [Beograd: Prosveta, 1960], pp. 275–359).

3   In the seventh century the territory that came to be known as Montenegro belonged to the Romans. On that territory the Serbs founded a state called Duklja, which was later annexed to Raška, the most powerful state where the Serbs lived. On the early medieval period and the state of Duklja see John V. A. Fine, *The Early Medieval Balkans* (Ann Arbor: University of Michigan Press, 1991), chap. 7, "Duklja and the Central and Eastern Balkans from the Death of Basil II, 1025, to the 1180s," pp. 202–47.

The state of Montenegro was formed in 1450, under Stefan Crnojević. In 1513 Turkey placed another Crnojević as a Skender-beg, the top ruler, of Montenegro. But in 1523 an edict was issued decreeing that "since Montenegro is an impassable and rugged country, and its people incapable of paying the usur (taxes), all taxes would be waived" (Babić et al., pp. 152–63).

Being of little use to the empire, Montenegro received a de facto independence from the Ottomans as early as 1718, paying a fixed tax of just one ducat a year.

4   In the pre-Slavic period the Roman Empire exploited the mines in the regions of contemporary Bosnia and Serbia, and recruited the indigenous population for armies. The Illyrians, who lived in Dalmatia, Istria, Epirus, northwestern Macedonia, Bosnia, Hercegovina, and western Serbia, earned a particularly high military reputation. (See Fine, *Early Medieval Balkans*, p. 9.)

5   On Croatia and Dalmatia in the early Middle Ages see Anto Babić et al., eds., *Istorija naroda Jugoslavije*, vol. 1 (Beograd: Prosveta, 1953), pp. 167–217; and Fine, *Early Medieval Balkans*, pp. 49–50, 286–87. In the sixth and seventh centuries the Slavic tribes, stemming from the area of Ukraine and led by experienced cavalry, followed the advances of Lombards and Avars. Roman dwellers retreated to the coastal towns of Dalmatia and the islands of the Adriatic. The newly arrived Slavic tribes lived under their tribal chiefs (*župani*).

6   Before the end of the sixteenth century the West mounted no resistance to the Ottomans. Protestant Lutheran princes in Germany calculated that an attack on the Muslims would help the papacy and refrained from any action. France not only failed to resist the Turks but urged Suleiman to attack the Hapsburg Empire, France's rival.

7   In the fourteenth century the state right notwithstanding, Croatian king Ladislav sold the entire territory of Dalmatia, stretching along the Adriatic coast, including the islands of the Adriatic from Krk to Korčula, to the Venetians for one hundred thousand ducats.

8 The institution of the Ban had existed prior to the Pacta conventa, that is, since the rule of King Krešimir, in 1063.

9 On the complex demographic, social, and political changes the forming of Krajina created in Croatia, see Babić et al., vol. 2, pp. 645–705. For a more detailed analysis of life in Krajina see Drago Roksandić, *Srbi u Hrvatskoj od 15. stoljeca do naših dana* (Zagreb: Vijesnik, 1991).

10 Babić et al., vol. 2, p. 652.

11 Watson notes that the granitschars were justly famous not only for their military prowess but also for their sturdy independence of character (p. 23).

12 The detachment of Krajina from Croatia shrank the latter considerably and thus also depleted feudal revenue. Croatian lords insisted on receiving rent from the land given to the Serbs. At first, land could be taken away from the Serbs, but in 1627 Ferdinand II gave the Serbs and the Vlachs (a widely scattered group of the descendants of the aborigines from the Roman province of Dacia, speaking a language derived from Latin), the right to stay on the land. This provoked bitter discontent among the feudal oligarchy (Gunther Rothenberg, *The Austrian Military Border in Croatia, 1522-1747* [Chicago: University of Chicago Press, 1960]; and Rothenberg, *The Military Border in Croatia, 1740-1881* [Chicago: University of Chicago Press, 1966]. On the economic impoverishment of Krajina throughout its existence see John R. Lampe, *Yugoslavia, Twice There Was a Country* [Cambridge: Cambridge University Press, 1966], p. 30).

13 Italian and German baroque influences are evident in Croatian churches from the end of sixteenth century.

14 Under Dušan, Serbia stretched from the river Danube, just south of Belgrade, all the way to the free city of Dubrovnik on the Adriatic coast, encompassing a part of today's Bosnia-Hercegovina and all of Montenegro. From there it stretched south, across Albania, to the Gulf of Corinth. From the west end of the gulf it spread east across much of contemporary Greece, toward the Aegean Sea, reaching the Gulf of Stirmon, just short of the city of Kavala. The border then cut back northward, across Greece and a good chunk of southwestern Bulgaria, toward the Danube. Dušan was crowned the emperor of Serbs, Greeks, Bulgarians, and Albanians, in Skopje, today the capital of Macedonia.

Back in the eleventh century, before the golden days of Dušan's empire, Serbia was Byzantium's vassal state. The Byzantine hierarchy—which originally recognized Roman papacy—broke away from Rome in 1054 and subsequently converted the pagan population under its rule, including the Serbs, to Christianity.

Having endured the assault of Bulgaria during its drive to Constantinople, Stefan Nemanja, who ruled Serbia in the twelfth century, created in 1138 a Serbian state joining the territory originally called Raška to the mountainous Zeta, today's Montenegro. With Byzantium weakened by the crusades and the wars with Hungary, Nemanja reached the Adriatic coast.

By the fourteenth century the Balkan states—Rumania, Bulgaria, Serbia, Croatia, Bosnia, Albania, and Greece—were either fully formed or well on their way to statehood. All were ethnically mixed and ruled not by a centralized power, but by alliances of local notables. As elsewhere in Europe, these alliances were shifting and unstable. On Serbia in the early Middle Ages see Babić et al., vol. 1, pp. 229–55; and Fine, *Early Medieval Balkans*, pp. 234–47. On Serbia in the late Middle Ages see John Fine, *The Late Medieval Balkans: A Critical Survey from the Late Twelfth Century to the Ottoman Conquest* (Ann Arbor: University of Michigan Press, 1987), pp. 286–344.

15 Late-fifteenth-century documents suggest that between 1473 and 1483 up to two hundred thousand Serbs settled in Hungary, in the provinces of Banat, Bačka, and Srem. The migration continued in the next century (Babić et al., vol. 1, p. 443; Fine, *Late Medieval Balkans*, p. 576).

16 L. S. Stavrianos, *The Balkans since 1453* (New York: Rinehart, 1958), p. 251 (cited in Barbara Jelavich, *History of the Balkans*, vol. 1 [New York: Cambridge University Press, 1983], p. 238).

Vuk Karadžić, the famous Serbian linguist, writing about his travels of the early 1800s, notes in Serbia "big villages of about one hundred houses, and others of about fifteen, but most have from thirty to fifty. In the hilly country houses are so scattered that a village of forty houses may cover more ground than Vienna" (cited in Duncan Wilson, *The Life and Times of Vuk Stefanović Karadžić* [Oxford: Clarendon Press, 1970], p. 13).

17 The territory was finally incorporated into Croatia on July 15, 1881.

18 At the end of the twentieth century the concept of Krajina autonomy, revived by Slobodan Milošević and a number of Serbian intellectuals, led to the Croatian war.

19 On the Illyrian movement see Seton-Watson, pp. 52–64, 118–28. See also the chapter by Branka Prpa-Jovanović in the present volume.

20 Seton-Watson offers a detailed documentation of the trial (pp. 174–208).

21 Robert J. Donia and John V. A. Fine insist that despite the claims to the contrary in the last five years, Bosnia had been a coherent entity through centuries. Bosnians never called themselves either Serbs or Croats, but Bosanci, or Bosnians, which identified them as members of a state rather than of an ethnic group (*Bosnia and Hercegovina: A Tradition Betrayed* [New York: Columbia University Press, 1994], pp. 7–8, 25, 72).

22 Ban Kulin was most likely a protégé of Byzantium but had to recognize Hungarian rule. He struck the first trade deal with Dubrovnik and allowed its merchants passage without customs (Babić et al., vol. 1, p. 517).

23 Salim Ćerić notes that the Bosnian state existed for four hundred years—from the mid-eleventh century to 1463—under sixteen rulers, six of whom were Bogomils, five Catholics, and four both Bogomil and Catholic (see *Muslimani srpskohrvatskog jezika* [Sarajevo: Svijetlost, 1968], p. 58).

Challenging the common belief among scholars that the Bosnian church was dualistic, or "neo-Manichaean," Donia and Fine insist that—unlike the Western neo-Manichaeans—the Bosnian Church retained the symbols of Catholic theology: the cross, the cult of saints, religious art, and a part of the Old Testament (p. 23). But the authors acknowledge that Bosnians were never strong Christians. All three faiths—Catholic, Orthodox, and Bosnian—were in fact weak (pp. 43–45). The famous medieval tombstones, *stećci*, generally associated with Bogomilism, were erected by the members of all three denominations and not just by Bogomils (pp. 24–25). On the origins of Bogomilism in Bulgaria see Fine, *Early Medieval Balkans*, pp. 171–78. Fine argues that the Bosnian mountain population, scattered in small villages, was hard to reach for the Franciscan clergy, the Orthodox priests, and the Bosnian Church officials alike (see John Fine, *The Bosnian Church: A New Interpretation: A Study of the Bosnian Church and Its Place in State and Society from the Thirteenth to the Fifteenth Centuries*, [Boulder, Colo.: East European Quarterly; distributed by Columbia University Press, 1975], pp. 384–85).

24 Bosnia fell to the Turks ten years after Mehmet II the Conqueror—a son of a Turkish sultan and a slave girl—conquered Constantinople. Following the 1463 Turkish capture of Jajce—a small city in central-western Bosnia, built on the hill above the Pliva River waterfalls—the Bosnian state became an Ottoman province. The Srebrenica region, however, remained independent for a few decades after the rest of Bosnia had fallen (Babić et al., vol. 1, p. 559; and Fine, *Late Medieval Balkans*, pp. 282–84).

The Bosnians were expected to partake in Ottoman military expeditions. In the 1727 Persian war, ten thousand Bosnian feudal lords and paid soldiers participated; a scant five hundred returned. In the 1735 war between Turkey and Russia, twenty thousand Bosnians were sent to the front; only 1,340 returned. The wars disrupted both agriculture and trade, and caused significant decay. Ever heavier taxes were levied on the peasant population, the poorest in the empire (Babić et al., vol. 2, pp. 515–75; Donia and Fine, pp. 13–70).

25 Members of the Bosnian Church converted not only to Islam but also to Catholicism or the Orthodox faith, while many who were Catholics or Orthodox became Muslims (Donia and Fine, p. 35).

26 Ćerić, p. 50.

27 The Orthodox were preferred to Catholics, however. Donia and Fine explain this by the fact that the Orthodox patriarch lived in the Ottoman capital, Constantinople, and was thus more easily controlled, whereas the papacy in Rome represented a wholly separate and antagonistic realm, launching crusades against the Ottomans. "The Franciscans," say Donia and Fine, "were seen as a potential fifth column" (pp. 38–39).

28 See also Vasa Čubrilović, "Poreklo muslimanskog plemstva u Bosni i Hercegovini," *Jugoslovenski Istorijski Časopis* 1 (1935): 368–403; and also P. F. Sugar, *Southeastern Europe under Ottoman Rule, 1354–1804*, vol. 5 of *A History of East Central Europe*, ed. P. F. Sugar and D. W. Treadgold (Seattle: University of Washington Press, 1977), p. 56. On the position of Jews in Bosnia see Noel Malcolm, *Bosnia, A Short History* (New York: New York University Press, 1996), pp. 109–14. On the Gypsies of Bosnia see Malcolm, pp. 114–18. On the position of Christians see Donia and Fine, pp. 63–69.

29 Donia and Fine argue that national awareness became a factor for the first time in the nineteenth century, under Austrian occupation. This had a strong ideological effect, as it was intended to have, "but in terms of the actual origins of these Bosnian Catholics and Orthodox, this conclusion was nonsense. The population was greatly mixed as a result of various migrations and many conversions. Thus it was not pos-

sible to determine with any accuracy, for example, if a modern Orthodox Christian was descended from a medieval Catholic or from a Bosnian Churchman. Moreover, the translation of one's religious denomination to Serb or Croat nationality also had no relevance to the area's population, since Bosnians before the nineteenth century had not described themselves as either Serbs or Croats" (p. 73). On the evolution of the national consciousness in the nineteenth century see pp. 79–85.

30 Of the total number of *kmets* (79,669), 3,653 were Muslim, 58,895 Orthodox, and 17,116 Catholic (Donia and Fine, table 5.1, p. 78). The Muslim begs, however, did not live a life of ostentation. Only 0.18 percent of all landlords had land holdings of over 2,473 acres (Ivo Banac, *The National Question in Yugoslavia: Origin, History, Politics* [Ithaca, N.Y.: Columbia University Press, 1984], p. 367).

31 This was not an easy task, not only because of poor transportation but also because Vuk was lame, suffering from rheumatoid polyarthritis. Most doctors agreed he would be unable to lead an active life.

32 For its part, Russia worried that British control of the Turkish Straits would allow Britain to attack the Russian Black Sea ports and to advance into the Caucasus. On Russia's role see Sumner Benedict Humphrey, *Russia and the Balkans, 1870–1880,* (London: Archon Books, 1962), pp. 399–424, 501–53.

33 See Lampe, p. 65. The monarchy encountered stiff resistance as Bosnian Muslim conscripts and many Bosnian Serbs joined Ottoman battalions in attacking the monarchy's convoys from the hills, eventually tying up over one-third of Austro-Hungarian military resources that turned out to be necessary to subdue the area.

But once it established its power, the dual monarchy applied a great deal of skill and tact in appeasement. Between 1878 and 1914 it spent considerable resources in developing Bosnia. Traffic was greatly improved, the mine works reactivated, and lumber plants and tobacco plants spurred. Electricity and sewage systems were installed in the cities; banks and mortgage agencies opened. And while the efforts at modernization were ongoing, the existing social pattern of obligations of Christian peasants to the begs remained in place, undergoing only small modifications. The Austro-Hungarian authorities placed their bet on avoiding upsetting the ingrained traditions. Yet that strategy caused the peasants, who did not benefit directly from the urban growth, to remain deeply dissatisfied and a potentially explosive social group.

The authorities tolerated political activities, including the work of different political parties and their presses, but also encouraged "bošnjaštvo," loyalty to Bosnia as a whole, instead of loyalty to separate ethnic groups. It did not take widespread root but attracted Muslim gentry, who embraced it as a shield against the emerging Serbian and Croatian nationalist autonomist movements. The movements were prodded by Belgrade and Zagreb, which encouraged its members, in violation of Bosnian tradition, to think of themselves as either Serbs or Croats. Each claimed that Bosnia and Hercegovina properly belonged to its nation. On "bošnjaštvo" see Donia and Fine, pp. 97–99; and Banac, pp. 361–64.

In the beginning of the twentieth century, a number of patriotic societies emerged in Bosnia and elsewhere among the progressive youth, including Mlada Bosna

(Young Bosnia), a predominantly Serbian student organization. Their common objective was Yugoslavism.

34 Jovan Cvijić, the famous Serbian geographer and ethnologist, expressed his deep discontent with the results of the Berlin Congress in *Aneksija Bosne i Hercegovine* (Beograd: Državna štamparija, 1908), pp. 6, 7.

35 On the significance of land distribution in Bosnia see Lampe, p. 80. Sabrina Ramet discusses the effect of the Berlin congress on contemporary developments in "Western Peace-Making in the Balkans: A Skeptic's View," *South Slav Journal* 17, nos. 1–2 (spring–summer 1996): 16–30.

36 The Muslims of Bosnia were reluctant to support either Serbian or Croatian national ambitions, aware that they only fragmented Bosnian identity, threatening an eventual partition of Bosnia—the event Bosnian Muslims were determined to avoid. Still, if they had to choose, they chose Croats over Serbs. The Serbs abased Islam while the Croats flattered it, calling Bosnian Muslims the best Croats.

37 Vladimir Dedijer, *Sarajevo, 1914* (Beograd: Prosveta, 1966), pp. 549, 552–53. Even if the group of eight members of Young Bosnia (Mlada Bosna) participating in the assassination was armed and trained by the Black Hand, which included some high-ranking Serbian army officers, it is likely, as John R. Lampe suggests, that the members of Young Bosnia sought out the Black Hand to help them in their terrorist acts, rather than the other way around (Lampe, p. 367 n. 27). See also Wayne C. Vucinich, "Mlada Bosna and the First World War," in *The Hapsburg Empire in World War I: Essays on the Intellectual, Military, Political, and Economic Aspects of the Hapsburg War Effort* ed. Robert A. Kann, Bela Kiraly, and Paula S. Fichtner (Boulder, Colo.: East European Quarterly; distributed by Columbia University Press, 1977), pp. 45–69.

38 Austrian authorities considered Bosnian Serbs to be traitors and all through the war carried out trials ending with internment in the camps (where many starved to death or died from mistreatment), long prison sentences, executions, forced exportations, and forced resettlement (Donia and Fine, p. 118).

39 About the difficulties in establishing the exact figures for the genocide see Srdjan Bogosavljević, *Drugi svetski rat—žrtve u Jugoslaviji*, Ogledi Edition, *Republika* (June 1995), pp. xi–xvi.

40 On the controversy among scholars about the groups that can be encompassed under the Illyrian name, and on the disagreements about the ethnic origin of the Albanians, see Fine, *Early Medieval Balkans*, pp. 9, 11.

   Serbian extremists claim that Kosovo has never been anything but "old Serbia" and deny that the Albanians are Illyrian and therefore the indigenous peoples of the region.

41 From that time dates the saying: "To the Armenians, the pen; to the Arnauts [Albanians], the sword." Yet despite the prevalent belief among the Ottomans that Albanians were Turks, a sizable third of Albanians remained Christian—Catholics in the north, Orthodox in the south.

42 The Kosovo myth at the center of Serbian national consciousness encompasses a number of legends and one whole epic cycle of folk poetry. The elaborateness of

the myth contrasts with the scarcity of established historical facts about the battle. Only basic facts are known: the date of the battle—June 15 (or June 28, according to the new calendar), 1389; the participation in the battle on the Serbian side of the prince Lazar Hrebeljanović, together with Vuk Branković and the Bosnian duke Vlatko Vuković, and on the side of the Ottomans, Sultan Murad with his two sons, Bayezid and Jakuv Ćelebija; it is also known that both prince Lazar and the sultan were killed. The time of their death, however, the size of their armies, the number of those killed on the two sides, and even the outcome of the battle are not known (Olga Zirojević, *Kosovo u istorijskom pamćenju*, Ogledi Edition, *Republika* [March 1995], p. 9).

Nation and Ideology: Essays in Honor of Wayne S. Vucinich, ed. Ivo Banac, John G. Ackerman, and Roman Szporluk (Boulder, Colo.: East European Monographs; dis-years, until the battle of Smederevo in 1459 (Sima Ćirković, *O kosovskom boju 1389* [Prizren-Beograd-Ljubljana: n.p., 1987], p. 560).

Immediately after the battle, a tale was spun on behalf of the Lazarević dynasty, which was to succeed prince Lazar. Between 1390 and 1419, ten new histories of the battle were created to nurture the cult of the fallen king, who was declared a saint by the church soon after the battle (Zirojević, pp. 10–11).

On the use of the cult of Kosovo in the process of Serbian national rebirth see Thomas E. Emmert, "Kosovo, Development and Impact of a National Epic," in *Nation and Ideology: Essays in Honor of Wayne S. Vucinich*, ed. Ivo Banac, John G. Ackerman, and Roman Szporluk (Boulder, Colo.: East European Monographs; distributed by Columbia University Press, 1981), pp. 61–86.

43   Leon Trotsky, *The Balkan Wars, 1912-13: The War Correspondence of Leon Trotsky* (New York: Monad Press, 1980), p. 293.

44   Tucović offered a scathing critique of Serbian policy toward the Albanians in *Srbija i Albanija* (Beograd-Zagreb: Kultura, 1946), pp. 78–119.

45   "Kacaklar" means an outlaw or a fugitive in Albanian.

46   See Banac, *The National Question in Yugoslavia*, p. 303.

47   Asked by Svetozar Pribićević at the beginning of the twentieth century who in fact were the Macedonians, Jovan Cvijić said: "Dear friend, they are neither Serbs nor Bulgarians, at least not today. Common people, peasants, know only that they are Macedonians. Those Macedonian Slavs, who at this moment would be the happiest to say they are Yugoslavs" (cited in Svetozar Pribićević, *Diktatura kralja Aleksandra* [Beograd: Prosveta, 1952], p. 163).

48   The Bulgars, originally a Turkic tribe of central Asia, arrived in the Balkans at about the same time as the Slavs, sometimes in alliance with them. On Bulgars in the early Middle Ages see Fine, *Early Medieval Balkans*, pp. 94–201.

49   On Macedonia see Babić et al., vol. 2, pp. 48–60, 575–78; and Banac, *The National Question in Yugoslavia*, pp. 307-27.

50   Banac, p. 315.

51   See Wayne S. Vucinich, *Serbia between East and West* (Stanford: Stanford University Press, 1954), pp. 24–30.

52   Banac, p. 322.

The Making of Yugoslavia: 1830–1945

Branka Prpa-Jovanović

"The whole world sees morning, but in the Balkans daylight never comes," begins a poem written in 1842 by Ognjeslav Utješenović Ostrožinski, a Serb from Croatia. It was a lament about the condition of the ignored, backward, and divided South Slavic peoples, who in the first half of the nineteenth century still lived under the rule of the Austro-Hungarian Hapsburg dynasty and the Turkish empire.

At the time Ostrožinski wrote, a movement for unification of South Slavs had just begun. It was not a movement led by political thinkers or reflecting popular discontent. Rather, the early movement for South Slavic unity was created by a group of Croatian scholars who called themselves Illyrians, after the oldest tribe known to have inhabited the Balkan peninsula, dating back to classical Greek times. The name also evoked memory of the Illyrian Provinces, as the Hapsburg possessions on the Adriatic, including Croat-speaking lands, were known when they were briefly annexed after 1805 to the modernizing empire of Napoleon Bonaparte.[1] But the name further expressed the desire for a historically neutral identity that all South Slavs could accept. The scholars who joined the Illyrian movement in the 1830s and 1840s tried to establish a common language as a means of uniting the South Slavs, who spoke and wrote in different idioms. A common language, they thought, would be the cornerstone of a unified national culture—a major step toward liberation from foreign domination.[2]

Yet in the Balkans, there were many dialects and languages, both vernacular and literary. Choosing one that would prove acceptable to all Slavic ethnic groups turned out to be a daunting task. In an admirable act of wisdom and restraint, the Croat Ljudevit Gaj, the leading figure among the Illyrians, opted not for the Kajkavian dialect spoken in his own place of origin, Zagreb, and the northwestern part of Croatia, but for the Štokavian, spoken in much of the rest of Croatia, a dialect in which, Gaj argued, "everything that heart and mind demand can be expressed" and which was also spoken by Serbs.[3] Gaj insisted that the Croatian community and other South Slavic communities should each give up something to allow the formation of a single literary language and a unified Illyrian culture.

To achieve their goal, the Illyrians sought to open schools, publish intellectual journals, start cultural associations, and, above all, standardize their written language. This was a way not only of strengthening Slavic unity but also of emphasizing cultural differences between the Slavs and the non-Slavs who ruled over them, whether German-speaking Austrians, Hungarians, or Turks.

The Illyrianism of the 1840s was revived in the 1860s, but under the name of Yugoslavism (*jugoslavjenstvo*), that is, unification of the South (*jug*) Slavs. The most famous representatives of the new movement were two members of the Croatian Catholic church hierarchy: Josip Juraj Strossmayer and Franjo Rački.[4] Their program, like that of the Illyrians, pursued national spiritual unification through establishment of a single literary language and development of the characteristics deemed unique to South Slav culture. Only through building their own distinct culture and linking up with their Slavic kin, such as the Czechs, Poles, and Russians, Strossmayer and Rački argued, could the Croats resist the continuing efforts of the Austrians and Hungarians to assimilate Croatia. Strossmayer, a wealthy Catholic bishop, generously donated his large fortune to support unification efforts. Not only was he instrumental in creating the University of Zagreb and the Yugoslav Academy but he also supported numerous other, lesser cultural institutions and publications.

Strossmayer hoped to unify the South Slavs then under Hapsburg domination through federalization, in which the numerous peoples of the Austro-Hungarian Empire (ranging from Italians to Romanians, Slovenes to Serbs, Germans to Ukrainians) would gain equality with the Germans, Austrians, Hungarians, and South Slavs. This form of Yugoslavism was called by some Austro-Slavism. Creating an independent state of all South Slavs would have been more desirable than uniting them under the Hapsburg roof, but Strossmayer and Rački insisted that the end of the empire was not yet in sight. In addition, the Serbs, who had gained more than the Croats or other South Slavs in terms of independent nationhood, were still not strong enough to push the Turks out of the Balkans. Under more favorable circumstances, Strossmayer and Rački argued, they would urge forming an independent Yugoslav state.

Simultaneously with the emergence of Strossmayer's Yugoslavism, a new movement of Croatian national affirmation developed, stressing the constitutional achievement of a strictly Croatian state rather than the unification of all South Slavs. This movement, led by Ante Starčević and Eugen Kvaternik, called itself the Party of Right (Stranka Prava).[5] It called for a reborn Croatian state legally founded on the ancient "Croatian state right" that had been recognized by the Hungarian and other foreign rulers of Croatia since A.D. 1102, when the previously independent Croatian kingdom was joined in a "personal union" to the Hungarian throne.

According to the ideology of Starčević and Kvaternik, Croatia had maintained itself as a distinct legal entity since A.D. 1102, and although it had been under long Hungarian and then Austro-Hungarian rule, its special legal character had never been abrogated. The party's focus on the Croatian state and Croatian medieval traditions implied a clear rejection of Strossmayer's Yugoslavism. In contrast to Strossmayer, Starčević and Kvaternik not only opposed the program of Croatian unity with other South Slavs under the Hapsburgs but also viewed some other South Slav groups as inferior to the Croats. The Slovenes were, they alleged, merely "Mountain Croats," with no legitimate identity of their own, while Serbs were held to be an "unclean, servile race" without culture.

By the end of the nineteenth century, educated Croatians, whose prosperity and sophistication had increased in the epoch of imperial investment and the rise of industry, were politically split. Some supported Strossmayer and Rački; others rallied to Starčević and Kvaternik. But the imagination of many young people was fired by a new movement, a political club of students at the University of Zagreb called Progressive Youth (Napredna Omladina). This group attempted to combine the South Slavic claims of Austro-Slavism with the particularism of the Party of Right.

Progressive Youth held that a pragmatic politics aimed at reconstitution of a Croatian state should be based on cooperation between Croats and Serbs, to oppose the march of German-speaking culture eastward (*Drang nach Osten*). In this environment, three men—Franjo Supilo, Ante Trumbić, and Josip Smodlaka—gave the ideas of Croatian statehood, as defined originally by the Party of Right, a new, Yugoslav orientation. In 1905 a

Croatian-Serbian electoral coalition was formed in Croatia. The concept of Croatian-Serbian integration thus gained broad currency and support in the period leading to World War I.

The Serbs viewed the rise of Yugoslavism from an entirely different perspective. Serbia had attained a considerable degree of national independence, and for a long period Yugoslavism was of interest to most Serbian political circles, if they took notice of it at all, only as a means to the reconstruction of a strong Serbian state. In 1804 Serbia was the first Balkan region to sustain a national rebellion, directed against the Ottomans. Although the progress of liberation was uneven, in 1830 the sultan granted Serbia broad autonomy under Turkish rule. Serbia was in a radically different position from any other South Slav nation, including that of the Croats, who remained subordinate to the Austro-Hungarian Empire. For the Serbs, Yugoslavism was not a very attractive alternative to the Serbian nationalism through which the Serbian state sought to strengthen itself, by expanding at the expense of Turkey and Austria-Hungary. Until the end of the nineteenth century no political party in Serbia included Yugoslavism in its program. For the Croats, by contrast, unification under the Yugoslav banner represented the sole probable means of their emancipation.

As early as 1844 a leading Serbian political figure, Prime Minister Ilija Garašanin, had developed what amounted to a blueprint for an expanded Great Serbia: the Načertanije or Memorandum.[6] Garašanin advocated the expansion of Serbian rule into Bosnia-Hercegovina, Montenegro, and northern Albania as essential for Serbia's national survival. Garašanin was also open to Strossmayer's Yugoslavism and suggested to Strossmayer in 1867 a loose plan for liberating Christians from Turkish rule and for the "unification of all South Slavs in one federal state." Serbia was to be the axis of unification. Serbian rulers followed the philosophy of Garašanin's Memorandum by pushing their frontiers into neighboring regions where Turkish rule had been weakened and where Serbian-speaking peoples were present. These territories also included large numbers of non-Serbian peoples, who were brought into the Serbian cultural sphere on the basis of historical arguments. The Obrenović dynasty (or Obrenovići in common parlance), then ruling Serbia, believed that a strong Serbia, absorbing all territories that could be claimed historically, was a preferable goal to that of a broader South Slav unification. Serbian political leadership therefore called for unity of all Serbs, many of whom lived in Croatia, Bosnia-Hercegovina, and southern Hungary.

However, at the beginning of the twentieth century, Serbian leaders saw expansion southward as the means to attain these objectives. Their ideas reflected the pragmatic reality of a decaying Turkish empire, hardly able to resist redivision, in contrast with a still militarily intimidating Hapsburg power to the north and west. Yugoslavism, which challenged the latter, therefore remained a secondary concern even as, in 1908, Bosnia-Hercegovina, under de facto Hapsburg rule since the late nineteenth century, was officially absorbed into the Austro-Hungarian Empire.

The oldest and strongest political party in Serbia, the Radical Party, simply rejected Yugoslavism as unrealistic, and its position remained unchanged from 1881 into the early twentieth century. The Radicals called for a union of Balkan states, but one that would merge Serbia, Montenegro, and Bulgaria. A new youth group called the Slav South (Slovenski Jug) was formed in Belgrade in 1904; it argued for a pan-Slavic unification, but its brand of Yugoslavism could make little progress in a Serbian political scene still dominated by nineteenth-century political thinking.

Serbia was transformed by the two Balkan Wars of 1912–13. In these conflicts, the four nations that made up the Balkan League (Serbia, Montenegro, Greece, and Bulgaria), with the support of czarist Russia, resolved to drive the Ottomans out of Europe. In the First Balkan War of 1912, the Turks were deprived of all their remaining European territories except for a small strip adjacent to Constantinople. The ensuing territorial settlement predictably produced a great deal of discord among the allies. As a result, in the Second Balkan War of 1913, Serbia, Montenegro, and Greece aligned themselves against Bulgaria to divide Macedonia, which they had seized from the Turks.

The Balkan Wars had varied results. Serbia acquired Kosovo and the largest portion of Macedonia, the territory around the upper Vardar River. Montenegro and Serbia seized and divided the Sandžak of Novi Pazar, which linked Macedonia to Bosnia, and this conquest gave Montenegro a common border with Serbia. Greece got Aegean Macedonia, and Bulgaria obtained Pirin Macedonia, the smallest part of all. In addition, Albania secured its independence.

Success against the Turks gave Serbia a great deal of self-confidence; if the Ottomans could be so easily defeated, why not the Hapsburgs as well? More important, it stimulated sentiment for a South Slav union. The Radical Party began to call for Pan-Slavic liberation from Austria-Hungary, with Serbia leading the way. In 1903 the Obrenović dynasty was overthrown in Serbia and replaced by the Karadjordjević dynasty (Karadjordjevići, in common parlance). This move helped shift Serbian politics toward Yugoslavism and increased tension with Austria-Hungary.

However much Serbia now enjoyed seeing itself as the liberator of the South Slavs, it was not strong enough to immediately confront one of Europe's great powers. Nevertheless, backed by imperial Russia, Serbia found itself at war with Austria-Hungary following the assassination of Archduke Franz Ferdinand in Sarajevo on June 28, 1914. Austria-Hungary seized the opportunity to settle accounts with Serbia; it accused Serbia of sponsoring the assassination plot and, supported by Germany and later joined by Bulgaria and Turkey, declared war on Serbia on July 28, 1914. Russia, with France and Great Britain, rallied to Serbia's side. At the beginning, Serbian objectives were defensive. But soon the Serbian leaders defined their war aims in terms of broader South Slav liberation. If the war with Austria-Hungary could not be avoided, it at least offered a possibility for Serbia, in case of victory, to create a powerful Slav state, uniting Serbs, Croats, and Slovenes.

Yugoslavia was thus born in the chaos and blood of World War I. In battle, as in the past, South Slavs found themselves fighting on opposite sides: Croats, Slovenes, and Serbs from Croatia and southern Hungary, in the trenches of the Hapsburg forces, fought against Serbs and Montenegrins in the armies of those two monarchies. In effect, Croats, Slovenes, and "exiled" Serbs were obliged to combat Serbia's stated goal of South Slavic liberation and unity.[7]

At the cost of 1,900,000 Yugoslav lives, war produced the collapse of Austria-Hungary.[8] Croatia saw nationalist and social uprisings, Hungary underwent a brief Soviet revolution, and the remaining non-German peoples who had been ruled by the Hapsburgs demanded their independence under the doctrine of self-determination enunciated by U.S. president Woodrow Wilson. At the height of glory and prestige, Serbia was jubilant, although it had lost one-fourth of its population and half its economic assets in the war. At long last, the chance to create, if not a Great Serbia, then at least a united South Slavic state was at hand.

The formation of the new state was outlined in 1917 when the South Slav Committee, consisting of such prominent Croatian figures as the sculptor Ivan Meštrović and the politicians Trumbić and Supilo, joined the Serbian government in issuing the Corfu Declaration, calling for a democratic, constitutional monarchy of Serbs, Croats, and Slovenes. At the same time, the Slovene politician Antun Korošec had organized a Yugoslav National Council, advocating South Slav unification. The movement for unity was fed by traditional fears of German cultural domination combined with anxieties over the ambitions of Italy, a member of the Allies whose leaders had demonstrated that their appetite for annexation of the Slovene- and Croat-speaking territories along the Adriatic from Trieste to Dubrovnik was not to be discounted.[9]

In the world destined to be defined by the Versailles Treaty, Yugoslav unity had ceased to be an abstraction and had become an urgent reality.[10] A revolutionary State of Slovenes, Croats, and Serbs quickly gave way to a new Kingdom of Serbs, Croats, and Slovenes, declared on December 1, 1918, and ruled by the house of Karadjordjević from Belgrade. The new state was recognized by the great powers at Versailles on July 28, 1919, although the United States, in which South Slavic immigrant political groups were active and articulate, had already recognized the kingdom in February 1919. To the former Serbian monarchy were added Slovenia, Croatia, Bosnia-Hercegovina, Montenegro, and Vojvodina, the latter being an area, formerly part of Hungary, with a considerable Serbian population and rich in Serbian tradition. Italy, the least influential of the victorious Allies, was the only power resolutely opposed to recognition; it saw in Yugoslavia a rival for control of the Adriatic.

This was a transcendent historical moment, the fulfillment of the dreams of generations of South Slav advocates. The South Slavs were coming together not only because of shared cultural and linguistic traditions but also in search of prosperity, modernization, autonomy, and equality in the new European order. The aggressiveness of Germans, Hungarians, and Italians had the effect of further strengthening the Slav union as a means of national survival. Yet the manner by which Serbs, Croats, and Slovenes would resolve their differences, once a united kingdom was proclaimed, remained unclear.[11]

The new state, under the rule of Regent Aleksandar in Belgrade, did not constitute an equal partnership. A new constitution picturesquely described Serbs, Croats, and Slovenes as "three tribes" of the same nation. The Montenegrins, however, were not recognized as a separate tribe because their parliament had voted on the eve of the new state's creation to incorporate themselves into Serbia. The Macedonians were not recognized as a nation because they had been part of the Kingdom of Serbia since the Balkan Wars and were treated as Serbs. The Muslims were recognized as a religiously separate entity and were allowed to have political parties but, like the Montenegrins and Macedonians, were not recognized as a separate tribe or nation. The large Albanian minority in Kosovo was simply ignored.

Other aspects of the political situation showed that profound tendencies toward the disintegration of the new state existed within it from the beginning. The distinct regions exhibited drastically different levels of economic development. Legal traditions varied greatly.[12] Virtually all the communities in the new state disagreed over one issue: Should the regime be centralized or should it be a decentralized federation? These differences deepened with time. Very soon the country resembled a construction being built during the day and destroyed at night.

Modernization encountered some insurmountable obstacles in addition to the frailty of democratic traditions and the variety of legislative and executive regimes inherited from the previous rulers. Since it was mainly a traditional peasant society, the whole Balkan region had seen a retarded process of urbanization and development of the middle classes. In 1921 agriculture was still the main occupation of some 80 percent of the Yugoslav population, and in 1931 of more than 76 percent.[13] But Yugoslav agriculture was in permanent crisis, and reform and mechanization were elusive. Landholdings were typically very small, often too small to be productive beyond securing immediate subsistence. In 1931 some two-thirds of farming households had less than five hectares of land; seven hundred thousand households owned less than two hectares, and the tendency was continually toward smaller and smaller, and less and less efficient landholdings. The crisis in agriculture was worsened by the low level of technical development and labor productivity, and by rural overpopulation.

Industrial development was also stunted, as well as being unequally distributed. The greater part of industry had been established in the former Hapsburg realm, in the northwest regions of Slovenia, Croatia, and Vojvodina. Slovenian industrial development was four times greater than Serbian and twenty-two times greater than Macedonian and Montenegrin industrial development. Compounding the problems facing the young country was the heritage of four different railroad systems, seven different bodies of law, and several different currencies.[14] The merging of these multiple systems was slow, and the kingdom, from the beginning, lagged well behind the rest of Europe in embracing twentieth-century methods.

Yugoslav leaders wanted to fashion the key features of the country's social and political system after European models of capitalist efficiency and political liberalism. In practice, the stability of the new state depended on the willingness of the Serbian, Croatian, and Slovene political elites to minimize their major conflicts in the interest of modernization.

The constitution of June 28, 1921, which became known as the St. Vitus Day Constitution (Vidovdanski Ustav), was intended as a major step in this direction. It defined the new state as a constitutional, parliamentary, and hereditary monarchy. The constitution enshrined the principles of European bourgeois life: the abolition of feudal obligations, the inviolability of private property, and guarantees of equality under the law and freedom of religion and of the press. This constitution promised modernization but in practice offered only a step in that direction. In a simpler context the liberalism of the constitution might have prevailed; in the Balkans, it could not.

The new constitution brought about several disputes. Because of maneuvering by Serbian politicians, the text was adopted only by a simple majority of the Constitutional Assembly, not by a two-thirds majority. The Slovenian and Croatian representatives bitterly objected to the adoption process, which institutionalized the domination of the Serbian majority over representatives of the other Yugoslav nationalities. Furthermore, the constitution conceived of a highly centralized state. That worked to the advantage of the Serbs, who ruled the state from Belgrade, but greatly exacerbated the sense of grievance of the non-Serbs. In theory, the national interests of the three "tribes"—Serbs, Croats, and Slovenes—were meant to be fused in a new nation. But as it turned out, the proposed Yugoslav nation-state consisted of nothing more than a geographic framework, while politically it remained the cockpit of conflicting Serbian, Croatian, and Slovenian national interests. Neither the force of the state machinery nor the strength of South Slav unitarian idealism could succeed in forging a genuine single people or nation out of these three. Consequently, the kingdom never became a true nation-state. The leading principle of the European liberal world—that of "one man, one vote," as promised in the constitution—abstractly represented progress. In the political practice of the multiethnic kingdom, however, it enabled the most numerous nation—the Serbs—to outvote and dominate the others.

Some leading Serbian personalities who spent World War I in exile in western Europe understood as early as 1918 that Yugoslavia could not be constructed on a centralist basis without provoking an irresolvable political crisis. They anticipated an inevitable collapse of Yugoslavia and tried to find solutions that would appease differing national interests. In 1918 Ljubomir Stojanović, a prominent Serbian linguist and professor at Belgrade University, predicted in a letter to Jovan Cvijić, a geographer and Belgrade University colleague, that Yugoslavia would end up like Austria-Hungary unless it adopted a federal structure in which Serbia, Montenegro, Croatia, Slovenia, and Bosnia-Hercegovina enjoyed equal status. Cvijić, for his part, theorized a Yugoslav community along federal lines which he called a United States of Yugoslavia.

Other members of the Serbian intellectual elite also considered the generation of old Serbian politicians—and especially the long-popular Nikola Pašić—unable to guide Yugoslavia in the direction of a modern European state, simply because they belonged to the past in their political practices and outlook. Cvijić said of Pašić, whose political career had begun in the era of revolutionary pan-Slavism, influenced by anarchist extremism at the same time that it was subsidized by the Russian czar, that "he did not understand and could not understand the mentality of Western Europe."

Yet, as the head of the Serbian government before and during World War I and as leader of the Radicals, Pašić enjoyed a decisive influence in the creation of the Yugoslav state. After unification, from January 1921 to April 1926, Pašić formed ten governments and remained the dominant figure on the Yugoslav political scene. His outmoded, centralist conceptions provoked increasing resistance from Croatian and Slovenian representatives. Croatians were especially sensitive on these matters because their whole political tradition was based on centuries of struggle against the centralism of Vienna and Budapest. The federalist Yugoslavism that Croatian intellectuals pursued during the nineteenth century was conceived as an alternative to the centralism of the Astro-Hungarian monarchy, not as a means for its substitution by another form of centralism. Croatia expected the new state to grant what it had been denied under the Hapsburgs: national sovereignty and a chance for unhindered economic and cultural growth. Croatian Yugoslavism, the current that triumphed during World War I over Croatian ultranationalism, gradually lost its sense of optimism and enthusiasm in clashes with real-life Yugoslavism. The Croatian public came to view the formula of three tribes in the constitution as a mask for Serbian expansionism and as the assimilation, if not the destruction, of the Croatian people.

The centralism established by the 1921 constitution encountered its most serious obstacle in the form of the dominant trend in Croatian politics after World War I: the Croatian Peasant Party. Its leader, the remarkable Stjepan Radić, exercised a commanding hold over the loyalties of the Croatian public, by combining peasant protest and an antimonarchical, pacifist program. The Croatian Peasant Party took up the crusade against centralism. A sense of common purpose—the preservation of the Croatian nation and its historical tradition of statehood, melded with a program of agrarian radicalism—bridged social differences.[15]

In the same period, Slovenian political aspirations tended either to Yugoslavism, or to nationalism. In a 1918 manifesto, some Slovenian intellectuals had criticized Slovenian "separatist political aspirations," but by 1921 another group had assembled yet another manifesto, declaring the impossibility of a mechanical unification of Yugoslavia and soon demanding Slovenian autonomy within Yugoslavia. Although the majority of Slovenian politicians and intellectuals saw Yugoslavia as a necessary vehicle for political unity, they would not grant it the power to forcibly combine the existing nations into one new Yugoslav nation. The initial good faith with which Yugoslavism had been received by Slovenes vanished and doubts mounted. Like Croats, Slovenes could not accept a state that was controlled by Serbia. The split between centralists and autonomists in Slovenia ended in a decisive victory for the latter.

The "three-tribe" nation thus stood divided from the very beginning. No awareness of distant, common Slavic ethnic origins and no unifying state policy could change this reality. Yugoslavia was viable only so long as its Serbian rulers did not openly seek to suppress the identity of any of the other constituent nations. That and the aggrieved agitation of the federalist opposition, especially as it gained momentum in Croatia, made open conflict between Croats and Serbs inevitable.[16]

Misunderstanding, distrust, and intolerance became the main features of political life in the kingdom.[17] The parliament was paralyzed, working less and less frequently: either it waited for the end of yet another extended ministerial crisis (some lasting more than six months) or it called new elections.

Moreover, this political struggle was carried out in an unfavorable economic environment. Economic liberalism was mandated by the constitution; the adoption of new legal codes should have stimulated development. Yet the social and economic differences between the regions persisted in profoundly influencing political life. The regions that were more developed industrially (Slovenia and Croatia), in which 75 percent of all industry had been located in 1918, increased that percentage between 1920 and 1930 to 80 percent. The underdeveloped southeastern regions showed much slower industrial growth. The predominantly agrarian economies of Serbia and Montenegro were especially hard hit by the worldwide recession of the early 1920s, in which commodity prices collapsed, as well as by the deeper world economic crisis that began in 1929.

The northwestern regions of the country sought to preserve their advantageous situation in the internal Yugoslav market, while the southeastern regions, especially Serbia, wanted to close the economic gap as quickly as possible. Hence, Croatians and Slovenes expected their economic position to win them political authority, while the Serbs expected their political authority to strengthen their economic position, mainly through the power of taxation. Disparities in economic and political power were dramatic: according to one calculation, Serbia accounted for a mere one-fourth of Yugoslav capital, but its representatives made up three-fourths to four-fifths of government personnel.

The crisis of the new state was also complicated by the special powers of King Aleksandar Karadjordjević, the first Yugoslav king and the son of the Serbian King Petar I. The prerogatives the constitution granted to Karadjordjević and the use to which he put his prerogatives weakened the parliamentary system, and the constitutional monarchy soon became an autocracy. The king was endowed with inviolability—that is, he could not be politically challenged or forced to account for his actions to parliament. The Belgrade government was responsible for all his actions, yet all state functions—the legislative, the administrative, and the judicial— were in the king's hands. In a form very distant from that of the European parliamentary monarchies, in which the ruler discreetly influenced government and did not in practice test the limits of royal authority, King Aleksandar, as he was known, constantly interfered in the political life of the country, above all in the choice of cabinet members. By frequently using his constitutional right to convene and disband parliament, by allowing the country to be governed by governments that lacked a parliamentary majority, and by nullifying governments that had a parliamentary majority, he undermined the basic principles of parliamentarianism.

For example, according to the testimony of Svetozar Pribićević, a politician who was very close to the king, of twenty-three cabinet crises, the parliament had provoked only two; all the rest were provoked by the king or by officials close to him and acting on his instructions.[18]

A critical turning point came ten years after Yugoslavia emerged from the ashes of World War I. On June 20, 1928, three deputies of the Croatian Peasant Party, among them the famed Stjepan Radić, were shot in parliament by Puniša Račić, a Montenegrin deputy and member of the Radical Party. Two were killed immediately, and Radić suffered a lingering death. With that tragedy, parliamentarianism also died, and with it many illusions about the future of a democratic Yugoslavia. The death of a person as popular as Radić deeply radicalized the Croatian national movement and irreparably aggravated the Serbian-Croatian split.[19]

King Aleksandar took advantage of the crisis created by the parliament murders to carry out a coup d'état. On January 6, 1929, he suspended the constitution, outlawed all political parties, and dismissed the National Assembly. Although the coup was publicly justified in the interest of peace and order in the country, in reality it represented the last attempt in the history of the Yugoslav monarchy to maintain a centralist regime. The king set up a dictatorship, suppressing all forms of parliamentary and democratic activity in the name of Yugoslavism. The Kingdom of Serbs, Croats, and Slovenes was officially renamed the Kingdom of Yugoslavia.

For a while, it seemed as though the king had found the formula for stopping the escalating crisis. His attempt to settle ethnic antagonisms by denying their existence—as in the renaming of the state—was welcomed by elements of Croatian and Slovenian public opinion who believed the Yugoslav king really wanted to establish inter-ethnic balance and prevent chaos. The king accused Yugoslav politicians of instigating strife among the people; he insisted that their opportunistic struggle for power was the basic cause of the political crisis in the country. He therefore offered a framework for the establishment of an "ideal" form of Yugoslavism; the "unifying king," as a symbol of the unified state, promised to communicate directly with the Yugoslav people. He eliminated the liberal legal-political structure in order to establish "direct democracy." Between the monarch and the people, he claimed, there should be no intermediary. But the success of these seemingly effective maneuvers was short-lived.

The refurbished version of Yugoslavism served the king as a political rationalization for authoritarian rule. The centralistic model created by the constitution was reaffirmed by a new administrative division of the state into nine provinces (*banovine*), named after major rivers. Dividing the Yugoslav territory geographically, the king sought to erase all trace of the state traditions of the different Yugoslav nations, as well as ethnic and religious borders. The constitution of September 3, 1931, which the king's supporters called the September Constitution and his opponents called the Imposed Constitution (Oktroirani Ustav), offered an illusion of democracy through a pseudo parliament.

Reality had exposed the false nature of monarchical Yugoslavism. Still, few expected the price to be paid in blood — and by Aleksandar Karadjordjević himself. Macedonian and Croatian extremists assassinated him in Marseilles in 1934. With him was buried the illusion of monarchical Yugoslavism.

The death of the king brought about a regrouping of political forces, but the democratic, liberal foundations of the Yugoslav state had been thoroughly eroded. On the one hand, Yugoslav parliamentarianism had been compromised by the parliament murders of 1928 and further subverted by royal dictatorship. On the other hand, fascist Italy and Nazi Germany, as well as Hungary, were encouraged to exploit Yugoslav national conflicts for their own objectives. The world economic crisis exacerbated the situation. These were the circumstances in the final chapter of Yugoslavia's short and turbulent life. A race against time began.

Demands for Croatian independence from the Yugoslav state continued to threaten the government with new crises. The question was put on the agenda in 1934, but not until February 1939 did Prince Pavle Karadjordjević open the way for settling Serbian-Croatian relations. An agreement signed on August 26, 1939, between the Serbian politician Dragiša Cvetković and the Croatian politician Vladimir Maček, successor to Radić as leader of the Croatian Peasant Party, initiated a reordering of the Kingdom of Yugoslavia. The state and its "imposed constitution" underwent a radical change, eliminating the thirty-three provinces that existed thus far, and creating instead nine regional units, or banovine. Croatian autonomy was recognized through the establishment of a special banovina of Croatia.[20]

Banovina Croatia, as it was known, was granted a specific territory and a separate government organization. Croatia now was qualitatively different from the nine previous banovine; it now enjoyed a degree of recognized statehood, which, although it was subordinate to the central government and king, held out the possibility of a federal Yugoslavia.[21]

But a federal Yugoslavia might have had a better chance at another time. It was now too late—not only because the Serbian-Croatian agreement was reached on the eve of World War II, in difficult international circumstances, or because the other Yugoslav nations were bitter about being left out, but also because the solution satisfied neither the Serbs nor the Croats. Croatian politicians were angered by the limited nature of autonomy and Serbian politicians by the loss of their dominion, the abandonment of centralism, and the new division of administrative powers. Nevertheless, the 1939 agreement began the revision of Yugoslavia's national foundations, a process that remained incomplete through failing to encompass Slovenia, Bosnia-Hercegovina, and even Serbia as separate units.[22] The national demands of the Macedonians and Albanians continued to be ignored.

Only eighteen months after the agreement was signed, Yugoslavia collapsed. There was hardly enough time for the range of national and party differences to be overcome. On April 6, 1941, Hitler's air force leveled Belgrade, dragging Yugoslavia into World War II on its own territory. The first South Slavic state perished as it had been born, in fire and smoke. The creative energy symbolized by the unification and the accumulation of human, intellectual, and economic potential had foundered on the phenomena of permanent political crisis and national antagonism. Yugoslavia had gambled away its first historical chances.

In less than two weeks, Hitler and Mussolini abolished the country of Yugoslavia. Its territory was partitioned between Germany and Italy, with parts also handed out to Hungary and Bulgaria. Once again, new borders were laid out by foreign powers, trenches were dug, barbed wire strung, bunkers built, concentration camps opened, armies formed, and local chiefs installed.

Society was reorganized on the basis of ethnic separation and inflamed hatreds. There began a war of all against all. Armed attacks on the occupying power began almost immediately in Italian-controlled Montenegro, which had ancient traditions of guerrilla warfare, as well as in Serbia, marked for "exemplary punishment" by the Nazis. With the German invasion of Soviet Russia less than three months later, the Communist Party of Yugoslavia, which had been a negligible political factor after a brief leftist upsurge in the 1920s, called for partisan warfare. The occupiers answered both non-Communist and Communist resistance with terror and mass executions, compounded by further atrocities by their local collaborators.

The pro-Axis forces that emerged to rule the ruins of the South Slav state included the Ustashe, or Rebels, the extremist wing of the Croatian nationalist movement, which had gained the patronage of Italy and Hungary in the period before the outbreak of war and which, with the fall of monarchist Yugoslavia, set up a puppet Independent State of Croatia that absorbed Bosnia-Hercegovina. The Ustashe, although a small minority of the Croatian population, also recruited among the Slavic Muslims of Bosnia-Hercegovina, for a program of brutal repression of Communists as well as outright genocide against the Serbian population within the "independent state." In addition, the Ustashe enthusiastically fulfilled Nazi demands for the extermination of the historic Jewish communities of Croatia and Bosnia-Hercegovina (in the latter case, a Sephardic Jewry of great age and distinction), as well as many Gypsies.

In Serbia, a collaborationist regime was also set up, run by military and police officers, and an array of ultranationalist formations, known as Chetniks (irregulars), began pursuing vengeance against Slavic Muslims, Croats, and Communists. In Vojvodina, the combined efforts of local German colonists and the Hungarian authorities resulted in the wholesale destruction of the local Jewish population and serious losses among the Serbs.

Against this range of extremely unattractive options, only one force existed that was committed to united South Slavic resistance to the invaders, that is, to something like the original ideal of Yugoslavia. That was the Communist Party under the half-Croat, half-Slovene Josip Broz Tito, which included many members of the International Brigades in the Spanish Civil War.

The rest of the old political organizations and parties disappeared. The royal Yugoslav government and its king found refuge in London, representing a country that no longer existed. The Allies, committed to supporting resistance efforts throughout occupied Europe, were faced with two such movements in Yugoslavia: a faction of Serbian Chetniks loyal to the king and led by General Dragoljub (Draža) Mihailović, formally representing the national Yugoslav army in its occupied homeland, and the

Partisans of the National Liberation Movement set up by Tito. Although both Mihailović's Chetniks and Tito's Partisans were members of the Allied coalition, the two movements never succeeded in uniting for a joint, patriotic fight against the German and Italian occupation. The Chetniks fought for a return to a Great Serbian, centralist monarchy, the Partisans for a socialist federation. Ideologically opposed, advancing conflicting war aims as well as different visions of the renewal of Yugoslavia, they would fight a war within the war. For all these reasons, World War II for Yugoslavia was not simply the bloody destruction of a conquered state by the Nazi-fascist coalition. It was also a civil war within each of the Yugoslav communities.

From this pandemonium of evil that broke loose in Yugoslavia only one faction emerged victorious—the Communists. Their historic victory would be difficult to explain had they relied on ideology alone. The Communists were a small, illegal organization, fiercely persecuted in pre-1941 Yugoslavia.[23] Soon after the war began, they launched sporadic and isolated armed actions. However, as the war progressed, it was clear they were alone in maintaining a consistent struggle against the invader. Their appeal to the Yugoslav peoples lay in their patriotic, local, and democratic, rather than ideological, principles. Thus, in Slovenia they allied themselves with the Christian Democrats; in Croatia they recruited followers of the Peasant Party as well as Dalmatian Croats angry at the Italians who sought to colonize the area and Serbs who had suffered under or feared the Ustashe regime; in Bosnia-Hercegovina they brought together Croats, Serbs, Muslims, and Jews; in Serbia and Montenegro they harked back to national traditions of mutual aid from and for "Holy Russia," now ruled by Stalin but, to many Orthodox peasants in the Balkans, no less Russia and no less holy. In the past political life of the kingdom, the Communists had unequivocally demonstrated their commitment to a federal Yugoslavia—to the principle of full equality for all the peoples living within it. During a war with all the features of a religious and ethnic war, the Communists offered—at the time when the renewal of Yugoslavia seemed entirely impossible—a new vision of Yugoslavia, expressed in the slogan "Brotherhood and Unity." Yugoslavism was reborn in blood, but on new foundations. The Communists hoped not to repeat the errors of their predecessors.

In 1943, the second session of the Antifascist Council for the National Liberation of Yugoslavia—the political leadership of the Tito Partisans—

decided to recognize Bosnia-Hercegovina, Montenegro, Croatia, Macedonia, Slovenia, and Serbia as federal units of a Democratic Federative Yugoslavia. National status was granted to the Macedonians, Montenegrins, and, implicitly, through recognition of Bosnia-Hercegovina, to the Muslims. The status of Kosovo and of Albania itself in the future Balkan socialist commonwealth was left unmentioned. The intention in forming the federation was to establish a national equilibrium and prevent any nation from dominating the others. It was on this platform and on the basis of their undeniable successes on the battlefield that the Communists won widespread support.

But the Allies recognized the Yugoslav government in exile and the Chetnik commander Draža Mihailović, the representative of the exiled king, as the representative of the country. As the war continued, however, it became increasingly clear that the Communists were the only real military force to contend with in Yugoslavia. British policy backed away from Mihailović's Chetniks as a political or military alternative. Churchill, in 1943, recognized the internationalist Partisans as the major partners of the Allies, shocking the royalist Yugoslavs exiled in London. The leadership of the Mihailović Chetniks held an underground congress, offering a reborn constitutional and parliamentary monarchy of Serbs, Croats, and Slovenes. But the attempt to make this an all-Yugoslav platform did not bring Mihailović the support of the Allies, nor did it reinforce his position in the country. The Allies concluded that the Mihailović Chetniks were not fighting the Germans and Italians but, rather, collaborating with them against the Communists. The Chetniks also compromised themselves before the Yugoslav people because of their violent Serbian chauvinism and the atrocities they had committed against Muslim, Croat, and other non-Serbian civilians. By 1943 the Communists faced no serious rivals in the anti-Axis camp.

From small groups committed to desperate and poorly organized actions against the occupiers, Tito's National Liberation Army grew to become a force of eight hundred thousand fighters. Tito triumphed in the halo of military success and ascribed his glory to the power of Communist ideology. The real victory, however, was that of the resurrected Yugoslav idea. Once again, Yugoslavs looked to the future with enthusiasm and hope. The first, post–World War I Yugoslavia had been created by intellectual and political elites. The new Yugoslavia that emerged from World War II was seen as a creation of the people. Despite the legacy of the ill-fated royal state, and despite the terrible crimes committed in the name of nationality during World War II, Yugoslavism provided a context for reconciliation. Common life was not only possible, but necessary.

NOTES

1 Napoleon saw his Illyrian provinces as "the guard set before the gates of Vienna" (cited in R. W. Seton-Watson, *The Southern Slav Question and the Habsburg Monarchy* [London: Constable, 1911], p. 26).

2 This was a response to the aggressive introduction of Magyar as the exclusive language in communication with the Hungarian authorities as well as in schools. In Croatia, Latin had been used in the courts, but in 1843 it was proclaimed that speeches made in Latin by the Croatian delegates should be ignored (Seton-Watson, p. 29).

3 Gaj, "a man of Western culture and fiery eloquence" (Seton-Watson, p. 29), founded three journals of great cultural and ultimately political influence: *Novine Hrvatske* (Croatian gazette); *Danica* (Morning star); and *Danica Ilirska* (Illyrian morning star). The journals advocated the eventual unification of the South Slavs.

4 Josip Juraj Strossmayer supported every South Slav learned society, including the work of the great Serbian philologists Vuk Stefanović Karadžić and Djuro Daničić. Franjo Rački was one of the first Croatian historians and drew his financial support almost completely from Strossmayer. On the Illyrian movement and beyond see Mirjana Gross, "Croatian National Integrationist Ideologies from the End of Illyrianism to the Creation of Yugoslavia," *Austrian History Notebook* 15–16 (1979–80): pp. 4–21. *Ed.*

5 In an affront to Austria, Ante Starčević said: "To exist, Croatia only needs God, and the Croats" (cited in Rudolf Horvat, *Najnovije Doba Hrvatske Povjesti* [Zagreb, 1906]).

6 On Garašanin see David MacKenzie, *Ilya Garašanin: Balkan Bismarck* (Boulder, Colo.: East European Monographs; distributed by Columbia University Press, 1985). Nacertainje was written as an internal document, and remained unknown to the general public until 1906. At its heart lay a romantic dream of uniting the South Slavs, but with Belgrade as the center. Garašanin failed to work out the place Croatia would occupy in the new union, but favored respect for all ethnic groups and cooperation with Croatian Catholic clergy. *Ed.*

7 Many Croats, like the Croatian Serbs, had no choice but to join the Hapsburg Balkanstreit Armee. The army included up to 25 percent Serb soldiers, assigned along with 50 percent Croats, to invade Serbia. On this paradoxical, but for the times typical, situation see Dimitrije Djordjević, *The Creation of Yugoslavia 1914–1918* (Santa Barbara, Calif.: Clio Press, 1980), p. 310. In 1914, over five thousand Serbian civilians were interned in camps; many suspected of aiding Serbian fighters were summarily executed; up to fifty thousand Serbs living in towns and villages along the Drina river were forced to abandon their homes; by mid-1917 up to one hun-

dred thousand Serbs were deported and held in concentration camps; in the town of Foča (which saw horrific scenes of ethnic cleansing in 1992–93), massacres and mass deportations of Serbs took place, amounting to what John Lampe has called "the first incidence of active ethnic cleansing" (p. 107 n. 11). *Ed.*

8   See Branko Petranović, *Istorija Jugoslavije* (Beograd: Nolit, 1978), p. 35. The loss of human life was staggering. In its epic retreat across Albania in 1915, for example, the Serbian army numbering 300,000 was halved; 630,000 died in concentration camps and in exile; 500,000 children were orphaned. *Ed.*

9   Support for unification grew steadily among the common people as the war was drawing to a close. In 1918 that support varied between 100 percent in Dalmatia and 60 percent in Croatia, Slavonia, and Bosnia-Hercegovina (see Milorad Ekmečić, *Stvaranje Jugoslavije 1790–1918*, vol. 2 [Beograd: Prosveta], pp. 829–32).

10 See Ivo Lederer, *Yugoslavia at the Paris Peace Conference* (New Haven: Yale University Press, 1963). The proclamation of the kingdom was bitterly protested by the Social Democratic Party, the Party of Pure Right, the Catholic clergy, and by Stjepan Radić himself, who insisted that Croatia should be an autonomous confederal unit. *Ed.*

11 The war's devastation only made the situation graver. The unstable new state encountered collapsed traffic routes, famine in the winter of 1918–19, a shortage of living space, the epidemics of typhus, diphtheria, and Spanish fever, and last but not least, an entirely undeveloped middle class (see Petranović, p. 41).

12 The legal system was fragmented, allowing for the parallel existence of diverse legal codes. This made it impossible to ensure uniform protection of legal security (see Petranović, p. 34).

13 Only 2.9 percent of the population held land in excess of twenty hectares (Petranović, p. 150). The failure of economic development between the two world wars exacerbated doubts about the wisdom of national unification. *Ed.*

14 See John Lampe, cited in Djordjević, p. 343.

15 Svetozar Pribićević says that Radić was a Croat from head to toe, but a Croat filled with Slavic sentiment. Radić told the king that the entire parliament was too rotten to offer a chance for a healthy political life; the reason is, said Radić, that the parliament was built from the top, by the use of terror and electoral corruption (see Svetozar Pribićević, *Diktatura kralja Aleksandra* [Beograd: Prosveta, 1952], pp. 69, 71). Ivo Banac quotes Radić's address to the Central Committee of the Zagreb National Council: "If the Serbs really want to have such a centralist state and government, god bless them with it, but we Croats do not want any state organization except a confederated federal republic" (*The National Question in Yugoslavia: Origins, History, Politics* [Ithaca: Cornell University Press, 1984], p. 226).

16 See Pribicević, pp. 150–60.

17 See Charles Jelavich, "Comments," *Austrian History Yearbook* 15–16 (1979–80): 38–41.

18 See Petranović, pp. 76–94.

19 On the assassination of Radić see Pribićević, pp. 59–75.

20 For a condensed interpretation of the period between the two world wars see R. W.

Seton-Watson and R. G. D. Laffan, "Yugoslavia between the Wars," in *A Short History of Yugoslavia from Early Times to 1966*, ed. Stephen Clissold (London: Cambridge University Press, 1966), pp. 170–207.

21 It is worth noting that as the Croatian banovina became more independent, the Serbs in Croatia complained with increased frequency of various forms of harassment, discrimination, and general ill treatment. See Bruce Bigelow, "Centralization versus Decentralization in Interwar Yugoslavia," *Southern Europe* 1, no. 2 (1974): 170; and *History of Yugoslavia*, ed. Vladimir Dedijer, Ivan Božić, Sima Ćirković, and Milorad Ekmečić (New York: McGraw-Hill, 1974), pp. 529–50. Banovina Croatia included on the south, Dalmatia and the Dubrovnik region; on the north, Srem and the town of Vukovar; and in the center-south, a good part of Bosnia and Hercegovina, including the town of Mostar. The Ustashe party, which returned from Italy after the signing of the Serbian-Croatian agreement (Sporazum), opposed the agreement and recruited its supporters (albeit not too successfully: only 5 percent of the Croatian population joined the Ustashe) claiming that the whole of Bosnia should be added to Croatia. In 1991–95, Franjo Tudjman aimed to add the regions of Bosnia-Hercegovina, recognized as a part of Croatian banovina, to the state of Croatia he proclaimed in 1991. *Ed.*

22 Petranović, p. 147.

23 On December 30, 1920, a new law, known under the name Obznana, prohibited all Communist activity and urged confiscation of all the party's offices and newspapers. Communist members went underground, but at that time their activity lacked any significant structure (see Ivo Banac, ed., *The Effects of World War I: The Class War after the Great War: The Rise of Communist Parties in East Central Europe, 1918–1921* vol. 13 of *War and Society in East Central Europe*, East European Monographs No. 137, (Boulder, Colo.: SSM, 1983), pp. 203–5. *Ed.*

Tito: 1945–1980

Mirko Tepavac

In 1941 the Kingdom of Yugoslavia collapsed under the assault of Nazi Germany and its Axis allies. The disintegration, twenty-three years after the foundation of a unified South Slavic state, was dramatic and appeared final. Few in the country or abroad believed the pieces could ever be put together again in a revived single state. Yet what had seemed impossible proved possible, in the hands of Josip Broz Tito.

Soon after the German invasion in April 1941, two figures emerged as apparent resistance leaders: General Dragoljub (Draža) Mihailović, who led the Chetniks, a faction of Serbian irregular forces loyal to the exiled king, and Tito, who directed the Partisans under Communist political control.[1] The Mihailović strategy was to avoid direct battle with the German and Italian occupiers so as to preserve the strength of the royalist Serbian nationalist forces, in anticipation of a return to power by the prewar Karadjordjevići dynasty. Tito's Partisans, in contrast, waged an uncompromising war against the invader and gained strength in the struggle. While Mihailović was able to rally only Serbs and Montenegrins to his stationary units in the mountains, Tito recruited his Partisan troops from among all the peoples in Yugoslavia and maintained a continuous military campaign against the occupation. Once the war ended, their sacrifices and successes in battle earned the Partisans unchallenged power.

Mihailović had promised a rebirth of the Kingdom of Yugoslavia, under Serbian rule. Tito promised a new, federal Yugoslavia, national equality, and a change in the prewar sociopolitical order, which was much disliked even by Serbs, notwithstanding their domination of the royalist state.

Tito called for an "all-out war against fascism," with the victory of communism as the ultimate goal. Mihailović called for defense of the Serbian nation and the defeat of communism. The war ended with the Allied powers overwhelmingly supporting Tito's Partisans, despite Tito's revolutionary objectives.

On November 29, 1943, the wartime Partisan parliament convened in the Bosnian town of Jajce, liberated from the occupiers, and voted for a new Yugoslavia that would, in its final form, be a federation of six republics, with two autonomous provinces, Kosovo and Vojvodina, joined to Serbia. Bosnia-Hercegovina was restored to its historic parity with Slovenia, Croatia, Serbia, and Montenegro; Macedonia was also granted full republic status. In reality, the shape of the new state was not fully clear until after the war. Only one thing was certain at Jajce: a new Yugoslavia had to guarantee national equality.[2] The Partisan parliament meant what it said, and, with the war over, it delivered much of what it had promised.

The victorious, strong Tito regime immediately tried and punished a range of pro-Axis war criminals, along with a sprinkling of nonfascist political opponents, and acted to suppress what it viewed as reactionary nationalistic tendencies, above all in Croatia and Kosovo. The slightest manifestation of nationalism was treated as a major crime.[3] But within two years, one could travel safely from one end of Yugoslavia to another, irrespective of nationality, religious beliefs, or language. In a country where one-tenth of the population had died fighting the occupation or had fallen victim to genocide, this amounted to a miracle. Tito's slogan "Brotherhood and Unity," which today is frequently an object of scorn, was not empty demagoguery in a country where one million seven hundred thousand men, women, and children had lost their lives, many because of ethnic hatred. The slogan reflected new hope in a population that had undergone a catharsis.[4]

Contrary to recent claims, Tito was a sincere Yugoslav, an internationalist and cosmopolite, unencumbered by his Croatian and Slovenian origins.[5] He bore no grudge against any of the Yugoslav nations, Serbia included. As a pragmatic politician, however, he saw Serbian nationalism, because it appealed to over one-third of Yugoslavia's total population and reflected a tradition of imperial rule, as a greater danger to the federation than, for instance, Macedonian or Slovenian nationalism.

If the concept of national equality was now clearly affirmed in Yugoslavia, the sociopolitical and economic vision of the future was, at best, cloudy and burdened with considerable ideological baggage. Abstract generalizations about socialism and social justice were the rule. A romanticized picture was conjured up, invoking a Soviet-style system with un-assailable values for Yugoslavia to emulate. The Communist leadership seemed to believe that the destruction of private capitalism—which had brought neither freedom nor prosperity to Yugoslavia—was sufficient to accomplish a social and political transformation.

The educated elite, which had supported Tito and gladly continued to do so after the war, did not really grasp the full scope and complexity of constructing an entirely new country from its foundations. In the early postwar years, their vision hardly went beyond the idealized Soviet model, of which few had any direct knowledge. Tito and several of his closest associates had experienced Soviet reality through visits to the USSR before the war. Tito himself worked for the Comintern in Moscow in 1934–36. He and his inner circle knew that Soviet communism was not flawless, but they, like other Communists, sought to ascribe the dif-ficulties to the growing pains of an otherwise positive system.[6] The Tito regime had genuine popular support and could, it thought, avoid the mis-takes of the Soviet leadership.[7] Many Yugoslav Communists honestly be-lieved that the Soviet Union would do everything to help Yugoslavia and other Soviet bloc countries deal with their problems.

It was not long before illusions about the Soviet Union were shattered by the Soviet leaders themselves.[8] A brusque, contemptuous, and provoca-tive letter from Stalin to Tito in 1948, which announced the split between Moscow and Belgrade, was a landmark example of dictatorial arrogance. Stalin resented what he viewed as the excessive self-confidence of the Yugoslavs. Foreign Communist leaders were supposed to be reverent, not proud and independent, and, of course, the last thing in the world Stalin wanted was a ruling communism he could not control. Stalin made it clear to Tito that the achievements of Yugoslavia's antifascists—whose movement was proportionately as great and combative as that among the Soviet peoples themselves and had excited the admiration of millions around the world—must be considered very small in comparison with the wartime exploits of the great Soviet Union. The main point of Stalin's message was that Yugoslavia must not imagine that it enjoyed a privi-leged position in the Soviet orbit. Stalin threatened, and carried out, a purge in the world Communist movement in response to Tito's defiance.

Only three years after war's end, Yugoslavia and Tito were again faced with a mortal danger, threatened this time not by a traditional foreign enemy but by the "greatest friend" and "elder brother of the Yugoslav peoples," as the Soviets had been described throughout the war. Tito categorically rejected Stalin's attempts to call him to account. However, some Yugoslav Communists, who honestly believed that the rejection of Soviet orders was the rejection of communism itself, believed that a socialist patriotism that was more faithful to one's own country than to the USSR was bitter betrayal. They were soon to find themselves labeled "traitors to their country and party" and were sent to prisons or concentration camps.[9]

Yet a historic, courageous, and resounding *no* had been delivered to Stalin, with the overwhelming support of the Yugoslav people. Tito, at the head of the Yugoslav Communist Party, emerged from this confrontation the authentic hero of all Yugoslavs, unquestionably the most admired figure in the history of Yugoslavia. His popularity made his people forget and forgive his many absurd and arbitrary policies.

In the late 1940s, for example, blind dogmatism led to the nationalization of all private businesses, to the collectivization of agriculture, and to the compulsory sale by the peasants, at state prices, of farm produce— policies intended to feed the populace as well as to undermine the political power of those "rich peasants" labeled kulaks. Tito had broken with Stalin but not with his political methods. The rigid Stalinist conception of state and society remained intact in the minds of Tito and his colleagues at the heights of their power, however much they hoped to avoid Soviet errors. In the end Tito was able to avoid some Soviet errors but not to surmount those errors that were strictly his own.

Titoist Yugoslavia enacted a constitution and laws for a one-party, unitary, strongly centralized state, in contradiction to its official multinational federal structure.[10] Private enterprise and property were reduced to a minimum. Political freedom and civil rights were restricted and the media placed under total state control. The West was willing to overlook all this because Tito had clearly demonstrated his geopolitical independence from Moscow.[11] With Western aid, the military was strengthened, disproportionately to the country's size, at the same time as internal security was modernized. On the surface, it appeared that the chief aim of the military, police, and other repressive organs of the Titoist state was to counter the Soviet threat. In reality, supported by his people and lauded by almost the entire world, Tito was carrying out exactly the same program he would have undertaken as an orthodox Communist, by establishing an uncontested dictatorship, regardless of his foreign policy toward Stalin.

While resisting the Soviet threat, Tito nevertheless always saw himself as a Communist first and foremost, even as he had become a patriotic symbol of Yugoslav honor and independence.[12] Ideologically distrustful of the "capitalist world," but now an outcast from the Communist one, he had no choice but to link his own and his country's survival to the West, which, pursuing its own interests, provided willing and effective assistance.

To develop an independent foreign policy for Yugoslavia, Tito had to navigate between the Soviet model, the commands of whose leaders he rejected, and a Western model, which he found ideologically distasteful. He turned out to be a master of such a difficult and delicate course.[13] The Soviets were unable to push him entirely over to the Western side, but neither did his dependence on the West force him to renounce Yugoslavia's socialism. Of course, he was not guided by principles alone. He defended his own power and everything he had personally accomplished. Fortunately, his personal ambitions and the interests of the country happened to coincide. He was a pragmatist, not a sage. But to work, pragmatism requires wisdom.

As much as Tito had been able to say no to Stalin, he found himself unable to say yes seven years afterward to Khrushchev. In 1955, the arrival in Belgrade of Nikita Khrushchev and Nikolai Bulganin, hoping to redress the wrong Stalin had done to Yugoslavia in 1948, was spectacular and historic. Tito's attitude was made visible before the eyes of the world. He turned away when Khrushchev attempted to embrace him in the Russian style. Khrushchev then made a repentant statement before live microphones, and he gestured to Tito to follow him to the podium; Tito responded by pointing coldly to an open car door. Tito offered the Russians no more than a diplomatically correct normalization of relations between two equal members of the international community. The Belgrade Declaration, a carefully worded document drawn up by the best minds in the Tito government, was published at the end of the visit and signed reluctantly by the disappointed Soviet leaders. Everyone was left with the impression that Yugoslavia's internal affairs and its socialism would never again be the object of interference by the Soviet regime or international Communism. Unfortunately, things did not work out that way.

Tito, however, followed Khrushchev's trip to Yugoslavia with a series of visits to nearly all the Soviet bloc countries. Wherever he went, he was given a hero's welcome as a "great revolutionary and Communist" whose words should be respected and advice sought. In many such countries, attractive offers were made for cooperation with Yugoslavia. Everything was done to soften the heart of Tito, the "comrade in arms and in ideology." Khrushchev himself, in his own struggle with Stalinist restorationists, needed a reconciliation with Tito; at the same time, the ineluctable imperial Soviet logic required that he attempt to dilute Tito's heretical independence.

Tito was not an innocent, but his ideological loyalties ran extraordinarily deep. In the end, they made him susceptible to Soviet overtures and incapable of recognizing that the new Soviet embrace was no less risky than the earlier threats. Tito believed that he had become the most influential leader in the Communist world, which was the only world in which he truly felt at home. Emboldened, the cautious statesman gradually, unwittingly acquiesced.

The Moscow Declaration, signed by Tito during his state visit to the Soviet Union in 1956, formalized cooperation between the Soviet and Yugoslav Communist Parties "in the common interest of the struggle for socialism." Over the next few years the USSR offered Tito, on a number of occasions, full readmission to the Warsaw Pact and other institutions of the Soviet bloc. Tito remained too shrewd to accept such membership as a favor, being aware that in 1948 the loss of the same membership had been a punishment.

But a shift in relations with the Soviet Union had taken place, with a strong impact for Yugoslavia. Ill at ease with liberal reformism and still burdened with the traditions of Soviet socialism, Tito began to obstruct attempts to loosen up the one-party political monopoly and free the economy from state supervision. Milovan Djilas, one of the four men closest to Tito during and immediately after the war and the first public advocate of a democratization of Yugoslav Communism, had already been removed from leadership in 1954. Attacks on Djilas were stepped up; he was arrested and given a long prison term.

The 1956 rebellion in Hungary, against the remnants of the harsh and violently anti-Tito Stalinist regime of Mátyás Rákosi, followed by the brutal Soviet intervention that crushed it, swept away many illusions that any fundamental change would come to the post-Stalin Soviet Union. Once again, Yugoslavia found itself resisting Soviet pressure, which now was encouraged by Tito's incautious acceptance of reconciliation. Still, like Khrushchev and Leonid Brezhnev after him, Tito never broke entirely with the basic Soviet style of governance, regardless of his defiance of Soviet hegemony. In the higher echelons of the Yugoslav party and state, democratically oriented officials had been arguing for years against making ideology the basis of relations with the socialist countries, given Moscow's history of manipulating ideology to disguise naked, aggressive imperialism. But these efforts were, of course, hopeless. In truth, the ideology of the Warsaw Pact countries was never fully abandoned in Yugoslavia; it was merely given a liberal interpretation.

The 1958 Program of the League of Communists of Yugoslavia—the new name of the ruling party—promised reform, with Yugoslavia professing a liberalism inconceivable in any other socialist country. The program planners envisioned a limit on one-party rule; a narrowing of state planning; evolution toward a full market economy; and economic efficiency as the test of the political system. The role of the state in general was to be circumscribed, with the introduction of "self-management," democratization of the federal structure and increased autonomy of the constituent republics, and, finally, greater openness toward the West. The "leading role" of the party was redefined as a "guiding role." The party would become a participant in decision making instead of the sole decision maker: it would argue for its positions instead of handing down orders.[14] The text of the party's program ended: "Nothing in our established practice may ever be considered too sacred for us to not move on and replace it with practices that are more progressive, freer, more humane." Sadly, dogmatic practices had already become too entrenched to be easily replaced. Yugoslavia's "soft totalitarianism" was incapable of fundamental change.[15] As rapprochement with Moscow proceeded in the coming years, the spirit and the letter of the 1958 program were defended with diminishing vigor; the program never fully came to life.

Fluctuations in Yugoslav domestic policies and in the country's role in the Cold War world centered on the sole reliable constant: Titoist Yugoslavia was and remained an authentically independent country. Yugoslavia continued using, to maximum advantage, its cooperation and close relations with the West, while avoiding the maximum damage of its relationship with the Soviet Union. Yugoslav success in this area stemmed partly from Tito's personal commitment to the new idea of nonalignment, that is, of a broad neutrality between the capitalist and Soviet powers on the part of nations in Asia, Africa, and Latin America. Tito was a leading figure in the Movement of Nonaligned Countries, which was launched in 1954–55, and he remained a prominent figure in it until his death. For the better part of two decades, the 1960s and 1970s, Yugoslavia was in the forefront of nonalignment and contributed effectively to the movement's leadership. Although Tito's involvement with the nonaligned movement has been fiercely criticized in the former Yugoslavia, nonalignment did at least as much for Yugoslavia as Yugoslavia did for nonalignment.

Tito may have exaggerated, for domestic consumption, the nonaligned movement's international importance, and he may have been overambitious in seeking to play a major part in world affairs. But nonalignment was very important for Yugoslavia's independent international position. The Russians were not happy about Yugoslavia's nonalignment and were even less happy when nonalignment gained favor in other Soviet bloc countries or led to the weakening of Soviet influence in some nonbloc countries. Still, the Soviet Union never dared to attack Yugoslav nonalignment or to demand that Tito renounce the movement. In any case, Yugoslavia could never have achieved the degree of liberalization it enjoyed —a liberalization surpassing by far that of the other Soviet bloc countries—had it not been aggressively open to the entire world. And that openness was necessarily intertwined with nonalignment.

Yugoslavia departed decisively from Soviet dogmatism in that it genuinely attempted to create a more democratic socialism, moving ahead under the impetus of postwar enthusiasm and significant foreign aid. Industrial growth reached impressive levels, above 10 percent annually. During the first two postwar decades, broad modernization and industrialization were accomplished, and the standard of living showed constant improvement. Yugoslavia became the showcase of socialism, surpassing Hungary and Czechoslovakia, which were much better developed before the war. Yugoslavia was the only country that was well off, indeed rather comfortable, under Communism, above all in regard to its living standard. Many inside and outside the country thought Yugoslavia had succeeded in finding an original road for socialism. But the essential prerequisite for maintaining growth and progress, a policy of fundamental democratic changes from top to bottom in the political system, was out of the question. Tito, who was actually a reluctant reformer, began putting the brakes on change. He preferred socialism to prosperity, if and when the two seemed to conflict. In 1968, he told Belgrade University student demonstrators that he agreed with demands for greater democracy, but he then turned around and blocked all change.[16]

In 1965 a broad economic reform had been launched, with the objective of establishing a market economy by removing administrative price controls. In Slovenia and Croatia, the richest regions, this led to a dramatic rise in production and income; in Kosovo, the poorest, it led by contrast to further stagnation. Prices for agricultural and industrial products soared, and the government responded by temporarily imposing new controls. From 1965 on, Yugoslavia attempted to keep its own brand of "market socialism." The attempt, however, was faint-hearted and generated no more than a hybrid economy plagued by the many problems implicit in an untested experiment, whose direction was not clear to Tito or anyone else.

Titoist Yugoslavia was, therefore, permanently characterized by a zig-zag progress between liberalism and authoritarianism. In 1974 the constitution was amended to redefine the complicated lines of authority between the federal government, the republics, and the autonomous provinces of Kosovo and Vojvodina. The new constitution granted the latter two complete economic and political autonomy, with a de facto status as full republics. But this effort at decentralization resulted in a more fragmented economy and society, with centralism intact as a policy of governance. Centralist power was simply transferred from the federal authority to the republics. Over time the republic leaders duplicated, in their own environments, the same centralism they resented when it had originated with the federal administration: the result was eight tightly controlled centralist regional governments. The 1974 constitution allowed them to act freely and openly in pursuit of their national interests, oblivious to those of the federation as a whole. In addition, regional leaders promoted their careers by offering their peoples a romantic vision of harmony within each single ethnic community. Within a few years of Tito's death in 1980, each republic and autonomous province had become a state within a state. The center no longer held. Gaps between the nations began widening uncontrollably.

Tito was not blind to signs of the eventual decomposition of the new Yugoslavia that was the product of his lifework. Yet he was aware he could not stop the trend without risking his unchallenged position. He opted for self-deception and acted as though he himself believed the popular song, heard more widely than the Yugoslav anthem, that went, "Comrade Tito, we pledge not to veer from your course." He believed that Yugoslavia was safe as long as he lived. Afterward, others would face the responsibility of having "veered from Tito's course."

One night in autumn 1971, aboard the presidential Blue Train on his return from a state visit to Romania, Tito began discussing, with the delegation that accompanied him, news of unrest at the University of Zagreb. Tito's associates condemned the rebirth of nationalist sentiment in Croatia. Tito had already made up his mind, although he did not disclose it, to purge the Croatian Communist leadership, which he blamed for the growing discontent. In the middle of the conversation, Tito suddenly looked up at his comrades and said, "If you saw what I see for the future in Yugoslavia, it would scare you."[17] There were many valid reasons for fear, and his words were obviously prophetic.[18] In the meantime, he was determined to come down hard on the Croatian Communist leadership. He was incapable of opening up the party and government to a democratic debate that would have explored the social and national problems that underlay Croatian nationalist concerns.

In the early 1970s, an article was added to the Yugoslav constitution stating, "Josip Broz Tito is President-for-life of Yugoslavia." A Belgrade University professor, among others, criticized this article during public discussion of the draft constitution. Tito undoubtedly lost no sleep when the professor was arrested, tried, and imprisoned. He could no longer face the new or abandon the old. He had ceased to be simply the head of state; he now was the state.

In 1971 and 1972, with the help of the conservative wing of the League of Communists of Yugoslavia, Tito purged the Communist leadership and the intellectuals in Croatia, crushing demands for federal reform.[19] The movement, although nationalist in its consciousness, embodied a broader democratic outlook. One year later, Tito repeated this performance when he repressed the reformist democrats in Serbia led by Marko Nikezić, the president of the Serbian Central Committee, and Latinka Perović, its secretary.[20] Ousted were also Stane Kavčić in Slovenia and Krste Crvenkovski in Macedonia. In contrast to the maspok leaders, in Serbia the leaders who came under attack were known as enlightened liberals and committed non-nationalists. They supported the democratic student movement of 1968 and promoted democratization not only for their own republic but for the entire federal structure. But genuine democratization remained a far greater potential danger to Tito's rule than nationalism.[21]

The confrontations with Croatia and Serbia were each followed by purges, including several thousand dismissals, at all levels. Prominent figures in academic and cultural life, and even in trade and industry, were targeted. The vacancies in the bureaucracy were quickly filled by Tito's loyalists. A new peace descended on the country, although the real problems remained untouched and the illusion of solidity and unity was emptier than ever. Tito's solutions were obsolete. He continued accumulating power even as it grew more and more problematic. Beneath the calm surface, the ground was turbulent. The foundation of Yugoslavia, weakened by the fragmentation into virtual mini states by the 1974 constitution, was increasingly shaky.

Another negative side emerged in regard to Tito's long-lasting ability to maintain Yugoslav independence. Still perceived as a country that had rebuffed the Soviet Union, Yugoslavia in the 1970s obtained cheap loans from many foreign sources. The federal government borrowed and spent ever more recklessly. Meanwhile, the 1974 constitution encouraged the republics to believe that mutual responsibilities would disappear in the near future. Concerning themselves only with their own affairs in the late 1970s and 1980s, the republics imposed on the federation an enormous foreign debt. Regional spending was not determined by economic criteria but orchestrated by local bureaucracies increasingly governed by nationalist selfishness. The facade of prosperity was maintained, but the economic underpinnings of Yugoslavia were crumbling. The overriding concern was to keep up the appearance of progress, measured by the fictitious standards of "self-management." In reality, Yugoslavs were squandering their future.

Titoist Yugoslavia, now in decline, had become nothing more than Tito's Yugoslavia. Tito was not only the supreme and unchallengeable first citizen of the country; he was, at the end, its only effectively functioning institution. All the levers of power operated through his hands. Government rubber-stamped his will. The League of Communists was not a political party, if for no other reason than that it was the only party; the parliament was a debating club and not much more; the army and internal security were Tito's private domains. The members of the federal government came to view any initiative on their own part in foreign policy, defense, or security as "meddling" in Tito's jurisdiction and carefully avoided these areas. The government had never been much more than a council for economic affairs, economy being the one area in which Tito preferred to avoid involving himself. While the ministers of defense and foreign and internal affairs were in constant personal contact with Tito, with access to him whenever they liked, the speaker of parliament and the prime minister could not see him even after repeated requests. He discussed the details of their work with the first three, but with the other two, he sent instructions through underlings.

However, Tito's direct contact with the republic governments and League of Communists leaders became more important as their autonomy increased. With these leaders he met regularly, if not frequently. As a result, relations among the republics, and their conflicts, were more and more removed from the purview of federation officials. Republic delegations officially reported to Tito and increasingly turned to him for approval of many measures they believed could not be adopted through constitutional channels. Furthermore, Tito was inclined to agree with everybody. When a problem arose between two or more republics, republic leaders learned to approach Tito separately instead of meeting together. Tito often would satisfy the parties individually, sometimes at each other's expense, and without resolving the underlying issues.

Tito liked to travel around the country meeting local leaders. He journeyed in high style and was welcomed and seen off by huge crowds; every word he had to say at a meeting or in a speech was carried in full by all media. He was generous with praise, and his public criticism was judicious. Whatever he said was received with gratitude, as "helping our work," and was enshrined by the government and party bodies. There is almost no record of anyone voicing criticism of Tito himself at such meetings or disputing his observations or evaluations. He believed that public acceptance of his word was proof of unity and unanimity and a demonstration of democracy, when it only masked the self-serving careerism of the republic leaders.

Tito would exclaim, "They say there is no democracy in our country, but aren't these talks with the people the highest form of democracy?" or "They say there is no criticism in our country, and I myself am the greatest critic of anything bad." He was hard on "weaknesses" and criticized his associates for not doing a better job. "I will single them out by name when the time comes," he would say and then leave everybody guessing whom he had in mind. He spoke out against lawbreaking, willfulness, ambition for power and extravagance, never imagining that for the growing number of skeptics in his audiences his reproaches should very obviously apply to himself. He had long since stopped seeing himself through the eyes of the "ordinary citizens" and "working people" to whom he most often addressed his words. Once, in a small circle, when the growing abuse of privileges in the construction of private vacation homes was mentioned, he grumbled, "I wouldn't mind building a place I would actually own, but one has to think about what the people would say."[22] It was clear that it never occurred to him that those present might consider private ownership of a vacation home a much humbler form of ownership than his own possession (if not ownership in the strict sense) of dozens of luxury vacation homes around the country, replete with servants.

The conservative nature of the system affected the selection of individuals for public service, including the political leadership. In early postwar Yugoslavia, the criteria for public responsibility had been meritorious war service, belief in the party's goals, and readiness to work hard. The party's choice and a person's public reputation were affirmed through a process of thoughtful appointment from above rather than democratic selection. Gradually, however, personal loyalty became the decisive element. In the 1970s an unconditional pledge to one's republic and ethnic leaders was required for advancement. "Negative selection," as the filling of offices with loyal cadres was called, gained momentum. Finally, in the 1980s, all restraint was lost and totally arbitrary promotion became the rule. Like mushrooms after rain, a multitude of power-hungry bureaucrats emerged from the pseudo-populist jungle of post-Tito Yugoslavia. To the leaders of the republics, the worst extremists became indispensable.

Still, only a few years before fighting broke out in 1991, Yugoslavism, or, more precisely, the principle of a Yugoslav federation, would have won a majority in any honest referendum in all the republics and autonomous provinces, without exception. Why then did Tito's Yugoslavia, after only fifty years, perish in a bloody ruin?

Was Communism to blame? The Communists were certainly not free of blame. Yet Balkan evils have a deeper history than does Balkan Communism. Being antinationalist and even, in theory, internationalist, Communism did not foster ethnic antagonisms. Many decades of Yugoslav Communism passed in genuine national and religious equality and tolerance. Laws against inciting national hatreds were unambiguous and harshly enforced. In any case, nationalistic offenses were rare until the 1980s. The constituent Yugoslav nations enjoyed, as nations, considerable equality of rights, unknown in any other socialist country. Missing in Yugoslavia were the universal democratic rights, regardless of national affiliation.

In its seventy years of existence, Yugoslavia tried monarchy and Communism, centralized and decentralized government, "self-management" —everything except genuine democracy. And only as a genuine democracy could Yugoslavia have held together or, if proven a failure, dissolved honorably.

Tito died in 1980, two days before his eighty-eighth birthday. Had he lived much longer, he still would have been unable to preserve the Yugoslavia he left behind. Tito was the courageous leader of Partisan antifascism, the uncompromising opponent of Stalin, the skillful guardian of his country's independence, the architect of post–World War II Yugoslavia, and the driving force behind the policy of national equality—long the best and most consistent aspect of Yugoslavia's governance. He was, however, also the watchdog of a political system that wavered between dogma and democracy. The collapse of Yugoslavia was a consequence of this unsustainable political system, not its policies, whatever their failings. Tito will not be forgiven for valuing the preservation of his own power above progress and greater democracy, and for condemning his country to survive him by no more than a decade. But it was not Tito who murdered Yugoslavia. The murderers are among us.

NOTES

1 See Jozo Tomašević, *The Chetniks* (Stanford: Stanford University Press, 1975), and Walter A. Roberts, *Tito, Mihailovich, and the Allies, 1941-1945* (New Brunswick: Rutgers University Press, 1973).

2 Milovan Djilas writes that Tito's inner circle was committed to national equality, and that its members hoped ethnic differences would disappear in the new communist society (see "Novi tok Istorije," *Socijalizam*, vol. 1 [1990]).

3 See Milovan Djilas, *Wartime* (New York: Harcourt Brace Jovanovich, 1977), pp. 448–49.

4 See Vladimir Dedijer, *Tito Speaks: His Self-Portrait and Struggle with Stalin* (London: Weidenfeld and Nicolson, 1953), pp. 244–46. On the confidence in the early postwar period that the problem of nationalism had been solved see Frederick Bernard Singleton, *Twentieth-Century Yugoslavia* (New York: Columbia University Press, 1976), p. 223.

5 A balanced portrait of Tito appears in Richard West, *Tito and the Rise and Fall of Yugoslavia* (New York: Carrol and Graf, 1994), pp. 196–98. By contrast, for the way Tito was viewed in the late 1980s see Stojan Cerović, *Bahanalije* (Beograd: Vreme, 1993), pp. 1–12.

6 Tito was aware of the totalitarian nature of Soviet communism as early as 1935. He told Vladimir Dedijer, his biographer, that he "witnessed a lot of careerism and

elbow pushing. . . . even in 1935 there were no end of arrests, and those who made the arrests were later themselves arrested. Men vanished overnight, and no one dared ask where they had been taken" (Dedijer, *Tito Speaks*, p. 13).

7 Vladimir Dedijer, *Tito* (Rijeka: Liburnija, 1981), p. 305. Tito lived in Moscow between 1934 and 1936, working in the Comintern. In 1937 he was charged with the task of organizing a Communist party in Yugoslavia.

8 Frederick Bernard Singleton, *A Short History of the Yugoslav Peoples* (Cambridge: Cambridge University Press, 1985), p. 212. The best coverage of the breakup with Stalin is in Milovan Djilas, *Rise and Fall* (London, 1985), and *Conversations with Stalin* (New York: Harcourt, Brace and World, 1962).

9 Tito did not falter and used the crisis to strengthen his position (see Milovan Djilas, *Tito* [New York: Harcourt Brace Jovanovich], p. 32).

10 Robert J. Donia and John V. A. Fine argue that the 1946 constitution, although closely modeled on the constitution of the Soviet Union, preserved the distinctiveness of Bosnia-Hercegovina and recognized its borders. The authors cite Dennison Rusinow, who claims those borders were "among the oldest and most continuous in Europe" (see Donia and Fine, *Bosnia and Hercegovina: A Tradition Betrayed* [New York: Columbia University Press, 1994], p. 161).

11 On massive Western aid to Yugoslavia in the fifties see Singleton, *Twentieth-Century Yugoslavia*, pp. 144, 171–73.

12 On Tito as a Leninist see Djilas, *Tito*, p. 39.

13 On "Tito's intuitive pragmatism" see Djilas, *Tito*, p. 33.

14 See Singleton, *Twentieth-Century Yugoslavia*, pp. 134–43.

15 Stojan Cerović makes the effective observation that Tito had always been both "a revolutionary and a restaurateur of his own monarchy" (p. 7).

16 *History of Yugoslavia*, ed. Vladimir Dedijer, Ivan Božić, Sima Ćirković, and Milorad Ekmečić (New York: McGraw-Hill, 1974), pp. 529–50.

17 The author was a member of the delegation on this occasion in the Blue Train. *Ed.*

18 Branko Petranović, one of the leading historians of former Yugoslavia, wrote in 1993: "Tito had no illusions. He knew only too well the kind of legacy he was leaving behind. But for this he cared little" (*Borba*, "Izolacija je smrt na duže staze," 24–25 April 1993).

19 On the national movement in Croatia in the early 1960s and 1970s see Ante Čuvalo, *The Croatian National Movement 1966-1972* (Boulder, Colo.: East European Monographs; distributed by Columbia University Press, 1989).

The major complaint of the Maspok, as the movement was called, had to do with the disproportionate amount of revenue that Croatia was obliged to deposit into the federal account, instead of keeping all of it for itself. Singleton notes, however, that while it was true that a great deal of income from tourism in Croatia was appropriated by the federation, it was "virtually impossible to draw a balance sheet." Without the federal investment in highways, hotels, transportation facilities, and ship building, Croatia would not have had its tourist boom. In addition, it had the advantage of importing cheap raw materials and food from the less developed regions (see Singleton, *Twentieth-Century Yugoslavia*, pp. 224–26).

20 Following the ouster of Marko Nikezić and Latinka Perović, the author, at the time foreign minister of Yugoslavia, resigned. Koča Popović, a treasured intellectual and a World War II army commander as well as a former foreign minister, withdrew from political life in protest. *Ed.*

21 Vladimir Dedijer, *Novi prilozi za biografiju Josipa Broza Tita* (Zagreb: Mladost, 1980).

22 Author's notes.

The Interlude: 1980–1990

Jasminka Udovički and Ivan Torov

Tito died on May 4, 1980, but the slogan "After Tito, Tito" lived on. The majority of Yugoslavs sincerely mourned him. Their lives had been incomparably better in terms of living standard and political freedoms than the lives of the citizens of any other Eastern European country after World War II. The slogan reflected a common perception, still current at the time of Tito's death, that he was the very incarnation of Yugoslavia.

The plan for the evolution of the country after his death, however, was vague at best, resting on the system Tito had proposed himself, of periodic rotation of all political posts—including the post of the Yugoslav president—among the representatives of different republics. The purpose of such a system was to prevent the domination of any single nation over others—a balancing act Tito tried to sustain throughout his political life.

The idea of a collective leadership, an oddity in the history of statesmanship, turned out very soon to be as awkward as it was risky for the transition awaiting the country. The leadership vacuum, a consequence of the experimental, tentative character of the rotation system, expressed itself most strongly in the absence of clear goals and of a sound concept of the changes necessary to overcome the approaching crisis. The eight-member collective presidency, one from each of the six republics and the two autonomous provinces—proved a weak institution, incapable of reaching a consensus on the pressing economic and political difficulties that were growing worse as the 1980s progressed.

The practice in the 1970s of building up foreign debt in response to the abundant offer of cheap Western credit boomeranged by the beginning of 1980s, the time of a worldwide recession. The debt would not have been nearly as grave had the borrowed funds not been mismanaged and misinvested in "political factories," giant operations built to satisfy political and not economic objectives. The malfunctioning of those industries, equipped with state-of-the art technology, and their failure to yield expected results, produced an economic calamity of staggering proportions.[1] Foreign debt increased 400 percent by 1980. From $6 billion in 1975, it climbed to $17 billion in 1979 and to $19 billion in the subsequent few years.[2] Interest on the foreign debt alone brought about three-digit inflation. Prices for food, clothing, electricity, and other daily necessities rose 60 percent approximately every six months.

Instead of imposing monetary controls to slow inflation, lifting restrictions on the functioning of the market, and allowing self-managing enterprises greater latitude in decision making, the federal government maintained the illusion of prosperity by regular emissions of fresh supplies of cash. The increasing economic chaos was reported in detail in the media. A tide of strikes for higher pay and lower prices for the basics — meat, bread, milk, and local farm produce — swept the country, amounting in 1987 alone to more than one thousand and involving up to 150,000 workers.[3] Still, many from the burgeoning middle class found it possible to maintain their lifestyle, eat at good restaurants, and furnish their homes with imported sofas and tiles, even if they were no longer able to afford winter vacations in Austria or France.[4]

As the crisis worsened, becoming the hottest media issue, disillusionment among directors of enterprises and many intellectuals grew.[5] The crisis reached a climax in the summer of 1990, when the banks revealed they could no longer cover their customers' foreign currency deposits — a private asset built over time and deeply treasured by Yugoslavs — because of the shortage of convertible currency in federal reserve. For the general public, this event signaled the total collapse of the economic system.

The system's structure was set in place by the federal constitution in 1974, when the republics and autonomous provinces were given much greater latitude than they formerly enjoyed. Republics and provinces alike were granted veto power in the federal assembly, and this power in fact transformed federative Yugoslavia into a confederation. The federal government was crippled and gridlocked whenever the leadership of any one of the republics or provinces judged its interests to be threatened. The constitution empowered the republics to manage their internal economies, set investment priorities and taxing policies, control their own banks, and maintain an independent balance of payment with their international partners. Capital investment was duplicated, economic and transport infrastructure fragmented, and the flow of capital between the eight federal units stifled as each tried to control as much as possible of its foreign exchange revenue. The director of the Institute of Economic Sciences in Belgrade, Zoran Popov, characterized this situation as "a feudal organization of economic life."[6]

Fragmentation, however, did not bring about liberalization. Instead of one state-controlled economy, the constitution of 1974 created eight, one in each republic and autonomous province. At the micro-level, the governments of the republics were free to interfere in the activities of enterprises and banks, even though, nominally, the system of self-management remained intact. Directors of large enterprises, including those engaged in significant trade with the West, publicly complained of the strict limitations of their mandate. They were burdened with maximum responsibility but had minimal leeway in running the enterprises.

The crisis invited two possible types of solution. One was to open the way to an overall economic and political liberalization. The other was to strengthen the conservative forces and by the same token exploit the volatile situation to entrench power. The first required the removal of state controls of prices, de-bureaucratization of the economy, and abandonment of the existing cumbersome rules of enterprise management. This approach would have freed up the energies in the socially owned firms, encouraged the launching of private businesses, and attracted foreign investment. A process of political liberalization and the eventual removal of the League of Communists of Yugoslavia (LCY) as the ultimate political, social, and economic arbiter would also have been under way. Eventually, Yugoslavia could have turned into a prosperous European country. This required a broader, long-term vision and a political commitment to endure in the face of a likely rise of unemployment and a period of increased social unrest.

Pressures for further liberalization of the economic and the political life were growing steadily throughout the 1980s. Belgrade was the country's center of glasnost, before the notion of glasnost ever entered the political vocabulary.[7] At the other end of the country, in the westernmost republic of Slovenia, even more substantial liberalizing currents were taking root in the second part of the 1980s, leading to bold attacks on the one-party monopoly and on the Yugoslav People's Army (YPA). Dissonant voices were heard first from the journal *Mladina*, questioning excessive federal funds allocated for defense. It instigated a debate about lifting the compulsory military service requirement—a previously unthinkable request. By the end of the 1980s, the Slovenes were demanding that the conscripts be given the option of conscientious objector status. In 1989 Slovenian politicians were already openly advocating political pluralism and a broad-scoped public debate on the nature and the virtues of a fully developed civil society.

The fall of Communism in Eastern Europe in 1989–90 profoundly changed the European political environment, offering a new context for the consolidation of cosmopolitan, democratic voices in Yugoslavia. The new prime minister of Yugoslavia, the Croat Ante Marković, responded to the changes abroad by calling for a substantial degree of privatization and for turning the Yugoslav economy into a fully market-oriented economy. Had those trends been allowed to take root, the future of Yugoslavia—of all Eastern European countries by far the most liberal and economically the most open—would most likely have been entirely different.

The new democratizing currents in the 1980s, coupled with the leadership vacuum and the economic crisis, predictably polarized the existing power structure, deeply threatening its conservative wing. The way out was nationalism. In nationalism conservative forces found an instrument against fundamental social, political, and economic change that threatened their social positions and privileges. All three social institutions (by their very nature the most conservative ones)—the party apparatus, the army, and the state-controlled media—rallied behind Slobodan Milošević, who became the president of Serbia in 1989. Franjo Tudjman, the Croatian president as of 1990, found support among the Croatian far-right political emigrants, whose Nazi past he pledged to revisit and reinterpret.

The propaganda Milošević, and later on Tudjman, set in motion appealed to the quite tangible, legitimate grievances of the common person: the falling standard of living and the political void.[8] The appeals evolved around the same core: the claim that current economic ills in each of the republics stemmed from the long practice of economic exploitation and political subordination of that republic by all others. In this sense Milošević and Tudjman's campaigns mirrored each other, although their ultimate objectives differed. In both cases nationalism served objectives that had little to do with ethnicity or grassroots ethnic sentiment, were politically motivated, and were fully orchestrated from above.

Milošević's campaign derived much of its energy from a concrete allegation that Serbia's current problems resulted from being economically crippled by the 1974 constitution, which had fragmented Serbia's territory into three separate parts, unjustifiably granting autonomy to its two provinces: Vojvodina in the north and Kosovo in the south.[9] The constitution vested Kosovo and Vojvodina with prerogatives analogous to those enjoyed by Serbia itself. The provinces profited from all the institutional benefits of semisovereignty—autonomous courts, police, health, and educational systems—and they had, like the republics, one representative each in all federal organs.[10] The sovereignty of the provinces was underscored by the right of their political representatives to take a turn as head of the Yugoslav state and the League of Communists of Yugoslavia—until 1974 the exclusive privilege of republics.

Despite its full equality with other federal units, Kosovo remained the least economically developed region of Yugoslavia.[11] Its underdevelopment remained an enduring source of tension between its ethnic populations: Albanians on the one side, Serbs and Montenegrins on the other.[12] In 1968 a series of demonstrations shook the region with demands for the annexation of Kosovo to Albania. Tito refused to grant this demand but gave Kosovo, as well as Vojvodina to the north, the status of a Socialist Autonomous Province. This immediately provoked concerns in Serbia that it was "losing" its territories.[13] Thirty leaders of the 1968 upheaval received three- to five-year jail terms.[14] Autonomy and arrests, however, did little to quiet the discontent. Throughout the 1970s, the arrests of groups and individuals working for the secession of Kosovo continued, amounting to six hundred persons for the period 1974–81.[15]

In the same period, the Albanian population increased from 40 percent to more than 80 percent. As the least developed region, Kosovo received from a special Federal Fund for Development, and from separate federal grants, substantial financial aid without repayment obligations. The total amounted to up to 3 percent of the social product of the more advanced regions, including the other Serbian autonomous province, Vojvodina.[16] Yet by the time of Tito's death it was flagrantly clear that financial aid hardly affected Kosovo's economy and the resolve of the Albanians to secede. One reason was the lack of economic progress in Kosovo, despite the steady influx of development funds. The expenditure priorities of local political elites proved to be catastrophic, and the misspending massive, including the construction of excessively lavish public buildings, oversized sports halls, and luxurious libraries, at the expense of industrial infrastructure that would provide jobs.[17] The donor regions had no control over the use of aid funds and in time became openly resentful of supporting poorer regions.

Almost immediately after Tito died, sporadic acts of arson and terrorism inflamed Kosovo once again, culminating, in spring 1981, with another wave of demonstrations in Priština, Kosovo's capital, and other towns; the demonstrators were demanding that Kosovo be granted the status of a separate republic.[18] The League of Communists, traditionally wary of the expression of any ethnically based form of discontent, proclaimed the 1981 rebellion "counterrevolutionary," sacked the Kosovo leadership, and appointed Azem Vlasi, a proven young Communist and an Albanian, to head the province. Hundreds of Albanian teachers, professors, and students were expelled from schools and universities shortly after, and a series of political trials, involving over a thousand persons over the period of five years (1981–86), only fanned Albanian discontent and poisoned further the relationships between Serbs and Albanians.

The economic crisis in Kosovo was left unaddressed, however, and found expression over the coming years in growing ethnic tensions. The complaints by Serbs about the unofficial but steady pressures put on them by Albanians to leave Kosovo increased significantly. Albanians responded by claiming that most Serbs left Kosovo for economic reasons, and not because of pressure or harassment.[19]

In Serbia this situation provoked a backlash, and the view gradually took hold that the young Kosovar Albanian bureaucracy used its post-1974 ascendancy not as an opportunity to foster economic growth and national reconciliation but as a chance to turn Kosovo into an exclusively Albanian region.[20] In a 1985 petition to the president of the Serbian party, over two thousand Serbs alleged that Albanians were forcing them out and that local authorities did nothing to protect them. There had been many previous complaints of both psychological and physical harassment of Serbs. Albanians, it was said, repeatedly and aggressively offered to buy Serb houses, making it clear to the owners that they were unwanted in the region; the crops of many Serb peasants were sporadically burned, their livestock blinded, goats or chickens killed, vegetable gardens destroyed. Rumors were magnified by fear, and the atmosphere was becoming one of increasing uncertainty and imminent jeopardy. Ordinary Serbs interpreted assault, murder, and rape—whether or not ethnically motivated—as part of an anti-Serb conspiracy.[21]

In an environment less emotionally charged and committed to giving protection to persons and property, such acts would have been prosecuted as criminal activity. In Kosovo, however, all forms of hostility were experienced as ethnic aggression.

In the mid-1980s the federal government and the authorities in Serbia preferred to ignore the grievances of the Kosovo Serbs and Albanians alike, rather than recognize them as expressions of a difficult, long-term problem that required open, candid, and, above all, evenhanded management. The ideological assumption of "brotherhood," never questioned in Tito's time, blurred existing political clashes and provided a peculiar alibi to the ruling hierarchies for failing to face such issues head-on. In 1986, burdened with the long-term legacy of political euphemism, federal political authorities and those in Serbia had neither the stomach nor the will, and perhaps least of all the necessary experience, to effectively tackle the worsening Kosovo situation.

Ivan Stambolić, the head of the League of Communists of Serbia until June 1986, feared the effect the Kosovo crisis might have on stability in the federation as a whole and thus opted for moderation and caution. He visited the province a number of times and tried to reason with the Serbs, and each time returned deeply disturbed by the rapid growth of Serbian dissatisfaction. He also pressured political authorities in Kosovo to seek solutions for protecting the Serbs. But he had no follow-up policy. The Albanian leadership tended to formally accept some of his demands and to put few into practice. Stambolić wished to tie Kosovo closer to Serbia but faced the problem of how to introduce changes into the constitution while at the same time preserving Kosovo's autonomy. He knew he needed time; that, however, left both the Serbs and the Albanians frustrated and restless.

In June 1986 Serbian peasants from the small Kosovo village of Batusi threatened to emigrate en masse to Serbia because of Albanian harassment.[22] In November, a group of two hundred Serbs from Kosovo traveled to Belgrade to protest the total lack of police and legal protection in Kosovo, citing two cases of rape, one involving an eleven-year-old girl.[23] The group was sent home with assurances that they would receive protection. The Serbian secretary for internal affairs, Svetomir Lalović, in addressing the Serbian parliament shortly afterward, pointed out the economic and political chaos in Kosovo, which he likened to the "Hobbesian state of nature." He cited corruption, minimal productivity, endemic unemployment, and the failure of the province to effectively collect taxes and other revenues. He pointed a finger at the regional hierarchy, hungry for power.[24] Yet nothing was done to improve the situation, then or later.

Slobodan Milošević, who in June 1986 succeeded Ivan Stambolić as the head of the Serbian League of Communists and was therefore expected to take charge of the situation in Kosovo, at the beginning showed neither knowledge nor interest in the region.[25] Ten months after he became the chief of Serbian League of Communists, on April 24, 1987, he went for the first time to Kosovo Polje, on the outskirts of Priština, to attend a Serbian rally. Ivan Stambolić, who had meanwhile become the president of Serbia, hoped that Milošević would calm the rally, by adopting the policy of gradualism.[26]

As the cars bringing Milošević and other party officials approached the local cultural center at five that afternoon, the square suddenly filled with fifteen thousand people shouting in unison: "We want free-dom! We want free-dom!"[27] Milošević appeared astonished. The police had to virtually carry him into the center, a hall barely big enough to hold three hundred. Police formed a cordon around the building, but the people broke through the police line, whereupon the police turned upon the crowd with batons and the crowd responded with stones, preparing to storm the center. Milošević seemed bewildered as he was carried forward by the people, who were yelling and pulling at him. Suddenly, an old man who found himself right next to Milošević yelled directly into his face: "They are beating us, President! Don't let them beat us."

The plea and the scene seemed to electrify Milošević. He pushed his way to the window and, standing in its frame, cried out to the frenzied crowd below: "Nobody must ever again dare to beat you!" A lull descended on the mob. The delegates were allowed to enter the building and address the politicians. Thousands who could not make it inside stayed in front of the building all night. Beginning at six that evening, until six the following morning, people delivered one personal testimony after another: about incidents of murder, rape, layoffs, destruction of property, burning of crops. Milošević listened throughout the night until the last person had spoken, and at 6 A.M. he approached the podium. To Albanian "separatists" and "nationalists" he sent the message that "in those quarters there will no longer be tyranny." To the gathered Serbs he promised "speed and efficiency" in addressing their grievances. He called mass departures

of Serbs from Kosovo "the last tragic exodus of European population."
"Yugoslavia and Serbia will not give up Kosovo," he said. "All Yugoslavia
is with you."[28]

"Sloba's *ours*," people were heard saying in the aftermath of the rally
all across Kosovo.[29] Milošević's triumph at Kosovo Polje turned him in-
stantly into the foremost Serbian politician. The silence enshrouding the
crisis in Kosovo seemed to have been finally broken. To the oversensi-
tized Serbian public, bewildered and frustrated by the apparent indifference of the regime to the fate of the Kosovo Serbs, Milošević appeared to
be the only politician "unashamed of his own people, unburdened with
guilt, and ready to right some self-evident wrongs."[30] The long pent-up
"people's movement" for the protection of human rights finally seemed
to be under way.

But hopes for a grassroots movement had never been more futile. Even
at the time when the federal and Serbian leadership appeared indifferent
to the Serbian complaints and mass rallies in Belgrade, the police had its
informants on the ground.[31] A Committee for the Organization of Mass
Meetings was established under the guidance of the retired police officer,
Mićo Sparavalo.[32] From that point on, the "spontaneous" rallies—billed in
Politika as an antibureaucratic movement and a widespread democratic
process of national revival—were carefully masterminded by specialized
groups.[33] The place of the rally, its organizer, the speakers, were all pre-
selected.[34] Even authentic workers' protests against the deteriorating conditions of life were derailed and turned into nationalist rallies. "They
come as workers, and leave as Serbs," is how Slavoljub Djukić described
the strikes at the Rakovica motor industry on the outskirts of Belgrade.[35]

Official television and the daily *Politika* were pivotal in constructing
Milošević's image and promoting his program.[36] The program had three
basic components: it urged constitutional reform to reintegrate Serbia's
autonomous provinces; it warned against the winds blowing from Slovenia and Croatia in anticipation of Yugoslavia's disintegration; and it
cautioned in ever shriller tones of the dire jeopardy facing Croatian and
Bosnian Serbs should they, in some future hostile arrangement, find themselves cut off from Serbia.[37] As time went on, hints of the possibility of
an armed conflict were increasingly present in the media. On the level
of oratory and rhetoric, Milošević identified his leadership with the will

of the Serbian people. He found allies in the chief editor of *Politika*, Živo-rad Minović, and on official television.

Politika had an exceptional status in the former Yugoslavia, and particularly in Serbia, where it was founded in 1904 by the Ribnikar brothers, two well-to-do sons of a Belgrade surgeon. The oldest and most widely read daily, *Politika* was a paper the public identified with the country's best liberal traditions.[38] Unlike any other daily or weekly, it had always enjoyed the aura of a national treasure. At the same time, on a more intimate level, common readers saw it as an inseparable part of their household life, a cherished family friend. At the end of the 1980s, building on the enormous trust it enjoyed, *Politika* gradually engendered in its reading public a deep sense of foreboding about the future and the perception that Milošević was Serbia's only hope.[39]

Milošević's political program also owed a great deal to a group of twenty-seven Serbian intellectuals, all members of the Serbian Academy of Sciences and Arts (SANU) in Belgrade. In the summer of 1985 this group had formed a committee for the preparation of a "memorandum on current social issues," intended as a response to the growing crisis, particularly in Kosovo. In September 1986 an unfinished draft of the memorandum was leaked to the press, instantaneously creating a political scandal. The first part of the document urged a reexamination of the 1974 constitution and the consolidation of Serbia's territories through the reintegration of the provinces. The second part focused on the allegedly unexamined issue of the inequality of Serbia in the federation; on the need for Serbia's tremendous human and material sacrifices in the formation of Yugoslavia, during World War I and World War II, to be recognized; and on the need for the Serbian people to formulate their national program in the interest of national prosperity.[40] The memorandum launched a new and virulent vocabulary, which in the next few years imbued the public discourse. Phrases such as "genocide against the Serbs," "the Serbian Holocaust," "Serbian martyrdom," "the tragedy of Kosovo Serbs," "the Serbian exodus," and many others entered the vernacular of politics, and particularly the media, and shaped the framework of many public discussions taking place at the dawn of the war.[41]

Slobodan Milošević—although at the time president of the Serbian Communists and thus the obvious person to issue a statement—remained completely silent regarding the memorandum. The document was criticized from within the academy itself and provoked much heated debate in political circles in the first half of 1987. Although the establishment outside Serbia was shocked by the undisguised nationalism of a document coming from the top of the intellectual hierarchy, criticism of the memorandum ceased completely after the Eighth Session of the Central Committee of the League of Communists of Serbia, the event that entrenched Milošević at the helm of Serbian politics.

The memorandum had provided an ideological platform for Milošević to develop his political program. His appeal to the preservation of Yugoslavia attracted the support of Yugoslav People's Army, the most powerful federal institution deeply invested in the survival of the federation for several reasons. On the institutional level, the disintegration of Yugoslavia threatened the very foundations on which the army had built its authority and might. On the personal level, disintegration implied a threat to the status, income, and often lavish privileges of the military personnel. General Nikola Ljubičić, the military minister, expressed his appreciation of Milošević's program by using his influence at the Eighth Congress to facilitate a purge Milošević masterfully carried out against all liberal politicians, media editors, and their supporters—all those in effect favoring gradualism and negotiations in Kosovo.[42] The purge culminated in the forced resignation of Ivan Stambolić, Serbia's president.[43]

The support of Ljubičić notwithstanding, Milošević would have had a much harder time in removing the moderate Stambolić had he encountered determined resistance on the part of other federal politicians. But it was early on in the game. Political leaders outside of Serbia not only underestimated Milošević, but also viewed the Kosovo crisis as a messy issue, one best avoided. Rather than obstructing Milošević's Stalinist-style maneuver, leaders of other republics were in fact quite anxious to see Serbian leadership do precisely what Milošević seemed to be doing: taking charge of Serbia's provinces.[44] Federal politicians chose to view the conflict between Milošević and Stambolić as an internal Serbian affair.[45] Because of the army's backing and indifference on the federal level, Milošević's hand was free.

Many common people in Serbia applauded the removal of Stambolić and supported what later came to be known as Milošević's "antibureaucratic revolution." In these times of economic hardship and political turmoil, the public fervently wished for a bold leader to set things right. In the view that emerged under the relentless media crusade, Serbs were under assault everywhere: at their ancestral home in Kosovo and, in fact, in the whole of Yugoslavia. The anger and pain of the Serbs rested on the misguided perception of suffered injustice, the perception that—as the leading Serbian economist Ljubomir Madžar has suggested—turned out to be stronger than reality.[46]

In the spring of 1988, Milošević offered a program of economic recovery.[47] A commission that came to be known as Milošević's Commission was charged with working out a plan to increase foreign investment, bolster private enterprise, and introduce market reforms and mixed property ownership. All this sounded quite liberal. To Serbs it held out the promise of wealthy socialism; to the potential critics in other republics it suggested that whatever they might think of him, Milošević was a man with whom one could do business. This helped soften the image of Milošević as a political hard-liner and earned him the political space to complete his "antibureaucratic revolution."

Mass rallies served as the major instrument of Milošević's purge of all those opposed to or even mildly skeptical of his politics. In the summer 1988, and again in September and October, Serbia was engulfed in an enormous tide of mass demonstrations involving tens of thousands, sometimes hundreds of thousands, of people expressing support for Milošević and demanding bold action. On July 9, 1988, on the streets of Vojvodina's capital, Novi Sad, a group of about two thousand Kosovo Serbs, protesting Albanian repression, was joined by tens of thousands of Vojvodina Serbs. Up until then the prosperous province had been quiet and free of protests of any kind. Its leadership was well aware of the nationalistic character of the rally and on July 16, after a series of heated meetings, accused Milošević of stirring nationalism, encouraging political demonstrations for his own political ends, and acting aggressively toward their province.[48]

In Belgrade the attack was immediately characterized as "factionalism," "a struggle for power," and "an attempt at revision of the Eighth Congress."[49] New demonstrations, requesting the resignation of the Vojvodina leadership proclaiming support for Milošević and demanding bold action, engulfed Serbia in the next couple of months.[50] On October 5 a mass rally of up to a hundred thousand people from Bačka Palanka, a Vojvodina town, joined by workers of the Novi Sad factory Jugoalat and led by their director, as well as masses from Kosovo and Belgrade led by Vojislav Šešelj, was staged in Novi Sad. The cry was for the Vojvodina leadership to step down. Once again, federal leaders remained silent, thereby allowing the forced resignation of the complete Vojvodina leadership to take place following the rally. On January 10 and 11, 1989, after mass rallies in Titograd, almost the entire Montenegro leadership resigned, too. Milošević's antibureaucratic revolution brought his supporters to power in both places effortlessly.

In Kosovo, whose leadership enjoyed the overwhelming support of the Albanian population, the process turned out to be much more complicated. The federal establishment, hoping to pacify Milošević, used its authority to force the Albanian leader, Azem Vlasi, to resign in November 1988. In response, Kosovar Albanians staged peaceful demonstrations that lasted five days and nights. The Yugoslav presidency declared a state of emergency and sent in the troops. Serbia sent its special police force. The demonstrations nevertheless ended without a single window or bottle broken.

On February 4, 1989, the miners of the Kosovo silver mine Trepča began mass strikes. Azem Vlasi, who visited the striking miners, was arrested and indicted as the strike leader. The arrest of Vlasi on March 3, and the "isolation" of about two hundred Albanian public personalities, was followed by a series of clashes, leaving sixty Albanians dead. On March 28 the amendments to the constitution of Serbia as a unified republic were adopted. Kosovo had been stripped of all attributes of autonomy. The trial of Azem Vlasi at the end of October 1989 caused another tide of Albanian demonstrations.[51] The arrival of Yugoslav People's Army tanks in Kosovo on February 1, 1990, choked off the protest, but before that happened, fifty-four Albanians were wounded and twenty-seven lay dead. Meanwhile, on December 6, 1989, Slobodan Milošević was declared the president of the presidency of the Republic of Serbia.[52]

In an act of defiance of the Serb authorities, on July 2, 1990, Albanian delegates of the Kosovo assembly declared Kosovo's sovereignty as an independent unit equal in every way to other units of the former Yugoslavia. Three days later, the Serbian regime disbanded Kosovo's assembly and all other organs of the Kosovo provincial government. A widespread purge of Albanians from government and state positions ensued. Nearly all Albanian media were suppressed. On September 7, in the small town of Kačanik, a group of delegates of the dismissed Kosovo assembly declared the constitution of the republic of Kosovo. But a mere three weeks later, on September 28, the new constitution of Serbia was enacted, which revoked the autonomy of both Kosovo and Vojvodina, reducing the two provinces to mere municipalities. The event was celebrated in Belgrade with fireworks. In Priština demonstrations broke out, leaving twenty-four persons dead.

In federal circles, many were prone to view Milošević's campaign in Kosovo as a kind of controlled catharsis of Serbian dissatisfaction. They were hoping the reintegration of Kosovo into Serbia would satisfy Milošević's ambitions. The Croatian leadership was also afraid that any firm opposition to Milošević would stir up Croatian Serbs, who were avidly following the events.

Milošević took advantage of the silence. The indifference and indecisiveness of his colleagues bought him time to harness the discontent of Kosovo Serbs as a detonator for a much more widespread discontent—of Serbs in Croatia and Bosnia-Hercegovina.[53]

With Milošević's assistance and prodding, on July 25, 1990, in the small Krajina village called Srb, a summit of Croatian Serbs was held that adopted the declaration of sovereignty and autonomy of the Serbian people—an occurrence Jovan Rašković, the leader of the Serbian Democratic Party (SDS), characterized as an "unarmed uprising."[54] This act of Serbian defiance was preceded by the victory of the nationalist Croatian Democratic Union (HDZ) on April 22, 1990, and the election of Franjo Tudjman as Croatia's president—events that electrified Serbs in Croatia.[55] The only force that could have undercut Milošević's project of stirring the Serbs in Croatia would have been a genuine effort on the part of Croatian leaders to demonstrate that the Croatia of the 1990s was not the Croatia of the 1940s; that every effort would be made to safeguard the safety of the Croatian Serbs and to uphold their political, cultural, economic, and human rights. Yet Franjo Tudjman saw his chance not in reconciliation but in an alliance with the most conservative forces inside the republic and abroad that harked back to the ultranationalist post–World War II Croatian emigration. Rather than calming the swelled tensions, Tudjman chose to exacerbate them and use the displeasure of many Croats at the rise of Serbian nationalism as a lightning rod for his own ascendancy.

The first convention of the HDZ, on February 24, 1990, made flagrantly clear many features of Croatian ultranationalism, which deeply disturbed not only Croatian Serbs but also many democratic-minded Croats. Present at the congress were many hard-core extremists, including the post–World War II emigrants with a record of ties to the wartime Ustashe regime. Tudjman brought the heated rhetoric at the congress to a climax by stating that the Ustashe state did not so much constitute a Nazi crime as the expression of the historical aspiration of the Croatian people for independence. This earned him a standing ovation in the auditorium. Among the Croatian Serbs and the Serbs in Serbia, however, the statement reinforced his reputation as an Ustashe apologist.[56] There is hardly anything else Tudjman could have single-handedly done to make Milošević look credible. Over the forthcoming years, Tudjman's ultranationalism served as the single most important ideological resource in sustaining Milošević as an uncontested Serbian leader.

Tudjman's main objective was Croatian independence. The rehabilitation of the Ustashe was closely tied to that primary ambition. Croats had been deprived of their national pride, Tudjman claimed, because Communist Yugoslavia had stigmatized them for the association of their government with Hitler. That had made it impossible to give equal recognition to all the victims of World War II, whether they had been Nazi collaborators or antifascists. Tudjman pledged to right the wrong. From the beginning, he ignored the epidemic of desecrations across the Croatian countryside of the monuments of antifascist heroes.[57] The names of notorious Ustashe appeared on schools, municipal buildings, and street signs in Zagreb and all across the republic.[58]

Redeeming Croatian national pride was intertwined with dismantling the legacy of Communism in Croatia. "Bolshevik Yugoslavia," which was dominated by the Serbs, Tudjman argued, had stifled Croatian growth, taking away a disproportionate amount of the hard currency the republic earned every year through its tourist industry. Separation from Yugoslavia was the only way to achieve economic progress. "De-Communization" served the same purpose. And since most of those linked to the Communist regime were Serbs, their representation in the state service was to be reduced in proportion to their demographic representation in the total population.

As a result, massive layoffs of Serbs took place almost immediately after Tudjman's election, striking Serbs in the police, army, the judiciary, and the educational institutions, and even extending to many employed in tourist offices and in some private firms. Any of those left holding a public office were required to pledge a loyalty oath to the state of Croatia as a condition of employment.

The Latin alphabet was declared the official alphabet in Croatia, thereby doing away on a symbolic level with the Cyrillic script, traditionally used by the Serbs.[59] State symbols were changed, and a historic Croatian coat of arms, the checkerboard (*šahovnica*), was placed on the national flag. Serbs condemned the šahovnica as a symbol that although historic, was also used, with a big letter *U* superimposed on the field, by the Ustashe regime during World War II and was thus morally unacceptable.

Finally, an official document called a Domovnica (a form providing proof of Croatian origin) was instituted and became an instrument of differentiation between Croats and non-Croats when it came to jobs and privileges. Opening a private business, obtaining medical coverage and the right to retirement pay, getting a passport or a driver's license, even in some cases being qualified to make withdrawals from one's own savings accounts—all these things hinged on the possession of a Domovnica.[60] Life turned out to be impossible for those who could not provide proof of Croatian origin, and they left. Among them, in addition to the Serbs, were many Muslims and Romanies.

All these changes were introduced in the first year of Tudjman's presidency. He took the power firmly into his own hands, reducing most other members of his government to mere appendages and introducing strict control over all media. In this atmosphere, a vote against a strong national program in Croatia was immediately labeled as unpatriotic and Serbophile. This ultraconservative platform was buttressed with a strong promise of prosperity and a Western standard of living, but only on condition of isolation from the federation. Croatian nationalism thus served as a powerful vehicle for sidelining all the liberal forces that would have favored comprehensive change, change that would have preserved the respect for minority rights and relied on gradualism and moderation.[61]

Tudjman's ultranationalism had the effect of deeply alienating the Serbs and lending authenticity to Milošević's warnings. In June 1990, the new government proposed amendments to the Croatian constitution. Encouraged by Belgrade, Jovan Rašković rejected the draft of the amendments, characterizing them as an "attack on the Serbian people." On July 26, 1990, he announced that in case of Croatia's secession, Serbs would hold a referendum where not only cultural autonomy but also "other solutions" would be considered.[62]

Zagreb declared the referendum unconstitutional, pledged to prohibit it by all available measures, and announced that there would be an inventory made of any and all weapons found in the possession of Serbian citizens. In August 1990 Croatian police tried to disarm the Serbian reserve police in Benkovac, a town in the vicinity of Knin, but the Serbs in the surrounding villages broke into the Benkovac police station, taking the stored weapons. On August 17, two days before the referendum, the Croatian authorities dispatched three helicopters and special forces with armored personnel carriers to Knin. Both were forced by the federal army to turn back.

Responding to the request of Croatian authorities to take a stand on the incident, Borisav Jović, a Milošević supporter and at the time the president of the Yugoslav presidency, boldly stated that the right of the people to express their political will or to political activity cannot be questioned. Encouraged, the SDS organized the local population to block all the roads toward Knin with logs. Armed civilians manned the barricades, stopping cars and checking the identity documents of passengers. Trucks and private cars were gridlocked at the peak of the tourist season, and Zagreb was cut off from its coastline. On August 18, Serbs held their referendum for autonomy. No identification was required, and many people voted twice and even three times. The SDS nevertheless considered the referendum legitimate and formally proclaimed Serbian autonomy on October 1, 1990.

On December 22, 1990, the new Croatian constitution was adopted, proclaiming Croatia to be "the national state of the Croatian people." Serbs interpreted the constitutional change to mean a demotion for them from the status of an equal-partner nation to that of a minority. On February 28, 1991, the Serbian National Council and the executive council of the Serbian Autonomous Region of Krajina (SAO Krajina) adopted a resolution in favor of the separation of SAO Krajina from Croatia. The local police in the Serbian regions of Croatia refused to put Croatian emblems on their uniforms and to join the new, centralized police force loyal to Tudjman's government.

As the atmosphere in Croatia grew hotter by the month, the Serbian official media, and the voices of some highly respected Belgrade intellectuals, became ever shriller.[63] The media warned that the transformation of Yugoslavia into a confederation, advocated by Slovenes and Croats, would lead to an eventual secession of the western republics, thereby threatening a renewal of the horrors of World War II. That is why, Miloševi insisted, Serbia could not and would not ever compromise on the idea of the confederation. The implication was that the Ustashe had returned.[64]

In Croatia Serbs were increasingly described as terrorists, and the police continued to threaten to use all legal means to restore order to the Krajina. The Croatian government rejected the suggestion by the federal government that a special unit be formed, made up of police from all the Yugoslav republics and to be sent to secure peace and communications in the Krajina. The rejection upset not only Serbs but many Croats as well. Searches and arrests of Serbs in western Slavonia and throughout the previously peaceful regions of Croatia began. The incidents became increasingly numerous as relations between Serbs and Croats worsened. Several thousand Serbs from Petrinja in Slavonia, northern Croatia, fled to the woods, and several thousand more took refuge in the federal army compound in Petrinja. Serbian extremists from Serbia and Montenegro began to offer "help," sending their volunteer units to Croatia. War was approaching.

The events in Slovenia in 1989 and 1990 speeded up the polarization in Croatia as well as the overall federal disintegration. More firmly than even Croatia, Slovenia was determined to break off from Yugoslavia. Like Croatia, Slovenia maintained that for its development as the most developed republic and thus one constitutionally obliged to participate in the federal budget with the greatest proportion of its revenue, membership in the federation was economically disadvantageous.[65] Slovenian leaders have held this position consistently since 1974, and particularly in the early 1980s, when they again campaigned for a weak federation and strong republics. The confrontation with Serbia, which under Milošević's leadership stood for a strong federation and would not even consider a confederation, intensified in 1989.

While they kept silent in 1987, and even supported the reduction of Kosovo autonomy in 1988, in 1989 the Slovenes took a different stand, organizing their own "truth and solidarity" rally in Ljubljana's largest concert hall, to hail the striking Trepča miners. The Slovene League of Communists leader Milan Kučan addressed the meeting, expressing enthusiastic support for the miners and linking their protest with the Slovenian right to secession and to territorial sovereignty.

Many in Serbia saw this as a cynical move.[66] Everything about the solidarity event, especially as reported by Serbian television and print media, enraged the Serbian public. In Slovenia, however, Kučan acquired the aura of a hero, becoming the most popular public personality in the republic.[67] He skillfully used the protest in Kosovo to portray Milošević as the enemy of democracy not only in Kosovo but in Slovenia as well, and to place in the center of the public debate in Slovenia the need for its own territorial autonomy.[68]

Milošević responded with a propaganda barrage against Kučan and his supporters, in an effort to split Slovene public opinion. On March 3, 1989, emergency measures were introduced in Kosovo, and Burhan Kavaja, Aziz Abresi, and Azem Vlasi were imprisoned, accused of having organized the Trepča strike. In November 1989, Milošević tried to organize a "truth rally" by the Kosovo Serbs in Ljubljana. Slovenia then, for the first time, addressed Serbia and Yugoslavia as an "independent sovereign state." It forbade the meeting to be held and warned it would prevent the Serbs, by force if necessary, from crossing the Slovene border. Milošević responded by declaring a trade war. This effectively ruptured economic relations between Slovenia and Serbia, at great cost to the Slovene economy but at even greater cost to Serbia, since a large part of its industry was technologically dependent on Slovenia. Appeals by Serbia's leading economists and industrial managers to reconsider were ignored. Everything made in Slovenia disappeared from the stores throughout Serbia. This damaged political relations between Serbia and Slovenia beyond repair.

It was in this atmosphere of great tension that the Fourteenth Extraordinary Congress of the League of Communists of Yugoslavia convened in January 1990. The Serbian delegation and Milošević brought a clear message: the LCY was to be a unified organization or it would cease to exist. This turned the congress into a battlefield of words between Milošević and Kučan, who rejected the Serbian concept of the party and the army as the two axes of Yugoslav unity and who argued that Slovenia was a sovereign state opposed to a unitary Yugoslavia. To circumvent the confrontation between Milošević and Kučan, a group of liberal delegates— Branko Horvat from the University of Zagreb and Zdravko Grebo and Nenad Kecmanović from the University of Sarajevo—tried to suggest that two parties be formed, one Communist and the other Socialist. Serbia and its bloc of delegates from Montenegro, Vojvodina, and Kosovo rejected the suggestion as ludicrous. Aware that the Serbian bloc made it impossible for the Slovenes to achieve the required majority vote, the Slovene delegation walked out of the congress, to frantic applause, and tears. With that walkout, the federal LCY had ceased to exist.[69]

This left the federal structure hanging in midair.[70] As though the mortar holding the country together had dried up and turned to dust, only six months after the LCY had withered, the federation itself began to fall apart. Slovenia declared its sovereignty on July 2, 1990.[71] Kosovo proclaimed its independence the same day, and Croatia its independence on July 25, 1990. On October 1, 1990, the Croatian Serbs proclaimed their independence. The Bosnian Serbs and Macedonia each followed with their proclamations of independence on December 21, 1990. In a community such as that of the former Yugoslavia, disintegration without the consent of all parties meant, to say the least, that none would be able to realize its objectives without a major conflict. In this atmosphere of profound political crisis, the proclamations of independence of states within former states anticipated further destabilization and a polarization of unpredictable consequences.

The collapse of the LCY coincided with a turbulent and initially successful year for Yugoslav prime minister Ante Marković, who took office in January 1989. A product of the managerial section of the Yugoslav school of socialist economics and committed to maintaining federal Yugoslavia, Marković immediately proceeded, with the help of Western economic advisers, to reform the Yugoslav economic system from the bottom up. On taking office, he made it one of his top priorities to sweep away "socially owned" property, encouraging the sale of shares in each enterprise to its employees and the privatizing of industry. His ultimate goal was twofold: to open the economy to private ownership and foreign capital, and to create a single integrated economic system for the entire country.

This project, with potentially far-reaching positive consequences, rested on two types of assumptions: that there would be an influx of aid funds from abroad to support the economic transformation and that a safety net could be built up for the workers affected by layoffs and the period of economic austerity. Jeffrey Sachs, Marković's adviser, anticipated a period of rising unemployment followed by radical cuts in social spending, and a massive loss of economic security in the social sector. Substantial Western aid was thus all the more urgent for the project to work. Without that aid, a sound social security net could not be built and social unrest was almost certain to erupt. Yet by 1989, the year of the end of the cold war, Yugoslavia had lost much of its global significance, and in the new political context, the West saw no urgency in backing Marković. In the end it failed entirely to deliver on its promises of financial help.

Despite Marković's popularity, owing to his success in bringing inflation of 2,800 percent down to 4 percent, his failure to offer, on the federal level, viable social protections had a significant political effect. To many people it now seemed that economic security hinged on the policies of the republics and not on the actions of the federation as a whole. Inevitably, this empowered Slobodan Milošević and Franjo Tudjman, both of whom promised to the constituencies in their republics prosperity without economic cost.[72] The assault on Ante Marković—whose project's survival rested on the strengthening of the federal government—was for both Milošević and Tudjman a vehicle of self-empowerment. Slovenia launched an anti-Marković campaign of its own. His program for economic and political integration of Yugoslavia threatened Slovenia's decision to leave Yugoslavia.

Thus the determination to bring about Marković's fall was fully shared by Ljubljana, Zagreb, and Belgrade. Threats and ultimatums were thrown at Marković and his team from all three sides. Economic programs were openly or subtly sabotaged. Slovenia, for example, decided to retain for itself all custom duties it collected along its borders with Italy and Austria and not transfer them to the National Bank, as it was constitutionally obliged to do. In October 1990, in anticipation of its secession, Slovenia contracted with Austria to print its new currency.

Ante Marković was convinced that a party supporting an undivided Yugoslavia, a market economy, and democratic rights and freedoms was the only option after the discredited Communists and right-wing nationalists. But he was blocked at every turn, until it was too late. On July 29, 1990, at the meeting on Mount Kozara in Bosnia, he announced the formation of the Association of the Reform Forces of Yugoslavia. The elections in Slovenia and Croatia had already taken place, however, and that made all the difference.

Marković hoped that elections in the republics would be followed at the end of 1990 by federal elections. Slovenian leaders, however, turned out to be politically more apt, and to have understood that holding republican elections first would foreclose the very possibility of holding federal elections and therefore would cancel the federal option altogether. Slovene politicians thus insisted on holding republican elections first, and they prevailed.

The elections were billed abroad as the "first democratic multiparty elections" in the former Yugoslavia. Yet each was held within the closed political space of separate republics, and each withheld the option of voting for the federation. Despite the participation of a host of political parties, the substantial portion of the public, which otherwise would have voted for Yugoslavia, was denied that option.[73]

Ante Marković resigned in December 1991, in protest against the appropriation of 86 percent of the federal budget for war purposes. The war machine rolled first into Slovenia in early summer 1991, then into Croatia in midsummer, and then into Bosnia-Hercegovina in spring 1992.

NOTES

1 Most of the factories were built without taking into consideration the proximity of resources or markets, or the low quality of extracted ore, bauxite, or other resources. The gravest examples include: FENI, the iron ore plant built in Macedonia; the Obrovac aluminum refinery in Croatia; the Smederevo steel plant (responsible for one-half of Serbia's total foreign debt); INA, an artificial fertilizer plant in Croatia; the Trepča lead and zinc plant in Kosovo; the Feronikl nickel plant in Kosovo; and the aluminum plant in Zvornik, Bosnia.

2 Harold Lydall, *Yugoslavia in Crisis* (Oxford: Clarendon Press, 1989), p. 67.

3 Zvonko Simić, "Konstrukciona greška ili komadić švajcarskog sira," *NIN* 29 November 1987, p. 19. The author points out that in the first nine months of 1987 the figure for the number of strikes was double that for the entire year of 1986.

4 The Italian Communists called the lifestyle of the Yugoslav middle class "il socialismo borghese" (see Dusko Doder, *The Yugoslavs* [New York: Random House, 1978], p. 43).

5 Josip Županov, *Marginalije o Društvenoj Krizi* (Zagreb: Globus, 1983). Županov's analysis was followed by a number of studies by other authors who wrote openly about the rapid decline of the legitimacy of the political leadership, owing to its failure to stem the crisis (see Branko Horvat, *Jugoslavensko društvo u krizi: kritički ogledi i prijedlozi reformi* [Zagreb: Globus, 1985], and Mirko Galić, "Dramatika našeg zaostajanja," *Danas*, 22 September 1987, pp. 12–15).

6 Lydall, p. 219.

7 Belgrade was known as the place where political dissidents from the entire country would find solid public support. See, for example, the interview with the Slovenian philosopher Slavoj Žižek, in Snežana Ristić and Radonja Leposavić, "Mitski prostor Balkana," *Vreme*, 11 January 1997, p. 44. In her monograph *Trauma bez katarze*, Ogledi Edition, *Republika* (June 1995), Drinka Gojković sketches the efforts of the Serbian Writers Association, beginning in 1981, to secure the right of free speech and artistic expression. (The author focuses on the analysis of the transformation of the association from a liberal group standing for civil rights in the beginning of the 1980s into a stalwart advocate of Serbian nationalism at the end of the decade.)

8   The thesis that the fires of nationalism were not stirred through appeals to eth-
    nicity per se is effectively discussed in V. P. Gagnon, "Serbia's Road to War," *Journal
    of Democracy* 5, no. 2 (April 1994): 117–31.

9   Vojvodina, with a Hungarian population of four hundred thousand, shares borders
    with Hungary; Kosovo, with a 90 percent Albanian majority, shares borders with
    Albania.

10 The education of Hungarian children in Vojvodina was conducted in Hungarian,
    that of Kosovar Albanian children in Albanian. Textbooks to be used in Kosovo's
    elementary schools and high schools, as well as at the University of Priština, were
    regularly imported from Albania.

11 In 1984 the Slovenian per capita social product was 7.5 times greater than that of
    Kosovo, a difference "analogous to that between England and North Africa" (Branko
    Horvat, *Kosovsko pitanje* [Zagreb: Globus, 1988], p. 98).

12 For the sake of brevity, in this chapter we shall refer only to the Serbs, which does
    not imply that we consider Montenegrins to be Serbs.

    The situation was quite different in Vojvodina—but Vojvodina was not under-
    developed, like Kosovo. On the contrary, it was always the most developed part of
    Serbia.

13 This perception was exacerbated by a demographic factor: between 1948 and 1991
    the number of Albanians in Kosovo increased from 727,820 to 1,956,196. The fastest
    demographic growth occurred between 1961 and 1971 (see Marina Blagojević, *Iselja-
    vanje Srba sa Kosova: Trauma i/ili katarza*, Ogledi Edition, *Republika* [November
    1995], p. iii).

14 On the unrest in Kosovo and on Serbian and Albanian nationalism in the late 1960s
    see Sabrina Ramet, *Nationalism and Federalism in Yugoslavia, 1962–1991* (Bloom-
    ington: Indiana University Press, 1992), pp. 178–98.

15 Ramet, p. 194.

16 Lydall, p. 193. Author notes that "compared with the volume of similar inter-
    national transfers between rich and poor countries," the size of transfer to the under-
    developed regions of former Yugoslavia (including to a lesser extent also Bosnia
    and Hercegovina, Montenegro, and Macedonia) "can be seen as a very considerable
    effort."

17 On misspending in Kosovo see Momčilo Čebalović, "Šta koči otvaranje pogona,"
    Politika, 10 December 1986, p. 8.

18 Ramet states that "hardly a municipality in Kosovo abstained from violence" in
    their demands for secession or demands for Kosovo to become a republic (*Nation-
    alism and Federalism in Yugoslavia*, p. 196).

19 Marina Blagojević argues that this explanation was inaccurate in most cases. Had
    the emigrations been economically motivated, most would have involved the head
    of the family only and not entire families; they would have encompassed mostly
    people of working age; the emigrants would have by and large moved to an envi-
    ronment offering them better economic chances. Blagojević cites a survey of five
    hundred families with 3,418 members that contradicts the assumptions cited above
    (p. vii).

20 That Albanians had always felt like second-rate citizens in former Yugoslavia, and that genuine political and institutional changes inaugurated by the 1974 constitution failed to alter that fact, was usually ignored.

21 The daily *Politika* gave the events a sinister coloring. The situation was described in such terms as "tragedy," "drama," "cancer wound," "Golgoth," "exodus," "the epic of the Serbian soul"; Albanians were called "separatists and terrorists," and somewhat oddly, "fantasized demonstrators," "monstrous," and "bestial" (see Srdja Popović, Dejan Janča, and Tanja Petovar, eds., *Kosovski čvor, drešiti ili seći?* [Beograd: Republika, 1990], pp. 124–25).

22 V. Zečević, S. Nikšić, S. Rabrenović, and M. Djekić, "Batuska seoba," *NIN*, 29 June 1986, p. 16.

23 D. Ivanović, B. Kaljević, and Z. Radisavljević, "Žitelji Kosova ponovo u Beogradu, Nećemo da se selimo, tražimo zaštitu," *Politika*, 4 November 1986, pp. 1, 5–6.

24 *NIN*, 9 November 1986.

25 Between 1966 and 1968 Milošević was an economic adviser to the mayor of Belgrade. He then became general director of the Belgrade firm Tehnogas, a post in which he remained from 1970 to 1978. He moved up to become the director of Beobanka, one of Yugoslavia's most important financial institutions, where he worked from 1978 to 1982. In 1982 he became a member of the presidency of the Central Committee of the League of Communists of Serbia. In 1984 he was named head of the Belgrade League of Communists. For a political biography of Slobodan Milošević see Slavoljub Djukić, *Izmedju slave i anateme* (Beograd: Filip Višnjić, 1994).

26 According to Stambolić, Milošević sought his advice before going to Kosovo, and he told Milošević: "That is a burning issue at a hot spot. That is fire. Pour cold water, but do not make them mad, make them listen" (Roksanda Ninčić, "Krunski Svedok," *Vreme*, 4 September 1995, p. 35).

27 People were calling *his* name. The name *Slobodan* is derived from the adjective *free*.
   Slavko Ćuruvija offers a lively description of the event, which he witnessed, in "I on se tresao kao prut," the second part of the ten-part series "Godine zapleta" (*Borba*, 19 January 1993, p. 15). The details of the description offered here rely on Ćuruvija's testimony.

28 All quotes in this paragraph are from S. Ćuruvija, "Godine Zapleta," pt. 3, *Borba*, 20 January 1993, p. 15.

29 Slavko Ćuruvija, "Godine Zapleta," pt. 4, *Borba*, 21 January 1993, p. 13.

30 Mihailo Marković, *Duga*, 28 May–19 June 1988, p. 17.

31 In his monograph, Nebojša Popov cites a high police functionary, Dušan Ristić, who revealed that the "people's movement" was deeply infiltrated by police informants (*Srpski populizam*, *Vreme*, special edition, 24 May 1993, p. 20 fn. 95).

32 This happened after the purge of the party Milošević carried out September 23–24, 1987, at the Eighth Session of the Central Committee of the League of Communists of Serbia, to be discussed later in the chapter.

33 Sava Kercov, Jovo Radoš, and Aleksandar Raić, *Mitinzi u Vojvodini 1988. godine* (Novi Sad: Dnevnik, 1990), pp. 195–270.

34 Popov, p. 22.

35   Slavoljub Djukić, *Kako se dogodio vodja* (Beograd: Filip Višnjić, 1992), p. 266.

36   On the role of television see chapter 5; on the role of *Politika* see the monograph by Aleksandar Nenadović, *Politika u nacionalistickoj oluji*, Ogledi Edition, *Republika* (April 1995).

37   Speeches Milošević delivered between 1986 and 1989 were published in the collection *Godine Raspleta* (Beograd: BIGZ, 1989). Milošević says, inter alia: "How should they [Kosovo Serbs] develop, how should they catch up with Yugoslavia, let alone with Europe, if one part of that population lives in fear of what may happen to them at the work-place, and an even greater fear about what they would find coming home from work—will they find their children alive and well? Will they find their houses intact? Because the laws of this country do not apply, in many regions of Kosovo, to the Serbs and Montenegrins" (p. 153). "We have been listening to the appeals for a cool and calm head, where Kosovo is concerned, for six years. Those politics turned out to have been demonstrably wrong" (p. 160). "Undue fear and the inferiority complex are leaving us" (p. 217). "The national inferiority complex was perhaps the strongest. It expresses a false belief that every struggle in the interests of the Serbian people is the same thing as nationalism" (p. 218).

38   *Politika* was, as Nenadović points out, older than Yugoslavia itself, a fact that greatly enhanced its status (p. ii). Yet, adds Nenadović, *Politika* has had its ups and downs and has not always been uncompromisingly critical of the regime, particularly in the post–World War II period.

39   "As time went on it became ever clearer that 'national enlightenment' and the use of *Politika* to create 'a unified and strong Serbia' knew no scruples or boundaries. *Politika* addressed all social strata—even, as you see, the invalids. This campaign encompassed all informative columns of the paper—from those on internal policy and foreign politics, to those on culture, and even the sports pages" (Nenadović, pp. vii–viii).

40   The integral text of the memorandum was published in *Naše Teme* 33, nos. 1–2 (1989): 128–163. For an analysis of the activities of SANU in 1986–92, see the monograph by Olivera Milosavljević, *Upotreba autoriteta nauke*, Ogledi Edition, *Republika* (July 1995), pp. i–xxviii; and Milan Milošević, "Srbija nije u ratu, akademija se ne bavi politikom," *Vreme*, 17 July 1995, pp. 40–47.

41   For the analysis of the role played by some well-known Serbian writers (among them several SANU members) in forging the virulent rhetoric of the end of the 1980s, see Gojković, pp. i–xi.

42   About the conflict between the two conceptions having to do with Kosovo—that of Slobodan Milošević and that of Ivan Stambolić—see Ćuruvija, pt. 4, p. 13.

43   Ivan Stambolić offers credible testimony of this extraordinary event in *Put u bespuce* (Beograd: Radio B-92, 1995).

44   Stambolić also suggests that political elites in other republics were getting impatient with Kosovo and were happy to leave the problem to Serbia (Ninčić, p. 38).

45   Ivica Račan, head of the Croatian Communists, and even Azem Vlasi, chief of the Albanian-dominated government in Kosovo, were among those who failed to raise any questions.

46   In his monograph *Ko koga eksploatiše*, Ogledi Edition, *Republika* (September 1995),

Ljubomir Madžar offers an economic analysis demonstrating that the allegations on the part of Serbia and other republics that they were subject to politically orchestrated economic exploitation were entirely unfounded.

47 In his public addresses, Milošević emphasized: "Our aim is not just to resolve the crisis we are in. Our aim is economic prosperity which will bring us closer to Europe, and a political and cultural development which will bring us closer to the ideals that inspired all revolutions of the twentieth century" (*Godine raspleta*, p. 156).

48 See Ivan Torov, "Politička tuča medju drugovima" in "Godine Zaspleta," pt. 7, *Borba*, 26 January 1993, p. 15. In her monograph *Jugoslavija kao zabluda*, Ogledi Edition, *Republika* (March 1996), p. ix, Olivera Milosavljević shows that the slogans at the 1988 rallies reflected the political objectives of Belgrade: for example, "An attack on the Serbian leadership is an attack on us"; "Slobodan is a heroic name"; "Slobo, help us"; "Slobo, carry on, we are with you."

49 Torov, pt. 7, p. 15.

50 Milošević responded to the critics of staged rallies by stating openly that there was nothing unconstitutional about the rallies. They were not nationalistic or aberrant; instead, they represented the most genuine expression of public sentiment.

51 Vlasi was acquitted on April 19, 1990.

52 This only confirmed the results of the referendum for the election of the president of the presidency, held in November 1989, when Milošević won 86 percent of the vote.

53 The celebration in a little village near Knin in the Croatian Krajina of the sixth hundredth anniversary of the battle of Kosovo on June 28, 1989, had the mark of all previous mass rallies orchestrated in Serbia by Milošević's rally committees. About forty thousand Serbs and some Croats attended the celebration, which would have ended up as a local event, had it not been for a train arriving from Belgrade, carrying a mob with banners, flags, bottles of brandy, and framed photographs of Milošević. The crowd descended from the train with shouts "This is Serbia!" and calls to Milošević to lead them into battle for Serbian autonomy.

A year later, at the end of July 1990, the leader of the Krajina Serbs, Jovan Rašković —who was in close touch with Slobodan Milošević—declared the sovereignty of Krajina. By August 1990 roads leading to many Serb-populated towns and villages in Croatia were blocked in defiance of Croatian authorities and guarded by people armed through a clandestine operation from Serbia.

In a letter in 1990 to Milošević, Jovan Rašković describes Milošević as "unambiguously the foremost figure in the modern history of the Serbian people. Our Serbian Democratic Party considers you its spiritual, moral, and certainly biological protector. . . . Finally, I assure you that I am one of those, whose number is not small, who consider you a paradigm of everything that is Serb" (Jovan Rašković, *Luda Zemlja* [Beograd: Akvarijus, 1990], p. 338).

54 Milan Četnik and Radovan Kovačević, "Odluka srpskog narodnog parlamenta u Srbu," *Politika*, 26 July 1990, pp. 1, 7–8.

55 The HDZ formed in 1989 but needed an electoral law to legalize its existence. The law was enacted six months before the elections.

56 Tudjman had also tried to use his authority as a historian to refute the number

of Serbian victims killed by the Ustashe in World War II, putting that number at about seventy thousand. This enraged the Serbs, who thought the figure was about ten times as high. The exact figure, however, may never be known. The authorities of former Yugoslavia, eager to leave the disturbing past behind, failed to record the war victims right after the war in 1945. Estimates of those killed were made in 1948, 1952, 1964, 1985, and 1989. The early studies suffer from a number of significant methodological imperfections. On the methodological problems regarding collection, classification, and interpretation of the data, see Srdjan Bogosavljević, *Drugi svetski rat — žrtve u Jugoslaviji,* Ogledi Edition, *Republika* (June 1995), pp. xi-xvi. Bogosavljević cites as most reliable the estimate that places the total number of victims at between 890,000 and 1,200,000, and the maximum number of Serbian victims at about 600,000.

57 Over three thousand monuments were either reduced to ruin, badly damaged, or sprayed with derogatory graffiti (see Marko Knežević, "Ustaški Mirko i Slavko," *Vreme,* 17 April 1995, pp. 24–25; and Svetlana Vasović-Mekina, "Stid od sadašnjosti," *Vreme,* 12 September 1994, pp. 33–37).

58 Marko Knežević, p. 24.

59 Most Serbs in Croatia, however, use the Latin alphabet anyway. The Cyrillic alphabet became significant to them only once it was banned. In Serbia the urban population uses both alphabets, shifting from one to the other at will. The rural population uses primarily Cyrillic.

60 See Ivan Zvonimir Čičak, "Srpsko porijeklo obitelji Tudjman," *Borba,* 23–24 January 1993, p. xii.

61 One redeeming feature of Tudjman's regime, in the eyes of the Western public, were its free elections. Yet Tudjman's HDZ party won only 41.5 percent of the vote, but benefited from the winner-take-all system to gain preponderance in the parliament. Susan Woodward discusses the body politic's lack of experience with this type of elections, giving the advantage to the most virulent messages, which appealed to the gut and not to reason (*Balkan Tragedy: Chaos and Dissolution after the Cold War* [Washington, D.C.: Brookings Institution Press, 1995], pp. 119–20, 123–25).

62 In December 1971 *Politika* informed its readers about a statement very much like that of Rašković and other Serbian leaders in the late 1980s and early 1990s. A stack of leaflets had been found in the office of Slobodan Subotić, the president of the Serbian and Montenegrin Bar Association, urging Serbs to prepare for the day when "Yugoslavia breaks up and Croatia becomes a sovereign state"; the leaflet urged that Serbian committees be set up in Croatia and Dalmatia in case of war, to defend Serbian interests. The bar association was then considered to be the stronghold of Serbian nationalism (see Frederick Bernard Singleton, *Twentieth-Century Yugoslavia* [New York: Columbia University Press, 1976], p. 229).

In May 1990 Rašković broke all contact with Tudjman. Tudjman had offered Rašković the post of vice president in the new government, but the latter informed the Croatian parliament that his party would boycott any public offices they were offered.

63 Referring to World War II, the poet Matija Bećković, for example, said that "Serbs

in Croatia are the remains of a slaughtered people." Images were conjured up, rhetorically and on television, of the worst tortures, executions, and massacres of the fascist era (see Gojković, pp. vii–viii).

64 Aware of the grave dangers of this situation, some Croatian intellectuals, such as Branko Horvat, Žarko Puhovski, and others, warned that the grievances of the Croatian Serbs had to be taken into the account. They charged that Tudjman's administration had done a great deal to antagonize the Serbs and warned, to no avail, that the removals of road signs in Cyrillic, the disappearance of Cyrillic subtitles from Croatian television, physical attacks on Serbian deputies in the Croatian parliament, arrests, persecutions, firings and demotions of Serbs, the imposition of a loyalty oath as a prerequisite for Serbs to keep their jobs, telephone threats—all these exacerbated the feeling among Serbs that they were under serious threat.

65 Ljubomir Madžar writes that membership in the Yugoslav community cost Slovenia roughly one-twelfth of its social product a year. "It is hard to find a viewpoint," says Madžar, "from which that amount would look negligible" (p. viii). See also Singleton, p. 227.

66 This position was in contrast to the economic stand Slovenia had already taken on Kosovo, when it was the first republic to refuse to contribute to the Federal Development Fund for Kosovo. In the second part of the 1980s, many press reports also warned of racist treatment of both Kosovar Albanians and Bosnian migrant workers in Slovenia. (Inter-republic migration escalated, particularly in the late 1960s, when a great number of Kosovar Albanians and Bosnians sought work in Slovenia and Croatia.) Singleton compares the treatment of Albanians and Bosnians in Zagreb and Ljubljana to the treatment the first generation of Asian migrants received in British cities (p. 223).

67 Kučan twice won the Slovenian presidential elections—once before Slovenia's declaration of independence and once after.

68 Susan Woodward argues that Kučan effectively introduced confusion in distinguishing between human rights and territorial autonomy; she cites Dimitrij Rupel, the foreign minister of Slovenia at the time, who admitted that Slovene politicians used Kosovo for their own nationalist purposes (p. 440 n. 32).

69 For a more detailed coverage of the event see Ivan Torov, "Godine Zapleta," pt. 9, *Borba*, 28 January 1993, p. 13; and "Godine Zapleta," pt. 10, *Borba*, 29 January 1993, p. 11.

70 Many believe that after the congress, Milošević knew he would never be able to beat Kučan and that he gave Kučan a nod for Slovenia's relatively painless secession from Yugoslavia.

71 Its elections were held on April 8 and 22, 1990.

72 The rhetoric of prosperity in Milošević's campaign contrasted sharply with the pessimistic forecasts—much more grounded in reality—that were offered by the opposition. The electorate opted for Milošević's party, which proclaimed, "With us, there is no uncertainty."

73 Susan Woodward argues that the first democratic elections "were thus not the opening of choice for Yugoslavs but its closure" (p. 118, 445 n. 19).

The Media Wars: 1987–1997

Milan Milošević

♠

For seventy years, Yugoslavs, regardless of ethnic background, lived daily in a multicultural environment. The music played at weddings, private parties, pubs, and restaurants was typically a mixture of the tunes and rhythms from across the country: Macedonian laments, Dalmatian sea harmonies, Bosnian love odes, Serbian rounds, Zagreb chansons, Slovene polkas. Television programming was also strongly multinational.[1] Until 1974, studios in different parts of the country coordinated their programming to make room for one another's productions. Entertainment, cultural, and news broadcasts of one TV center were regularly integrated into the programming of other centers. *Dnevnik*, the popular evening news program featured across the country in prime time, five in the afternoon and seven-thirty in the evening, was produced in a different regional capital every day.[2] Each program was aired in the regional language, prepared by local reporters and camera crews, and presented by local anchors and commentators. Although Yugoslav TV production never entirely broke free of political control, the regular participation in the common TV network of the TV studios across the country assured constant circulation of information.

After 1974, the year the new constitution was adopted, ushering in the process of strong political decentralization, media policies gradually began to change. As the political climate in the country evolved toward increasing regional autonomy, TV centers slowly abandoned the traditional multiethnic style of programming. More and more frequently, each center opted for developing its own network of affiliated studios and relying on local programming. The daily and weekly press was caught up in a similar process. Media subsidies were transferred from the federal budget to the budgets of the republics, enabling regional politicians to take full control of the media. Slobodan Milošević and Franjo Tudjman, the presidents of Serbia and Croatia, elected in 1987 and 1990 respectively, both gave top priority to completing the total isolation of the media in their republics and making them impermeable to other views. Television served as a springboard for Milošević and Tudjman's nationalistic agendas, as regional media turned into pulpits for the advocacy of local powers.[3] By the end of the 1980s, media editors and directors and their party secretaries in Belgrade, Zagreb, and Ljubljana alike had almost completely eliminated the programming of other republics from local channels. As it soon became clear, the media fragmentation favoring strident nationalism was at least as fatal for Yugoslavia as was its economic and political fragmentation.

A mental conversion was necessary before the majority of Yugoslavs could tolerate nationalist slogans. Despite the claims of foreign journalists and politicians, in the former Yugoslavia mutual trust was in ample supply. For the war to become thinkable, trust that had steadily grown since World War II despite some tensions between the ethnic groups had to be rooted out first, and confusion, doubt, and fear implanted in its stead. That is what Belgrade television achieved over three and a half years preceding the war in 1991. TV studios proved to be colossal laboratories of war engineering.

Still, television failed in the main purpose of any war propaganda: to arouse the will to fight. Conscription of reservists in Serbia in the summer of 1991 turned out to be excessively difficult. Hundreds of thousands of young men went into hiding or fled the country to avoid having to put on a uniform. According to General Veljko Kadijević, head of the chiefs of staff, the Yugoslav People's Army was eighteen divisions short at the beginning of the Croatian war because of draft resistance.[4] Several reservist uprisings occurred, one after another, in units in the heart of Serbia—in Valjevo, Kragujevac, and Topola.[5] None of this was ever reported on television.

Milošević's politics in Serbia since his rise to power in 1987 were viewed by the antiwar opposition in Belgrade as "Caesarism by plebiscite."[6] One of the political tools of such a policy was the use of visual kitsch. Milošević's first television mega-spectacular took place on June 28, 1989, St. Vitus Day, an important date in the Serbian religious and historical calendar. The day commemorates the 1389 Battle of Kosovo between the armies of the doomed Serbian empire and the expanding Ottoman Empire. The 1989 event took place at Gazimestan, the site of the historic battle. The commemoration had all the trappings of a coronation staged as a Hollywood extravaganza. Milošević descended by helicopter from the heavens into the cheering crowd; the masses were the extras. The cameras focused on his arrival. In some vague way, the commentator placed Milošević at the center of the Serbian ancestral myth of Prince Lazar, the hero and martyr of the Kosovo battle. Exactly six hundred years before, the voice-over told the viewers, on this very soil, Prince Lazar had chosen the kingdom of heaven over his earthly kingdom, the glory of death over survival in defeat. The relics of Prince Lazar, killed in the battle, were carried a month previously, in a procession accompanied by unprecedented media pomp, through virtually all Serb-populated regions where war would later break out.

At Gazimestan, for the first time Milošević explicitly mentioned the possibility of war.[7] He did not have in mind the later wars in Croatia and Bosnia-Hercegovina. He was speaking of Kosovo itself. The TV spectacular at Gazimestan was designed to promote the myth of Kosovo as the cradle of Serbian medieval culture and, hence, the cornerstone of every Serb's national identity. The territory, belonging to Serbia until 1974, had been unjustly uncoupled from Serbia by the 1974 constitution, insisted TV commentators, and ethnic Albanians would try, sooner or later, to wrench Kosovo from Serbia altogether and unite it with Albania. Serbia had to reestablish its authority over Kosovo.

Milošević had addressed an allegedly self-evident, justified, and painful grievance of the Serbs, now victims in the heart of their own ancestral land, denied by Albanians their historic right to live where they belonged.[8] By suggesting that he would stand up for the Serbs, Milošević was making an appeal to justice. When, shortly after the event, the Serbian army and the police force were sent to subdue Kosovo, terminating its political and cultural autonomy and banning Albanian-language media, many of Milošević's TV viewers believed he was doing what had to be done to restore justice. Looking straight into the TV cameras, Milošević struck many as a real hero.

Staged mass meetings like the one at Gazimestan proved a powerful tool for political mobilization over the next three years.[9] Each meeting was a painstakingly thought-out, coordinated, and promoted media event, exploiting messages drawn from the old national myths. Gradually, a familiar socialist ideology was being replaced by a foreign, fervently nationalistic one. At mass rallies, television shots were framed to give the impression of overwhelming popular attendance and support. In smaller towns the people from the crowds were delighted when they later saw themselves on television. To them this was official proof that something important had occurred and that they were at the center of events.

Gradually, mass meetings and the folk rhetoric adopted by the electronic media brought about an ideological switch, and a switch in mass psychology as well. The Serbs would vindicate their honor again and see to it that the historical pattern of injustice was broken once and for all. Every day, television featured programs lauding the capacity of the Serbs to survive the wrath inflicted on them in the past. A vague but stubborn link was suggested, time and again, between the five hundred years Serbs endured under the Turks and their current suffering caused not only by the Kosovar Albanians but also by the revamped Croatian fascists and by foreign media, especially those of Germany and the Vatican.[10]

In its effort to augment the sense of grievance in the population at large, television especially exploited World War II history. The goal was to plant the idea that the official history of World War II did not tell the complete story and that the full extent of Croatian atrocities had been covered up. The number of Serbs who perished during the war in the Croatian death camp Jasenovac and from Croatian persecution, TV claimed, was much greater than had been calculated. The "demystification of history" was launched, with television as the main medium. The campaign was in part a response to Franjo Tudjman's book *Bespuća* (Wilderness), published in 1989, a year before his election as president of Croatia, in which he alleged that official Communist history had greatly exaggerated the wartime crimes of the Croatian side.

To prove Tudjman wrong, a bizarre process of systematic unearthing of World War II Serbian mass graves was undertaken in the summer of 1989 and throughout 1990 in the glare of Belgrade television. To establish the "true" number of the dead, concrete-sealed mass graves in limestone terrain in the Krajina, and afterward in Hercegovina, were opened and the skeletons displayed and bones counted. After funeral services at the site, the remains were reburied and the graves resealed, with TV cameras eagerly recording the event. The ceremonial and official character of these events slowly awakened the sense that the past might have been far worse than anyone had imagined.

Simultaneously in Croatia, Partisan graves and war monuments were desecrated in an effort to shake off the Nazi legacy. In particular, the monuments marking the sites of the infamous death camps run by the Ustashe were defaced or destroyed. The Croatian media insisted the time had finally come to make peace with the past that had plagued the Croatian national consciousness since 1945. Zagreb TV repeatedly accused the Yugoslav Communist regime of rubbing Croatia's war guilt in the face of its people. Television presented Croats as victims of the Communist conspiracy to brand them with a permanent shameful stigma.

In this context, new tactics of characterizing the leaders of other republics as monsters served to discredit other nations as a whole. In the Serbian media, Franjo Tudjman was described as "genocidal," "fascisoid," the "heir of Ustashe leader Ante Pavelić," a "neo-Ustashe Croatian viceroy"; the Croatian media meanwhile portrayed him as "wise," "dignified," "steady," "a mature statesman." By contrast, according to the Croatian media Slobodan Milošević was a "Stalinist and Bolshevik," "Stalin's bastard," a "bank robber," an "authoritarian populist," while according to the Serbian media the same man was "wise," "decisive," "unwavering," "the person who was restoring national dignity to the Serbian people."

Demonizing Chetniks and "Serbo-Chetnik terrorists" was another major assignment of the Croatian media. When the first uprising occurred among Croatian Serbs in 1990, the Croatian media responded by referring to Serbs in general as "bearded Chetnik hordes," "terrorists and conspirators," "a people ill inclined to democracy." Meanwhile, in the official media of Belgrade, rebellious Serbs in Croatia were hailed as "people spending sleepless nights defending their homes," "boys with heads held high," "defenders of their centuries-old hearths from Ustashe evil."[11]

Once the war broke out in Croatia in 1991, Croatian propaganda played more and more on the moral advantage of the victims. Television returned time and again to Vukovar in ruins, Dubrovnik in flames, and Zagreb under air-raid warnings, but it failed to show any of the Serbian villages in Croatia being torched. Long after the fighting had stopped, in 1992 and 1993 Croatian television still greeted its viewers with: "Defenders of the homeland, good morning."

TV Belgrade made its viewers amply aware of the desecrations of the Partisan graves in Croatia, and of the determination of the new regime in Croatia to minimize the World War II genocide against the Serbs. The ugly head of Croatian nationalism was rising again, the viewers were told. Serbs had to "defend their own homes." This rhetoric continued unabated into the 1992–93 Bosnian war, completely eclipsing coverage of the genocide perpetrated against Bosnians. As the army shelled Sarajevo, TV viewers in Serbia watched mutilated Serbian corpses, Serbian homes in flames, Serbian children orphaned—or at least that is what they thought they were watching. TV Belgrade showed Serbs demonstrating in Western European cities against the false image the West had constructed of Serbia as the aggressor. The message was that the world had conspired, together with the mujahideen and the Ustashe, to wipe out the Serbian nation. No one ever explained why the world had come to so hate the Serbs, but after months of watching television the hatred itself seemed to many common people to be fact. Television had defined the Croatian and later the Bosnian war as indigenous ethnic conflicts, as civil wars whose only tragic target were the Serbs themselves.

Written-to-order telegrams lauding Milošević gave the impression of popular backing for his policies and provided a chorus of support to his government. Some telegrams were written at TV Belgrade itself.[12] The strength of the Serbian nation was a constant media theme: in their history the Serbs had survived horrors much beyond anything the new world order could think up; the Serbs were not only a "just people" but, indeed, a "chosen people," given their endurance and their spirit of defiance.[13]

A new language—a compound of formulas from folk history, the old Communist rhetoric, and the new nationalist ideology—was being generated day by day. Architect Bogdan Bogdanović, one of the most prominent Belgrade antiwar dissidents who analyzed the new language as it was taking shape, suggested that "the dizzying repetition of pseudo-patriotic terminology has a shamanistic effect."[14] When Bogdanović's book appeared, the Belgrade official daily *Politika* declared: "Serbia is sick and tired of people like Bogdan Bogdanović."[15] Repeated attacks on prominent intellectuals such as Bogdanović were a way of discrediting the opposition. Every voice raised against the official chorus was labeled traitorous or at least indifferent to the plight of the Serbian nation facing its worst hour.

As the spiraling inflation of 1992 put the daily papers in Serbia out of reach of the family budget, television became the only source of news and information for most people. The independent media lost ground, almost financially crushed by the international economic sanctions. Independent TV Studio B, a privately owned progressive Belgrade TV channel, and

Radio B-92, an equally progressive small radio station that became world-famous during the 1996–97 protest, had tremendous problems trying to finance basic essentials. The network of the Association of the Independent Media clustered around Radio B-92 encompassed many small local radio stations in the towns of Požarevac, Bajina Bašta, Smederevo, Cetinje, and Podgorica. Radio B-92's young crew eventually expanded its activities into publishing and video production,[16] joining the few courageous groups that managed to do quite extraordinary things in tough times.

The privately owned antiwar print media, *Borba* and *Vreme*, were never sure they would have enough newsprint or paper for the next issue. In 1992 newspaper circulation hit its lowest level in thirty years, dropping to somewhat less than three hundred thousand for the four largest dailies combined in Serbia—the circulation figure for just one of them only a year and a half earlier. In a country where the population was so impoverished that only 8 percent could afford a daily paper, the official TV channel, the only one with total territorial coverage, became the single information source. The alternative, independent media thus bore the brunt of the sanctions. In this respect, the sanctions, rather than weakening the regime, effectively strengthened Slobodan Milošević.

Before the war started, early in 1991, Yutel, an independent Yugoslav TV studio that was objective in its news coverage and committed to the preservation of Yugoslavia and to tolerance and liberalism, was established in Belgrade. At first Yutel was carried by all the regional TV channels throughout Yugoslavia, but only after midnight. A sizable audience, especially in the larger towns and cities, waited late into the night to watch Yutel news and commentary, because it was the only way to find out what was really going on in the already overheated situation. Quite soon, however, Yutel was labeled treasonous in both Serbia and Croatia. In this regard, the two leaderships were in total agreement—any activity supporting a multinational concept of Yugoslavia had to be silenced.

When in late 1991 the Serbian government confiscated a transmitter Yutel planned to install on Mount Avala, just outside Belgrade, Yutel sought refuge in Sarajevo. The editorial staff knew that in Sarajevo all programming was still the work of, as before, multiethnic teams of Muslims, Serbs, and Croats. But in the spring of 1992, only a few months after Yutel moved to Sarajevo, the first attacks on the city occurred, and the Yutel transmitter in Bosnia was blown up. Yutel was cut off from its Belgrade audience. From the exclusively Serbian television studio in Pale, the Serbian stronghold on the outskirts of Sarajevo, the barrage against Yutel was often fiercer than against the television centers of the war enemies.

Using a biased voice-over, poisonous commentary, and its own type of death-porn, official Serbian television exploited the war to consolidate the powers that be as the only guarantee of national survival. The sophisticated cosmopolitan tone formerly cultivated on Belgrade TV and Yutel gave way to a closed, parochial approach. One cultural program on Serbian TV, "Friday at 22," aired late on Friday nights. Occasionally featuring foreign guests like the British actor Kenneth Branagh and the French philosopher Jacques Derrida, it somehow managed to survive for a surprisingly long time despite its determinedly antinationalist orientation. But overall, the editors of official TV sought to eliminate European names and European topics and to create an isolated and self-sufficient cultural model. "Friday at 22" faded from the air as its editorial staff gradually was dispatched on an "extended vacation." The educated public, deprived first of Yutel and then of one of its favorite cultural programs, sensed that dark days lay ahead. If foreign guests were featured on the TV shows at all, they were no longer of the Branagh and Derrida type. They were supporters of Italian fascists in late 1991, and of the Russian far right in 1993. TV cameras filmed the Russian playwright Edvard Limonov—given a celebrity welcome at his arrival in Pale—firing a machine gun in the direction of Sarajevo from a hill overlooking the city.

Those who proved themselves "soldiers of the media army" filled the jobs of those who were laid off. Rebellious colleagues were labeled "obstacles to the government's effort to restore order." News anchors, commentators, and staff members of drama programs were fired for including a Slovene writer on a list of best TV dramatist. Musical program editors were fired for broadcasting over Radio Belgrade "four times more Croatian and Slovene music than Serbian music." The general manager of Radio Belgrade, Momir Brkić, divided his staff into "reliable Serbs" and "bad Serbs" (loši Srbi), the latter relegated to the same category as non-Serbs. His hit list was broadcast on official radio in April 1992 several times and read on prime-time TV news. Before long, a large number of undesirable journalists and other media professionals had left Belgrade TV.

Serbs in the parliamentary and, especially, nonparliamentary opposition, who had openly voiced their protest against Serbian politics under Milošević, were crudely assaulted. In the summer of 1992, Belgrade composers organized a demonstration in front of the Serbian presidential offices that lasted for several days. The following letter was delivered to the demonstrators from Radio Belgrade's general manager, Brkić: "Ladies and Gentlemen, Composers: You have given your full support to a woman who slipped an Ustashe song into a Radio Belgrade program. Since then, I believe nothing you say, and nothing you do can surprise me."[17] The composers believe that the same hand also wrote the next message: "Anti-Serb riffraff! Just keep on barking, you won't last long. All of you will be eliminated and your places taken by real composers, real people, real Serbs."[18]

The TV news program routinely referred to all of the opposition and all free-thinking intellectuals as traitors. Thugs in the olive-green uniforms of military irregulars often ambushed such people at night in front of their own homes, shouting "Beat him up! Show him!" Several opposition figures, like Obrad Savić, a Belgrade philosopher, were beaten. In 1991, and again in 1992, the offices of the Belgrade Citizens Association, the most prominent antiwar organization, were demolished and office telephones and computers taken away.

Yugoslav prime minister Milan Panić was proclaimed a "bad Serb" when he decided to run against Slobodan Milošević in the December 1992 presidential elections. The media pounded him: he was a traitor because he insisted on negotiations with the "Albanian separatists" in Kosovo; he was Bush's secret agent, sent to Yugoslavia to undermine Serbia's true patriots; his real intention was to make sure the new Yugoslavia remained under sanctions indefinitely. Television attacks on Panić were accompanied by documentary inserts of civilian casualties caused by the U.S. intervention in Panama. In the minds of the viewers this left an impression of Panić's personal involvement in the Panama intervention, and of his inclination to bring about something similar in Yugoslavia. Belgrade TV showed filmed statements by individuals interviewed in the United States alleging in the crudest terms that Panić was involved in criminal activities and claiming he had close friends among the American Ustashe immigrants. Panić was particularly attacked for having admitted in foreign interviews the existence of war criminals and for even having named some. According to the Belgrade media, he was preparing another Nuremberg for Serbia. Incredibly, despite the propaganda barrage against him, Panić won 34.2 percent of the vote, compared to Milošević's rigged 56 percent.

The favorite target of the Serbian official media in its mudslinging campaigns was the writer Vuk Drašković, leader of the Serbian Renewal Movement. From being initially a strident nationalist in 1988 and 1989, and also part of 1990, he had evolved into a moderate in open opposition to Milošević. His leadership in organizing the protests to liberate TV Bastille, as official TV was called by the opposition, made him a favorite TV target. During the 1990 Serbian presidential campaign, Belgrade TV released a report claiming that the CIA had bought a house in Geneva for Vuk. In March 1991 he was arrested for organizing a week-long demonstration in Belgrade that same month and charged with "inciting the destruction of Belgrade." Under pressure from demonstrators demanding his release, he was let go. During the antiwar demonstrations in Belgrade in June 1993, both Vuk and his wife, Danica, were arrested in the street and clubbed by the police until they were semiconscious. Their lawyer and family members were prevented from seeing them for several days. Neither received medical treatment for almost two weeks for serious skull and spine injuries inflicted during the beatings. Only days before the event, Danica had spoken out on TV Studio B against the murder of Muslims in the Bosnian town of Gacko, Vuk's birthplace. The police assault on them was a warning to all by the "war lobby."

At the same time that it conducted its campaign of slander against the opposition, Serbian TV contributed widely to the promotion of the most hard-core extremists. The Chetnik leader Vojislav Šešelj was second to none regarding the TV time he received in 1991, 1992, and the first half of 1993, while he was on good terms with Milošević. The nightly TV news featured him calling for physical attacks on journalists, declaring prominent individuals traitors, and naming "spies" and "bad Serbs." Official TV commentators referred to Šešelj as "the only voice of reason in a dark tunnel." During the 1992 campaign, Slobodan Milošević rated him the opposition deputy he respected most. As the TV hero of 1992, Šešelj won 30 percent of the vote for parliamentary candidates.

Željko Ražnjatović-Arkan—a criminal wanted by Interpol for armed robbery and terrorist activity in Western Europe, a person widely suspected of having been a hit man for the state security service (UDBA) during the Tito years and a member of the paramilitary forces responsible for some of the worst war crimes in Croatia and Bosnia—was another TV favorite. His "restless youth" image was romanticized by attaching to it the aura of a Rambo. As a war hero and patriot, Ražnjatović won a seat in the 1992 parliamentary elections. A flattering TV film portraying his irregulars as defenders of Serbs was shown on the eve of war in Bosnia-Hercegovina. The accompanying script treated the accusations against him as part of the hostile Western effort to set up a war crimes tribunal aimed only against the Serbs.

A local Vojvodina studio belonging to the official Serbian TV network, TV Novi Sad, feted in 1992 a favorite extremist of its own, a certain Ostoja Sibinčić, arrested and charged by the court in the town of Sremska Mitrovica with organizing the expulsions of Croats and Hungarians from a small Vojvodina village called Hrtkovci. The prosecution had accused Sibinčić of using psychological and physical pressure to drive non-Serbs from their homes in the village where Croats, Hungarians, and Serbs had lived together and in harmony for more than two hundred years. Before Sibinčić was given a suspended sentence in the spring of 1993, TV Novi Sad aired "a documentary" about Hrtkovci. Sibinčić and his codefendant Rade Čakmak were described as "legendary commanders" of the war in Croatia. Only their supporters in the village were interviewed. No non-Serb, and no Serb favoring the right of the Hungarians and Croats to stay in their village, were asked to express their opinion. TV Novi Sad censured the statement made by Milan Panić, at the time still prime minister of rump Yugoslavia, that expulsions of Croats and Hungarians were a disgrace to Serbia.

In the spring of 1993, the Civic Association, the Serbian Renewal Movement, and the Independent Association of Journalists collected signatures to protest the media policy of spreading hate and intolerance. Television support of the war had led many public personalities in Belgrade to refuse offers of participation on official TV talk shows. This left a void, more and more frequently filled by trash shows exploiting the supernatural, the eccentric, or featuring explicit pornography. During the second year of the war, mysticism became rampant on Belgrade TV. Milja Vujanović, an actress turned astrologist, was a regular guest on an occult show. She would cut an apple in half to point out to her audience "the diabolical pentagram" at the heart of this symbol of New York City. She would then declare, facing the cameras, that New York, the "diabolical fortress of conspiracy against Serbia," was doomed to ruin. The evil Western world that refused to hear Serb grievances would get its due in the natural-supernatural course of events.[19]

A smoke screen of unreality had been generated, defusing the awareness of relevant events. Fabricated news, the most frequently used instrument of propaganda, deepened the distortion. The first spark of armed conflict in Croatia was ignited on February 16, 1991, by fabrication. Special correspondents of Montenegro TV announced on that day that at least forty people had been killed in the small town of Pakrac in Croatia. Radio Belgrade picked up the report but cited the death toll as six. The report on TV Novi Sad was eight dead, and TV Belgrade found an Orthodox priest among the dead. The dead priest appeared live on television a few days later with a statement of his own. The Yugoslav presidency finally came up with a communiqué, officially stating that nobody had been killed in Pakrac. But by that time it was already too late. The fabrication had produced the desired effect.

During the 1991 siege of Dubrovnik, General Milan Gvero gave a TV interview in which he stated categorically that not even a "grain of sand" had fallen on the Old City. Meanwhile, TV channels around the world were showing images of the town in flames. In Vukovar one of the frontline officers responsible for the town's devastation, Major Veselin Šljivančanin, was filmed shouting "This is my country!" and physically preventing journalists and European Community observers from entering the Vukovar hospital after the town's destruction. Šljivančanin explained the devastation by saying: "Leveled but free!" Images of Vukovar in ruins were shown for weeks on television accompanied by commentary describing the town as "liberated."

In Serbia and in Croatia, TV fabricated and shamelessly circulated war crime stories. Television thrived on death porn. In interviews with TV Belgrade Serbian soldiers told of Croats they had imprisoned wearing necklaces made of children's fingers. Croatian TV showed witnesses who accused Serbian soldiers of having "gouged out the eyes before cutting the throats of their Croatian victims." Throughout the second half of 1991, parents and children had the opportunity to watch on television victims of the most heinous crimes, with lingering close-ups of the massacred and torched. The war was carried directly into private homes by audacious reporters sent to the scene to document "genocide against us." Most extremely graphic and shocking reports explained nothing: neither why nor in whose name the killing was taking place. The official studios in both Belgrade and Zagreb abandoned any form of news analysis in favor of a sensationalized "human interest" approach that made the war scenes frighteningly direct while playing on the confusion of the audience about what was actually happening.

As the constant exposure to inexplicable horror continued, less and less room was left for common sense. Irrational, intense fear grew in the viewers in proportion to the incomprehensibility of the total picture.

It was not unusual for Croatian and Serbian television to borrow each other's victims. The same victim would be identified on Zagreb screens as a Croat, on Belgrade screens as a Serb. A dossier on TV Novi Sad, published by the opposition Belgrade monthly *Republika* in May 1992, recorded that during the Vukovar offensive a notice on the TV studio bulletin board instructed that any and all corpses filmed be identified as "Serbia corpses."[20] A stunning variety of instruments of death and torture was shown. A large butcher knife was presented as a "Serb chopper" and many other implements as "eye gougers." Interviews with "war criminals," usually some distraught prisoners unsure whether they were being interrogated or interviewed, were treated as "documents of war" on Belgrade and Zagreb TV alike.

When the fighting began in Bosnia, propaganda strategists in Belgrade were thrown into a quandary. For the first time, Serbian TV found it wiser to hide the pictures of war than to promote them. The war began in April 1992 with shots fired by Serbian irregulars from the roof of the Sarajevo Holiday Inn into a huge peace demonstration. Despite the presence of a TV Belgrade team on the site, the TV report in Belgrade consisted of a blank screen and a voice-over. "I can't say for sure what happened in Sarajevo today," the report went, "except that some men broke into the Holiday Inn Hotel." The better informed TV Novi Sad said that "so-called pro-peace forces" had gathered in Sarajevo to overthrow the government and form a new, pro-Moslem and anti-Serb government. Only Independent TV Studio B, with its limited transmission range, covered the start of the war in Sarajevo and the subsequent peace demonstration in Belgrade.

The antiwar demonstrations were covered by TV Sarajevo, which ran them live, with a written message on the bottom of the screen saying: "Nations of Bosnia-Hercegovina unite, don't shoot!" The general manager of TV Sarajevo stated in those first few days of the war that the Bosnian government accused TV Sarajevo of wanting to help produce a coup.[21] Nenad Pejić, a Bosnian journalist, wrote in the beginning of the second week of the war: "TV Belgrade and Zagreb journalists are lying shamelessly. They write what they are told to write. They are creating an atmosphere favorable to bringing into Bosnia more and more volunteers from Serbia and Croatia. The war in Bosnia is being fought by people who do not live here!"[22]

The claim that the war in Bosnia was being fought by outsiders and not by Bosnian Serbs, Croats, or Muslims eventually formed the core of the propaganda of the Bosnian government. But this was simply propaganda and not much else. It was indeed Bosnians who fought the war, even if with a good deal of outside help.

For two months, TV Belgrade showed no film footage to go with its reports of the shelling of Sarajevo. At TV Novi Sad written orders were displayed on the walls that reports must not be accompanied by film. Archive footage and static maps were used instead, and the side doing the shelling was not identified. On May 31, 1992, at 6 P.M., however, a Serbian government resolution was read condemning the shelling of Sarajevo by Serbian forces. The condemnation was issued two hours before the UN Security Council was to meet and vote on the first sanctions resolution against Serbia. At that point, owing to the government's last-minute attempt to avert the sanctions, a large part of Serbia's television audience for the first time discovered what was happening in Sarajevo.

The Vase Miškina Street massacre a few days earlier—when a breadline was hit by a mortar and a score of people killed—was immediately reported by TV Sarajevo showing images of the victims lying in blood. Serb-controlled TV Pale reported the massacre as a self-inflicted act by the Bosnian side, a part of the strategy devised to force international intervention. A month later, Serbian television interviewed a woman who claimed that the Moslems had staged the massacre; otherwise, she said, the TV Sarajevo team would not have been able to reach the scene so promptly. To settle the issue, viewers in Serbia were told that an anonymous UN official had "confirmed" that staged incidents were a possibility. The news about the concentration camps discovered in Bosnia in the summer of 1992 were either ignored or represented as a part of a Western conspiracy against Serbia.

The first organized action of the antiwar opposition in Belgrade was aimed at freeing television.[23] In the March 1991 demonstration, eighty thousand people demanded the fall of TV Bastille. When students joined the demonstrators, tanks rolled into the streets of Belgrade. Nevertheless, the demonstrations lasted five days. Two people were killed and hundreds injured, but no changes were made in official TV. The struggle for free television continued through the following years at the cost of deaths, physical attacks, injuries, loss of jobs, threats, court indictments, and self-imposed exile. The 113-day protest of the winter 1996–97 was also in great part a protest to free the media.

In the fall of 1991 over a hundred journalists at the Belgrade radio and television stations walked out of their jobs in protest against the media warmongering. The protest was joined by a large number of citizens and spread to other Serbian towns and cities. At the Terazije Square in Belgrade, a live "TV News Hour," part street theater, part straight news reporting, was held every evening. Reporters, writers, and opposition figures discussed the events and provided in-depth analysis. This evening protest gained momentum and gave a boost to the antidraft movement.[24] In September, however, groups of extremists were sent to break up the news hour.

The fight for professional independence and a free press continued unabated. A student antiwar protest, including a protest against media control, began in the spring of 1992 and lasted into the summer. One of its slogans was "Turn off Your TV and Open Your Eyes!"[25] That same spring, during one of many protest strikes at Radio Belgrade, the management drew up lists of employees who were permitted to come to work but were required to sign a "loyalty oath." Striking journalists spoke of two burly men stationed in chairs in the director's office. Staff members allowed to reach their workplace said the halls were patrolled by police officers carrying machine guns.[26]

The Serbian government proclaimed strikes by journalists blatant violations of the law and demanded that measures be taken against the strikers. Threats of dismissal or suspension followed, especially against the members of the Journalists' Independent Trade Union, founded in 1991 to oppose government control.[27] In late December 1992, fifteen hundred journalists and technical staff of Belgrade TV—all union members—received notice of an "extended holiday," a form of dismissal with pay. Reasons cited ran from absenteeism to "insufficient facial optimism" in commenting on the election victory, only days before, of Milošević's Serbian Socialist Party. Top staff positions were filled by people with no professional standing, political careerists, and correspondents and reporters from the war-torn regions.

A mid-1991 periodic survey of the Institute for Political Studies in Belgrade concluded that only 8.4 percent of the Serbian TV audience was well informed about events of vital importance to the whole country. Surveys conducted a year later indicated that over 60 percent of television audiences expressed no doubt about the truth of the information transmitted by the TV images. Only 7 percent said they did not believe the images.

The success of the TV propaganda was measurable by the increasing confusion of the public at large. The collective loss of perspective enabled the government to defuse the dissatisfaction of the population trapped in radically deteriorating economic, cultural, and social conditions. The repetition of propaganda formulas from program to program, day after day, year after year, helped create a virtual reflex in the minds of the viewers against everything out of line with the TV-constructed reality. The culprits of the crisis were being found everywhere but in one's own midst. The growing gap between the simulated TV reality and the one the viewers themselves experienced daily caused profound confusion. Caught among rising contradictions in a hopeless situation, many found it easier, and safer, to accept the fiction.

At the end of 1993, following the decision of Slobodan Milošević to present himself in international negotiations as an agent of peace, the official media changed their tune. A collective-memory reconstruction was under way. The ruling party of Slobodan Milošević was being presented as having always advocated peace. Verbal warfare was launched on Šešelj's radicals—the same ones who had been celebrated only a year earlier. In this new media projection, it was the radicals and extremists who were war-crime culprits. They were now referred to as "war profiteers" and "criminals."

Simultaneously, however, the independent media came under attack in a new way. Thirteen foreign reporters (including those working for CNN, Radio Free Europe, *Le Monde*, Sky News, and the *Christian Science Monitor*) had their accreditations revoked because of "the shameless media war being carried out against Yugoslavia from its own territory."[28] Domestic reporters were blamed for supplying CNN and other foreign agencies with lies and for being part of a foreign conspiracy. "What Belgrade reporters write," said Milorad Vučelić, the director of official television, "is there so that it may be quoted by foreign media. Satanization of the Serbian people has its roots in Belgrade."[29] At the point when the government was officially adopting the pacifist rhetoric of independent media, those media, paradoxically, faced graver conditions than ever before. The time of open threats and pressures had passed, but the regime mounted a more insidious offensive against the alternative media. In addition, not only were funds at a pitifully low ebb, but after many years of war, the public had grown tired and largely indifferent to assaults dealt by the government.

At the very end of 1994 the regime made an attempt to destroy the daily *Borba* once and for all by annulling its status as a holding company and nationalizing it. The majority of the editorial board, however, refused to accept the fait accompli and immediately founded *Naša Borba* instead.[30] The same happened to the weekly *Svetlost*, published in the Serbian town of Kragujevac, where now in addition to the official *Svetlost* the former editorial board launched *Nezavisna Svetlost*.[31] *Vreme* contributed the paper for the first two issues and helped to consolidate the editorial boards by publishing the paper under the masthead *Vreme za Svetlost* (Time for light).

The crisis of the Independent TV Studio B, dating back to the second half of 1993, provides another striking example of the internal media-takeover war. By the end of the summer of 1993, after about three years of existence, Studio B had solidified its status. In the regions beyond its reach, local TV stations showed videotapes of its programs. But having proved to be a valuable information station—which is how it was identified from the very beginning—Studio B now had to sharpen its profile and technical skills and show that it was also a professional TV station that adhered to standards of excellence. For this, additional funds were necessary, and they were hard to come by. Official TV channels were funded by all citizens.[32] Studio B, by contrast, maintained itself only through advertising. Yet the only firms that needed and could afford to advertise in tough economic times were those closely tied to the regime by playing a part in the underground economy, in violation of the economic sanctions, and in war profiteering.

Studio B was free to sell its airtime to the political parties competing in the parliamentary elections scheduled for October 20, 1993, and to make money that way. This offered the opportunity for the regime to try to destroy the station's image. The ruling party refrained from buying any airtime, but the Party of Serbian Unity led by Željko Ražnjatović-Arkan offered to buy a lot of it. Without consulting its workers, the Studio B management decided to accept. Arkan failed to win the elections, but collapse of confidence in Studio B was tremendously accelerated. The management's decision had precipitated a deep and far-reaching internal crisis. The best reporters resigned in protest immediately, followed by about a hundred others who resigned in the beginning of 1995.[33]

The quality of Studio B programming deteriorated precipitously. News that was unavailable on other channels was still broadcast, but this could not compensate for the lack of a firm editorial policy. After two years of financial hardship and a period of professional duplicity, Studio B was faltering. In February 1996, following the ruling of the Supreme Court, Studio B was deprivatized and became a state-owned enterprise.[34]

Following the signing of the Dayton Accord, the Socialist Party and the Yugoslav United Left Party, led by Mirjana Marković, the wife of Slobodan Milošević, monopolized all media space.[35] Official channels celebrated with pomp the signing of the peace accord and the partial lifting of the sanctions against rump Yugoslavia, but public response remained lukewarm. Devoid of politics and saturated with trash entertainment and fantastic projections of the future, the state-owned media were featuring speed rails, Internet communication, and a thriving economy. It seemed as though the tele-fiction of a consumer world had replaced the reality of 50 percent unemployment and ninety-three dollars average monthly income—a reality, that is, devoid of consumers.

Through all this, the public seemed to have remained paralyzed, like those victims of terrible natural disasters. Reporters often express surprise at seeing such people, whose houses have been destroyed and whose families have perished, resigned and apathetic, watching breathless teams of helpers. That appeared to have happened to the Yugoslavs. A passive, listless body politic, thoroughly depoliticized—the product of almost ten years of what some have called the "media gulag."[36]

But in November 1996 something unexpected happened. In Belgrade, Novi Sad, Niš, Kragujevac, Loznica, and many other cities across Serbia, people took to the streets in unprecedented numbers. This happened following the attempt of Slobodan Milošević to annul the November 17 municipal elections victory of the opposition Zajedno (made up of the Serbian Renewal movement, led by Vuk Drašković, the Democratic Party, led by Zoran Djindjić, and the Civic Association, led by Vesna Pešić), which carried fourteen of the most important cities in Serbia. This was a triumph, particularly considering that Zajedno was denied access to the official media in the pre-electoral campaign.

The attempt of the Milošević government to annul the elections trig-

gered an avalanche of protests. For the first time since the beginning of
the war, students, intellectuals, clerks, and homemakers, as well as many
retired people otherwise unlikely to join the marching crowds, found
themselves united in saying a resolute *no* to the Serbian regime. In Belgrade the main slogan of the student movement was "Belgrade is the
world," suggesting a wish for the Serbian people to overcome the insu-
larity brought on them by xenophobic nationalism and war, and to find
in themselves some universal values that would connect them with the
rest of the world.

The official media noticed the universalistic character of the protest,
which contrasted sharply with the self-pitying bathos of the government
media in the previous years. A vicious propaganda campaign against
the demonstrators, characterizing them as pawns of foreign powers, was
launched by official television and the daily press. These characteriza-
tions only emboldened the protesters. At times there were four hundred
thousand people in the streets of Belgrade. Every night at 7:30, the time of
the official TV news hour, thousands of people joined the demonstrations,
beating on drums and pots and pans from their balconies and apartment
windows, in a symbolic attempt to drown the lies of official television.
Together with the students, all social groups and professions—from actors
to clergy, from writers to judges—faced the police cordon in full gear and
twice endured its brutal wrath. In some way Serbia was cleansing its soul.
For some, this was an opportunity to wash dirty hands in the rosy waters
of a dignified, cosmopolitan, whimsical, and above all peaceful protest.

When in January 1997 Milošević ordered Radio B-92—the only reliable
source of audio information, whose reporters were on the streets day and
night—to be cut off, an information blackout ensued for five days. The
voice of the official media reported that sporadic small groups of hooligans were trying to destablize Serbia under German and U.S. flags.

Determined protest and international pressure forced Slobodan Milošević to reestablish Radio B-92, claiming that the reason for the cutoff was
water in the cable network. When in February 1997, after months of daily
demonstrations, Milošević yielded to Zajedno, acknowledging its victory,
Independent TV Studio B was reborn. Some of its reporters who resigned
in 1993 and 1995 rushed back to Belgrade, one of them from Chicago,
where he had been a taxi driver since 1995.

A new round of struggle for the freedom of the media is now under way.
The monopoly held by official television remains intact. The struggle is

still a struggle between a David and Goliath, only David is now faster on his feet, and has gained a bit of savvy.

NOTES

1 This study examines the official Belgrade media within a wider context of the media's role in the entire former Yugoslavia.

2 *Dnevnik* was produced at TV Zagreb (Croatia), TV Belgrade (Serbia), TV Ljubljana (Slovenia), TV Priština (Kosovo), TV Sarajevo (Bosnia-Hercegovina), TV Titograd (Montenegro), TV Skopje (Macedonia), and TV Novi Sad (Vojvodina).

3 Many members of the Belgrade opposition maintain that since the 1930s in Germany no propaganda has been as effective as the TV Belgrade and TV Zagreb propaganda was in shaping popular perceptions and choices.

4 Veljko Kadijević, *Moje vidjenje raspada: Vojske bez države* (Beograd: Politika, 1993).

5 Dragan Todorović, "To nije njihova kolubarska bitka, Grad slavne ratničke tradicije opire se razapinjanju na krst srama," *Vreme*, 28 October 1991, pp. 24–25.

6 Nebojša Popov, *Srpski populizam*, special monograph edition, *Vreme*, 24 May 1993). See also Slavoljub Djukić, *Kako se dogodio vodja*, (Beograd: Filip Višnjić, 1992), p. 136.

7 Milošević said: "Six centuries later, today, we are once again in the battles and facing battles. Those battles are not armed, but armed ones cannot be excluded either." *Politika* published the transcript of the entire speech on June 29, 1989, pp. 3–4; the above citation is from p. 4.

8 See Slobodan Milošević, *Godine Raspleta*, (Beograd: BIGZ, 1989).

9 Darko Hudelist, *Kosovo, Bitka bez iluzija* (Zagreb: Centar za Informacije i publicitet, 1989), and "Prohujalo sa jogurtom," *Stav*, special edition, pts. 2 and 3, 24 February 1989 and 31 March 1989.

10 See "Predlog srpskog crkveno-nacionalnog programa," *Glas Crkve*, no. 3 (1989): 11.

11 Such descriptions became part of television vernacular in 1991. Personal notes of Milan Milošević.

12 A former Serbian TV editor claimed that one of the network's directors wrote a "telegram" in verse that ended on a defiant note: "There's nothing they can do; we are stronger than destiny" (author's personal notes).

Orchestrating of public support was used from the very beginning of the so-called antibureaucratic revolution of 1987 and 1988. During the Eighth Session of the Central Committee of the League of Communists of Serbia, the delegates received copies of insulting telegrams aimed at the opponents of Milošević, and also of telegrams favoring Milošević. Following the protest of Špiro Galović (today a Belgrade lawyer), Milošević suggested that the telegrams be used only by the members of the Central Committee and not by the press (see the book of stenograms *Osma sednica CK SK Srbije* [Beograd: Komunist, 1987], p. 378).

13 Even the disaster of international economic sanctions was made to yield an advantage. Life under the economic sanctions was daily becoming more unbearable, but

at least Serbs had the moral satisfaction of showing the biased, unscrupulous, evil world that their cause was just and that nothing could bring them to their knees.

14   Bogdan Bogdanović, *Mrtvouzice* (Zagreb: August Cesarec, 1988).

15   Aleksandar Nenădović, the former general editor of *Politika* and currently a member of the Independent Association of Journalists, commented on the manipulative technique whereby the letters of readers were used, in the *Politika* column "Echoes and Responses," to push a political message. See Aleksandar Nenădović, *Politika u nacionalistickoj oluji*, Ogledi Edition, *Republika* (April 1995), pp. 16–30.

16   The videotape documentary satire *Tito for the Second Time among the Serbs* represents Radio B-92's most lucid production. The director, Želimir Žilnik, followed an actor impersonating Tito as he made his way through the center of Belgrade. The actor was outfitted in Tito's marshal's uniform, and people spontaneously entered into playacting conversations with him. What was striking about the conversations was people's deep sense of disillusionment and personal pain about the tragic collapse of Yugoslavia—a much stronger reaction than was outwardly apparent among the population on a day-to-day level.

17   The quote is drawn from author's personal documentation.

18   Author's documentation.

19   Dragoš Kalajić espoused a similar philosophy in "Americi recimo zbogom," *Duga*, 9–22 May 1992, pp. 69–72; and Dragoš Kalajić, "Mi živimo poslednje vreme jednog sveta obmane i iluzije," *Pogledi*, 24 April–15 May 1992. See also Smilja Avramov, "Graktanje evropskih lešinara," *Duga*, 23 December 1991–6 January 1992, pp. 6–8.

20   An investigative team of the Independent Association of Journalists of Vojvodina recorded the events in "Sukobi i Raspleti na TV Novi Sad," *Republika* (May 1993): 19–30.

21   In January 1992 Alija Izetbegović made the statement for television that he was not going to sacrifice a sovereign Bosnia for peace. He was afraid that the peace demonstrations, in which many demonstrators carried banners with photographs of Tito, might have been organized by pro-Yugoslav generals (author's notes).

22   *Vreme*, 13 April 1992.

23   On the views of the antiwar intellectuals and journalists see the collection of Belgrade Circle discussions in *Druga Srbija*, ed. Ivan Čolović and Aljoša Mimica (Beograd: Plato, Beogradski Krug, Borba, 1992).

24   The failure of the draft drive in Serbia and the low morale in reservist units made the regime quite nervous. In closed sessions of the Serbian parliament, demands were made for deserters, draft dodgers, and those who publicly encouraged them to be brought before a military court. The proposals for extreme repression were not accepted, but the regime did not loosen its control over the broadcast media.

25   On the protests see Milan Milošević, "Mart 92, Beograd," *Vreme*, 16 March 1992; Milan Milošević, "Srbija u razbijenom ogledalu u Nojevoj barci," *Vreme*, 29 June 1992. Between March and December 1992, both *Vreme* and *Republika* published a number of reports and analyses of the protests written by Milošević, Miloš Vasić, Ivan Radovanović, Ljubiša Rajić, Dragan Popadić, Ljuba Stojić, Ksenija Radulović, and Predrag Milidrag.

26 Author's personal notes.

27 The trade union had a large membership, but lack of funds severely restricted its activities.

28 Dejan Anastasijević, "Veliko spremanje," *Vreme*, 25 April 1994, pp. 51–54.

29 Ibid., p. 54.

30 *Borba* means "struggle" and refers to the paper's origins in the 1920s, when it was the voice of the then illegal Communist Party. *Naša borba* means "our struggle."

31 *"Svetlost"* means "light," and *nezavisna svetlost* means "independent light."

32 In July 1993 a ruling was issued saying that every user of electricity also paid for the opportunity to watch official television—i.e., that official television took a cut from electricity payments. Prior to that, TV watchers were supposed to pay a monthly fee—although many avoided such payments.

33 Milan Milošević, "Direktan prenos zatvaranja," *Vreme*, 24 February 1995, pp. 12–13.

34 The opposition issued a strong protest, but that did not change anything, in sharp contrast with the events of March 1991, following the police break-in of Studio B and the banning of its programming, when students had launched a long wave of demonstrations with the slogans "We Want Truth" and "Studio B! Studio B!" This time the democratic opposition threatened to defend the freedom of independent media, including Studio B, through demonstrations, but it was no longer able to inspire mass action.

   For commentary on the end of Studio B, see Rade Veljanovski, "Na ivici ponora," *Republika* (January 1–31, 1996): 19, and the report of *Voice, Peace, and Human Rights*, Bulletin No. 9 (Beograd: Centar za Antiratnu Akciju, March 1996), p. 1.

35 The Yugoslav United Left is a pro-Communist party of the orthodox ilk, led by Mirjana Marković, the wife of Slobodan Milošević.

36 Zoran Djordjević, "Srbija u medijskom Gulagu," *Republika* (February 1–28, 1995): 15.

The Army's Collapse
Stipe Sikavica

In 1992, for the first time in the history of the Yugoslav People's Army (YPA), December 22 — the army's official anniversary — went unmarked by a celebration. On that day in 1941, Josip Broz Tito had presented the newly formed first regular army unit of the wartime Partisan forces with its battle colors. Fifty-one years later, in 1992, neither Yugoslavia nor the Yugoslav People's Army existed any longer. Croatia and Slovenia had seceded from Yugoslavia in the summer of 1991. In the spring of 1992 the Bosnian war broke out following the unsuccessful attempts by General Nikola Uzelac and General Milutin Kukanjac (both of Serbian origin) to avert it. General Ratko Mladić and General Momčilo Perišić had the support of the regime of Slobodan Milošević, and they prevailed. On April 27, 1992, the Federal Republic of Yugoslavia — the "rump Yugoslavia" — was proclaimed. The remnants of the YPA were renamed the Army of Yugoslavia. Only a year later, 170 generals of the YPA were forced to retire in successive waves of purges, leaving in place only those who could be counted on to wholeheartedly support nationalism.

When at the outset of World War II Germany launched its attack on the Kingdom of Yugoslavia on April 6, 1941, with no prior declaration of war, it encountered armed forces entirely unprepared for battle. The Kingdom of Yugoslavia had no aviation, no mechanized units, no heavy artillery, no military industry to speak of. It took the Nazi war machine only twelve days to crush the royal army. The young King Petar and his government fled from Belgrade to London, and Yugoslavia's neighbors who had joined the Axis coalition were rewarded with parts of the defeated Yugoslav state. Italy, Bulgaria, Hungary, and Romania each received a sizable piece.[1]

At the time of the German attack, the Yugoslav Communist Party, headed by Tito, had only eight thousand members. It was, however, a tightly organized group and included a high proportion of university students, professionals, and intellectuals. With the king in exile, the Communists turned out to be the only force able and willing to rally the Yugoslav multinational community against dismemberment and occupation. Within two and a half months of the German assault on Yugoslavia, Hitler attacked the Soviet Union and the party initiated the Partisan war. It set up a nationwide clandestine press and underground network. Party cells in towns and cities formed immediately and began harassing the enemy with various forms of sabotage. The party leadership also turned to some willing officers and soldiers of the royal army, enlisting them to fight with the emerging units of the new military force. Directives were sent out for the collection and hiding of weapons and ammunition. Despite a German military proclamation warning that after April 17, 1941, anybody caught with a firearm would be shot on the spot, by the end of June the party was ready to order Partisan action against the occupation in all parts of Yugoslavia.[2]

Initially, Partisan units were kept small and local, numbering from twenty to thirty members, to give the liberation struggle the broadest possible base, especially among young peasants and workers. By early September, the party had organized seventy-five hundred armed men and women in twelve higher-level Partisan detachments. By the end of the same month, Partisan forces had grown to between fourteen thousand and fifteen thousand men and women in twenty-three detachments. Heading the forces were older prewar Communists, party and nonparty members who had fought for the republic in the Spanish Civil War, and a smaller number of officers and rank and file of the royal army.[3]

The party had formed a Military Committee in Zagreb on April 10, 1941, just four days after Germany's initial attack. In time, the Military Committee became the high command of the National Liberation detachments. The basic idea was to wage a Partisan war by forming a united front for all patriots—regardless of national and religious identity or political allegiance—to join together to save their country. The new army would be controlled by the Communists but would lead a popular, united resistance against the enemy throughout Yugoslavia. From the start, the cornerstone of the Partisan policy was "Brotherhood and Unity," the only basis on which a popular war against fascism could be waged and Yugoslavia restored.

Like the Communists, the Croatian fascist Ustashe Party, which founded the Independent State of Croatia (NDH), organized its forces immediately following the outbreak of war, with one of its primary objectives being to exterminate one-third of Croatian Serbs.[4] The first massacre of Serbs came only weeks after the German invasion. In the town of Bjelovar, 184 Serbian civilians were killed by Croatian firing squads in late April. Mass killings quickly spread to the predominantly Serb-populated areas of Croatia (the Krajina) and to Hercegovina. For many Croats opposed to the Ustashe state, the Partisan movement offered the only alternative.

Soon Yugoslav antifascists found themselves confronting a second nationalist threat. In 1941 the Yugoslav government in exile appointed Draža Mihailović—a colonel in the Yugoslav royal army who had remained in Yugoslavia after the collapse to rally the remnants of the former army to resistance in the name of the monarchy—to serve as minister of war. Mihailović, like the Yugoslav royal family itself, was a Serb, and he identified the monarchy's interests with Serbian hegemonic ambitions. As a monarchist, Mihailović saw in the Communists his real archenemy; he viewed the people's liberation movement as nothing but a Communist ploy for power. He blamed the Croats and Muslims for the war and advocated a "Greater Serbia," territorially extended and ethnically pure. Chetnik massacres of the Muslim population in eastern Bosnia and in the Sandžak in Serbia during 1942 and 1943 were demonstrations of Mihailović's policy of vengeful nationalism. Nevertheless, until September 1943 Mihailović and his forces were publicized abroad as the leading antifascist resistance movement in occupied Yugoslavia.

Two other Serbian ultranationalist groups, one led by Milan Nedić and the other by Dimitrije Ljotić, collaborated openly with the Germans and were responsible for the deaths of many Croats and Muslims as well as large numbers of antifascist Serbs. Nedić headed the quisling government installed by the occupation forces. Tito's national liberation movement thus found itself waging its fight on two fronts—against the Nazi occupation and against ethnic strife.

By the end of 1941, Partisan forces had grown tenfold, to about seventy thousand in forty-three detachments made up of numerous smaller units.[5] The time had come to reorganize the Partisan forces into a regular army. On December 22, 1941, the first regular unit of a new Yugoslav army, the National Liberation Army, was officially formed and presented with its colors by Tito, its commander in chief.

In their earliest days, the summer and fall of 1941, the rapidly growing Partisan forces had been able to proclaim the first liberated territory in occupied Europe: the town of Užice and its surrounding area of seventy-six hundred square miles in the heart of occupied Serbia. The Užice Republic had only recently come into being, but in addition to a great deal of arms and ammunition captured during its liberation, the existence of a freed territory gave a tremendous boost to the morale of the army being formed. The Partisan forces would wage their war entirely on their own until mid-1943, when, after several decisive but bloody battles, they received recognition and assistance from Allied forces. The first military supplies from the Allies were air-dropped to the National Liberation Army in September 1943, only eighteen months before the end of World War II in Europe. It was only at that point that the public abroad heard of the existence of the Partisan movement in Yugoslavia and of its army, which would emerge from the war as the third strongest Allied army in Europe.

While the Communist Party insisted from the outset that the Partisan forces and subsequently the National Liberation Army were free of all ties to any political group or party, the fact is that the party was the organizational and conceptual force behind the only effective all-Yugoslav antifascist movement. The red five-pointed star soon became the insignia of the Partisan soldier, and the hammer and sickle quickly appeared on the flags of the National Liberation Army. As the war progressed, the identification of the liberation war with the Communist revolution increased, until the two concepts became virtually inseparable. In the immediate aftermath of the war, the leadership of the new Yugoslav state, headed by Tito, viewed the army as its surest support and guarantee of survival in the emerging constellation of international forces and shifting allegiances within Yugoslavia.

Today nationalists of all stripes mock brotherhood and unity, the underlying principles of the liberation war. Many see them as empty concepts manipulated by Tito. But irrespective of this strong revisionist tendency, brotherhood and unity—the all-Yugoslav, grassroots character of the Partisan war—were the pillars of Tito's strategy. On December 22, 1952, the tenth anniversary of its official birth, the armed force received its definitive name: the Yugoslav People's Army.

In the immediate postwar years, not surprisingly, Tito decided to maintain a strong army. In 1946, the three traditional services—land forces, air force, and navy—were four hundred thousand strong. In the first four postwar years, the economically most difficult for the country, 20 percent of Yugoslavia's gross national product was earmarked for the military. By 1955, the military budget dropped to 10 percent of GNP. By the 1960s Yugoslavia's military-industrial complex was supplying more than 50 percent of domestic military needs. During the 1970s, that percentage rose to above 80 percent, and in the 1980s to a full 90 percent.[6]

Tito, as president for life of Yugoslavia, was simultaneously the commander in chief of its armed forces and the general secretary of the Communist Party, the second unchallenged authority next to the military. The party kept a close check on the political pulse at all levels and a constant guard against ideological deviation. Party membership was required for an officer's commission and "recommended" for noncommissioned officers. Ninety-eight percent of all command personnel were party members. Although Tito and the party may have kept the army in its proper political place, blind submissiveness became an important factor in the army's failure to respond adequately to the tragic course of events in the late 1980s.

Another important factor was the mediocre level of education of military commanders, who would by the 1990s control the army's arsenal of highly sophisticated weaponry. During World War II the National Liberation Army had consisted overwhelmingly of peasants and workers. A bare one-half of its command personnel had an elementary education, and only one in five commissioned officers had finished high school. After the war, the army relatively quickly organized a wide range of schools and academies of its own, from secondary-school through university-graduate level. But the officer corps, although soon well schooled, never became broad-minded. Tito's later choices of key military personnel would further undermine the caliber of military leadership.

In 1953, Tito had chosen as his minister of defense General Ivan Gošnjak, a Croat by origin but a Yugoslav by commitment, a distinguished veteran of the Spanish Civil War and the Yugoslav liberation war. In 1967 Gošnjak was suddenly dismissed, without explanation, and replaced by General Nikola Ljubičić, a man of little accomplishment and with an undistinguished war record. Ljubičić would prove to be a shrewd political manipulator, blindly loyal to Tito—which is what Tito deemed important. With this key appointment, the practice of "negative selection" took root in the army. Gradually, qualifications, ability, and integrity lost out to conformity. The officer corps began its slide toward mediocrity—a trend that was never reversed.

Military spending would also contribute to the various conflicts tearing Yugoslavia apart in the 1990s. The military budget was part of the Yugoslav federal budget, to which all the federal republics and autonomous provinces contributed equally. For Slovenia and Croatia, the two most developed republics, this amounted to a total figure greater than that paid by other republics, because Slovenia and Croatia were richest. This became an irritant to the two republics. Complaints in their press, not only about what they considered to be their disproportionately large contributions to the army but especially about the lack of any outside control on how the army spent its funds, were becoming ever more frequent. In 1987, the army found itself targeted publicly for the first time in its history. Shrill voices were heard first in the Slovenian journal *Mladina*. Why did Yugoslavia need such a large army, *Mladina* asked. How was the military budget being spent? *Mladina* requested that military spending be reduced, that all recruits be allowed to serve in their republics of origin, and that an alternative for military service be devised for those who did not want to bear arms.[7] Some media in Croatia joined the chorus. Instead of realizing that times were changing and that the army had to change with them, the military high command reacted as though every question was a direct, personal attack on each of its officers.

Financially, the army was a world unto itself. It provided the housing for all its personnel, including the civilians it employed. It had its own medical, educational, and recreational facilities, and even its own farms. Although it fostered a public image of close identity with "the people" and claimed that every military unit was a "Yugoslavia in miniature," the gap slowly widened between the standard of living of civilians and that of army personnel of all ranks. By the mid-1980s an economic crisis had been building in the country for some years, and Yugoslavia's economic difficulties were becoming more acute by the day. As the result of strong pressure, the military budget was reduced by 1 percent compared to the 1981 budget. The resulting 5.20 percent of GNP the army absorbed was still considered by many an excessive burden for the tottering economy.

The army was shutting itself off in an ivory tower more than just economically. Even after his death in May 1980, Tito continued to be venerated in virtually mystical terms as commander in chief. The slogan at every military post, on banners, on walls, and at muster was "After Tito, Tito."

Tito had never been publicly scrutinized in his lifetime. Healthy investigative and sometimes critical appraisals began to flood the media and the bookstores in the late 1980s, suddenly taking an ugly turn, especially in Serbia. Sensational articles and books dissected Tito's private life, some digging into his earliest youth. Never having made the necessary adjustments to the death of their commander in chief, the army's leaders found their sense of security seriously shaken by the sustained posthumous attack on Tito. The Communist Party, impotent in the face of economic, political, social, and ethnic crises, saw corroding of its authority. The army was soon to find itself at sea alone, with no experience navigating on its own, much less in a storm.

Before Slobodan Milošević undertook to consolidate his power in Serbia beginning in 1986, he had never shown any interest in the army, nor was the army ever known to have registered his existence. Having begun his play for power, however, he realized that success would depend on having the army on his side. To this end, he opted for the subtle tactics of a discreet courtship. He avoided voicing any criticism of the army himself and discouraged it among his staff, associates, and the Serbian media. Throughout 1987 and 1988, Milošević never missed a chance to make public, favorable mention of the minister of defense, Admiral Branko Mamula; Milošević also carefully echoed the army position on all issues afflicting the Yugoslav community in deep crisis. Little by little, he brought the army around to supporting him on issues critical to his ambitions.

The first test of his ability to manipulate the army presented itself in the beginning of 1989, when the Albanian majority in Kosovo, demanding autonomy, organized demonstrations throughout the province. Milošević, and the army, diagnosed the upheaval as a "counterrevolution." "Chop it off at the grassroots!" was the command. In the spring of 1989, tanks were sent to Kosovo. When twenty-two young Albanians and two young Serbian policemen were killed in the armed confrontation that followed, a senior army officer was heard saying, "What of it—two of ours were killed, but we got rid of twenty-two of theirs." None of the other high-ranking officers present disagreed.[8]

Some Yugoslav and foreign analysts predicted that war would break out first in Kosovo and that the fighting would start with an armed uprising by the Albanians. This might well have happened had Kosovo's Albanian community not wisely sidelined its extremist nationalists and opted for a policy of civil disobedience in response to Milošević's policy of force. With dignity, the community has maintained a life of its own below the surface of Serbian occupation and in contravention of that occupation.

Slovene and Croatian media were the first to ask why the army leaders went along with the dangerous approach Milošević had chosen for Kosovo. The army leaders, for their part, insisted repeatedly on the inherent danger of "every nationalism." They made it clear, however, that they found the Slovenian and Croatian nationalism particularly irritating. With Serbs vastly overrepresented in its officer corps, the army was inclined to look the other way in case of Milošević.

In 1988, Veljko Kadijević, whose father was a Serb and mother a Croat, was named minister of defense. He was considered one of the army's most highly educated generals and was respected for his modest lifestyle. Kadijević also openly supported the antinationalist program of Yugoslav Prime Minister Ante Marković. Nevertheless, without showing signs of disagreement, Kadijević allowed Milošević to gradually spread his influence in the army. The signs of the growing closeness between the army and the Serbian president provoked the media throughout Yugoslavia (with the exception of Serbia's official media) to cry out in dismay: "Whose army, for God's sake, is this?" Kadijević never responded to this outcry, directly or indirectly.

After the collapse of the League of Communists of Yugoslavia on January 22, 1990, the Yugoslav crisis entered its final stage. The idea of a military solution then became a virtual obsession of the hard-liners of the general staff, who had advocated since the mid-1980s that the army should take the deteriorating situation in hand. Three events that took place in March 1991 polarized the positions among the higher army echelons and pushed the army further into Milošević's camp.

On March 9 the opposition in Belgrade, requesting freedom of the media, staged massive demonstrations involving 100,000 people. The demonstrators, led by Vuk Drašković, demanded that Channel 2 of Belgrade TV be designated as a "nonparty channel," open to nonpartisan information.[9] The call was for Milošević to resign. The demonstrations could have ended peacefully. But Borisav Jović, at that time the federal president and a supporter of Milošević, urged the collective presidency to allow the use of tanks, thereby hoping to exacerbate the tensions.[10] He succeeded in his request and the tanks rolled into the streets of Belgrade. Two people were killed in the mayhem that followed, over two hundred injured, and one hundred fifty-eight taken to jail. The army had taken sides.

That same month in Croatia, President Tudjman attended the first parade of his National Guard Corps (ZNG), a parallel armed force formed by putting to use Croatian territorial defense units and arming them with clandestinely imported arms. Territorial defense units had existed all across the country for close to thirty years, to boost local readiness to respond to hypothetical attacks from abroad. These units were made up of reservists under the command of local army officers but were at the same time integrated in the broader network of the federal armed forces. In the beginning of the 1990s, however, both Croatia and Slovenia used their territorial defense units as the basis for the buildup of internal armed forces that would eventually be used for the conflict with the YPA.[11] In January 1991 the Yugoslav government issued an order that all armed formations the army did not directly control had to be disbanded. But in March 1991 the Croatian government rejected even the possibility of negotiations with the YPA.

The general staff did agree on confiscating the weapons purchased by Croatia, but at the same time the army was almost openly arming Croatian Serbs.[12] The attempt to disarm the territorial defense units provoked violent demonstrations in Split, a commercial port on the Adriatic coast and the home port for the Yugoslav navy. On May 6, 1991, demonstrators surrounded the naval headquarters. In the confusion and violence, with the Croatian police and the army shooting at each other, a young Macedonian army recruit was killed. The Croatian government expressed no regrets. Belgrade's propaganda machine portrayed the young Macedonian's death as final proof of the Ustashe revival and rehashed it on television for a full six weeks.

With the naval headquarters besieged by a violent civilian crowd, General Kadijević announced that the country now faced a "state of civil war" and informed the presidency that the army would respond with force to every attack on its members, units, or facilities.

The third event in March 1991 took place when Slovenian authorities declared they no longer had the intention of sending their conscripts to serve in the YPA. Like the Croats, the Slovenes left no room for negotiations. Slovenia was also importing military equipment from abroad and intensively training its own territorial defense units. Sparks of open conflict spread fast into Slovenia to the north. When in June 1991 the army rolled its tanks into the city of Maribor, its people poured into the streets in protest. In the general chaos one civilian was killed under the wheels of an armored car. All of Slovenia was in an uproar.

The event accelerated the tempo of developments in both Croatia and Slovenia. On June 25, 1991, the Croatian parliament in Zagreb, and a little later in the day, the Slovenian parliament in Ljubljana, adopted declarations of independence for their states. The Slovenes immediately put words into action and established customs and security control over what they now proclaimed as their state borders with Austria and Italy, forcing federal officials to abandon their border posts.

With independence celebrations in Slovenia at their peak, armored army units moved out toward international border crossings and Slovenia's largest international airport, Brnik.[13] General Blagoje Adžic, speaking for the general staff, made a public statement claiming that the decision to move into Slovenia had been taken by the federal government to ensure that the federal customs services might resume their obligations at the border crossings.

Customs collection was one of the most important sources of revenue for the federal budget, on which the army was deeply dependent. But the goal was probably more ambitious than that. Some army commanders had hoped to return Slovenia by force to the Yugoslav fold, counting on a show of force to be sufficient to accomplish the task and, in addition, to stop the process leading to secession that had already begun in Croatia. However, the YPA did not use the entire military power at their immediate disposal, but only a few armored units with neither infantry nor air support. Out of twenty thousand YPA troops stationed at the time in Slovenia, only one-tenth was used for the operation. This odd strategy prompted many analysts to assume that a deal had been struck beforehand between the Slovenian presidency and Slobodan Milošević that Slovenia would be let loose. If that was the case, YPA simply went along and simulated an attack.

Other analysts insisted that the army simply fell short of performing a professional job. Kadijević himself later stated that he could have reduced Slovenia to ruin but that the toll in human life would have been too high. The fact is that the humiliating defeat of the YPA was carried out by the best organized and most disciplined territorial defense units in the entire former Yugoslavia, whose combat readiness proved to be superior to that of the army. Territorial defense units moved with lightning speed to surround and blockade army garrisons throughout Slovenia. This tactic effectively paralyzed army ground forces. The army lost forty men, mostly nineteen-year-olds who had begun their compulsory military service only four months earlier. The Slovene side listed nine deaths.

At the time of the military intervention, Slovenia had 15,000 territorial defense forces, including officers; it also had 85,000 reservists and, from territorial defense arsenals, about 120 tanks and 20 armored vehicles. The army had, stationed in Slovenia, the first line of the former Yugoslavia's westernmost defenses: some 25,000 enlisted men and officers, who were joined during the military action by a few thousand more from Croatia. It had 250 tanks (100 more were sent in from Croatia), about 300 other armored vehicles, 90 fighter planes, and 50 combat helicopters. The military standing force at the time totaled 200,000 enlisted men and officers, with 150,000 in the land forces, 35,000 in the air force, and the rest in the navy. The army had 1,850 tanks, 240 reconnaissance planes, 990 armored personnel carriers, 1,950 heavy artillery weapons, 490 fighter planes, 165 helicopters, 10 submarines, and 4 frigates.[14] Yet this great military force lost out to the incomparably smaller Slovenian territorial defense.

The Brioni Agreement of July 7, 1991, had called for the YPA to withdraw its troops to the barracks. On July 28, 1991, two days after the proclamation of Slovenian independence, the high command ordered the withdrawal of all army effectives from the Slovenian territory. The withdrawal of the YPA from a large portion of Yugoslav territory signaled that the process of the disintegration of Yugoslavia was entering its terminal stage. Slovenia's secession opened the door to the secession of other Yugoslav republics.[15]

Training of the Croatian troops, the ZNG, was initially kept behind the scenes. Once the Croatian war began, its military might rapidly increased in personnel and weaponry. The largest arms purchases of various types of weapons came from Germany.[16]

The second principal source of weaponry for the Croatian forces was through confiscation or capture of arms and ammunition from the Yugoslav People's Army barracks.[17] The number of incidents involving the Croatian police and the Croatian Serbs (whose towns had already been infiltrated by Serbian provocateurs) mounted in 1991. The army stepped in with its military firepower to protect the Serbian population.[18] During the summer of 1991, Croatian armed forces followed the Slovenian example of obstructing the YPA by blockading army garrisons.

But in addition to the YPA and the territorial defense units, a number of other "private armies" sprang up in Serbia and Croatia. Vojislav Šešelj, the leader of the ultranationalist Serbian Radical Party, formed the Chetniks. Vuk Drašković, the leader of the Serbian Renewal Movement, organized the Serbian Guard. Željko Ražnjatović-Arkan, a person wanted by the Interpol for drug trafficking and other criminal activity, founded the Serbian Volunteer Guard, also called the Tigers; two other groups, the White Eagles and Dušan Silni, were also operative.[19] In Croatia the ultranationalist Croatian Party of Right, led by Dobrosav Paraga, organized the Croatian Defense League (HOS).[20] It was joined by two other right-wing groups, the Zebras and the Black Legions. On the Muslim side, the best-known paramilitary formation was the Green Berets, formed and led by Jusuf-Juka Prazina, a prewar Sarajevo criminal with a somewhat romantic reputation. The brutality of the men under his command led to his expulsion from Bosnia. He was killed following his escape abroad.[21]

All paramilitary groups relied on volunteers often recruited from the underclass. Paramilitaries were allowed to train quite openly on their national territories. They developed a rhetoric of strident patriotism, accusing reservists who avoided conscription or refused to volunteer of being cowards and traitors. Most paramilitaries had no qualms about robbing, murdering, massacring, or raping. The so-called weekend volunteers from Serbia and Montenegro put on their uniforms and went into war areas only on weekends and only to pillage. As the war continued, the number of these bands multiplied, and they could be thirty to a thousand strong. Former bar owners, self-employed truck drivers, and warehouse clerks popped up as their commanders, bringing with them new uniforms and insignia designs for the local armies. Drunken orgies were the recreation of these bands. Both Serbian and Croatian regimes made sure to lend the paramilitaries a veneer of legitimacy. A large number of the members of such bands became rich from the war, filling their trucks with the entire furnishings of homes and apartments and selling their booty on a flourishing black market. Many volunteers invested their profits in legal and illegal businesses.[22]

That the YPA also opened its ranks to volunteers of all stripes irrevocably and profoundly changed its identity.[23] The decision to invite volunteers to join was made in 1991 to alleviate the very low turnout of reservists and frequent rebellions in the units.[24] On July 2 a group of several hundred mothers of recruits had forced their way into the federal parliament building in Belgrade and occupied the building for two days requesting that their sons be sent home from Slovenia.[25] Desertion was rampant, and so was mass emigration (some 150,000 men left the country to avoid mobilization). Those who could not find the means to flee abroad opted for internal emigration and went into hiding with relatives or friends. In a number of Serbian towns (Kragujevac, Valjevo, Arandjelovac, Ada, Senta), the conscripts staged loud rebellions.[26]

Faced with a recruitment problem of staggering proportions, the federal presidency issued a nine-item command on October 12, 1991, that "volunteers" be included in the armed forces of Yugoslavia in case of imminent danger of war.[27] The admission of volunteers was not selective. They were armed and allowed to fight side by side with regular units but moved quickly beyond the control of their army superiors. Paramilitary leaders asked nobody's permission before going into action and were not called to account before a military or civilian court for their mass crimes. Where regular army units might shrink from certain actions, paramilitary units were ready for the job. Some leaders of the paramilitary formations were celebrated in their communities as national heroes despite the terrible war crimes they had committed. In Serbia, critics of such criminal activity were called Serbo-Ustashe by the "patriots."[28]

Some volunteers joined the forces after their homes and families came under direct attack by extremist bands or military forces of the other side. These people fought the war in the sincere belief that they had to defend their land and their lives. Some "volunteers" were forced to join, trapped in the midst of the fighting with nowhere to flee. They were given no choice by extremist bands except to join, often under threat of death to themselves or their entire families. It was common for men of this group to be forced to prove their loyalty by murdering a neighbor of a different national origin.

In July 1991 the prime minister Ante Marković, a committed Yugoslav of Croatian origin, confronted the YPA and the minister of defense, Kadijević, about the illegal action in Slovenia. In mid-September he requested Kadijević's resignation. Kadijević refused. A Serbian member of the Yugoslav presidency accused Marković of "openly threatening war." The general staff called a general mobilization in the "remaining Yugoslavia" and the order went out: "To Vukovar!"

Veljko Kadijević claimed that the Croatian town of Vukovar, situated on the Danube at the border with Serbia, was part of the "backbone of the

Croatian army" and that therefore it had to be "liberated." The army periodical *Narodna Armija* (People's army), in its November 20, 1991, issue, wrote that "Vukovar had for decades been prepared to support German military penetration down the Danube." Before the war, the Vukovar municipality had a population of 84,000, almost 44 percent Croat, 37 percent Serb, and 20 percent "others."[29] Serbian official propaganda insisted that Vukovar was a Serbian town.

Vukovar was probably doomed to become the symbol of Croatia's defense against Milošević's expansionist ambitions, simply because it was the first large town in the path of the Yugoslav People's Army, which was incomparably stronger than any armed force Croatia could field when the YPA openly marched on Croatia. Tudjman, in all his rhetoric, never suggested that Vukovar was the "backbone of the Croatian army."

On August 20, 1991, Croatian territorial defense units blockaded the two small YPA garrisons in Vukovar. The Croatian forces were reinforced by paramilitary HOS units led by the neo-Nazi Dobrosav Paraga. In reaction to the Croatian blockade, the army began by concentrating forces outside the town. On the night of September 24, the army moved in with 390 trucks carrying reservists, 400 tanks, and 280 other vehicles across the fertile plain surrounding Vukovar. Operation Vukovar began on September 30, under the command of General Života Panić.

The civilian population of Vukovar, consisting of Serbs and Croats, was not evacuated from the city. And even though no battle of significance to military strategists took place, the town was pounded indiscriminately for two months by several hundred weapons of various calibers, warplanes, and ships anchored in the Danube, while the population huddled in cellars and catacombs, dying of disease and starvation. After the town had been destroyed, tanks with infantry support, including volunteers and elite units, moved forward. The ratio of attackers to defenders was between thirty and fifty to one, depending on the direction of the assaults.

No definitive number of casualties has become available yet, but it is certain that many civilians, both Croat and Serb, died along with young, untrained soldiers on both sides. Although the devastation of Vukovar might appear a wanton act of madness, an underlying logic did exist. With its mixed population living in harmony, Vukovar was targeted, as were many towns after that, with the intention of eradicating every possibility that Serbs and Croats would continue to live as neighbors. That was the point of the war in general. The destruction of Vukovar was televised day by day. The YPA units returned to Belgrade, passing through an "arch of triumph" constructed for their procession. Officers were promoted, decorated, and congratulated for destroying Vukovar, "the toughest and fiercest Ustashe fortress."[30]

Dubrovnik could never be described as a Ustashe fortress. The Croatian police and ZNG units in the city and its environs numbered only a few hundred. No YPA garrison had been blockaded there. There could be no talk of an endangered Serbian population there either. Despite efforts during the summer of 1991 by the Serbian propaganda machine to circulate rumors about victimization of 10,000 Serbs in and around Dubrovnik, only 4,735 Serbs lived in the area—6.5 percent of the local population.[31] When the 12,000 local people began leaving the area, they headed almost entirely toward Croatia or, in virtually equal number, into Dubrovnik's Old City, to seek safety behind its thick stone walls. When the army artillery began firing on Dubrovnik on October 2, 1991, nobody in Serbia or Croatia could say why.

But at the Serbian parliament session of fall 1991, Mihalj Kertes, an ardent Milošević supporter, mentioned in one of the standard warmongering speeches of the time, that Dubrovnik would be the capital of Serbian Hercegovina.[32] The claim was outlandish. Yet in the summer of 1991, almost a year before the war began in Bosnia-Hercegovina, two army reservist corps had moved into the heights above Dubrovnik in eastern Hercegovina, allegedly to prevent clashes in that region. By fall, they had dug into a position directly above the Dubrovnik Riviera. The siege of Dubrovnik would eventually also include poundings by the navy from the Adriatic and by the air force.

Serbian appetite soon encompassed the entire Croatian coastal belt from the mouth of the Neretva River, northwest of Dubrovnik, to the Croatian-Montenegrin border southeast of the city. Bosnia's Serbs under Radovan Karadžić had still not stopped talking about their "right" to an outlet to the sea. Army reservists and irregulars carried death and destruction northwest of Dubrovnik. In the southeast, Montenegrin army reservists and irregulars took the field. Using the excuse that they were blockading an important army garrison overlooking the Montenegrin Bay of Kotor, they crossed into Croatia and moved up the coastal belt to the outskirts of Dubrovnik. They devastated everything in their path, stopping only to load their trucks with livestock, washing machines, freezers, television sets, furniture. For days, trucks returning full of loot and drunken soldiers passed through the Montenegrin resort town of Herceg-novi, only a few miles from the Croatian-Montenegrin border. Official Serbia and the army consistently referred only to the "liberation" of the Dubrovnik Riviera.

On December 6, 1991, the Old Town of Dubrovnik was shelled directly. Among the casualties within its thick stone walls were twelve dead. The Old City suffered widespread damage.

Late in December 1991, Milošević signed the Vance Peace Plan for Croatia, even though he had always insisted that Serbia itself was not at war with anybody. Early in January 1992, Kadijević resigned as the Yugoslav minister of defense, alleging ill health. Soon the YPA would start withdrawing from Croatia, primarily into Bosnia-Hercegovina. Already 10,000 tons of war supplies had been withdrawn from Slovenia, half of it into Bosnia-Hercegovina. By the start of 1992, the army had a standing force of at least 150,000 troops and immense firepower concentrated there. The Bosnian government, however, made no effort to hold discussions with the YPA.

Tito's military strategists had placed Bosnia at the core of Yugoslavia's defense system. Concentrated there were huge numbers of military effectives, more than 60 percent of Yugoslavia's military industry, a large air force base and other bases for logistical support, and four military airfields, the most important one at the town of Bihać.

The Bihać airfield had five runways, each from 7,500 to 10,000 feet long. An electronic state-of-the-art hangar had been provided in four underground tunnels for about one hundred planes and their maintenance. Its many additional underground facilities made this airfield among the best-fortified air bases in Europe. A system of thick, vertical steel pipes, deeply sunk over every 150 feet of the entire installation, could be filled with explosives if the danger of the base falling to an enemy ever became imminent. When the fighting started in Bosnia-Hercegovina, the army decided to prevent the Bihać facilities from falling into Croatian or Bosnian hands. On May 16, 1992, the army filled the pipes with explosives, and the Bihać airfield and its underground facilities, built at the cost of eight billion dollars, were destroyed in one mega-explosion lasting only minutes.[33]

Earlier that spring, on the eve of international recognition of independent Bosnia, President Alija Izetbegović asked the commands of YPA units stationed in Bosnia to remain and help build the armed forces of the new state. The generals responded with disdain and sent a shower of bombs on points alleged to be Ustashe strongholds in western Hercegovina.

When Bosnia received international recognition on April 6, 1992, the YPA became a foreign force on its territory. The Bosnian government ordered a blockade of YPA barracks and demanded that the YPA withdraw from Bosnia. The army announced that 80 to 90 percent of the force stationed in Bosnia had originated there and could not be forced to leave its land of origin. Accordingly, 20 percent was withdrawn to Serbia and Montenegro. The withdrawal was supposed to be completed by the end of May but dragged out until the fall. Eighty thousand troops who were Bosnians stayed.

By mid-May Serbian politicians and some generals were already claiming that not a single member of the YPA was fighting in Bosnia. On May 21, 1993, however, the following notice appeared among the obituaries of *Politika*, the leading official Belgrade newspaper:

> One year has passed since the death of our joyful, our beloved son and brother Marko Hrnjak, born July 5, 1972, a freshman in construction engineering at the University of Belgrade, doing his military service as a parachutist with the Airborne Brigade. He was killed on May 23, 1992, in the vicinity of Mostar, at a time when, allegedly, not a single soldier, citizen of the Republic of Serbia, was sent outside of Serbia. For a year we have been asking generals and politicians why he was killed and who is responsible for Marko's death. We are met by silence or untruths. We will continue to ask. Mother, Budislavka; sister, Ana; and father, Vladimir.

On May 13, 1992, YPA troops and officers who had remained in Bosnia were transferred to form the army of the self-proclaimed Serbian Republic of Bosnia, under the command of General Ratko Mladić, a career officer who commanded the Knin Corps of the YPA and had earned the rank of general at Vukovar. General Mladić ordered the first shelling of Sarajevo on May 6 and 7, 1992, from artillery in the hills surrounding the city.

In 1993 the army of the Serbian Republic of Bosnia had between seventy thousand and eighty thousand conscripts under arms, not counting the multitude of irregular formations or outright extremist bands formed on its own territory or in Serbia. Its striking force included 400 tanks, 20 armored personnel carriers, and some 500 artillery pieces. Its air force had

20 fighter-bombers, 20 helicopters, and 4 missile systems. It was believed also to have squadron of MIG-21s.[34] This made the Bosnian-Serb army by far the strongest in Bosnia. In 1992–93, it plowed over its territory in all directions with unrestrained use of its firepower and unprecedented brutality, until it held 70 percent of the country.

The Croatian Defense Council (HVO), a well-armed, fifty-thousand-strong force, acted as the extended arm of Tudjman. In 1993, it rapidly increased in heavy firepower, especially its artillery and armored vehicles. On the territory it held, the HVO was financed by the Croatian regime and by Hercegovinan Croatian émigrés living in Western Europe.

The Bosnian army, which included Bosnian Muslims, Croats, and Serbs fighting for a unified Bosnia-Hercegovina and numbered two hundred thousand troops, had sidearms but little heavy weaponry. It received some support in troops and weapons from Iran, along with a trickle of Muslim volunteers, called mujahideen, and limited financial and moral support from some other Muslim nations.[35] In 1992–93 any serious effort to arm the Bosnian army was shackled by the arms embargo, but especially by the fact that every route for bringing in heavy weapons had to pass through Croatia, and the Croatians were not in the least inclined to allow war supplies to reach "the Muslims." By 1994, however, the Bosnian army emerged much better organized and equipped than before, owing to the supplies obtained through Croatia from the former Warsaw countries but primarily to the shipments from Iran via Zagreb—the operation to which the United States turned a blind eye.[36]

The new Army of Yugoslavia replaced the YPA on May 8, 1992. It was formed from the earlier army units stationed in Serbia and Montenegro and from those withdrawn from Slovenia, Croatia, Bosnia-Hercegovina, and Macedonia.[37] The new army has some 135,000 recruits and officers; FROG, SAM, Neva, and Volhov missile systems; 140 combat helicopters; 1,000 tanks; 950 armored personnel carriers; 1,360 heavy artillery pieces; 5 submarines; and 4 frigates.[38]

Today, however, Slobodan Milošević relies not on the army but on the eighty-thousand-strong police force as the bedrock of his regime. Counting the reservists, the number of police increases greatly. The units are outfitted with state-of-the-art military technology, including 120 mm mine launchers, 82 mm antiaircraft tanks, transporters, helicopters, and other typical military equipment. The police academies resemble schools for military training.[39] The police forces are paid incomparably better than army personnel, which only adds to the disenchantment of the army officers.[40]

The restructuring of the army involved a series of mass purges of generals and top-ranking officers, until only Serbian and Montenegrin officers loyal to the politics of Slobodan Milošević remained.[41] Not one non-Serb top-ranking officer remained in the land force, navy, or air force. In mid-1992 the purge was extended to cover civilians employed by the army. Non-Serb civilian employees were given yellow passes for entry into army facilities, in contrast to the blue passes of their Serbian colleagues. The parallel with the yellow star of David was too obvious, and the use of these passes shocked both civilian and army employees. The wholesale dismissal of non-Serbian civilian employees was under way.

For many army personnel of all ranks who before the war sincerely believed they were serving in an institution dedicated to the protection of all of Yugoslavia and all the Yugoslav peoples, the "transformation and revitalization" of the YPA (as the operation was called in military circles) was a tragic process. Many of them, including some disabled veterans, find themselves now without rank, income, or hope in the future.[42]

NOTES

1   Hitler's aim was to destroy Yugoslavia and to punish Serbia for its role in World War I (Branko Petranović, *Istorija Jugoslavije, 1918-1978* [Beograd: Nolit, 1978], p. 198).

2   After the first successful attempts to disarm Italian garrisons in Cevo, Virpazar, and Cuci in Montenegro, small groups were formed to set up ambushes along the roadways, which eventually led to the uprising of the entire population (Milovan Djilas, *Wartime* [New York: Harcourt Brace Jovanovich, 1977], pp. 21-25).

3   Petranović, p. 227.

4   On the ethnic war between Croats and Serbs see Djilas, pp. 91-184.

5   Petranović, p. 253.

6   See Slaven Letica and Mario Nobilo, *JNA—rat protiv Hrvatske* (Zagreb: Globus, 1994), pp. 55-56; Mensur Ibrahimpašić, "Četrdeset pet godina oruzanih snaga SFRJ," *Narodna armija*, special edition, 12 April 1986; Slobodan Inić, "Osveta oružja," *Monitor*, 23 February 1996, p. 21.

7   Zoran Petrović Piroćanac, "Dimitrije Rupel," *Start*, 4 February 1989, pp. 15-20; Adrijano Kirsić, "Striptiz smrti???" *Mladina*, 18 December 1987, pp. 16-17; Zoran Medved, "U sjenci šapke," *Danas*, 17 April 1990, pp. 20-22; David Tasic, "Slovenija, Slovenija," *Polet*, 5 February 1988, pp. 11-13.

8   Stipe Sikavica, "Njihovi i naši," *Borba*, 4 April 1989, p. 2.

9   Drašković had started out as a nationalist, but he changed his outlook and by 1991 he put up a stiff resistance to Slobodan Milošević.

10 Dragoslav Grujić, "Dan koji je potresao Beograd," *Vreme*, 7 March 1994, p. 32, and Milan Vasić and Filip Švarm, "Povratak u stanje," *Vreme*, 25 December 1995, pp. 15–16.

11 The nationalist euphoria that had swept Croatia following the victory in 1990 of Franjo Tudjman and his strongly nationalist party, the Croatian Democratic Union (HDZ), was seen as a direct provocation by the many active and retired army generals living in Belgrade. The rise of the HDZ was interpreted as an Ustashe revival. The statements of some high army officers warning of the danger threatening Serbs in Croatia added fuel to Serbian nationalism. The military leaders were particularly alarmed in 1991 when information about the buildup of a separate armed force in Croatia leaked out. On January 25, 1991, at prime time, Belgrade television aired a military intelligence documentary on the clandestine methods and routes used by army officers in Croatia to illegally smuggle weapons into Croatia to arm territorial defense units. At the end of January 1991, federal military prosecutors requested the arrest of General Martin Špegelj, the Croatian minister of defense, for having illegally armed Croatian paramilitary forces.

12 In August 1991, when news was received of the military coup in Moscow against Mikhail Gorbachev, the Yugoslav army general staff celebrated the seizure of power by the Soviet hard-liners as being favorable for the Yugoslav hard-liners. A more moderate group, headed by Defense Minister Kadijević, sat paralyzed by indecision. Military coup or not? Kadijević never made up his mind.

13 Who ordered the movement has never been made clear. At the time, the presidency of Yugoslavia was paralyzed over disagreement as to which of its members should fill the office of president, the term of the former president having expired in mid-May. In short, the army was without a commander in chief.

14 Aleksandar Vasović, "Rat u Sloveniji," *Independent Radio B-92*, 14 April 1992; "Istina o oružanom sukobu u Sloveniji," *Narodna Armija*, special edition, 26 January 1991, pp. 14, 22; Stevan Šićarov, "Janša ukrao Alijine rakete," *Borba*, 14–15 August 1993, p. 4.

15 Had their real purpose been preserving the Yugoslav state, as they claimed, Kadijević and Milošević would not have allowed Slovenia to depart so easily. In retrospect, it seems reasonable to assume that Milošević was willing to permit Slovenia's quick departure precisely because he knew that it would fortify Croatia's secessionist ambitions, making war inevitable. He wanted war, and this was one way to provoke it. Overnight, his propaganda machine dropped the call for the "preservation of Yugoslavia" and gave top priority to the "protection of Serbs in Croatia from genocide" and the "liberation of Serbian regions in Croatia."

Milošević clearly assured the generals that the "remaining Yugoslavia," the "state of those peoples who want to live in it," would look after the army and their families and safeguard their status. The attitude of the officer corps had for some time been that as long as there was a Yugoslavia, their elite place within it was secure, and that their best hope rested with Milošević.

16   Fran Višnar, "Moć singapurske veze," *Danas*, 9 April 1991, pp. 7–8; editorial, "Istina o naoružavanju terorističkih formacija u Hrvatskoj," *Narodna Armija*, special edition, 26 January 1991, p. 54; editorial, "Hrvatska je vojska četiri puta jača od snage pobunjenih Srba," *Globus*, 6 August 1993, p. 2; Miroslav Vujović, "Hrvatsko kršenje embarga," *NIN*, 10 February 1995, pp. 58–59.

17   By mid-1993, the Croatian army had 105,000 enlisted men and officers and about 150,000 reservists, 350 tanks, 4,000 artillery pieces, and 140 fighter planes (see Miodrag Dinić, "Vojna sila nedefinisanog stila," *Borba*, 10 January 1992, pp. 13–14; Veljko B. Kadijević and Branislav Djordjević, "Kako odbraniti Krajinu," *Duga*, 27 May–9 June 1995, pp. 32–36; Michael Stephanson, "Hrvatska vojska od Vukovara do Okučana," *Globus*, 26 May 1996, p. 14).

18   In his book *My View of the Disintegration* (in the chapter entitled "Significant Events of the Final Phase of the Destruction of the Federative Republic of Yugoslavia"), Veljko Kadijević says: "The objective of the YPA in the first phase of the armed conflict in Croatia was: to protect Serbian people in Croatia from the attack of the Croatian armed formations and to facilitate the consolidation of Serbian defense; simultaneously, to prepare the YPA for the war with Croatia, once Croatia attacked the YPA. The task was to be accomplished in the framework of 'prevention of interethnic conflicts,' as defined by the Presidency of Yugoslavia" (*Moje Vidjenje raspada: Vojske bez države* [Belgrade: Politika, 1993], p. 127). The claim regarding the "prevention of interethnic conflicts" masked the brutality of Kadijević's YPA.

19   R. V., "Orlovi potsečenih krila," *Vreme*, 3 August 1992, pp. 27–29.

20   Fifteen thousand strong, HOS adopted the Nazi salute "Sieg Heil." The unit engaged a large number of criminals and foreign mercenaries acting on their own. HOS was guilty of war crimes committed both against the Krajina Serbs and later on against the Bosnians.

21   On some smaller paramilitary units on the Bosnian side see John F. Burns, "Two Gang Leaders in Sarajevo Face Crackdown in Bosnia," *New York Times*, 27 October 1993, p. A6; John F. Burns, "New Horror for Sarajevo, Muslims Killing Muslim," *New York Times*, 31 October 1993.

22   Milutin Mitrović, "Oficir, zvani Gotovina," *Vreme*, 20 March 1995, p. 21; and N. N., "Novi Desant na Drvar," *Borba*, 22 September 1993, p. 10.

23   On the decision to open the army to volunteers see Aleksandar Ćirić, Dragan Todorović, and Branko Bogdanović, "Otimači armijskog nasledja," *Vreme*, 15 July 1991, p. 5.

24   Because the Serbian regime insisted that Serbia was not at war, general mobilization could not be carried out. But the military police collected young men early in the morning at their homes, in discotheques, coffeehouses, and even public transportation. "The regime faced a stubborn, mass resistance," writes Milan Milošević, "more overwhelming than public manifestations of marginalized pacifist groupings." This fact was suppressed not only by the regime at home but also by the international community (Milošević, "Cepanje Poternice," *Vreme*, 27 January 1996, p. 11).

25   At least forty thousand conscripts took part in the rebellions of 1991 (Milan Milošević, "Garda je njegova," *Vreme*, 15 July 1991, p. 9). Mothers would demonstrate again in Belgrade and in Skopje as the war continued.

26 *Vreme* reported in July 1991 that the situation resembled total military disintegration (see Ćirić, Todorović, and Bogdanović, "Otimači armijskog nasledja," p. 5).

27 The transcript of the command to include volunteers in the armed forces was printed in *Vreme*, 30 December 1995, p. 29.

28 Arkan and his followers fought alongside the YPA at Vukovar and sowed death and destruction in many other places of Croatia and later on in Bosnia-Hercegovina. Arkan was nevertheless elected a deputy in the Serbian parliament at the same time that he took control of Belgrade's underground.

29 *Statistički bilten*, No. 1934 (Beograd: Savezni zavod za statistiku), p. 16.

30 On December 26, 1995, the Belgrade Military Court handed down a guilty verdict to the retired General Vladimir Trifunović, the commander of Thirty-second Corps YPA in Varaždin, for having negotiated with the Croatian authorities for a withdrawal from their garrison of 260 nineteen-year-olds serving their obligatory service when war broke out. Their barrack was blockaded in September and October 1991, and the garrison was surrounded by the overwhelmingly stronger Croatian forces. Rather than risking massive annihilation of his garrison, General Trifunović opted for an agreement with Croatian authorities for a safe passage. In the absence of the agreement, he would have been able to hold out only for about six days. General Trifunović was tried three times, receiving between seven and fifteen years. He was finally acquitted following massive public protest and relentless pressure on the part of *Vreme* (see "Spotlight Report No. 17," *The Humanitarian Law Center* [March 1995]: 1–7; see also *Vreme*, 2 January 1995, pp. 24–26; 26 June 1995, pp. 24–25; 27 November 1995, pp. 22–24; 4 December 1995, pp. 16–18; 30 December 1995, pp. 16–17; 27 January 1996, pp. 14–16).

31 *Statistički bilten*, No. 1934, p. 14; Ljubiša Stojmirović, "Vukodlak Mesić i majka Tereza," *Narodna Armija*, 9 November 1991, p. 5.

32 Miloš Vasić and Filip Švarm, "Generalski crni petak," *Vreme*, 30 December 1995, 30.

33 Borislav Soleša, "Kako je razoren aerodrom Bihać," *Borba*, 2 March 1993, p. 16.

34 Karl Gorinšek, "Napad je najbolja ucjena," *Feral Tribune*, 9 October 1995, p. 9, and Borislav Soleša, "Balkan se sporo gasi," *Borba*, 7–8 November 1992, p. 5.

35 On the arming of the Bosnian side see "Moć utihlog oružja," *Vreme*, 18 December 1995, pp. 14–15, which consists of information from the International Institute for Strategic Studies in London; Antun Masle, "Snažna bosanska vojska koju su naoružale islamske zemlje ne postoji," *Globus*, 2 June 1995, pp. 5–6; Miroslav Lazarinski, "Jedan avion i 80,000 ljudi," *Politika*, 21 June 1993, p. 7.

    Regarding foreign mercenaries on all three sides see Filip Švarm, Perica Vučinić, and Radenko Udovičić, "Vojni otpad," *Vreme*, 24 February 1996, pp. 15–17.

36 About the routes of armament see Miloš Vasić, "Trik sa embargom," *Vreme*, 3 October 1994, p. 24; Vasić, "Nebo nad Tuzlom," *Vreme*, 13 March 1995, p. 10. It is important to note, however, that the Bosnian government imported only light arms, that is, it did not import artillery of a caliber above 75 mm, whether with tanks, armored vehicles, or aviation equipment.

37 The Macedonian contingent was obtained by peaceful agreement with the government of Macedonia.

38 Miroslav Lazarinski, "Jugoslavija nema viška oružja," *Politika*, 26 November 1993,

p. 9; "Oslonac na sopstvene snage," *Vojska*, special edition, 10 May 1994, pp. 1–30; Karl Gorinšek, "Rat i politika," *Pečat*, 25 October 1994, pp. 15–21.

39   Filip Švarm, "Plavo gore, plavo dole," *Vreme*, 25 July 1994, p. 25.

40   In contrast to army personnel, who receive only $147.7 million annually in salary, police troops are given many privileges and salaries amounting to $238.6 million annually (Roger Cohen, "Strains in Belgrade, Army vs. Serbian President," *New York Times*, 25 October 1994, p. 6; see also Miloš Vasić, "Armija Senki," *Vreme*, 6 December 1993, p. 26).

41   Miloš Vasić and Filip Švarm, "Četvrti plenum za ponavljace," *Vreme*, 19 March 1993, pp. 26–28; Filip Švarm, "Generalske smjene," *Vreme*, 10 May 1993, pp. 22–23; Miloš Vasić and Filip Švarm, "Dvorski puč u toku," *Vreme*, 24 May 1993, pp. 18–21.

42   On the process of the army's transformation see Miloš Vasić and Filip Švarm, "Povratak u stanje," *Vreme*, 25 December 1995, pp. 12–16; Vasić and Švarm, "Generalski 'crni petak'," *Vreme*, 30 December 1995, pp. 28–31.

On the role of the police in the new system of power in Serbia see Jovan Dulović and Miloš Vasić, "Stub lične vlasti," *Vreme*, 1 August 1994, pp. 12–15.

The arms control agreement, signed June 13, 1996, in Florence outlines the reduction in armaments as follows: (1) Tanks: Federal Republic of Yugoslavia, 1,000; Republic of Croatia, 400; Bosnian-Croatian Federation, 267; Republika Srpska, 133. (2) Armored vehicles: Federal Republic of Yugoslavia, 700; Republic of Croatia, 280; Republic of Bosnian-Croatian Federation, 800; Republika Srpska, 400. (3) Military aircraft: Federal Republic of Yugoslavia, 150; Republic of Croatia, 60; Bosnian-Croatian Federation, 40; Republika Srpska, 20. (4) Military helicopters: Federal Republic of Yugoslavia, 50; Republic of Croatia, 20; Bosnian-Croatian Federation, 13; Republika Srpska, 7 (Miloš Vasić, "Natezanje u Oslu," *Vreme*, 15 June 1996, p. 13).

Croatia: The First War

Ejub Štitkovac

I spent May Day 1991, a mere month before the war in Croatia would begin, on assignment in Daruvar, a large multiethnic town in Slavonia, in the northeastern Croatian region bordering with Hungary.[1] Daruvar was a spa town, with waters especially recommended for the treatment of rheumatic diseases. The spa attracted its full quota of visitors year-round. When I came, it was full of them.

But as I heard from a number of people immediately, for several nights before my arrival Yugoslav People's Army (YPA) tanks had been rolling through the town. That did not bode well, the Croatian friend I visited said. He refused to come along with me to the house of our common friend, a Serb, his childhood buddy and best man at his wedding. "We'll leave that visit for better times," he said. "If Serbs like him don't wake up and realize Milošević is about to push them into war with us, all hell will break loose. I'm sure," he added, "Milošević will just use them and leave them high and dry. Mark my words."

Trying to sleep in my hotel room that night, I heard small-arms fire from the woods around Daruvar, and the tanks rumbling through the town. Few must be sleeping well, I thought. But in the morning, the streets looked calm again. Had the people already grown accustomed to tanks under their windows and gunfire from the woods?

At mid-morning, the Serbian friend whom I went to visit alone seemed exasperated. "You journalists are nuts," he said. "Instead of staying in Belgrade where you are safe, you come here, where the lid's about to blow off. Don't you feel it in the air? Catch the first train back. Later you might not be able to get out." He told me that the Croats were preparing to massacre the Serbs; the local Croatian Democratic Union (HDZ) was drawing up lists of Serbs to be shot. "We'll have to take to the woods again and fight. The army is our big hope, but it's falling apart. Nobody can expect Croatian officers to fight against Croats. The generals will go over to Tudjman, and us here, we'll be sitting ducks." My Serbian friend took off into the woods two days later. He became known by his war name, Struja (Electric).

The local radio station that day reported that a bomb was thrown at a gas station in Pakrac, a town some fifteen kilometers to the south. The incident took place half an hour after the Belgrade local, the train connecting Daruvar and Belgrade, had passed through. In Pakrac, where the majority of the population were Serbs, graffiti on the walls of buildings read: "Serbs get out. This is Croatia." In a number of other small towns I visited in Slavonia that time, including Pakrac, the streets were full of police and men in a uniform I had never seen before. The next day, the Belgrade local failed to arrive. The same day, May 2, 1991, things exploded in Borovo Selo.

Borovo Selo itself is little more than a village, but its importance derives from the neighboring town of Borovo, home of the Borovo Manufacturing Company, in the last fifteen years a major manufacturer of rubber goods as well as fashion shoes. Borovo Selo lies right next to the town of Vukovar at the Croatian-Serbian border.

As in Daruvar, the Serbs here and in towns and villages throughout Croatia harbored many fears. Over the past three years the official media in Serbia had gradually awakened a haunting sense of uncertainty and jeopardy in the Serbian community. To compound the sense of acute crisis, in 1990 the Knin Corps of the YPA, under the command of Ratko Mladić, distributed a large arsenal of weapons, allegedly for self-defense, among the already formed Serbian paramilitary groups. The victory of the nationalist Croatian Democratic Union (HDZ) in the elections of April 1990 had reinforced the fears.[2] Many Serbs could be heard discussing *Bespuća* (Wilderness), a book written by Franjo Tudjman, in which he attempted to revise the official death count for the World War II Croatian death camp, Jasenovac, whose principal victims had been Serbs.[3] Hundreds of thousands had died in the camp, but Tudjman placed the figure at well below one hundred thousand.[4] This was part of his effort to free Croatians from the historical guilt (commonly referred to as the "Jasenovac complex") brought on by the role of the Croatian Fascist Party, the Ustashe, during World War II. After his election, Tudjman launched a national reconciliation campaign with the Ustashe and the Croatian army regular forces, the Domobrani. They, too, were victims of the war, Tudjman claimed, but in contrast to the antifascist Partisans, they remained unmourned. The

Communist regime had placed a mark of shame on them—a stigma that had to come off.[5]

Ordinary Serbs were horrified when, as a token of reconciliation with the past, the streets and squares across Croatia commemorating victims of Fascism and heroes of the liberation war were renamed after figures infamous for their association with the pro-Hitler regime. On July 25, 1990, the Croatian Sabor (parliament) adopted a number of amendments to the Croatian constitution allowing for Croatian state symbols to be changed. The Yugoslav flag with its red-star emblem was replaced by the Croatian flag with a white and red checkerboard. Croatians saw the checkerboard as their ancient emblem and insisted passionately that the Serbs had no right to object to a symbol with such deep historical roots. Many Serbs, however, argued that the emblem had been defiled because it was also used by the Ustashe government.[6] The use of symbols that provoked associations with genocide were politically and morally unacceptable, Serbs argued. The checkerboard, however, was soon being flown everywhere, on official flagpoles and buildings and at private homes, shops, and cafés. At night, Serbs would remove it, raising the Yugoslav flag in its place; in the morning Croats would return to the sahovnica. Tensions grew.

The checkerboard did not only disturb the Serbs as the flag under which they had suffered during World War II, but also as a symbol of what they saw as Tudjman's current intentions. On February 24, 1990, at the first HDZ rally, Tudjman had spoken the astonishing words: "The NDH (the Independent State of Croatia under Hitler) was not simply a quisling creation and a fascist crime; it was also an expression of the historical aspirations of the Croatian people." What would come next?

On December 22, 1990, Croatia, at the time still a member of the Yugoslav federation, made a large change in its old socialist constitution. Croatian Serbs were no longer recognized as Croatia's "constituent nation" but became instead its "national minority." No one was clear as to what this meant in practical terms, if anything, but soon after, mass layoffs of Serbs took place. They were fired not just from the police force, where they had been overrepresented in the past, but also from educational and medical institutions, the tourist industry, private firms, and even from mountaineering associations.[7] What had been fear among many Croatian Serbs turned to panic.

Belgrade's official television gave these events a sinister cast. In the peak viewing hours, for more than a year before the outbreak of fighting, news programs and TV shows were dominated not only by loud commentary on the moves of the new Croatian government but also by detailed reports and reruns of attacks by Croatian extremists—routinely referred to as "Ustashe"—on Serb property in Croatia: houses, apartments, restaurants, shops, farms. Images of shattered roofs, windows, garages, broken furniture and china, destroyed orchards, and dead pets flooded TV screens. Panel discussions orchestrated to warn of the imminent extermination of Serbs in Croatia became a regular feature of official programming. The word *genocide* came into frequent use for the first time since World War II.

Tudjman's every new step seemed to lend credibility to Milošević's outrageous warnings that unless due measures were taken, the Serbs could never feel safe again. It followed from Milošević's statements that if Croatia continued insisting on leaving Yugoslavia, the only way to protect the Croatian Serbs would be to attach the regions with a significant Serbian population to Serbia. By the spring of 1991, it was no longer relevant that such claims were widely exaggerated. Even some Belgrade intellectuals had embraced them as self-evident. In the Serbian community the perception of an acute, palpable, and inherent danger hovered like a dark cloud over the home of each individual Serb in Croatia. The lack of police investigations or court actions in actual cases of violence against individual Serbs or their property was yet another factor making the Serbian community feel that it was under attack and unprotected. It was during these months that armed extremist groups from Serbia—the Chetniks led by Vojislav Šešelj, the Tigers led by Željko Ražnjatović-Arkan, as well as other smaller groups such as Dušan Silni, Beli Orlovi, and others—began to infiltrate the Serbian communities in Croatia, fanning the national paranoia already aflame and urging the Serbian population to arm.

In the early spring of 1991, in settlements with a Serbian majority in Croatia, armed civilians were organized to guard the entrance routes to their towns and villages. The barricades placed to prevent the entrance of Croatian militias created a cold-war atmosphere a full six months before actual fighting began. Borovo Selo, with its Serbian majority, was quick to set up its own roadblocks, elect its own local authorities, and appoint its own armed guards. An agreement was reached with Croatian authorities officially banning entry to Borovo Selo to any Croatian members of the police force without the explicit permission of the local Serbian authorities.

On May 1, 1991, two Croatian policemen in a marked police car entered Borovo Selo without permission. They were immediately arrested. On May 2, the Croatian authorities sent some twenty policemen to liberate them. Their vehicle was met by a shower of gunfire from Serbian irregulars, some of whom were local, some from Serbia. The Croatian authorities then sent in 150 policemen in buses as reinforcements. A fierce, armed confrontation ensued, leaving seventeen dead.

Three versions of the incident were immediately provided. Contradictory interpretations from different sources were to become the rule later. The first version was sent out by HINA, the newly formed official Croatian Information News Agency: Croatian policemen numbering 150 had come to Borovo Selo for a meeting agreed to by both sides. They encountered a barrage of gunfire from the local population and terrorists from Serbia. Twelve "guardians of law and order" and fifteen residents were killed on the spot.

The second version was put together by journalists from statements by local residents: The police entered the village and began shooting at everything that moved. Thirteen policemen and one local man were killed. The police took women and children as hostages, but the local people, without any outside help, freed the hostages and defeated the police.

A third version was given live on Belgrade TV. It was taped by the self-appointed Chetnik commander Vojislav Šešelj and shown several times. According to this version, fourteen of Šešelj's men had led the battle against "the Ustashe." Fighting Šešelj's boys were six local men and two members of the Serbian Renewal Movement from Nova Pazova, a town just outside Belgrade. Šešelj reported that one civilian and one hundred Croatian policemen died.

The event, marking the beginning of the Croatian war, demonstrates the overall war strategy in a nutshell. The Croatian police patrol entering Borovo Selo in violation of the previously reached agreement was a provocation. In the already heated atmosphere, any remaining trust between the Serbian and Croatian communities was destroyed once the shooting took place. The escalating Serbian nationalism had been equated in the Croatian official media with Bolshevism—the same Bolshevism that was allegedly to blame for the loss of national pride in Croatia, and for the loss of a large portion of its revenue since the 1950s.[8] Milošević's Bolshevism, Croatian media argued, had brought to peaceful Croatian towns and villages ultranationalist paramilitary groups from Serbia, roadblocks, and guns. The loss of mutual trust in towns like Borovo Selo weakened the position of the Croats who did not support secession or accept Tudjman's strident anti-Communism and ultranationalism. As events unfolded, more and more Croats saw secession as the only alternative.

Local Serbs, on the other hand, were equally terrified by the alleged need for the presence of the Serbs who were organizing and arming people door to door. The temperature in the town was at the boiling point. In Borovo Selo as elsewhere, the authentic deep-seated fears of ordinary people for their lives and the survival of their families were used by Belgrade as justification for armed conflicts and, ultimately, for the war for territories. The objectives of Franjo Tudjman and Slobodan Milošević complemented each other. After Borovo Selo, war seemed inevitable.[9]

Croatia, as well as Slovenia, enjoyed support for secession abroad, especially in Germany and Austria. Yet it was clear that Serbia would not accept their departure peacefully, but would use it to advance its own ends, and this spelled war. European leaders did nothing for about six months after the Yugoslav crisis had entered its critical stage. When they finally recognized that the crisis was not heading for a resolution, in the late spring and early summer of 1991, they embarked on diplomacy, but their effort lacked coherence, a strategy, and real authority. Most important, their diplomacy never appropriately identified the fundamental issue driving the conflict, referred to in the former Yugoslavia as the "Serbian question."

Of eight million Serbs in the former Yugoslavia, three million were dispersed outside Serbia, primarily in Croatia and Bosnia-Hercegovina. The only way for the international community to dampen the conflict was to unflaggingly insist that personal, political, cultural, and all other rights of minorities be firmly guaranteed in every state seeking secession. Had genuine guarantees of minority rights been obtained from Croatia, the wind would have been knocked out of Milošević's sails. He would also have been forced to consider similar guarantees for the Albanians in Kosovo. But minority-rights guarantees were not requested of anyone.

Milorad Pupovac, a Serbian professor of linguistics at Zagreb University and president of the antinationalist Serbian Democratic Movement in Croatia—not to be confused with the nationalist SDS (Serbian Democratic

Party)—tried in every possible way to bring some sanity to the situation and establish a dialogue between Croatian Serbs and Croats. His efforts were in vain as both official Zagreb and Belgrade vilified him for his "conciliatory politics," pointing at him as the agent of the other side. Both Belgrade and Zagreb did everything to neutralize, or to physically eliminate, all those who stood in the way of war. Nor did such groups and individuals receive any official recognition from the international community.

On June 25, 1991, the parliament of Croatia unanimously adopted a declaration proclaiming the republic's independence and full sovereignty and setting in motion the procedures for ending its union with Yugoslavia. Unanimity was achieved in the absence of the parliament's Serbian representatives, who had walked out of the session in protest.

That same day, the republic of Slovenia also declared its independence. To give this act symbolic support, the Slovene border authorities, without consulting the federal authorities, immediately took down the signs at the border crossings with Austria and Italy reading "Yugoslavia" and replaced them with new signs reading "Slovenia"—a slap in the face bound to provoke a stiff reaction.

At the time, twenty thousand YPA troops were stationed in Slovenia. Of that number, only one thousand were mobilized after the change of signs at the borders. An additional army contingent was sent from southern Serbia and another one from Croatia. During the last days of June and in early July, television satellites transmitted to the world pictures of what essentially was a ten-day war about borders.

The international community assumed that Milošević, by sending troops to Slovenia to protect the border crossings, was trying to save Yugoslavia. But the opposite interpretation is equally viable. The number of troops placed on the battlefield was strikingly inadequate. Milošević needed some troops in Slovenia to support his rhetoric of preserving Yugoslavia, but in fact he most likely calculated that the departure of Slovenia would tip the overall situation in his favor.

The Slovenian ten-day war was televised from the beginning. For public consumption, the YPA was defeated in ten days by Slovenia's own territorial defense forces. On July 8, 1991, a truce was negotiated between Slovenia and Yugoslavia, and Slovenia continued on its way to independence. In the background, unseen on the television screens, armed Serbs and Croats had their sights on each other. The Croatian war, about to begin, would claim twenty thousand lives, in contrast with the Slovenian war, in which a total of nine Slovenian civilians were killed.

The murder, on July 1, 1991, of Josip Reichl-Kir, the young chief of police of Osijek, the largest town in eastern Slavonia in Croatia, offered another proof that neither Croatia nor Serbia was interested in calming the hysteria of fear among the citizens in the two republics. Tudjman himself had appointed young Reichl-Kir to the sensitive position in this town with a significant Serbian population. But Reichl-Kir, like Milorad Pupovac, was one of the people who recognized that the final hour had come for people of authority to speak out and make every effort to defuse the tensions.[10] In an attempt to build on the remaining vestiges of trust between the Croats and Serbs, Reichl-Kir made many visits to the smaller towns and villages of his district, meeting tirelessly with representatives of local Serbs, reassuring them that his forces would guarantee their safety, and asking them to remove the roadblocks and allow normal traffic through the region. The murderer of Reichl-Kir, as it turned out, was not a Serb but a Croat, Antun Gudelj, an Australian émigré commissioned to kill Kir by Branimir Glavaš, ultranationalist HDZ member and secretary for the defense of the Osijek municipality.[11] Branimir Glavaš, who organized Croatian extremists from the region into a secret army, did not favor Reichl-Kir's pacifism. In addition, Glavaš seems to have known that Reichl-Kir had generated a fat dossier about Glavaš's activities.

The murder gave a clear signal to the people of eastern Slavonia that as far as HDZ was concerned, there would be no peace with the Serbs. For their part, the Serbian extremists were strengthening their own nationalist campaign in eastern Slavonia. They made sure to remind everyone who might have forgotten that Serbs in Osijek lost their jobs following the HDZ electoral victory and that unless they armed themselves, Serbs would now lose their lives too.

For the rank-and-file Serb in eastern Croatia, the idea of a Greater Serbia meant little, but fear for their own survival made them paranoid and bitterly aggressive. Until 1990, people's World War II memories had remained at bay, not because they were forcibly suppressed but because over time past horrors had lost their edge and lives in common had taken solid root. Generation after generation had grown up in a Yugoslavia where few believed another genocide was thinkable. In that context, the shock of new ultranationalism proved even more deadly, raising the fears to fever pitch.

Serbian nationalist extremists were instrumental in stirring the fears. In small towns such as Glina, about forty miles south of Zagreb, the extremists brought in from the outside did everything to shatter the unity of the multinational Croatian Democratic Party, which enjoyed strong support among local Serbs. Serbs supported the party, despite the fact that in 1941 the Ustashe had massacred eight hundred Serbs from the town in a single day, locking them up in the Orthodox church and setting the church ablaze. For forty-five years after the war, Serbs and Croats in Glina had lived in peace.

On June 26, 1991, a group of Serbian extremists attacked the police station in Glina. The attack was not carried out by the local Serbs but by the so-called Martićevci, (named after their leader Milan Martić), a group of Serbian extremists imported from Knin, the remote south Krajina region. The Martićevci had been active for months, infiltrating local institutions, spreading alarming rumors about the plans of the Croatian government, provoking intolerance, and, as always, handing out firearms.

In August 1990 the Knin Serbs were the first to think of setting up roadblocks made of tree trunks at the entrances to their towns and villages. Knin was a poor region, with no agriculture or industry to speak of. However, the town's function as the railroad junction for all lines to the Dalmation coast lent the region great strategic importance. This geographic advantage had never brought riches to anybody, but Tudjman knew that without Knin, Croatia's communication lines and tourist industry would be crippled. For this reason, one of his first tasks upon getting elected was to bring the Knin region under the strict control of Zagreb.

Knin was the site of the first organized Serbian demonstrations for equality in Croatia in the summer of 1989. In response to the unrest of that summer, Croatian authorities arrested and threatened the local Serbian leadership. The Serbs from the Kninska Krajina, many of whom had joined the nationalist Chetniks in World War II, took the Croatian government's harsh reaction to their protests as a signal that it intended to suppress Serbian culture and deny all rights to the Serbian community in Croatia. That Tudjman and the HDZ had prevailed in Croatia in 1990 was confirmation for the Knin Serbs of the renewal, right before their eyes, of the Ustashe movement. They felt that the movement had to be stopped, immediately and by all means. A local dentist, Milan Babić, and a local police inspector, Milan Martić, took things into their own hands. Both were inimical to compromise, insensitive to finesse and nuance, and bel-

Romanies were also victims of war. A Romany family in northern Croatia:
January 1996. Photo by Maja Munk. Courtesy of the photographer.

ligerent. From total anonymity, they shot to the top of the Serbian political scene. Generously supplied with weaponry by Slobodan Milošević,
they soon turned out to play his game in Croatia.[12]

The Martićevci struck terror in the non-Serbian population of the Krajina. As their paramilitaries made advances, villages emptied, the villagers not even taking the time to lock their homes before fleeing. The
homes, locked or unlocked, were robbed from cellar to attic. Most of the
booty ended up on a burgeoning black market.

For many irregulars, looting was the principal motive for going to war
in the Krajina and elsewhere. In the village of Miokovićevo, less than
twenty kilometers from Daruvar, self-proclaimed politicians came and
went making promises. "We will beat the Croats and then wherever Serbs

live will be Serbia, they told us," said one peasant to me in the spring of 1993. "I don't deny that I myself did some shooting, but the worst crimes were committed by the irregulars who came in from Serbia. First they looted the homes of Croats. When they came back a second time, they surged on Serbian houses, because the Croatian houses had already been cleaned up. Now we are being blamed for the murder of all those Croats. We will never be able to go back home again."[13]

Many Serbs in Croatia were against the war and refused to be turned against their Croatian neighbors. For this, many paid with their lives. Others, under explicit threat that their families would be wiped out, ended up joining the paramilitaries. Sometimes, however, Serbs and Croats fought side by side against either Croatian or Serbian attacks on their homes. Sometimes they fled together. Another villager from Mioko-vićevo told me that in August 1991 some YPA officers came to the village, handed out weapons, and left an old tank: "They told us to defend our village and that army officers and soldiers would come to help us. For six months nobody came. Croats from our village fought with us against the Croatian troops. They were defending their homes just as we were. For the whole time, we stayed in Miokovićevo. We didn't fight on any other front. After six months, we were ordered to evacuate the village and head to Bosnia. Bosnia was still quiet. So we left Miokovićevo in a huge column, and we finally reached Banja Luka. About twenty kilometers before Banja Luka, Serbian Radicals stopped the column and took all our money and anything else of value on us, like our weapons, even hunting rifles. They gave us some sort of worthless receipts. With us were the Croats who had fought alongside us. But in Banja Luka, they separated us. I have never been able to learn where the others were taken, to find even a trace of them. I only know for sure that they didn't dare return to Croatia because they would have been shot for fighting for their village on our side."[14]

On August 19 Serbian forces surrounded the eastern Slavonian town of Vukovar, on the Croatian side of the Danube River. Some of the best restaurants used to be situated on Danube's green banks. Belgrade is about eighty kilometers downstream, and the Hungarian border half as many kilometers upstream. From August to November 17, 1991, the old baroque center of Vukovar, like the rest of the town, came under constant shelling by the YPA and the Serbian paramilitary formations, Šešelj's Chetniks and Arkan's Tigers. The people of Vukovar withdrew into basements where they spent the entire time of the siege. The main hospital moved all its operations into the basement of the hospital building. Twenty-three hundred people died during the siege, and thousands others were wounded. Those who emerged out of the basements and into the light on November 17 had before them a scene of total devastation.[15] Out in the streets, they treaded the rubble of broken bricks, crumbled plaster, shattered glass. All around were twisted iron, the remnants of wood supports, beams, and decorative elements scorched by shell fire. The homes were without roofs, walls, doors, or windows. Vukovar was a ghost town.[16]

Numerous defenders of Vukovar were executed after the town fell. An evacuation was arranged to Croatian territory of 420 patients of the Vukovar hospital. About two hundred men were separated from the rest and, in groups of sixty, were loaded on YPA buses, which took them to the farm called Ovčara, lying between the towns of Vukovar, Negoslavci, and Sotin. There they were placed into farm-equipment storage rooms and beaten. By nightfall, groups of twenty were loaded on a truck that returned about twenty minutes later for another group of twenty. In 1992, about two kilometers southeast of Ovčara, a mass grave was found with the remains of hundreds of people. Apparently, 320 were shot during the first night alone.[17]

Into the houses of Croats who were killed or who left, Serbs from eastern Croatia, themselves refugees and homeless, moved in. Many had also lost close family. Others would be invalids for the rest of their lives. In Vukovar, a year after the "liberation," these people were still pushing wheelbarrows through the streets, searching through the rubble for perhaps an unbroken plate or a piece of wire usable to put together an electric heater to get them through the coming winter.[18]

It remains unclear whether the Croatian government tried to attract the attention and gain the sympathy of Western governments by stubbornly denying Vukovar sufficient military support and allowing it to be leveled. Many refugees from Vukovar who were transferred to Zagreb after the fall of Vukovar maintained that Tudjman sacrificed the town for the sake of the publicity and that the town could have been defended provided there had been effective military support.[19]

The Croatian strategy in Dubrovnik—whose shelling by YPA artillery began in early October 1991—suggests that publicity may have also played a significant role here. Dubrovnik was dear to Yugoslavs as their most splendid city, internationally known as the Pearl of the Adriatic. The YPA artillery inflicted considerable damage to the Old City and was much

November 19, 1991, the day the siege of Vukovar (Croatia) ended and people emerged from their underground shelters. Photo by Vlada Dimitrijević. Courtesy of *Vreme* news agency.

more destructive in the surrounding newer districts. The destruction in Dubrovnik placed the full irrationality of the fighting in the Balkans before the eyes of the world. Television viewers who had visited Dubrovnik years earlier and had photographs of themselves taken beside the walls of its Renaissance palaces were now seeing the smoke rising out of the Old City and the holes opened in its old fortifications by the YPA artillery. The wanton destruction stunned the world and gained Croatia much international sympathy. What was less obvious was that the Croatian government, in a maneuver aimed at provoking an ever fiercer YPA attack, placed sharpshooters in the walls surrounding the city.[20] This was a high-risk game, the kind that made sense only if, for its final objective — independence — no price was considered too high. Croatian allegations of Serbian expansionist ambitions, Bolshevism, brutality, and primitiveness found their material confirmation with each new shell that hit Dubrovnik. International support for the recognition of Croatia's independence was gaining momentum.

Konavoski Dvori, a small, agriculturally rich and culturally distinct strip of about twenty kilometers along the Adriatic coast south of Dubrovnik, was leveled. Serbian and Montenegrin irregulars and YPA reservists went on a rampage, sparing nothing and nobody. Resistance was out of the question; the predominantly Croatian population fled, to the last person. Small villages and farms were plundered and everything from television sets to cows and chickens carried off. The pillaged homes and farms were burned to the ground, fire was set to fields and orchards, livestock were slaughtered wholesale. Konavoski Dvori burned for days. Along the coast, luxury hotels were destroyed and hundred-year-old palm trees, silver pines, and the bougainvillea cascading down steep banks to the shore were reduced to ashes. The Serbian forces wanted Konavoski Dvori so as to gain control over the Prevlaka peninsula, to this day an area contested by Montenegro and Croatia.

The brutality perpetrated by the Serbian forces eclipsed the violence of the Croatian side, thereby obscuring the fact that Serbian towns and villages throughout Croatia were also being torched and razed by the HDZ supporters and right-wing Croatian extremists; that scores of Serbs from Gospić, Daruvar, Karlovac, Virovitica, Sisak, Ogulin, and other towns were massacred; and that a half million Serbian civilians had to abandon their homes to escape Croatian reprisals.[21]

On November 23, 1991, Cyrus Vance and Lord Carrington negotiated a cease-fire between Croatia and the Krajina Serbs. Between that date and the finalization of cease-fire on January 2, 1992, the houses of rich Serbian farmers in the villages in Western Slavonia and Baranja were torched and Serbs forced to leave.[22] To dramatize the situation, Serbian authorities urged the refugees to mount their tractors and load their possessions on open trucks. The ten kilometers-long convoy headed toward Banja Luka and Serbia.[23] According to the UN-negotiated settlement, the YPA had to withdraw from the Croatian territory by November 29, 1991, and was to be replaced by UN "blue helmets."

The November 1991 cease-fire was the precondition for recognition of Croatia in December, but it provided no political settlement.[24] The political status of Krajina and of the Croatian Serbs was not addressed. The German foreign minister Dietrich-Genscher urged the Croatian government to determine constitutionally the rights of minorities and to institute a human rights court, but he did little when Franjo Tudjman failed to provide any constitutional guarantees and instead adopted, in May 1992, a constitutional law that left out the Serbs altogether.

The fact that Croatia had gained international recognition but that one-third of its territory had been cut off, causing insurmountable communication and economic difficulties, created an unstable situation of neither war nor peace.[25] In an attempt to place the Krajina under Croatian control, Croatia maintained a state of low-level warfare throughout 1992 and 1993.[26] In September 1993, Croatian forces attacked the so-called Medak pocket, a group of villages in the Adriatic hinterland just north of Zadar. On September 17, the territory was handed over to the United Nations, but not before it had been completely emptied of its Serbian population, which offered no resistance. All houses were torched, livestock slaughtered, farming equipment destroyed, wells poisoned. In October, the UN observers wrote a report on the wasteland that was left behind.[27] Until a new cease-fire was negotiated on March 29, 1994, the self-proclaimed Republika Srpska Krajina faced a manpower crisis, since only a few hundred of its sixty thousand draft-age refugees who had fled to Serbia responded to recruitment calls, despite threats of job loss and expulsion from the Serbian territory.[28] By the beginning of 1994 Slobodan Milošević was ill inclined to risk his status as a peace negotiator by helping the Serbs in Croatian Krajina. From that point on, every Serb in Croatia had every reason to feel infinitely more threatened than at any time since World War II.

Until August 1995 the then president Milan Martić of Republika Srpska Krajina refused all negotiations with the international mediators or the Croatian authorities. When Martić finally accepted the agreement with the special envoy of the United Nations, Yasushi Akashi, it was too late. The Croatian army, trained and clandestinely armed by the United States, was ready to reintegrate Krajina by force.[29] On the morning of August 4, 1995, Croatian forces launched Operation Storm on the Knin region and the next day at noontime hung a twenty-meters Croatian flag on top of the Knin fortress. Krajina was subdued without any resistance. The army of the Krajina Serbs, which had no more than fifty thousand soldiers and outdated equipment, dispersed, leaving the population to fend for itself.[30]

Close to two hundred thousand people without food or water crowded the sun-drenched roads toward Banja Luka and Serbia—the greatest single exodus of the entire war. On August 7 the Croatian army and the army of Bosnia shelled fleeing civilians and burned villages, killing everyone who had stayed.[31] Places like Kistanje, a small village of two thousand about twenty kilometers southwest of Knin, were completely destroyed. The Helsinki Human Rights Committee in Zagreb maintains that perhaps six thousand persons disappeared during Operation Storm and about one

Serbian women and children from Krajina (Croatia), brought by a UNHCR truck to Sremska Rača, Serbia, after Operation Storm: May 1995. Photo by Elil Vaš. Courtesy of *Vreme* news agency.

thousand after it.[32] Most of those killed were the old and incapacitated, unable to flee. Some were also tortured, some burned to death in their homes.[33] The slayings continued into October and beyond.[34]

By that time, however, it was hard for the world to see Serbian civilians themselves as victims needing protection. "There is a sense in Western capitals that if something happens to the Krajina Serbs, they deserve it," said one Western official less than a week before the exodus of two hundred thousand from Krajina.[35] Home to a largely Serbian population for four hundred years, Krajina was swept off the map in a mere forty-eight hours.

Civilian refugees seeking shelter in Serbia encountered an indifferent state and an irritable, if not unconcerned, public. Many Serbs painfully found out through the war that—nostalgia notwithstanding—they were much more similar to the Croats, among whom they had lived for hundreds of years, than to their "kin" in Serbia. Most would give anything now to be allowed to return.

A Serbian woman in front of her house in Krajina (Croatia): May 1996.
Photo by Maja Munk. Courtesy of the photographer.

NOTES

1 The population of Daruvar was a mixture of no less than twenty-six ethnic groups—
the reason I had a special affinity for this town. Croats, Serbs, Slovenes, Montenegrins, Jews, Muslims, Albanians, Germans, Czechs, Hungarians, Romanies, and
a few other smaller groups, including Italians, all lived there.

2 The HDZ won only 41.5 percent of the vote in the parliamentary elections, but under
the Croatian electoral system it was capable of taking 58 percent of the seats. The
Serbian Democratic Party (SDS) left the parliament on May 20.

3 Jasenovac was the only World War II death camp not established and run by the
Germans. In addition to the Serbs, its victims were tens of thousands of Jews, Gypsies, and Communists.

4 No definite figures exist. Estimates of the number of deaths resulting from the
Ustashe genocide in Jasenovac and overall vary from 185,000 to 700,000 and higher

(see Aleksa Djilas, *The Contested Country: Yugoslav Unity and Communist Revolution 1919–1953* [Cambridge: Harvard University Press, 1991], pp. 125–27). *Ed.*

5   To this day, Tudjman insists on turning the Jasenovac memorial into a common memorial for the Ustashe victims and the Ustashe themselves, an idea tantamount to turning Auschwitz into a common memorial of Jews and Germans. The architect of the Jasenovac memorial, Bogdan Bogdanović, pledged in March 1996 that he would get all international organizations, the media, and all his personal connections involved to prevent this from happening ("Tudjmanov kulturocid," *Vreme*, 16 March, p. 5).

6   The official Ustashe emblem featured a prominent *U* above the checkerboard shield.

7   Gordana Suša, "Nemam domovinu, tražim neku drugu," *Borba*, 17 February 1993, p. 8.

8   The argument among many ordinary people and the politicians was that the income yielded by Croatia's tourist industry had been withheld from Croatia and allocated instead to Tito's Bolshevik federation, which was dominated by Serbia.

9   Late spring and early summer of 1991 were marked by a series of futile meetings at which both Milošević and Tudjman were present to discuss "avoiding" war. The last such meeting took place on June 6, 1991. It was a meeting, like so many before it, of the presidents of the remaining Yugoslav federal republics. Kiro Gligorov, president of the republic of Macedonia, and Alija Izetbegović, president of the republic of Bosnia-Hercegovina, tabled a proposal for forming a community of independent republics of Yugoslavia. Tudjman, Milošević, and Milan Kučan, president of the republic of Slovenia, rejected it outright. The Serbian leadership had already turned down proposals for a Yugoslav confederation. In truth, no proposal to save Yugoslavia could have won the support of all the parties. *Ed.*

10 Slavonia and Baranja were particularly vulnerable because in 1945 they were colonized by Serbs and Croats from poor regions of Bosnian and Croatian Krajina, and from Dalmatinska Zagora and western Hercegovina. The campaign of forced colonization was supposed to offer the people from poor regions a livelihood and a future. But this population found the adjustment to an entirely different culture, landscape, and climate extremely difficult. Reichl-Kir showed that the incidence of multiethnic animosities was ten times higher in the colonized villages than in the noncolonized ones. Colonists, said Reichl-Kir, are people who had been uprooted and are discontented and subject to manipulation (Miloš Vasić, "Osijek, na Dravi," *Vreme*, 2 December 1991; Vasić, "Neprijatno hapšenje," *Vreme*, 4 December 1995, p. 14).

11 Antun Gudelj killed three people on July 1, 1991: Milan Kneževic, the deputy in the municipal council of Osijek; Goran Zabundžija, vice president of the executive council of the Osijek municipality; and Reichl-Kir, the chief of police in Osijek. Gudelj was arrested on November 19, 1995, in Frankfurt am Main, Germany (Miloš Vasić, "Neprijatno hapšenje," p. 14).

12 The character of a Knin native has its roots in the seventeenth and eighteenth centuries, when Serbs, invited by the Hapsburgs, started settling in the region, then

part of the Hapsburg Empire. Serbs were offered sanctuary from Turkish persecution and were given land in exchange for fulfilling military obligations to the Hapsburg monarchy. In this way, the Hapsburgs built a live defense wall, the military frontier, or Vojna Krajina, against encroachment by the Turks. A local frontier culture developed in the region. The rules of war became the rules of life; honor, dignity, and heroism were measured in military terms. Whereas the Serb peasants in Serbia were on the whole peaceable, the Knin Serbs were armed freemen owing military service and allegiance to the Hapsburg monarchy. They could be called to serve anywhere. By the nineteenth century, many were stationed permanently as part of the regular forces in the different military districts. The descendants of these Serbs gradually came to speak the Croatian variant of Serbo-Croatian and to accept the customs of the local Croatian population, even though they did not convert to Catholicism, despite the animus of the Catholic church. Today, except in their churches, there is virtually no visible difference between the Krajina Serbs and the Croats with whom they have lived; in language, dress, and behavior, and in the internal and external appearance of their homes and the way they bring up their children, they are indistinguishable.

But in the nineteenth century, in contrast to the Croats, who were loyal to their own government, the Krajina Serbs were subject to three ruling powers: Austria, Hungary, and Croatia. What suited the Hapsburg monarchy did not always suit the local Croatian viceroy. Scattered throughout Croatia, the Serbs, whose military ethos the Hapsburgs encouraged, were viewed as a thorn in the side of the Croatian authorities. The status of an unwelcome minority whose relevance to the Hapsburgs was only that of a military tool conditioned the emergence in the Krajina of a Serbian culture quick to take offense, intolerant, and bellicose.

13   Interview by Author (April 1993).

14   Interview by Author (April 1993).

15   On the indictment of the Sabor of Croatia by the dwellers of Vukovar see Božo Knežević, "KOS i HOS," *Vreme,* 2 December 1992, p. 8.

16   Many nineteen-year-old Yugoslav army recruits sincerely believed they were risking their lives on the Vukovar front for the liberation of Vukovar.

17   Miloš Vasić, "Strašna tajna Ovčare," *Vreme,* 2 November 1992, pp. 17–18.

18   On the desperate state of Vukovar a year later see M. Dražić et al. "Vukovar, godinu dana posle," *Borba,* 18 November 1922, pp. 14–15; Dragiša Drašković, "Strašna Zemlja smrti, Vukovar 12 meseci posle," *Borba,* 21–22 November 1992, p. xi; Stojan Cerović, "Vukovar, mrtvorodjenče, Korov i trava," *Vreme,* 23 November 1992, pp. 8–9; James Ridgeway and Jasminka Udovički, "War without End," *Village Voice,* 10 November 1992, p. 36.

19   Božo Knežević, "Kos i Hos," *Vreme,* 2 December 1991, p. 9.

20   Susan L. Woodward, *Balkan Tragedy: Chaos and Dissolution after the Cold War* (Washington, D.C.: Brookings Institution, 1995), pp. 182, 236. Woodward argues that the Croatian government thus attracted "world attention to the internationally protected city that even the total destruction of Vukovar could not obtain" (p. 236). *Ed.*

21   Most of the atrocities have remained insufficiently examined by experts. On the Gospić massacre, including the list of eighty names of those killed by the end of 1991 by Croatian forces, see "Tajna Katine jame," *Vreme*, 25 July 1994, p. 30.

22   Affected were the agriculturally rich regions at the foot of the Papuk and Psunj Mountains as well as the areas of Daruvar, Pakrac, and Slavonska Požega, as well as Bilogora, Bjelovar, and Grubišino Polje in Baranja.

23   Milenko Marić, "Suze zbog plajevine i izdaje," *Borba*, 17 December 1991, p. 5; Zoran Radovanović, "Duga, izdana kolona," *Borba*, 18 December 1991, p. 20; Milenko Marić, "Cijelo imanje u najlon kesi," *Borba*, 18 December 1991, p. 9; D. Bisenić, "Neko nas je, eto, izdao," *Borba*, 19 December 1991, p. 19.

24   Having recognized Croatia, the international community left Alija Izetbegović, president of Bosnia-Hercegovina, with only two possibilities: either to follow in the steps of Tudjman and seek independence or to join rump Yugoslavia. Both options were fatal.

25   The Zagreb-Split railway connection was cut in two; the Zagreb-Split highway was interrupted and thus unusable; Zadar and Šibenik, two large cities on the Adriatic, sporadically had their water supply cut off (Filip Švarm, "Tanka pontonska linija," *Vreme*, 26 July 1993, p. 12).

26   In the winter and early spring of 1992, Serbian positions were attacked on the line between Zadar, Biograd, and Benkovac. The hinterland of Zadar was under continued sporadic shelling by one side or another throughout 1992 and 1993. In January 1993 the Serbian village Islam Grčki was set on fire. Artillery exchanges continued in the Benkovac-Jasenica-Maslenica-Obrovac area. In March 1993 the villages in the hinterland of Skradin (Cista Mala, Cista Velika, Morpolača and Bratiskovci) were in the line of artillery fire. The distance between Serbian and Croatian entrenchments was often between 50 and 150 meters (see, for example, Z. Šaponjic and S. Radulović, "Čuvaj Glavu u Velikoj Glavi," *Borba*, 4 February 1993, p. 7).

27   Duška Anastasijević and Denisa Kostović, "Zločini, rezultat strategije," *Vreme*, 11 July 1994, p. 23.

28   B. Oprijan-Inić, "Suprotno medjunarodnom paktu o pravima," *Borba*, 18 February 1993, p. 11. A recruitment drive was also launched in Banja Luka.

29   On the U.S. Balkan policy preceding the summer of 1995 see Roger Cohen, "U.S. Cooling Ties to Croatia after Winking at Its Buildup," *New York Times*, 28 October 1995, pp. A1, A5. Cohen reports that the Croatian army was counseled by a company from Alexandria, Virginia, run by a group of retired U.S. officers and called Military Professional Resources Inc.—"the greatest corporate assemblage of military expertise in the world." With the United States looking the other way, Croatia was able to violate the arms embargo and purchase arms worth one billion dollars, including tanks and MI-24 armored assault helicopters.

Anthony Borden, the director of the London-based Institute for War and Peace Reporting, wrote: "The U.S. support of the action in Krajina beforehand and the open, if strained, justification of it afterward signal an explicit return to the use of a client state and power politics amidst a regional conflict" ("Zagreb Speaks," *Nation*, 28 August/4 September 1995, p. 188). *Ed.*

30 Filip Švarm, "Pogled iz tvrdjave," *Vreme*, 7 August 1995, pp. 9–10. Stephen Kinzer reported in July 1995 that since mid-June Serbian police squads had been rounding up Serbian refugees from both Croatia and Bosnia and delivering them to the front lines—"a real Gestapo-type operation with police surrounding cafés and restaurants, raiding dormitories, stopping busses and busting into homes in the middle of the night with guns and handcuffs" ("Yugoslavia Deports Refugee Serbs to Fight Rebels in Bosnia and Croatia," *New York Times*, 6 July 1995, p. A6).

31 Uroš Komlenović, "Slom i seoba," *Vreme*, 14 August 1995, pp. 4–7. An old immobile woman who lived alone in Knin watched helplessly from her bed as Croatian soldiers looted her apartment. The water, which they left running, flooded the apartment (Darko Barac, "Pljačka staraca," *Vreme*, 2 March 1996, p. 25).

32 Yves Heller, "How Croatia Reclaimed Its Accursed Land," *Guardian Weekly*, 31 March 1996, p. 14. Thirty-eight thousand houses were destroyed (B. Bekic, "Napučivanje Krajine," *Vreme*, 18 September 1995, p. 21).

33 Chris Hedges, "Nine Aged Serbs Found Slain in Croat Town," *New York Times*, 5 October 1995.

34 Immediately, Franjo Tudjman called Croatians in the diaspora to settle in the Krajina, but few were interested (see Borjan Vekić, "Napučivanje Knina," *Vreme*, 18 September 1995, pp. 18–22).

35 Raymond Bonner, "Croats Widen Threat to Rebel Serbs, and Diplomats Seem to Acquiesce," *New York Times*, 1 August 1995, p. A6. Forcing out two hundred thousand birds from a habitat—observed a Croatian priest—would have triggered a hearty protest from environmental and other groups. Yet when two hundred thousand Krajina Serbs were driven away in a single sweep from their homes in Croatia, few people in Europe or elsewhere seemed to notice (see Milorad Pupovac, "Srbin nije ptica" [Serb is not a bird], NIN, 5 July 1996, p. 21).

Bosnia and Hercegovina: The Second War
Jasminka Udovički and Ejub Štitkovac

◆

Since 1990, seemingly as embattled adversaries, Slobodan Milošević and Franjo Tudjman have joined in a peculiar strategic game that at one and the same time advanced their own and their opponent's objectives. The unacknowledged partnership of foes became even more impudent during the war in Bosnia-Hercegovina.[1]

In 1990, upon becoming president, Franjo Tudjman made a number of public statements in which he claimed the historical right of Croatia to a part of Bosnia, based on the borders of the Independent State of Croatia (NDH) that encompassed Bosnia.[2] Milošević was more cautious than Tudjman in making claims about partition. He grounded his anticipation of joining parts of Bosnia to Serbia on political, and biological, necessity. Serbs in Bosnia, he asserted, must never be cut off from the mother state — and that would happen if Bosnia sought independence. In March 1991, in Karadjordjevo — Tito's favorite hunting estate north of Belgrade and a place he favored for talks with his associates — Tudjman and Milošević worked out a map of Bosnia's partition.[3]

The Croatian war fed the ambitions of both Serbian and Croatian nationalist extremism, and it had the overwhelming effect of silencing nonnationalist forces that existed before the summer of 1991 in both states. The sea change in the political and moral landscape of the former Yugoslavia produced a critical mass of fear and ethnic intolerance that radically undermined the prospects for Bosnia's peaceful disengagement from Yugoslavia.

The international recognition of Croatia in January 1992 added to the complexity of the situation by forcing the Bosnian president, Alija Izetbegović, to choose between following in the path of secession or remaining in rump Yugoslavia. Izetbegović saw the choice as one between "leukemia and a brain tumor" but remained convinced well into the spring of

1992 that war in Bosnia was unlikely. He counted on the lack of will for war among the Serbian conscripts, many of whom had fled rather than be recruited for the Croatian war, and on the economic weakening of Serbia itself owing to its overextension.[4]

Other Bosnian leaders such as Adil Zulfikarpašić—the descendant of an old and distinguished Muslim family who lived in Switzerland after World War II—were much more cautious. Zulfikarpašić saw an independent Bosnia as a dangerous fiction. Despite his belief that in Bosnia "the roots of good neighborly relations run deep," Zulfikarpašić warned that if the war broke out, it would be a war "to destroy an entire nation and to empty the territory of its Muslims; it is not an exaggeration to say it would lead to their total extermination."[5] To avoid the catastrophe, Zulfikarpašić advocated great caution in seeking international recognition. He favored making an agreement with the Serbian leadership that would satisfy both sides.[6] The effects of Milošević's propaganda—successful in instilling in the Bosnian Serb population a genuine, haunting fear of being cast adrift from Serbia—must not be underestimated, Zulfikarpašić maintained.[7] To a common Serb on the street, the slogan "All Serbs in one state" suggested not that the Serbian regime had imperialist ambitions in Bosnia but that it sought to safeguard the future of Bosnian Serbs. Zulfikarpašić understood the psychological appeal of the call to Serbian unity, and the potential it had to mask the territorial designs of Belgrade. Unable to bring Alija Izetbegović to see things his way, Zulfikarpašić broke away from the Party for Democratic Action (SDA), where Alija Izetbegović held the majority, and formed the Muslim Bošnjak Organization (MBO) two months before the November 1990 Bosnian elections.[8]

Participating in the elections were forty-one miniparties and five larger ones. Two of the larger parties, Party of Democratic Change and Alliance of Reform Forces, led by the prime minister Ante Marković, represented the liberal wing of the former Communist elite, standing for Yugoslavism and multiethnicity. The other three large parties—the Muslim-led Party of Democratic Action (SDA), the Serbian Democratic Party (SDS), and the Croatian Democratic Union (HDZ)—were ethnically based and organized around nationalistic programs. The Serbian and the Croatian nationalist parties in particular had their own extremist wings, whose message was that the civil war in Bosnia was imminent.

This was pluralism, but it was not multiculturalism or democracy. Rather than promoting the emergence of free political will, the multitude of parties had a strong disorienting effect, which amounted to what Lidija Basta-Posavec called "repressive pluralism."[9] The chances for success of virulent electoral rhetoric of Serbian and Croatian extremist groups were greatly enhanced under such conditions. Heavily financed by the Serbian and Croatian regimes, these groups monopolized the interpretation of the political options and styled themselves as the only guarantors of "national interest" of their ethnic constituencies. The SDA, HDZ, and SDS won the elections, each within its own ethnic majority.[10]

Although hostile to each other, the three ethnically based parties functioned in reality as a powerful block against the pro-Yugoslav forces of the Reform Party, founded by the popular federal prime minister Ante Marković. "The Reformists," as the party was called, would have prevailed over any one of the nationalist parties in isolation, but the compounded effect of three nationalisms reduced Reformists in the second round of the elections to a negligible percent of the total vote.

After the elections, the SDA, SDS, and HDZ proclaimed that they would govern in partnership and in the interest of all under the presidency of Alija Izetbegović. Continued pressures from Serbia and Croatia, however, rendered a trilateral partnership virtually impossible. Party flags went up in the centers of towns and villages; party graffiti were painted on private homes and public buildings and loyal party cadre placed in municipal offices. The republic was being partitioned on a symbolic level long before the brutal process of its territorial partition took root.

Ethnic divisions were in flagrant contradiction with the ethnic composition of Bosnian municipalities, only 30 percent of which were ethnically homogeneous.[11] Islamic, Catholic, and Orthodox houses of worship faced each other on the squares of Bosnian towns.[12] In more recent times, and certainly in the secular post–World War II environment, services at the churches and mosques were attended mostly by the elderly people. A saying that was commonly heard in the Muslim community was: "There'll be time to go to mosque; wait till you get old."[13]

Contrary to many interpretations of pent-up ancient hatreds in Bosnia, the tightly knit multiethnic community disintegrated for the first time in World War II. The roots of the conflict rested not in a "historical predisposition" of the Bosnian population mix, but in the Nazi-inspired policies of Ante Pavelić's puppet regime, which controlled a good part of Bosnia.[14] There was no historical precedent for the 1990s war. It was the very threat of disintegration—expressed through the outcome of the elections and through the demand for secession by the Muslim and Croatian legislators on October 14, 1991—that unleashed the forces of war.[15]

The Bosnian-Serb legislators responded to the call for secession by walking out of the October 14, 1991, session in protest. On November 9 and 10, to seize the opportunity of consolidating the grip on the Bosnian Serbs, their leadership organized a plebiscite among the Bosnian Serb population on the issue of secession. Ill adapted to plebiscites that had no tradition in Tito's Yugoslavia, frightened by the ongoing war in Croatia, panic-stricken by the news of large-scale firing of Serbs in Muslim and Croatian regions of Bosnia (even though the same, in reverse, had taken place in the Serbian regions), and, finally, confused by Serbian propaganda of Alija Izetbegović's alleged fundamentalism, the Serbs in Bosnia overwhelmingly voted to remain in Yugoslavia.

Muslims and Croats charged that the plebiscite expressed the will of only one group in Bosnia, and not of all Bosnians. Responding to the charge, the Serbian leaders pointed to the analogy with the May 19, 1991, referendum carried out in Croatia.[16] The European Community considered the referendum valid, even though it reflected the will of only one group, the Croatian majority. The EC consequently used the referendum as a basis for granting Croatia's independence. Karadžić and others around him argued that the same rules had to apply in Bosnia and that the precedent validating the plebiscitary will of the Bosnian Serbs had been set.

Serbian leadership thus ushered in a dual basis of political legitimacy in post-1990 Yugoslavia. After the first precedent was set in Croatia, nationalist-plebiscitary populism was used repeatedly as an instrument of nationalist politics.[17] The international community not only failed to question the constitutional validity of plebiscitary populism in the former Yugoslavian context but also tied its own decisions to the outcomes of referenda and plebiscites. Having decided by the end of 1991 that there was no way to prevent the breakup of Yugoslavia, the Arbitration (Badinter) Commission selected December 24, 1991, as the deadline for any republic wishing to apply for international recognition of its independent status. But the commission at the same time ruled that the claim for independence would be considered valid only if a sufficient proportion of voters within each of the three ethnic communities supported secession.[18] Thus, the commission conditioned international recognition on the consensus of the majority within each of the three ethnic groups, not on the approval of a simple majority within the total population. This was consonant with the Bosnian constitution but played into the hands of Serbian nationalist extremists.[19]

Alija Izetbegović decided to ignore the outcome of the Serbian plebiscite and on December 24, 1991, applied to the European Community for recognition of Bosnian independence. The problem arose when Radovan Karadžić told the Bosnian Serbs to boycott the February 1992 referendum called by Izetbegović and required by the Badinter Commission. The Bosnian Serb population overwhelmingly boycotted the referendum, excluding themselves entirely from the voting process. Bosnian Muslims and Croats, together forming the simple majority, voiced their overwhelming support for secession. This satisfied the democratic criterion of majority vote but did not satisfy the criterion of the Badinter Commission.

Both the Badinter Commission and the European Community—which eventually acted in violation of the ruling of the Badinter Commission— were caught up in a conflict between the pragmatic and the democratic concerns underlying their policy. The commission's invitation to the republics to request international recognition was a landmark decision and a radical intervention into the Yugoslav crisis. As it turned out, the decision, considered pragmatic at the time, also had radical consequences, not least because the Badinter Commission left unaddressed the key issue of Bosnia's war and peace: the so-called Serbian question. What guarantees of their political status, their sovereignty, and their human rights were the Bosnian Serbs to expect after Bosnia's eventual secession from Yugoslavia? The commission failed to recognize the significance of this question, all the more urgent because ethnic tensions in Bosnia were gaining momentum by the day. By stipulating that the request for international recognition be supported by the majority within each ethnic group, the Badinter Commission tried to give its intervention a democratic form. By overriding the stipulation of the Badinter Commission and recognizing Bosnian independence on April 6, 1992, despite the overwhelming boycott of the referendum for independence by Bosnian Serbs—a full one-third of the Bosnian population—the EC made matters worse. Its recognition of Bosnia appeared to place the will of Bosnian Muslims and Croats above the will of the Bosnian Serbs. This had the unwanted effect of strengthening the hand of Radovan Karadžić by providing fodder to his claim that, then as in the past, the outside powers were bent against Serbian sovereignty. The crisis was now brought to a wholly new level. A full-scale war erupted in Bosnia immediately following the EC's recognition of Bosnia's independence.[20]

In mid-October 1991, Radovan Karadžić had warned the Croatian and Muslim members of the Bosnian parliament: "You have no way of breaking off from Yugoslavia. Serbs can prevent both Croats and Moslems from leaving. The path you are taking is the path that led Croatia to a hell, except the hell in Bosnia-Hercegovina will be one hundred times worse and will bring about the disappearance of the Muslim nation."[21] On January 9, 1992, Bosnian Serb representatives, insisting that the Bosnian government no longer represented them, abandoned the republic's parliament, proclaimed they considered Bosnian laws nonbinding, and declared their autonomy. Eight months earlier, on April 26, 1991, they had proclaimed the Municipal Community of Bosnian Krajina and chose the northwestern town of Banja Luka as its headquarters. By September 1991 the Serbian Autonomous Region of Hercegovina (SAO Hercegovina) was proclaimed in southeastern Bosnia, around the town of Trebinje.[22] A number of other autonomous regions sprang up thereafter in northwest Bosnia and around Mount Romanija. The self-proclaimed autonomous entities were not recognized de jure by the international community but were recognized de facto, through the involvement of Radovan Karadžić as legal interlocutor in all internationally sponsored peace talks.

The Belgrade antiwar independent weekly *Vreme* reported in October 1991 that the Bosnian Serb leadership had gone beyond simply declaring autonomy and had taken measures to organize armed units in every Serbian village and town in Bosnia.[23] The article included details on the origin of arms destined for the towns and villages and made it clear that the YPA was deeply involved in the operation. The arms flow had begun back in 1990 and continued in 1991, as a part of the secret operation that became known under the acronym RAM, whose prime protagonist was a certain Mihalj Kertes, a Hungarian by origin, later to become chief of the Serbian secret police. Kertes liked to say that he owed everything he had achieved in life to Slobodan Milošević and that he was ready to die for the man. Under Kertes's command, uncounted camouflaged trucks loaded with arms crossed from Serbia into Bosnia. Ante Marković, the prime minister of Yugoslavia at the time, had publicly revealed the RAM operation as early as September 1991.[24] His information came from a tapped telephone conversation between Slobodan Milošević and Radovan Karadžić, in which RAM, Greater Serbia, and the Yugoslav army had all been mentioned. Having come into possession of the tape, Marković, a Croat strongly committed to Yugoslavia, accused the Yugoslav army of having "placed itself directly in the service of one side" and requested the resignation of General Veljko Kadijević. Kadijević did not resign, but three months later, on December 20, 1991, Marković issued his own resignation. This resignation, in protest against the overwhelming use of the Yugoslav budget for military needs, failed to affect Milošević's hold on Serbia's public opinion. The organized buildup of arms and food reserves in Bosnian Serb towns and villages went on. Reporting in December on the Serbian mobilization for war in the town of Banja Luka, *Vreme* described Bosnia as rapidly becoming a vortex of quicksand.[25]

Gunrunning in Bosnia had been rampant almost a year before the war began. In downtown Sarajevo, in front of the Hotel Europa, petty thieves and smugglers offered pistols, small-caliber sniper rifles, Kalashnikovs, and bazookas.[26] In the more conservative heartland, the strategy was more elaborate. In a village populated by a Serbian majority, an arms dealer would gather a group of better-off men, warning them "in confidence" that he had information the Muslims of a neighboring village were preparing to attack. He would then offer arms for self-defense. The story would spread rapidly through the village. Not knowing what to believe, people would come to check out the sale. Seeing others buy, they would buy themselves; it seemed imprudent not to. Often, all arms would be gone in a day. The dealer would then move on to the neighboring, predominantly Muslim village and would repeat his story, this time about the Serbs preparing to attack. Many people were borrowing money or selling livestock to buy a gun.[27]

In parts of Bosnia where during World War II Muslims and non-Muslims had protected each other, a more brutal approach was necessary. In Bosanska Krupa, a town in the northwest Cazin region, a story was circulated in the summer of 1992 about a Serb, an owner of a dairy farm, who had found his wife murdered among the cows in his barn. Several cows had also been shot in the head. Beside his wife's body a piece of paper was left, signed by his neighbor. The neighbor was a Muslim, whose farm was just across the bridge over the Una River. Whether the signature was authentic or not, the Serb could not tell. In the past the two had never had reason to exchange written messages. The Serb never became fully convinced that his neighbor was the one who murdered his wife. But he could not be entirely sure, either, that he hadn't. News of the murder spread like wildfire through the Cazin region.[28] The murder achieved its purpose. Among the Serbs, who knew neither men, a belief gradually set in that Muslims could not be trusted.

The shooting and killing that started in Mostar as early as the fall of 1991, and in Bosanski Brod in early spring 1992, considerably worsened the already tense situation. The Croatian war had spread to these two strategically important Bosnian towns much before the Bosnian war itself had begun. Bosanski Brod, lying just across the Sava River from the Croatian town of Slavonski Brod, was the first town to be ruined in the Serbian-Croatian duels over Bosnia during March 1992.

In Mostar the quiet was broken by machine-gun bursts and bomb explosions between the Serbs and Croats even earlier, in the fall of 1991.[29] Mostar, the largest town in Hercegovina, was 35 percent Muslim, 34 percent Croatian, and 19 percent Serbian. Its misfortune was to be located on the intersection of Serbian and Croatian interests in southern Bosnia. During World War II the region had been a major Ustashe stronghold. In 1991 it once again became the home of the most extremist Croatian nationalists, who hoped Mostar would eventually become the capital of their own ministate, Herceg-Bosna. The Serbs insisted that Mostar remain within Yugoslavia, and for that purpose army reservists were sent to Mostar, to "maintain peace." The Muslims felt that the town belonged to an indivisible Bosnia.

In December 1991, Mostar's municipal government requested that the city be demilitarized. Two infantry garrisons, an air force base, a flight school, an army factory, and several thousand Serbian and Croatian reservists brought in from the outside remained entrenched. Machine-gun fire and explosions shook the city incessantly, turning Mostar into a hotbed of violence and fear.

The clashes between Serbs and Croats over Mostar were a bitter warning to the ordinary people that peace had become precarious. The analysis of the situation by common people was deeply conflicted. Intuitively, most Bosnians could not contemplate an all-out war in their republic. Yet the signs from Mostar and Bosanski Brod were alarming. There was also a great deal of clamor about the annexation to Serbia (in the course of

Bosnia's secession) of the SAO Krajinas, which had proclaimed autonomy. This was deeply worrisome and indicated to many people that they had better get ready for the worst.

Alija Izetbegović nevertheless seemed to remain unperturbed and failed to take any action. He adhered to the belief that isolated incidents of hostilities in Bosnia were possible but that war was unlikely. Yet the barricades in western Hercegovina and in Mostar were up. On March 1, 1992, violence erupted at a Serbian wedding party in the predominantly Muslim section of Sarajevo. Serbian flags were waved at the wedding, and a gunman, who remains unidentified, fired at the celebrating crowd, killing the groom's father and wounding a guest. Immediately, barricades—first Serbian, then Muslim—sprang up in Sarajevo and elsewhere in Bosnia. Yet the people guarding the barricades were still quite reluctant to engage in any real confrontation. Many pulled stockings over their heads to hide their identity from one another, believing the tension could not last. A mere couple of days later, the barricades came down. A joke went around Sarajevo: "You look better without the stocking, trust me!" one neighbor was telling another. A song called "A stocking on your face" was sung for weeks afterward as neighbors once again sat together in local cafés.[30]

On the barricades shots had been fired, leaving more than ten people dead across the republic. But the Sarajevans also found a way to speak out against everything the barricades represented. Throughout the city, neighborhood women set up counter-barricades, where they served Bosnian delicacies—*ćevapčići* (local grilled meatballs) and cheese pie. Cigarette peddlers raised their barricades, hawking their wares as available "on credit." And even at the official barricades, Sarajevo's love of burlesque prevailed. When a Muslim barricade received warning of an imminent Serbian attack and the Serbs failed to arrive, one of the masked barricade guards yelled suddenly, provoking a round of hearty laughter: "*Rajo*, I'm off to make sure nothing's happened to the guys!"[31]

As soon as the official barricades went down, tens of thousands took to the streets of Bosnia's towns shouting, "We want to live together." Similar demonstrations had already taken place in Sarajevo. In November 1991, an antiwar demonstration organized by workers in front of the parliament building in Sarajevo drew tens of thousands from all over Bosnia. The crowd of workers, high school and university students, young women and men, and many elderly people, carrying Tito's picture and "Brotherhood and Unity" banners, covered the large parliament square.

The Old Library in Sarajevo: February 1996. Photo by Maja Munk.
Courtesy of the photographer.

A miner from Tuzla, Izet Redžic, addressed the crowd. The workers of Bosnia-Hercegovina, he said, would not allow fratricidal war. "We won't let our sons die for the purposes of others. We are workers, not soldiers. My national identity is 'miner.'" Many people held banners saying "Yugo, We Love You!"[32]

This, and the antiwar demonstrations that shook Sarajevo during the last month before the siege, fed Izetbegović's belief that the destructive forces hovering over Bosnia could not prevail. Yet simultaneously, the Yugoslav army's presence in Bosnia had been greatly strengthened by a contingent transfer from the battlefields of Croatia following the January 1992 cease-fire. President Izetbegović visited none of the sites to investigate the alleged "military exercises" taking place throughout the republic.

Eight months earlier he had shown greater realism. In September 1991, he had brought to the attention of the Conference on Security and Cooperation in Europe (CSCE) the fact that 60 percent of Yugoslavia's military industry was located in Bosnia and that the larger part of the officer corps was stationed there. Izetbegović requested that the CSCE use its influence to aid in dismantling this military complex and to help start a retirement fund for the army officers, anxious at the prospect of being left without a job and income. The retirement fund, he explained, would help prevent the army officers from joining the Serbian side for fear of losing their jobs. The European conference, however, ignored the appeal, remaining blind to the rapidly mounting tensions.

An attempt to avert war was made on March 18, 1992, when the Portuguese EC mediator José Cutileiro called Moslem, Serbian, and Croatian representatives to Lisbon and presented them with a draft of the "Cutileiro peace plan" for Bosnia. The plan organized the republic into three territorial units, or cantons, and stipulated that the representatives of all three national groups were to partake in the power sharing. Croats and Serbs accepted the plan.[33] Yet Alija Izetbegović, who first said yes, changed his mind a week later and reneged on the agreement.[34] The Cutileiro plan was a last-ditch effort to prevent the worst. It was followed by the EC's recognition of Bosnia on April 6—the fifty-first anniversary of the day Belgrade was leveled by Hitler's bombardment.

Recognition had the effect of handing the Bosnian Serb leadership a pretext for war. The principle of self-determination underlying the EC's decision to recognize Bosnia was echoed by Radovan Karadžić, who claimed that foreign powers, in a familiar historical pattern, stood in the way of Serbian self-determination.[35] Karadžić argued that the international community was biased and that it applied the principle of self-determination selectively, thus capriciously. The argument convinced many Serbs in Serbia and in Bosnia, for whom self-determination had special historical significance, that going to war was just.

Radovan Karadžić thought he would win the war in six days. He had on his side not just Slobodan Milošević in Belgrade but the fully equipped YPA and the well-armed paramilitary formations, closely tied to the Belgrade government.[36] Yet Izetbegović seemed to believe that the Serbian leadership would be satisfied with the territories it had proclaimed autonomous without bloodshed, despite the fact that in the final days of 1991, trenches for multibarrel artillery aimed at Sarajevo were discovered on Crepoljsko and Bukovik, the two hills surrounding the city.[37] Five months later, the shelling of Sarajevo would begin from these hills. No system of defense existed and no person in the Izetbegović government was in charge of the defense of the capital in case of war. Immediately following the international recognition of Bosnia, Serbian General Ratko Mladić ordered the artillery to launch fire on the city from the hills, throwing Izetbegović's government into bitter disarray. Sarajevo was shelled relentlessly throughout the summer and fall of 1992 and beyond, in an effort to break its morale and thus destroy Bosnia as a viable entity.[38]

In the first phase of the war the Serbian offensive had two objectives in addition to reducing Sarajevo to ruin: one had to do with conquering the eighteen-mile-wide strip along the Serbian-Bosnian border, marked by the Drina River, and the other with consolidating Banja Luka as the proclaimed capital of Republika Srpska. On April 4, 1992, the Tigers — paramilitary units led by Željko Ražnjatović-Arkan, the person responsible for some of the worst atrocities in the Croatian war — swept from the north into Bijeljina, a town in the northeastern tip of Bosnia. A slaughter, before the war officially began, was necessary to mark the point of no return. Foreign reporters were allowed to film the Tigers kicking corpses and stepping on the skulls of their victims. The images showed Arkan's men outfitted in flattering fatigues, clean, high leather boots, and black caps covering their faces, with just slits for the eyes. The eastern strip, to be conquered in the following weeks and months, would include, after Bijeljina, the towns of Zvornik, Bratunac, Srebrenica, Žepa, Rogatica, Višegrad, Goražde, and Foča, as well as a number of smaller towns. From the outlying neighborhoods of Han Pjesak, a small town about twenty miles west of Srebrenica, all but two Muslim families fled. Sonja Pirić, a Muslim refugee, described the expulsions upon the arrival of her evacuation convoy in Belgrade on November 13, 1992:

A neighbor, a Serb, broke into the house early one morning, about three months ago. His son had been killed in Sarajevo, and our house was there, near the cemetery where his son was buried. He didn't speak a word, he just came and shot at our window. He then broke down the door, entered, and started shelling the furniture. Then he barged into our room. The two of us, Mother and I, with my little one, opened the window trying to jump out. Another man, waiting in the street, shot at me and the baby. I was lightly wounded. My little one, she was killed. We ran away, I was carrying her, I did not know she had been hit, killed. Mother remained in the window. She was hit by the one in the street. They were yelling at us to get out, that they were cleansing the place. Yes, that's what they said.[39]

Other towns, like Modriča, belonging to the northern corridor along the Sava River separating Bosnia from Croatia—changed hands several times. The towns were first assaulted by heavy artillery and aircraft; then, paramilitaries would sweep in. Modriča was leveled, and one of the casualties was its well-known Institute for the Rehabilitation of the Mentally Ill. The 240 patients were transported to a nearby village and put under tents. Only one woman doctor, of the former twenty-five, sixteen nurses, and one cook, remained with the patients. In late fall 1992 a reporter from *Borba* found the patients wandering barefoot in the rain, some naked to the waist. None of them knew which calendar year it was. Some were aware a war was being fought around them but had no idea who was fighting.[40]

In the proclaimed capital of the Serbian republic, Banja Luka, in northwestern Bosnia, expulsions of Muslims began as early as April 1992. Banja Luka was in the throes of suffering attacks from local criminals, militias, bands, and other types of groups emerging from the underground. Those elements formed the SOS (Serbian Defense Forces), whose members were fully armed and free to act according to personal whim.[41] The businesses of the well-known townspeople were attacked first. Bombs were thrown into the restaurants, coffee shops, eyewear stores, boutiques, and into courtyards and private homes. Armed bands were known to barge into a house a little after midnight, beat up the inhabitants, and take away everything of value. No official protection was available. Banja Luka, the former vibrant cultural center of western Bosnia, descended into a state of terror and anarchy.[42] On the streets, soldiers and paramilitaries were free to request to see a person's papers and to beat up anyone they chose. Muslims and Croats were pulled out of private cars and left on the street while their cars were driven away. On the Venecija Bridge people were ordered off their bicycles and watched as the bicycles were thrown into the Vrbas River without explanation. Those who lost their jobs and for lack of money had to peddle their home belongings often had their stands overturned and the wares kicked around and destroyed. A red van was known to cruise the Banja Luka streets, playing deafening music. People were captured at random, thrown into the van, and beaten, sometimes to death, with baseball bats. Serbian authorities claimed these were the acts of extremists who could not be controlled. Yet the terror was organized by the municipality, to force the Muslim and Croatian minority to leave. The transport of the forced exiles, who were allowed one plastic bag as "luggage" and whose empty houses were immediately taken over by the Serbian military, turned into a profitable business.[43]

The bombing, on May 5–6, 1993, of the Ferhadija Mosque (dating from 1574) and the Arnaudija Mosque (dating from 1594) added to the sense that life in Banja Luka was altogether impossible for the minorities. The minaret of the Ferhadija Mosque remained standing after the blast, but the order came for it to be blown up the next night "for security reasons." The Islamic community asked to be allowed to collect the remaining stones. Instead, the authorities sent two bulldozers to the site and took the rubble away.[44]

In the villages surrounding the town of Prijedor, about twenty miles from Banja Luka, no Muslim dreamed of staying past fall 1992. Serbian forces took over all power in the region on April 30, 1992. They used the TV repeater on Mount Kozara to spread incessant propaganda that the non-Serbian population wanted war and had organized against the Serbs. All communications in the municipality were cut off and all non-Serbs fired from their jobs. In May 1992 the region around the village of Kozarac, at the foot of Mount Kozara and seven miles east of Prijedor, was assaulted from all sides and most of its population killed. On May 30, the army drove its tanks through Prijedor. In July the villages on the left bank of the Sava River, which were filled with the Prijedor refugees, were subjected to a sustained artillery attack, set ablaze, and fully destroyed. Thousands were killed in the vicinity of their homes and the rest taken to the notorious Omarska or Keraterm concentration camps.[45] From there, hundreds were transferred to the Manjača and Trnopolje camps. The number of prisoners arriving every day was so great that one mass murder a day was necessary to make room for the newcomers.[46] The camps were discovered in the summer of 1992 and subsequently closed. On August 21, 1992, between 150 and 200 Muslims, just released from Trnopolje and driven away from the camp in a truck, were stopped in the vicinity of Vlašić village by a group of Bosnian Serb soldiers, led by Dragan Mrdja. The men were ordered to line up facing a ravine and shot in the back of the head.

Some were shot more than once as they fell. Afterward the campsite was turned into a refugee center. Thirty-five thousand women, men, and children from the region, who all knew about the massacre committed by Mrdja's men, chose the former camp to await resettlement rather than stay at their own homes, where they would be at the mercy of Serbian authorities. They all could see their homes, or the remnants of their homes, in the distance.[47]

Some Serbian civilians in the Bosnian villages tried to avoid conscription as best they could and to help their Muslim and Croatian neighbors, despite the jeopardy this brought on themselves and their families. In the town of Prijedor a Serb saved four Muslim families by driving them in his truck to his father's isolated farm, where the families remained, working the farm to feed themselves. When Prijedor fell, however, the Serb was forcefully conscripted into the armed forces—a common pattern dreaded by the local population. Conscription was often carried out under the threat of liquidation of the entire family. The new conscripts were usually placed in the front line and forced to prove themselves by killing "the enemy." The Serb who saved the Muslim families was forced to join a unit sent to Kozarac, where the infamous massacre of most of the Muslim population took place.[48]

Fearing for their lives, local Muslims sometimes joined the Serbian side, hoping, at least at the beginning of the war, that conscription guaranteed they would not be driven out. In Trebinje, a region in southeastern Hercegovina where Muslims and Serbs lived as friends until the end of 1992, a greater percentage of Muslim members of the community responded to the draft than did the Serbs. Nonetheless, in January 1993, the order went out for all Muslims to leave the town immediately. Alarmed, the Muslims sent a delegation to speak to the town council. They were told that official authorities had nothing to do with the order. Yet extremist groups from out of town were breaking into private houses unhindered, taking money and valuables away. Then the torching started. First to be set ablaze was the landmark Beg house that used to function as a museum-restaurant. The Mosque of Osman Pasha, situated within the old town walls, was next. When homes of the old and reputable Muslim families came under attack, the Muslim exodus became massive.[49] Open terror accomplished its objective of creating ethnically homogeneous territories by inciting panicked, collective departures.[50] The manifold instances of terror included public executions, torture, concentration camps, and rape, all conducted as a sort of a public blood sport.[51]

In Trebinje local bus owners made big money. For a one-way ticket to Denmark, Sweden, or Turkey, they charged DM 280 (close to U.S. $200). Those who could not afford the ticket had to seek shelter in an over-crowded refugee facility; within weeks or months they usually had to move to another equally precarious location. As a rule, refugees were allowed to carry only small hand-held bundles. Their homes and everything in them became the booty of irregular forces.[52]

In June 1992, a little over two months after the outbreak of war, the UN secretary general, Boutros Boutros-Ghali, received a report drawn up by the UN officials in Zagreb, stating that the Croats were increasingly confident because "they were now heavily armed," and charging that Croatia was using the international focus on the Serbian shelling of Sarajevo as a smoke screen to pursue its own aims in Bosnia.[53] Perceived as a victim of Serbian brutality in the 1991 war, and as a country where democratic elections had taken place, Croatia enjoyed special treatment in most of the U.S. mainstream press. In the first two years of the Bosnian war, the actions of the Croatian armed forces were covered only sporadically, thus obscuring the fact that in Bosnia two parallel wars against Bosnians were unfolding at the same time: one carried out by the Serbs, the other by the Croats.

In the 1990 elections, the HDZ won the majority of the Bosnian-Croatian vote, but soon afterward the HDZ split between the hard-liners, whose goal was partition and creation of a Croatian state, Herceg-Bosna, and the moderates, who favored the preservation of multiethnic Bosnia. Men loyal to the hard-line faction were assigned immediately after the elections to start building a military force. They enjoyed the political and financial support of Franjo Tudjman and the "Hercegovina lobby," the ultra-right Croatian émigrés. Tudjman replaced the elected HDZ leader, the moderate Stjepan Kljujić, with the ultranationalist Mate Boban, a former supermarket manager who had made a name for himself as a successful arms dealer and a proponent of Bosnian partition. With a large part of the funds funneled in by the Croatian emigrants from Canada, the United States, Latin America, Austria, and Germany, Mate Boban armed the HDZ forces for the coming conflagration.

In part, the import of weapons for the Croatian side was conducted as an offshoot of the smuggling route that Iran, assisted by Turkey, opened in 1992, to supply the Bosnian government. Of the total amount of weapons designated for Bosnia, Croatia kept about one-third. The supply route involved Saudi Arabia, Pakistan, Brunei, and Malaysia, as well as Hungary and Argentina.[54] A wide variety of weapons were supplied by Russia and its former satellites—Czechoslovakia, Poland, East Germany, and Hungary, the countries that after the Cold War found themselves with large military arsenals and little cash.[55]

On July 3, 1992, aware of his military superiority over the Bosnian government, Mate Boban proclaimed an independent republic of Herceg-Bosna, and soon after he integrated the ultranationalist units of the Croatian Defense League (HOS) into his own militia force. The European Community responded by threatening Croatia with sanctions. Franjo Tudjman claimed ignorance and placed the blame on Boban's adventurism. Meanwhile, Boban's influence, along with that of the HDZ hard-liners in Zagreb, grew. Boban's forces were aided by forces of the ultra-right wing of the Croatian Party of Right, led by Dobrosav Paraga.

Virtually unobserved, Boban expelled Serbs from the areas in western Hercegovina he considered "the heart of the Croatian nation." He eventually completely controlled the police, the schools, and the economy in the occupied territory, and liked to say that Muslims should be grateful to him for having liberated them from the Serbs.

His assaults on the Serbian civilians notwithstanding, Boban was in regular contact with Radovan Karadžić. On May 7, 1992, they met in Graz, Austria, and signed a document outlining the strategy for Bosnia's partition—the enduring objective of both sides. On July 3, Boban declared the independence of the Croatian Union of Herceg-Bosna.

The same month, the Agreement on Friendship and Cooperation was signed between the Croats and the Bosnian government, whose forces were poorly armed and in dire need of military support. Even earlier, there had been some cooperation between the Bosnian and Croatian forces, resulting, in the case of the region surrounding the town of Konjic, situated halfway between Sarajevo and Mostar, in the opening of the concentration camp in the Čelebić tunnel for the Bosnian Serb civilians. The treatment of the prisoners here mirrored that of the Serb-run camps Keraterm, Omarska, and Trnopolje.[56]

The Bosnian-Croatian Agreement on Friendship and Cooperation turned out, however, to be of little consequence for the situation on the ground. In the summer of 1992, the HVO used the artillery rented from the Serbian side to attack the forces of the Bosnian government. In 1993 Bosnian Croats paid 4 to 4.5 million German marks to the Serbs for equipment and munitions.[57] All along, Bosnian-Croatian leaders, together with an elaborate network of criminals, were running profitable deals with the Serbian government in Belgrade, supplying the Serbian army with fuel and holding meetings with General Major Momir Talić, the Serbian commander in Banja Luka, and Colonel Vladimir Arsić, the commander in Prijedor.[58] Ivan Zvonimir Čičak, president of the Croatian Helsinki Committee, stated in 1993 that Croatian-Moslem cooperation "never existed."[59]

The Agreement on Friendship and Cooperation between the Bosnian government and Croatia broke down by the end of October 1992, after which Croatia obstructed arms deliveries to Bosnia by taking a substantial cut for itself. At the beginning of 1993, Croatian and government forces were engaged in intense fighting in the area of Gornji Vakuf.[60] This marked the breakdown of the Vance-Owen Peace Plan, offered to the three warring sides in Geneva in January 1993.[61] The Croatians agreed initially to the plan because its map afforded them more territory than they had captured. The Izetbegović side objected to the projected weak role of the central government and to the three-way division of Bosnia. Radovan Karadžić saw the role of the central government as too strong and called the agreement "hell." It required the Serbs to relinquish control over much of the conquered territory and prevented the territorial linkage of Republika Srpska, as proclaimed in August the previous year. Slobodan Milošević, present in Geneva and weakened at home despite having won the rigged elections in Serbia in December 1992, pressured Radovan Karadžić to accept. Karadžić signed but said that the parliament of Republika Srpska had to ratify his signature. The parliament ratified the agreement by fifty-five to fifteen on January 20, 1993, the day of Bill Clinton's inauguration. But before the details of the plan could be fully worked out in Geneva, the plan collapsed because of the Croatian-Bosnian confrontation around Gornji Vakuf, followed in early spring by the heavy assault of Serbian artillery on Srebrenica.[62]

In April a full-scale war between Croatian and Bosnian troops broke out northwest and south of Sarajevo and continued through May. In Vitez and Mostar masked Croats went house by house killing Muslims. This paral-

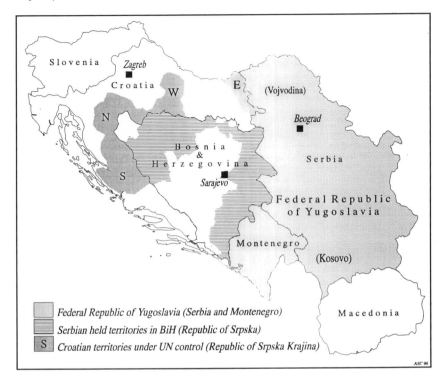

Territorial divisions in ex-Yugoslavia: 1992.
Courtesy of *Vreme* news agency.

leled the stepped-up offensive by the Serbs on the eastern Bosnian enclave of Goražde. The Bosnian government then turned to Slovenia, spending over thirty-six million German marks to purchase, at exorbitant prices, the leftover supplies of YPA arms and war technology Slovenia as a go-between had obtained on the black market from the former Warsaw Pact countries.[63]

In late spring 1993 the pressure to accept the Vance-Owen plan was renewed. This version of the plan allotted Bosnian Croats a share of territory equal to that allotted to the Bosnian government, although the Croatian population in Bosnia was two and a half times smaller than the Muslim population. Once again, Croats were to be granted not only the territory they had occupied by force but also additional territory where Muslims were in the majority. Predictably, the Croatian representatives signed the plan immediately and without complaint, but simultaneously they were the first to continue the war in order to win on the ground what the plan granted them on paper.[64]

The Vance-Owen plan met total failure, however, when on May 5 the Bosnian Serb parliament rejected it in defiance of the strong words Milošević delivered on Mount Jahorina, where he traveled to urge Radovan Karadžić to accept.[65] According to this plan, the Serbs were required to give back a greater portion of the land they had occupied. The Serbian leaders claimed the plan gave them pastures and awarded the other two parties the natural resources, industrial regions, and electrical plants. After voting no, the Bosnian Serb parliament told its guests—Serbian president Slobodan Milošević, president of rump Yugoslavia Dobrica Ćosić, and president of Montenegro Momir Bulatović—they had better

Territorial divisions in Bosnia: 1993.
Courtesy of *Vreme* news agency.

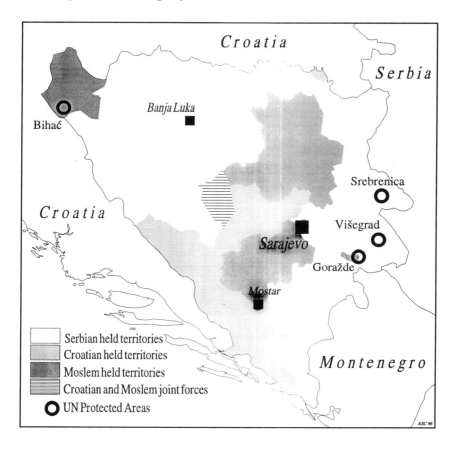

take a good breath of Jahorina mountain air, because it was most likely the last time they would be allowed on Bosnian territory.[66]

In fall 1993, Croatian forces were continuing their heavy bombardment (which they had started in May) of Mostar, the town they considered the capital of Hercegovina, and had divided the city along the Neretva River into the western, Croatian, part, and the eastern, Muslim, part. The town's old Turkish quarter, on the left bank of the Neretva, with its seventeen historic mosques, was obliterated in the Serbian siege at the beginning of the war and in the Croatian siege that followed. In November 1993 the HVO, openly displaying symbols from the Ustashe era, completed the months-long demolition of the Old Bridge (Stari Most), thus consolidating on a symbolic level the partition of the city. The bridge was commonly considered the most handsome Ottoman structure in the Balkan region. More than that, however, the bridge was perceived by most Bosnians as an emblem of a diverse community of faiths and ethnicity.

In August 1994 a makeshift bridge was constructed to replace the Old Bridge. In late July 1994 an old crane was hauled in from somewhere to test the waters of the Neretva and establish if the pieces of the Old Bridge had sunk deep enough into the riverbed to allow for a risk-free dive from the improvised structure that replaced Stari Most. Amid the ruins, preparations for the diving contest from the bridge drew a cheering crowd.[67] The hope was that the situation in Mostar would be normalized.

Overt hostilities between Croats and the Bosnian government had ended following the February–March 1994 cease-fire negotiations in Washington and the March 18 signing of the loose Bosnian-Croatian federation.[68] Among the hard-liners in Hercegovina the proclamation of the federation came close to provoking an armed rebellion, even though among others it raised hopes that eventually Herceg-Bosna would be united with Croatia.[69] To prod the process, Herceg-Bosna adopted the new Croatian currency, the kuna. Trying to appease the hard-liners even further, Franjo Tudjman promoted to the rank of general the former Croatian army commander Slobodan Praljak, who was responsible for the final destruction of Mostar's Old Bridge.

The federation, however tenuous, marked the cessation of hostilities between the two sides, but in its first year it turned out to function primarily as an alternative to the lifting of the arms embargo.[70] In the early summer of 1994 the Bosnian general Mehmed Aligić told the NATO commander for southern Europe, Sir Michael Rose, that he did not see the federation as a step toward peace but as a tool for more successful war operations.[71] Croatian forces refused to aid the Bosnian government on the battlefield, but the influx of arms into Bosnia intensified in proportion to the organization and training of the highly motivated Bosnian troops. This emboldened Alija Izetbegović to pursue winning back the land militarily.[72]

In the summer of 1994, the Contact Group (made up of the representatives of the United States, Great Britain, France, Germany, and Russia) pressed for a peaceful solution, and Slobodan Milošević—who wanted the sanctions against Serbia lifted—pledged to seal the borders along the Drina River and cut off the lifeline between Serbia and Republika Srpska. Nevertheless, in August and September 1994 the Serbs conducted another wave of ethnic cleansing in Bijeljina, Rogatica, and Banja Luka and cut off the supply routes to the safe havens of Srebrenica, Žepa, and Goražde, aiming to starve the local population.[73]

Despite these advances, however, in the early summer of 1994 the significant weakening of the Serbian forces was already evident. Not only were fuel and parts in short supply, but the morale of the infantry had dropped precipitously, and the will of the draft-age refugees to join the troops was at an all-time low. In Herceg Novi, the Montenegrin town on the Adriatic coast, for example, out of eight hundred and fifty draft-age refugees, only two reported to be drafted.[74] The military police of Republika Srpska resorted to catching people late at night at home, ordering them into vehicles parked in front of the house, and forcing them to sign that they were joining the armed forces voluntarily. Those who refused to put on the uniform were beaten, called deserters, and sent to the trenches.[75] The shortage of manpower was both an index of the lack of will to fight among the population at large and a sign that Republika Srpska was holding a much vaster territory than it was able to defend and control.

The summer of 1994 signaled a turning point in the war, marked by a series of military successes of the Bosnian army. The Serbian forces were also hard hit by the Belgrade blockade along the border on the Drina River. In August the Bosnian Fifth Corps recaptured the strategically crucial area of the Bihać pocket from the forces of the renegade Bošnjak businessman and politician Fikret Abdić, forcing thirty thousand of his supporters, all Bošnjaks, out of the region.[76] From there, the Bosnian offensive spread to the Grabež plateau, expelling ten thousand Serbs. Together with the Croatian troops, Bosnian forces captured the town of Kupres in central

Bosnia, forcing the Bosnian Serbs to flee, abandoning some tanks and artillery.

Aware that he must expect further assaults on the part of the Bosnian-Croatian Federation and that Republika Srpska was likely to suffer added losses, General Ratko Mladić mobilized his forces in July 1995 to secure what had been the paramount war aim of the Serbian side from the beginning—the continuous thirty-kilometer-wide band of territory along the western bank of the Drina River, including the safe havens of Srebrenica, Žepa, and Goražde.[77] On July 6, Mladić's forces started their advance toward Srebrenica, stopping on July 11, two kilometers from the center. The Bosnian troops withdrew from the town, abandoning the civilians. The civilians then divided into two large groups. One tried to escape into the Dutch battalion base in Potočari. The peacekeepers in Potočari, however, made it plain they could not protect the civilians.[78] Instead, on July 13, they were evacuated from the base on buses overseen by Bosnian-Serb authorities. General Ratko Mladić arrived in Potočari on July 12 with a TV crew and promised the Dutch representatives that the civilians would be treated fairly but immediately ordered all males above sixteen years of age to be separated from their families and taken to Bratunac, and from there to Karakaj. There a massacre took place.

During the night of July 11–12, the other group of about fifteen thousand, including thirty-five hundred Bosnian army troops, tried to escape toward Tuzla through the woods, across rivers and minefields, carrying small children and the old and feeble. The column was ambushed in Bulje and scores of people were killed. The group then splintered into two. One group, mainly soldiers, reached Tuzla safely. The other encountered a number of ambushes. Some people surrendered, assured by the Serbian authorities that nothing would happen to them. They were liquidated on the spot.[79]

The UN Security Council issued a resolution requesting the immediate withdrawal of the Serbian forces from Srebrenica. But by that time the population of the town, to the last person, had been driven away, and the very concept of a safe haven had collapsed. On July 13, 1995, Serbian forces turned their artillery on Žepa and captured it on July 25. The fate of Goražde hung in the balance.

At 2 A.M. on August 30, 1995, NATO launched the bombing of Serbian artillery posts, antiaircraft positions, ammunition depots, and arms factories

In Sarajevo, boys playing war: February 1996.
Photo by Maja Munk. Courtesy of the photographer.

around Goražde, Sarajevo, Tuzla, and Mostar.[80] The command and communication capacity of the Bosnian-Serb forces was decimated, forcing
Mladić to abandon the plan to capture Goražde and precipitating overwhelming losses of Serbian territory to the Bosnian and HVO forces in the
coming months.

In mid-September, Serbs lost a wide section in western Bosnia along
a major highway running between Bihać and Donji Vakuf. Fifty thousand Serbian civilians, in a forty-four-mile-long line of tractors and horse-
pulled carts, flooded the roads. To the south, Drvar and Šipovo, the towns
that had always had an overwhelming Serbian majority, fell to the Croats.
The Serbs also lost Jajce, Bosanski Petrovac, Mrkonjić Grad, and in central
Bosnia many strategic points on Mount Ozren.[81] By the end of September
the map of Bosnia was beginning to change radically.[82]

In October 1995, the Bosnian army captured 150 square miles of land, including the towns of Sanski Most, west of Banja Luka. Only a few weeks earlier, on September 21, in this same region, arriving in buses with Vukovar license plates, the paramilitary troops of Željko Ražnjatović-Arkan conducted one of their most brutal ethnic cleansing operations. In some of the villages, most of the male population was missing. In October, however, fortunes were reversed. The Bosnian army advanced to a position twelve kilometers away from Banja Luka, driving fifty thousand Serbs out of the villages surrounding the Prijedor region. Tens of thousands in crowded private cars, on tractors, horse-drawn carts, and trucks, crowded the roads to Banja Luka and the Serb-held town of Omarska. The abandoned Serbian villages were pillaged and houses left burning for days. Republika Srpska lost on the ground the territories it had refused to grant the Bosnian government around the negotiating table. Radovan Karadžić and Ratko Mladić now needed a peace plan to be able to keep what was left.

The peace plan preparations coincided with the takeover of Serb-held territories. After months of shuttle diplomacy, Richard Holbrooke, the U.S. secretary of state, convened the representatives of the three sides in Dayton, Ohio, for final negotiations on a peace deal. As indicted war criminals, Radovan Karadžić and Ratko Mladić were banned from the talks. Heading the Serbian delegation was Slobodan Milošević, and the Croatian delegation, Franjo Tudjman. In Dayton, computer-generated, virtual-reality maps of Bosnia, projected floor to ceiling, allowed for simulated flights along the cease-fire line 650 miles long.

The peace accord was signed on November 22, 1995.[83] It brought an end to the fighting but suffered from a series of built-in contradictions. The solution offered for the future political map of Bosnia remained equivocal. Bosnia was defined as a state made up of two "entities," the Bosnian-Croatian Federation (receiving 51 percent of territory) and Republika Srpska (receiving 49 percent).[84] By giving de facto recognition to Republika Srpska, the agreement legitimated the formation of "ethnic territories," even though it proclaimed democracy. It required the three sides to endorse the repatriation of refugees as the cornerstone of peace but provided no specific program or strategy for repatriation and outlined no measures to be taken in cases of the obstruction of repatriation. War criminals were to be prosecuted by the war crimes tribunal in the Hague, but no strategies for capturing even the most notorious among them were

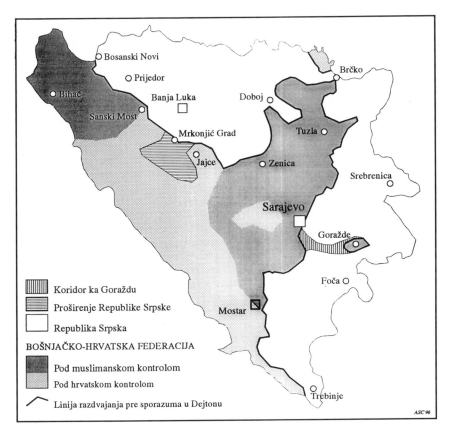

Pre- and post-Dayton map of Bosnia: 1995.
Courtesy of *Vreme* news agency.

in place. Peace was promised, but a pledge was also given to outfit the Bosnian army for more war. Free elections, to take place in September 1996, were envisioned as a mechanism for ousting the extremists, but the agreement failed to acknowledge that the time to prepare the conditions for free elections was too limited, and the period preceding the elections too volatile for the climate favorable for free elections to take hold. Above all, the Dayton talks addressed those who had brought about the war and failed to involve in the process any of the moderate forces standing for multiethnicity and democracy. These forces, active throughout the war but marginalized by the extremists on all three sides, remained anonymous beyond the local confines, lacking visibility and the legitimacy necessary for the September elections.

Sarajevo was to remain a multiethnic city, and its outskirts were to revert to the Bosnian government by March 19, 1996. The process of reunification of Sarajevo started in the suburb of Vogošća in the third week of February. Had there not been an intentional spread of hysteria among the Serbian population in the outskirts—orchestrated by the Bosnian-Serb Resettlement Force by dictate of Radovan Karadžić, for whom the loss of Sarajevo meant the collapse of his entire project—reunification would have taken place much less dramatically.[85]

To be successful, reunification required careful planning on the part of the UN and NATO. The paramount task was to create a sense of security among the local population. Only a determined show of the intention to safeguard the civilians could have altered the perception among many Serbian inhabitants that the UN never protected Serbs during this war, and that to have expected anything different now would have been an illusion. Instead of organizing to safeguard a smooth transition, the UN and NATO officials corroborated the perception that Serbs could expect no support. Peter Fitzgerald, chief of the UN operation to monitor the transition, stated openly that, indeed, "*Nobody* can guarantee people's safety here."[86] Not only was the deployment of the international police in the suburbs inadequate, but the UN and NATO officials failed to even put sufficient pressure on Alija Izetbegović to make good on his multiethnic rhetoric by delivering a timely, sincere pledge that the safety of the Serbian population would be ensured.[87]

All this played into the hands of the Pale campaign.[88] In addition to the authorities' constant television barrage, gangs of Serbian toughs were sent to the outskirts in defiance of NATO forces, to openly light fires in the apartment buildings, loot shops, shoot from their weapons, threaten, and even murder those who made no preparations to leave.[89] By the March 19 deadline, in an atmosphere of chaos, burning fires, and widespread vandalism, sixty thousand Serbs left Sarajevo, taking with them into homelessness not only windows, doors, firewood, bathtubs, water heaters, and electrical appliances, but also their dead.[90]

Mostar, whose integration was considered as important for peace as that of Sarajevo, held its elections as scheduled, in the beginning of July 1996; it resulted in a split vote between the Croatian and Bosnian nationalists. Regardless of the outcome, however, the leadership of Herceg-Bosna, stationed in Mostar, had already carved out a separate state, in defiance of the Dayton stipulation that Herceg-Bosna was to dissolve by January 1996. That state has become the extension of Croatia into the heart of Bosnia. Mostar and the rest of Herceg-Bosna use Croatian currency, car plates, identity cards, and even postage stamps. In 1996, the vice president of Herceg-Bosna, was Pero Marković, someone who in the summer of 1993 planned and organized the incarceration of thousands of Muslim men in underground tunnels near Mostar. His administration, which until the summer of 1996 had prevented the return of a single Muslim family to western Mostar, worked hand in hand with the Mostar mafia, which controls the town's political and economic life and was responsible for twenty killings in the first four months of 1996.[91] The presence of the UN and NATO has done little to control the Mostar HDZ.

Bosnia tested the practical utility of the international law of war and humanitarian law: the Convention on the Prevention and Punishment of the Crime of Genocide of 1948, the Nuremberg Principles, the Geneva Conventions and Additional Protocols, and the Helsinki Accords.[92] However significant these documents may be on the declarative level, they have had scant effect, from the legal standpoint, on the situation on the ground. The principles outlined in the documents served better as a foundation for moral indictments of the war and its protagonists than as a basis for building an applicable, effective policy for curbing the atrocities, protecting the victims, and preventing the continuous escalation of the war.

At the root of the impotence of the international law of war lies its ineffectualness in compelling the international community to step beyond the threshold of damage control. The international organizations, including NATO, have either engaged in a hygienic action of providing humanitarian help or in maintaining the cease-fire lines. However important humanitarian help has been, and however vital the maintenance of cease-fire lines, in the long run such actions had little strategic significance. Practicing engagement but noninvolvement, international organizations functioned satisfactorily as witnesses, not as agents to prevent mass-scale war crimes, even when they were happening in the very presence of the UN monitors, as was the case with Srebrenica. Rather than honoring the principles of international humanitarian law as the overriding norms for action, great powers allowed alternative interests to take precedence and shape events. Probably the only effective measure in the face of a humanitarian catastrophe of this magnitude would have been the establishing of a protectorate over Bosnia and Hercegovina, not in 1996 or even in 1993, but in February or March of 1992 at the latest. The war in Croatia offered

Parents tending a grave of their son in Tuzla cemetery, Bosnia: September 1995. Photo by Maja Munk. Courtesy of the photographer.

a preview of what was to follow in an environment infinitely more complex and volatile than that of Croatia. The assumption of "ancient ethnic hatreds" as the key factor, however, served to dampen the urgency of the humanitarian conventions, to project this war as an atypical case to which the conventions could not be effectively applied, and to absolve the international community of its duty according to the conventions. Moral indictments, however strong at times, were compromised by inaction.

NOTES

1   For reasons of brevity referred to from here on as Bosnia.

2   In June 1990 Bosnian authorities strongly protested the statement Tudjman gave to the German magazine *Der Spiegel,* to the effect that "one does not have to be

a historian to recognize that Bosnia makes a geopolitical unit with Croatia" (cited in "Predsjedništvo RKSSRN BiH, Odbijamo svako tutorstvo," *Borba*, 22 June 1990, p. 6). On the efforts in Croatia to build the NDH episode into the history of Croatian statehood and present it as a period of continuity and revival of the statehood, see Dušan Janjić, "Bosna i Hercegovina—otvorena pitanja državno-političkog identiteta multietničke i multikonfesionalne zajednice," in *Bosna i Hercegovina izmedju rata i mira*, ed. Dušan Janjić and Paul Shoup (Beograd: Dom Omladine, 1992), p. 26.

3   Ivan Zvonimir Čičak, the president of the Croatian Helsinki Committee, stated in an interview for *Borba* (30 June 1993, p. 11) that the map of partition was given to the Zagreb daily *Globus* by Tudjman's own adviser, Mr. Lerotic, himself a participant in the Committee for the Division of Bosnia.

In an interview in March 1996, Čičak argued that a tape of the Karadjordjevo talks existed, and that the person who taped the talks had been found dead on the bank of the Danube River in Belgrade. The reason cited for the death was suicide (*Naša Borba*, 31 March 1996, p. viii).

Susan Woodward suggests that the talks between Milošević and Tudjman on the partition of Bosnia-Hercegovina started much before Karadjordjevo, perhaps as early as July 1990 (*Balkan Tragedy: Chaos and Dissolution after the Cold War* [Washington, D.C.: Brookings Institution, 1995], pp. 172, 463).

4   Borisav Jović, Yugoslav president at the time, says the following in his diaries about the catastrophic results of conscription efforts: "Peace negotiations and war preparations are two parallel processes. But for both, conscription is key. We wanted about five thousand conscripts to begin with. The response was terrible: only 25 percent. That is very worrisome. It is not clear that the situation would be any different should the war erupt. . . . In eastern Slavonia Vojvodina brigades fled from the scene" (*Poslednji Dani SFRJ* [Beograd: Politika, 1995], pp. 385, 386).

In the fall of 1991 draft-age men emigrated or went into hiding in overwhelming numbers. The definite count has not been established; estimates vary between 150,000 and 200,000 (see Aleksandar Ćirić, "Svi smo mi dobrovoljci," *Vreme*, 31 May 1993, pp. 20–21).

5   Cited in Nadežda Gaće, "Velika Srbija na mala vrata," *Vreme*, 27 November 1991, p. 27.

6   On behalf of Alija Izetbegović, Adil Zulfikarpašić and Muhamed Filipović met in June 1991 with Radovan Karadžić, Nikola Koljević, and Momčilo Krajišnik and reached an agreement regarding the status of Bosnia. Bosnia would remain in a Yugoslav confederation but was to be sovereign and undivided, encompassing three constitutive nations of Muslims, Serbs, and Croats; the area of Sandžak in Serbia was to receive cultural and administrative autonomy; the Croatian and the Bosnian Krajinas were to abandon the idea of unification. Adil Zulfikarpašić went to Belgrade to get the approval of Slobodan Milošević on the plan. Milošević consented and also promised to give Bosnia 60 percent of Sandžak. Alija Izetbegović, who initially greeted the agreement with enthusiasm, subsequently changed his mind and abandoned it (*Okovana Bosna: Razgovor/Adil Zulfikarpašić, Vlado Gotovac, Mika Tripalo, Ivo Banac*, ed. Vlado Pavlinić [Zurich: Bošnjački Institut, 1995], pp. 80–102).

7   "What matters is not only the facts," Zulfikarpašić claimed, "but also the feeling

among the people" (cited in Nadežda Gaće, "Osjećao sam da mržnja buja," *Borba*, 8–9 August 1992, p. xiv).

8 Zulfikarpašić considered Izetbegović unqualified to lead Bosnia at the time of its deepest crisis (Gaće, p. xiv). In 1991 Zulfikarpašić accused Izetbegović of passively allowing the Bosnian Serbs to partition Bosnia even before the war broke out, by forming their own Krajina republic after the referendum of November 9–10, 1991.

9 "Ustavna demokratija i nedemokratska konstitucija društva," in *Raspad Jugoslavije produžetak ili kraj agonije*, ed. Radmila Nakarada, Lidija Basta-Posavec, and Slobodan Samardžić (Beograd: Institut za Evropske Studije, 1991), p. 110. Basta-Posavec argues that repressive pluralism had its origins in the political culture of the Titoist period, which failed to foster an independent body politic.

10 Susan Woodward argues that elections in Croatia, Bosnia, and Serbia alike did not represent a genuine opportunity for the common person to express a true political identity; the time for new political identities to be formed was too short (pp. 123–24).

11 The ethnic makeup of Bosnia's 4.5 million people made the region a powder keg: 43.7 percent of its population was Muslim, 31.4 percent Serbian, and 17.3 percent Croatian. Slightly over 5 percent declared themselves to be Yugoslavs (see Slobodan Inić, "Razbijeno Ogledalo—Jugoslavija u Bosni i Hercegovini," in Nakarada, Basta-Posavec, and Samardžić, p. 121).

One-fourth of all marriages in Bosnia-Hercegovina involved people of different nationalities. A striking commentary on this fact was transmitted to Jasminka Udovički by Salim Kovačević, a Muslim refugee from the small Bosnian village of Kotorsko. Mr. Kovačević was once asked by a Western reporter if ethnic hatreds in Bosnia were old and deep. According to Mr. Kovačević, he said: "Let me ask you something first: Do you love your wife?" The reporter nodded yes and Mr. Kovačević responded: "And why do you suppose we in Bosnia marry each other? Couldn't be because we hate each other, could it? Have you ever heard of anyone marrying out of hatred? We aren't that different from you, you know."

With his Serbian friend, an expert in civil engineering, Kovačević had developed in the early spring of 1992 a detailed rescue plan involving train and truck transportation—in the hypothetical case of an armed attack—for the thousand or so inhabitants of his village. Two alternative scenarios were worked out: the attack by the Serbs, to the east, and by the Croats, to the west. When in fall 1992 the village was attacked by the Serbs, all its inhabitants, short of five, were rescued according to the plan. Kovačević was seriously wounded during the evacuation and had to undergo eleven operations on his leg (interview of Salim Kovačević by Jasminka Udovički, April 1993).

12 Dušan Janjić cites a very low score for "ethnic distance" among Bosnians in a 1991 survey. Only 11.87 percent agreed that "nationality is a very important or a generally important criterion for friendship." An overwhelming 72.36 percent thought that "those are not important characteristics of a person." The responses changed in regard to marriage. Only 8.18 percent of those who had declared themselves to be Yugoslavs thought that nationality was important in marriage. Among other ethnic groups the percentage of those who thought ethnicity was a very important cri-

terion in choosing a marriage partner was lowest among the Serbs: 25.29 percent; among Croats it was 39.03 percent, and among Muslims 42.66 percent (Janjić, p. 19).

13   Interview of Salim Kovačević by Udovički. The issue was not religious repression: more often than not, being a Muslim implied ethnicity, not religious affiliation.

14   Old hatreds are cited as the underlying causes of the war even by some knowledge-able analysts. See, for example, Leonard Cohen, *Broken Bonds: The Disintegration of Yugoslavia* (Boulder, Colo.: Westview Press, 1993), p. 238.

15   Robert J. Donia and John V. A. Fine insist that the "current Bosnian crisis is, in the context of Bosnian history, an *historical aberration,* albeit with a single important historical precedent: the inter ethnic slaughter of the World War II era" (*Bosnia and Hercegovina: A Tradition Betrayed* [New York: Columbia University Press, 1994], p. 220). Stevan K. Pavlowitch has claimed (talking about Serbs and Croats, but the same can be applied to all three ethnic groups) that "because of the way they were intermixed and related, those among them who want them separated irreparably must commit irreparable crimes" ("Who Is Balkanizing Whom? The Misunderstanding between the Debris of Yugoslavia and an Unprepared West," *Daedalus:* 123, no. 2 [spring 1994], p. 208).

16   The referendum issue had to do with secession. Over 94 percent voted for "a sovereign and independent country." Serbian-controlled SAO Krajina boycotted the referendum (Nakarada, Basta-Posavec, and Samardžić, p. 140).

17   On July 1–2, 1990, a referendum was held in Serbia to, first, adopt the new constitution and then hold the elections. On March 31, 1991, a referendum was held in Borovo Selo on joining Slavonia, Baranja, and Western Srem to Serbia. In March 1992 Montenegro held a referendum about forming a common state with Serbia. On May 12, 1991, SAO Krajina held a referendum on its annexation to Serbia. On June 20, 1993, Republika Srpska Krajina held a referendum on its merger with Republika Srpska (in Croatia) and the possibility of a merger with "other Serbian states."

18   The committee was named after Robert Badinter, who headed it, and included the presidents of the constitutional courts of five Western European countries. Donia and Fine state that the committee "clearly felt that the EC should not recognize Bosnia as an independent state without the concurrence of the Bosnian Serbs" (p. 232). They also point out that "the EC failed to recognize the importance of negotiation and compromise in multiethnic Bosnia, where no nationality constituted a majority. . . . The referendum for recognition was inherently destabilizing, for it led the Bosnian Serbs to accelerate their campaign to avoid inclusion in an independent Bosnian republic" (p. 234).

19   The question left unexamined was whether, in a situation of a pending armed conflict and undemocratic voting conditions, a simple majority vote of the total population, or the majority vote within separate social groups, offered a more democratic solution. It remains an open question whether the democratic principle, defined in terms of a simple majority vote, should be considered the overriding principle in situations of imminent all-out war. (We are grateful to Sabrina Ramet for drawing our attention to the complexities of this issue.)

20   The question of the status of the Serbian minority after secession was the issue

that decided whether there would be war or peace in Bosnia, just as in Croatia. In Bosnia, moreover, the percentage of Serbs in the total population was almost two and a half times greater than in Croatia.

21 Roksanda Ninčić et al., "Drina bez Ćuprije," *Vreme*, 21 October 1991, p. 20.

22 It served as a launching terrain for the military operations during the Croatian war in Dubrovnik.

23 Ninčić et al., p. 21.

24 *Vreme* reported on the existence of RAM immediately. "Zbrisaće nas sa kugle zemaljske," 23 September 1991, pp. 5–12.

25 Ninčić et al., p. 24. Donia and Fine argue that by the time the January 1992 cease-fire in Croatia was signed, the YPA was already "poised to seize as much of the Bosnian countryside as possible" (p. 229).

26 Zehrudin Isaković, "Rovovi u duši," *Vreme*, 16 December 1991, pp. 24–25. Zehrudin Isaković also argues that all three sides had been arming, and that even some respectable members of the presidency of the Bosnian republic, parliament, and party headquarters functioned as "executive directors of the enterprises in the newly established economic sector—arms smuggling" (p. 24).

27 Personally witnessed by Ejub Štitkovac.

28 Interview of Zijad Musić, from Bosanska Krupa, who lost his leg in the Cazin region fighting with the Bosnian army, by Jasminka Udovički (March 1993).

29 Dating from Turkish times, Mostar was famous for its picturesque center and for its Old Bridge, completed in 1566 by Hajrudin, a contemporary of the great Ottoman architect Sinan (himself of Christian Balkan origin).

Up until 1990 Mostar was a favored site of the unofficial local summer "Olympics." The challenge was diving from the Old Bridge's eighty-foot-high peak into the green Neretva below. The media usually filmed the event, which was broadcast across Yugoslavia.

30 Ejub Štitkovac, "Svi su ljepši bez čarapa," *Borba*, 14–15 March 1992, p. vii.

31 *Rajo* (vocative of *raja*) is a turkism for "Hey, folks." See letter to *Borba* by Rade Vukosav, 22 October 1992, p. 21.

32 Ejub Štitkovac, "Uz rat, ni 100 maraka," *Borba*, 13 November 1991, p. 4.

33 In January 1992 Tudjman held talks with one of the two Bosnian Serb representatives in the Bosnian presidency, Nikola Koljević, regarding the partition of Bosnia between Serbs and Croats. The Cutileiro plan fit into this general scheme.

34 In an interview with Ljiljana Smajlović, Warren Zimmermann, the U.S. ambassador in former Yugoslavia, denied that he encouraged Alija Izetbegović to withdraw his signature. "Moja uloga u Bosni," *Vreme*, 27 June 1994, p. 18.

35 On the hazards of adopting the principle of self-determination to grant independence to groups living in multiethnic communities see E. Gayim, *The Principle of Self-Determination: A Study of Its Historical and Legal Evolution* (Oslo: Norwegian Institute of Human Rights, 1990), cited in Vojin Dimitrijević, "Upotreba ljudskih prava," in Nakarada, Basta-Posavec, and Samardžic, pp. 80–81. Citing Ruth Lapidoh, "Sovereignty in Transition," *Journal of International Affairs* 45, no. 2 (winter 1992): 336, Julie Mostov argues that although international conventions assume

that all peoples have the right to self-determination, a generally accepted agreement on what is a "people" was lacking ("Democracy and the Politics of National Identity," in *Yugoslavia: Collapse, War, Crimes,* ed. Sonja Biserko [Belgrade: Centre for Anti-War Action, Belgrade Circle, 1993], p. 32). See also Jasminka Udovički, "Nationalism, Ethnic Conflict, and Self-Determination in Former Yugoslavia," in *The National Question: Nationalism, Ethnic Conflict, and Self-Determination in the Twentieth Century,* ed. Berch Berberoglu (Philadelphia: Temple University Press, 1995), pp. 305–6.

36 As of May 1992, the YPA changed its name to the Army of Yugoslavia, which was composed of troops from Serbia and Montenegro. The decision to have the paramilitary or "volunteer" groups join the official army units was made in June 1991, when the difficulties in conscribing the reservists first became apparent. The Croatian and Bosnian side also had paramilitaries, bringing the total number of paramilitary formations in former Yugoslavia to about forty-five. All were under the command of an individual or were integrated into the action plans of regular armies. Serbian and Croatian paramilitary groups recruited, trained, and armed many criminal elements. Training centers for Serbian paramilitaries were located in Erdut, Petrovaradin, and Knin (see Aleksandar Ćirić, "Svi smo mi dobrovoljci," *Vreme,* 31 May 1993, pp. 20–21; and, particularly, Duška Anastasijević and Denisa Kostović, "Zločini, rezultat strategije," *Vreme,* 11 July 1994, pp. 19–23).

37 The Serbian general Vojislav Djurdjevac insisted that the trenches faced away from Sarajevo and were meant for anti-air attacks (see Isaković, "Rovovi u duši," p. 25).

38 Serbian reservists arriving in Sarajevo in April and May 1992 were told that all Serbs had fled the city to escape the terror of the fundamentalists. Every step of the way, however, the reservists ran into Serbs determined to stay. That provoked much confusion, but on the whole the soldiers accepted the official interpretation that these Serbs were traitors. They were treated the same way as Muslims and Croats. Željko Bajić, a Serbian editor of a Sarajevo magazine for the blind offered the following testimony:

> My part of town, called Aerodrom, was blocked off on May 1.... On Wednesday, June 17, the shelling and shooting started a little before 5 A.M. An hour later I heard loud swearing at our entry. A spray of machine-gun fire broke the glass, and an armed man rushed up the stairwell shouting: "Surrender or I'm throwing a grenade." His machine gun burst around our front doors, at the walls of the hallway, and ceilings.... Some thirty of us men were crammed into the neighboring basement. One bearded soldier swore at us, calling us "fundamentalists" and "Turkish bastards." His superior entered and barked in disgust: "Toss 'em a couple of pears!" He meant hand grenades.... Just before nightfall, two soldiers appeared bragging how they had "done in six each." Faced with these, even our guards were meek.
>
> ... After six days of constantly changing expectations and the wildest stories, word went around that we would be allowed to return to our apartments. My mother was impatient and rushed home. She came back on the verge of passing out. Everything, literally everything of any value, was stolen. The soldiers

threatened and swore at us, because here they were fighting on behalf of us Serbs, while we were having a good time.

(Željko Bajić, "Noć je pokretala vampire: Kako su me oslobodili," *Borba*, 25–26 July 1992, p. vii).

39   Quoted in Snežana Nikolić-Adamović and Goran Rosić, "Mi nismo normalni ljudi," *Borba*, 13 November 1992, p. 5.

40   Perica Vučinić, "Bez duše prema duševnoj bolnici," *Borba*, 16 October 1992, p. 7.

41   See Amir Osmančević, *Banja Luka, Vreme Nestajanja* (Zagreb, 1995), p. 43.

42   Between April and June 1992 more than five thousand people escaped from the city, most of them Muslims, but also a number of Serbs fearing possible conscription. On the extremely low response of reservists to the conscription call of Nikola Uzelac, the commander of the Banja Luka corps, see *Spotlight Report No. 3* (Belgrade: Humanitarian Law Center, 10 May 1993), p. 1. On the developments in Banja Luka between 1993 and 1994 see *Spotlight Report No. 14* (August 1994), pp. 1–10.

43   All details about Banja Luka derive from Jasminka Udovički's interviews of a Banja Luka Muslim-Croatian couple who requested anonymity (December 1995). The couple argued that Banja Luka and other towns in Bosnia that were not in the international media spotlight were subject to everyday terror of the kind Sarajevo did not experience.

44   *Spotlight Report 14*, p. 2. According to the Yugoslav Islamic community, between April and August 1992 alone, Serbian extremists destroyed no less than 430 mosques. Some of these were shelled and bombed during the fighting, but many, like those in Bjeljina, Trebinje, and Banja Luka, were destroyed by terrorist acts aimed at adding pressure on the Muslims to leave.

45   Keraterm was the site of the former tiles factory in the vicinity of Prijedor.

46   Anastasijević and Kostović, p. 22.

47   Perica Vučinić, "Strah preko Vlašića," *Borba*, 15 October 1992, p. 4. In mid-August 1993, *Borba* published a transcript of the testimony of one of two Bosnian women who spoke at the UN World Congress for Human Rights in Vienna (see "Molitva za smrt metkom," *Borba*, 14–15 August 1993, pp. xvi–xvii). The woman in question, fifty-four years old and from Prijedor, was imprisoned for three months at the Omarska camp, a site that before the war had been an ore mine. The name of the woman has been withheld. This is part of her testimony:

> Every day people were being brought to the camp. I knew many of them from before. As far as I know, five thousand men, two hundred forty boys age eleven to fourteen, and thirty-six women were there. Serbian authorities aimed primarily at the intellectuals, then at the members of Muslim and Croatian parties, and finally at important townspeople. But there were also ordinary people, and people seventy and eighty years old.

> I worked at the restaurant. Prisoners came in once a day in groups of thirty. The meal consisted of one piece of bread and a bit of cooked stuff, mainly beans. Of course that was insufficient; people would faint from physical weakness and hunger, particularly children. But the worst was that the meal had to be gulped up in two minutes; if you did not finish in two minutes you were beaten on the spot. People died in the restaurant, in front of our eyes.

The hardest thing was that in addition to the work in the restaurants, women were required to clean interrogation rooms, too. Those were full of blood, and we had to wipe off the blood.

. . . . We had to watch torture every day. They used large iron objects, wide rubber pipes, special cables. I was desperately hoping I would be killed with a bullet.

One hundred to two hundred people died every day from torture. Trucks took the bodies away every day, we don't know where. Perhaps the bodies were being thrown into the old mining shafts, and the shafts were leveled to get rid of the evidence.

. . . . We women slept in the two interrogation rooms, eighteen of us per room. At night anybody could come in. They came in usually drunk. They would call out the one they wanted and did what they wanted with her. We held each other by the hand and waited for our turn. We weren't saying anything. There was nothing to say. Five women, my colleagues, did not survive.

48 Interview of Alija Midžić, a Prijedor refugee, by Jasminka Udovički (April 1993). Mr. Midžić, who lost a leg when a shell hit his third-floor living room in Prijedor, never found out what had happened to the Serb, whom he knew personally, and whether that person also ended up having to kill in Kozarac. It is hard to imagine he did not. Asked why the Serb had not run away when he knew he was sure to be drafted, Alija said, "And where would you have wanted him to run? Prijedor was completely surrounded. There was no place for either me, or him, to hide when they closed in on us."

49 Dragan Banjac, "Samo Srbi u Hercegovini," *Borba*, 29 January 1993, p. 9.

50 Trying to defend his friend Alen, a Muslim and orphan since childhood, Srdjan Aleksić, a Serbian actor from Trebinje, died at the Trebinje hospital from the beating he received for being a "bad Serb" who defends Muslims (see Banjac, p. 9). Such cases were common and had the effect of emptying the area of the unwanted populations.

51 Donia and Fine maintain that the distinction between the ethnic cleansing practiced in the Bosnian war and the extermination practiced in Hitler's Germany resides in the deliberately open character of wholesale terror in the wars of the former Yugoslavia. By contrast, German operations were kept secret until the very end (p. 247).

On rape and the effect of the war on women see Lepa Mladjenović, "Pobedniku slede gresi," *Borba*, 1–2 August 1992, p. xii; Snežana Bogavac, "Specijalna forma genocida," *Borba*, 17 December 1992; Milena Dražic, "Sila ni boga ni ljubav ne moli," *Borba*, 21 December 1992, p. 13; Jelena Grujić, "Ženska strana rata," *Vreme*, 4 December 1995, pp. 50–51; Katerina Bertini, "Žene jedu poslednje," *Vreme*, 2 March 1996, pp. 46–47; Alexandra Stiglmayer, *Mass Rape* (Lincoln: University of Nebraska Press, 1994).

52 Loot was the primary motive for many of the worst crimes. The participants were encouraged by their superiors to take away whatever they found—cars, appliances, TV sets, video recorders, jewelry, cash (see John F. Burns, "A Serbian Fighter's Trail of Brutality," *New York Times*, 27 November 1992, p. A8). Raymond Bonner reported on the shop that Željko Raznjatović-Arkan set up in Erdut, near Vukovar, to sell

the booty from the loot of eastern Slavonia, and on the plunder of the Volkswagen factory in Vogošća, near Sarajevo ("In the Balkans, Doing Well by Doing War," *New York Times,* 26 March 1995, p. A4).

53 Judy Dempsey, "Croats Undermining UN," *Financial Times,* 29 June 1992, p. 3. Dempsey argues that in the summer of 1992 Croats were also involved in their own ethnic cleansing of Serbs from the UN-protected zone of Krajina, in Croatia.

54 John Pomfret and David B. Ottaway, "U.S. Allies Fed Covert Arms to Balkans," *Manchester Guardian Weekly,* 19 May 1996, p. 20. The authors claim that U.S. officials learned in 1992 that the smuggling route had been opened. George Bush's administration issued a strong protest when in September 1992 an Iranian plane landed at Zagreb airport with a cargo of four thousand assault weapons. Clinton's policy of turning a blind eye, the authors add, "marked a break with the Bush administration."

55 Large-scale imports were received in September and October 1991 from Hungary, Germany, Austria, Poland, Singapore, and even Czechoslovakia (Miloš Vasić, "Češka veza," *Vreme,* 23 November 1992, pp. 30–31).

56 On March 20, 1996, the tribunal in The Hague indicted the commander of the camp, Zdravko ("Pavo") Mucić; the coordinator of the Bosnian and Croatian troops in the region, Zajnil Delalić; the assistant commander of the camp, Hazim Delić; and the camp guard, Esad ("Zenga") Landzo. The Humanitarian Law Center supplied the Hague Tribunal with the testimonies of camp prisoners. Some were civilians from the Bradine village, which was burned to the ground. Prisoners testified about regular, heavy beatings that left the walls of the tunnel, built as an atomic shelter, covered with blood; being forced to drink their own urine as "juice"; having their tongues burned and hot needles driven through their tongues and nails; burning cables being wrapped around their bodies; hot knives placed on their palms. Many prisoners died from torture, malnutrition, and lack of water. The prisoners were also forced to testify in front of Arab journalists brought into the camp that they had raped and slaughtered Muslim civilians (see Filip Švarm, "Logor Čelebić," *Vreme,* 30 March 1996, pp. 14–15).

57 Miloš Vasić et al., "Privatna inicijativa," *Vreme,* 14 March 1994, pp. 14–17. "No war is clean," write the authors, "but our wars degenerated in record time into cynical business and plain robbery."

58 Ed Vulliamy, "Croats Supped with the Devil," *Manchester Guardian Weekly,* 24 March 1996, p. 7.

59 All too often, added Čičak, Franjo Tudjman referred to the Muslims as "dirty stinky Asians" and to the Serbs as "our Christian brothers" ("Milošević negativni genije, Tudjman politička nula," *Borba,* 29 June 1993, p. 7).

Donia and Fine stress that in contrast to their World War II predecessors, the leading Franciscans of Bosnia-Hercegovina supported the idea of a multiethnic Bosnia (pp. 250–51, 254–55).

60 Croatia sometimes kept 70 percent of weapons paid for by the Bosnian government. Other times it sent to the Bosnian government old Romanian kalashnikovs from its own arsenal and kept modern armaments (Miloš Vasić, "Nebo nad Tuzlom," *Vreme,* 13 May 1995, p. 11; see also Woodward, pp. 304–5).

61 Vance and Owen, the cochairs of the International Conference on Former Yugoslavia at Geneva, sponsored by the European Community and the United Nations, drafted a ten-point plan for the political organization of Bosnia. They called for the establishment of a highly decentralized, demilitarized state of three constitutive units made up of ten provinces. The plan urged "regionalization" rather than ethnic "cantonization." Provinces would have a mixture of ethnic groups. The central government would be based in Sarajevo, the tenth province. The UN, the European Community, and Conference on Security and Cooperation in Europe would monitor constitutional elections, the court, and the formation of a multiethnic army and police forces.

62 Both Cyrus Vance and Lord Owen insisted that Bill Clinton put American troops on the ground in Bosnia. But instead of forming any kind of policy on Bosnia, in February 1993 Clinton's administration opted for air drops of food to the safe havens in eastern Bosnia, which was besieged by the Serbian forces. In mid-April fifty-six civilians were killed in the center of Srebrenica.

63 Svetlana Vasović-Mekina, "Slovenački posao stoleća, Osovina Janša-Čengić," *Vreme*, 18 July 1994, pp. 32–33.

"Slovenia grew rich selling war technology at scandalously high prices," writes Miloš Vasić ("Nebo nad Tuzlom," *Vreme*, 13 March 1995, p. 11). On the arms trade through the Maribor airport see Svetlana Vasović-Mekina, "Sova, Vis, Moris," *Vreme*, 9 August 1993, pp. 32–33. On the Slovenian government's trade with Žirinovski (the leader of Russian ultra-right) see Svetlana Vasović-Mekina, "Maska za 2 Slovenca," *Vreme*, 17 October 1994, pp. 27–28.

64 Stojan Cerović, "Žrtve po planu," *Vreme*, 17 May 1993, p. 12; and Cerović "Klub prijatelja Bosne," *Vreme*, 24 May 1993, p. 10.

65 For a transcript of the Vance-Owen plan see *Borba*, special supplement, 7 May 1993.

66 James Ridgeway and Jasminka Udovički, "Uncivil War," *Village Voice*, 18 May 1993, pp. 19–20. Radovan Karadžić organized a referendum on May 15–16, 1993. Predictably, the plan was rejected. The observers said it was impossible to conduct a referendum in a war-torn area such as Bosnia. Judging by the vote, however, many ordinary Serbs in Bosnia seem to have still been convinced that the Bosnian war was fought to defend Serbian homes from the fundamentalists and the Ustashe. To have implanted and sustained this conviction among the ordinary Serbian population was the real feat of Karadžić's and Milošević's social engineering.

67 "Neretljanska Hirošima," *Vreme*, 1 August 1994, p. 9.

68 Present at the negotiations and the signing were, on the Croatian side, the Croatian foreign minister Mate Granić, Krešimir Zubak (the person Franjo Tudjman installed to replace Mate Boban), and the Bosnian prime minister Haris Silajdzic.

69 Jelena Lovrić, "Federacija s duplim dnom," *Vreme*, 6 June 1994, p. 63.

70 Michael T. Clarke, "The Guns of Bosnia," *Nation*, 22 January 1996, p. 23–24. The Croatian minister of defense Gojko Sušak revealed in November 1994 that Croatia had purchased arms regularly from Russia, Poland, and Bulgaria, for itself and for the Bosnian government, and said that Croatia was now assembling MIGs in a factory near Zagreb and tanks in the Djuro Djaković factory in Slavonski Brod (Roger

Cohen, "Arms Trafficking in Bosnia Goes on Despite Embargo," *New York Times,* 5 November 1994, pp. A1, A5). Cohen writes that the "embargo appears to have become largely a fiction."

On the Iranian shipments, mostly by air, and the ample evidence that the United States had of the shipments, see Douglas Jehl, "U.S. Looks Away as Iran Arms Bosnia," *New York Times,* 15 April 1995, p. A3; and Chris Hedges, "A Secret Arms Deal between Iran and Croatia Comes to Light," *New York Times,* 24 April 1996, p. A1.

71 Miloš Vasić and Filip Švarm, "Ratna Sreća," *Vreme,* 6 June 1994, p. 13.

72 In February 1994, following the killing on February 5 of sixty-eight civilians and the wounding of two hundred in the Markale marketplace in Sarajevo, the United Nations issued an ultimatum to the Serbs to withdraw their heavy weapons and stop shelling Sarajevo. (Until now it has not been definitively established who—Serbs or Muslims—threw the grenade on the Markale marketplace [see David Binder, *Vreme,* 15 June 1966, pp. 26–28].) On February 28, for the first time in the war, NATO downed four Serbian planes, forcing the Serbs to end the shelling of Sarajevo and to unblock the Tuzla airport.

In March 1994, despite the threat of NATO air attacks, the Serbs forced Muslims to flee the town of Zvornik and in April entered Goražde.

73 In September 1994 three thousand more Muslims were driven from Bijeljina. On Vojkan Djurković, a Bijeljina warlord who identified the houses he wanted in Bijeljina and then took the owners to the front lines, forcing them to cross over the battlefield, see Filip Švarm, "Djurkoviću, mlad majore," *Vreme,* 12 September 1994, pp. 18–19. On the events in the region in August and September see Chuck Sudetic, "Bosnian Serbs Drive 2,000 Muslims from Their Homes," *New York Times,* 30 August 1994, p. A8.

74 Vasić and Švarm, "Ratna sreca," 12.

75 Since 1991 the refugees in Serbia had lived in constant fear that they would be discovered and sent to the front. Radical extremists in Serbia helped the police by collecting lists of all the refugees from the Croatian and Bosnian Krajina who were between eighteen and fifty-five years of age and submitting them to the military police. Radical extremists also helped in rounding up the refugees and sending them to the front. In 1994 and 1995 the campaign of conscription of refugees gained new momentum (see Uroš Komlenović, "Jeftine glave izbegličke," *Vreme,* 31 January 1994, pp. 29–31; *Spotlight Report No. 18: The Conscription of Refugees in Serbia* [Belgrade: Humanitarian Law Center, June 1995]; Filip Švarm, Dejan Anastasijević, and Jelena Grujić, "Čišćenje Srbije," *Vreme,* 9 June 1995, pp. 15–17; Dejan Anastasijević, Jelena Grujić, and Filip Švarm, "Danak u krvi, *Vreme,* 26 June 1995, pp. 13–15; Filip Švarm and Miloš Vasić, "Danajski poklon," *Vreme,* 3 July 1995, pp. 16–19; Goran Svilanović, "Surovi lov na ljude," *Republika* [January 1995]: 11–12; Dragan Todorović, "Pozadinski rat," *Vreme,* 25 September 1995, pp. 18–20).

Vreme (3 July 1995, p. 63) published a desperate letter by a Serbian refugee from Croatia saying: "I received the citizenship, I exchanged my house, and I started to work and live in peace in Serbia. Now I have been hiding for days as a most hard-boiled thief or killer, and yet I am an intellectual. I scream: People, brothers, stop the harangue, scream yourselves, so that the whole world may hear once and for all. Do not let them beat me and incarcerate me—don't you know, I am an exiled Serb?"

76 At the Bosnian elections of 1990, Fikret Abdić won more votes than Alija Izetbegović, but he decided to leave the presidency because he considered Izetbegović too orthodox. On September 29, 1993, he proclaimed an Autonomous Region of Western Bosnia and made his own peace treaty and trade contracts with both Serbs and Croats, organizing a thriving enclave around the town of Velika Kladuša. On the Autonomous Region of Western Bosnia see T. Mičić, "Abdić otcepio Krajinu," *Borba*, 29 September 1993, p. 3; and Filip Švarm, "Babo deli dedovinu," *Vreme*, 28 June 1993, pp. 18–19. On the government offensive in the Bihać pocket see Igor Mekina, "Kladuška opštenarodna odbrana," *Vreme*, 18 July 1994, pp. 12–13. On the aftermath see Raymond Bonner, "Bosnian Splinter Group Is Exiled and Unwanted," *New York Times*, 22 August 1995, p. A7.

77 The safe havens fragmented the territory and represented potential threats to the integrity of this strategically important region. Mladić used as a pretext for his assault on the safe havens a June 1995 attack on a nearby Serbian village by Bosnian soldiers stationed in Srebrenica. For his operation, Mladić engaged a number of paramilitary troops: the White Eagles, Šešelj's militias, the Drina Wolves, Special Police, and the Tigers of Željko Ražnjatović-Arkan (see Barbara Crossette, "Talking Tough, U.N. Condemns Bosnian Serbs," *New York Times*, 30 November 1995, p. 12).

78 Before the war, Srebrenica had only eight thousand inhabitants, but its population swelled during the bloody spring of 1992, when the Bosnian-Serb army forces and paramilitaries overran the left bank of the Drina River. Srebrenica was not captured, which, as Miloš Vasić writes, was attributable to the skill of the defense commander of the enclave, Naser Orić, a former policeman and bodyguard of Slobodan Milošević. Yet during fall and winter 1992, local Bosnian units staged a number of attacks from the foothold of Srebrenica and Žepa. To bring an end to those attacks, Mladić in the beginning of 1993 launched an assault on the area. This time Srebrenica was saved because of the intervention of Philippe Morillon, and, together with Žepa and Goražde, it was proclaimed a safe haven (Miloš Vasić, "Pad Srebrenice," *Vreme*, 17 July 1995, p. 8).

79 The liquidations happened between July 13 and July 22. At Konjević Polje alone one thousand were killed (Stephen Engelburg et al., "Srebrenica: The Days of Slaughter," *New York Times*, 29 October 1995, pp. 1, 14–15).

80 The pretext for the NATO bombing was the launching of a 120 mm grenade that killed thirty-seven people and wounded eighty-five in Sarajevo.

81 See Zoran Kusovac, "Borba za Tudjmanov jelovnik," *Vreme*, 18 September 1995, pp. 8–10; and Miloš Vasić and Filip Švarm, "Fifti, fifti," *Vreme*, 25 September 1995, pp. 8–10. Although the gains were a product of a joint Bosnian-Croatian offensive, the possibility remained, particularly after the capture of the significant stretch in western Bosnia that bordered on Croatia, that in the end Tudjman might opt to abandon the federation and make a deal with the Serbs for the division of Bosnia.

82 The Bosnian-Croatian forces advanced by using their numerical advantage in in-

fantry and engaging the much weaker Serbian infantry on a number of locations simultaneously along a wide stretch. In the beginning of September the Croatian government called for the capture of Banja Luka. The fall of Banja Luka would not only have crushed the Serbian republic but would have represented a great prize for Croats in case of some future division of Bosnia.

83   For an overview of the Dayton Accord see Ljiljana Smajlović, "Tajna 11 aneksa," *Vreme*, 27 November 1995, pp. 5–9.

84   The demarcation line between the federation and the entity overlapped almost completely with the line of cease-fire. The only two exceptions were a five-mile-wide corridor, linking Sarajevo and Goražde, awarded to the Bosnian government, and a forty-kilometer square around Mrkonjić Grad and Šipovo, awarded to the Serbs.

85   Karadžić promised to assist in the resettlement of tens of thousands of Serbian refugees, by, for example, providing feeding stations and rest stops, and also housing in Pale. None of these things turned out to be available (see Stephen Kinzer, "Serbs on Trek: Weighed Down and Terrified," *New York Times*, 23 February 1996, pp. A1, A6). Mirko Pejanović, the president of the Serbian Civil Council in Sarajevo, dubbed Karadžić's orchestrated campaign "a crime against the Serbian people" (Anthony Borden, "Moving Dayton to Bosnia," *Nation*, 25 March 1996, p. 19).

86   Kinzer, 6.

87   On a statement by senior UN officials that NATO had failed in its mission to protect the remaining families in the suburbs, see Chris Hedges, "NATO to Move against Anarchy in Serb-Held Suburbs," *New York Times*, 11 March 1996, p. 3.

88   See Chris Hedges, "Bosnia's Checkerboard Partition: Instability More Likely," *New York Times*, 20 March 1996, p. A12; and Stephen Kinzer, "Serbs Are Pressed by Their Leaders to Flee Sarajevo," *New York Times*, 21 February 1996, pp. A1, A3.

89   Chris Hedges reported on a gang that murdered a man and his daughter who tried to argue with people to stay ("NATO to Move against Anarchy," p. 3).

90   Christine Spolar, "Serbs Flee from Sarajevo Suburb," *Manchester Guardian Weekly*, 3 March 1996, p. 16.

91   Werner Stock, a German police captain who works for the European Union, stated in late April 1996 that the entire "HDZ in Mostar is the mafia," gangsters working hand in hand with political leaders. Two of those gangsters, Mladen Naletić and Vinco Martinović, make millions of dollars and have been involved in the killings (see Chris Hedges, "A War-Bred Underworld Threatens Bosnia Peace," *New York Times*, 1 May 1996, p. A8).

92   On the war in the former Yugoslavia and international law see "International Humanitarian Law and Yugoslav Wars," in Biserko, pp. 141–274. In that collection see, in particular, Milan Šahović, "International Humanitarian Law in the 'Yugoslav war'" (pp. 141–59); and Vladan A. Vasiljević, "Grave Breaches of International Law of War and Humanitarian Law—International and National Criminal Law," pp. 193–227.

International Aspects of the Wars in Former Yugoslavia

Susan L. Woodward

Few inside or outside Yugoslavia believed the dire predictions in 1990 or earlier that the country would disintegrate in bloodshed, or the forecasts in 1991 that violence would spread. The European Community mediators and foreign ministers who rushed to the scene in June 1991 assumed that their very presence would induce Yugoslav politicians to reason and to negotiate their differences. As late as December, the foreign ministers of states such as Germany, Austria, and Italy thought that recognition of Slovene and Croatian independence would end the violence and leave the rest of the country to form a rump Yugoslavia. There would thus be three states where there had been one. In July 1991, despite the overpowering atmosphere of uncertainty about their political future, most people in Yugoslavia also found it difficult to imagine that there would be war.

Even after the war erupted in Croatia in the summer of 1991, Western security still seemed to many to be protected by the NATO alliance, by the norms and conflict-resolving institutions of the Conference on Security and Cooperation in Europe (CSCE), and by agreement among the powers to act in concert. In fact, these assumptions could not have been further from the truth. The major powers had to confront the fact that they did not agree on the parameters of a permissible outcome or the means to achieve it. They could agree that maintaining a united front was more important than any particular outcome in the Balkans, but this was not the same as leadership to achieve a goal.

The failure to prevent the escalation of the war was a failure to understand its real causes. Two distinct views formed almost immediately. One view was that this was a civil war, ingrained in the history and temperament of the Balkans, particularly Bosnia, and inclining its population inevitably toward ethnic conflict and war over territory whenever imperial or dictatorial protection collapsed. The other explanation—expansionist aggression by a revanchist Serbia—accused leaders in Serbia of having a deliberate plan to annex territory in neighboring republics where Serbs lived and create a Greater Serbia. Outsiders insisted that Yugoslavs were not like them, that violent atrocities always characterized the troublesome region. Western leaders defined the conflict as anachronistic, rather than as a part of a contemporary upheaval including their own national competition to redefine Europe and respond to the end of the Cold War. Even the morally outraged used a language of distinctions in their label of barbarism: the "otherness" of nations capable of such evil. This act of dismissal—itself profoundly nationalistic in its core—justified inaction.

Inaction was also the result of the changed role of Yugoslavia in the aftermath of the Cold War. With Gorbachev's reforms, Yugoslavia lost the strategic relevance it had for forty years. It had enjoyed a special relationship with the United States, including the implicit guarantee of open access to Western credits in exchange for Yugoslav neutrality and military capacity to deter Warsaw Pact forces from Western Europe. By 1991, Yugoslavia was being moved from a category in which it stood alone, or shared its status with southern Europe, and returned to its pre-1949 category, defined geographically, of eastern and southeastern Europe.

The ominous signs after August 1990 of armed clashes in Croatia and of open talk of independence in Slovenia brought warnings from diplomats, scholars, and intelligence agencies about the danger of "Balkanization" and Yugoslavia's violent disintegration.[1] For the most part, these were dismissed out of hand. No longer needed to contain the Soviet Union, not considered capable of sparking a wider war, since great-power competition in the Balkans was a thing of the past, Yugoslavia and its fate were not significant to the major powers. But more important than any specific calculations of threat and interest at the time were the general euphoria and self-confidence in the West, based on the belief that the peace dividend and economic interests would define the next period of global order. Only much later did the West's unwillingness to take the threat seriously boomerang, sapping that ebullient mood.

At the same time, both the Slovene and the Croatian governments were helping to shape Western opinion, in their efforts to gain outside support and to prepare the way for independence. The political strategy of the Slovene government elected in April 1990—to win international public opinion over to its position—was to send governmental and parliamentary delegations to Western capitals to represent the case for independence, to test the waters for likely reaction, and to construct a climate of foreign opinion that would see Yugoslavia as an artificial state that was now irretrievably doomed. Tudjman's government in Croatia also made preliminary soundings at the time about the best strategy for independence. These included, first, inquiries in Sweden and Norway about how they had managed their separation in 1905 and then consultations in Bonn. The Vatican openly lobbied for the independence of the two predominantly Roman Catholic republics, exerting decisive influences through Episcopal conferences on the Bavarian wing of the ruling German party, the Christian Social Union (CSU), and hence on Kohl's Christian Democratic Union (CDU). Jorg Reismuller, publisher of the *Frankfurter Allgemeine Zeitung*, one of the most influential German newspapers, was particularly sympathetic to the Croatian national cause and waged a campaign against Slobodan Milošević and Serbian nationalism that had a major role in shaping German opinion about the conflict. Whereas Austria was outspoken in its support of Slovenia (a relatively low-risk position since its only common border was with Slovenia), the Hungarian government publicly supported Yugoslav integrity. But Hungary's clear sympathies with the Croatian and Slovene cause could no longer be denied when it was revealed in September 1990 that it had illegally sold between thirty-six thousand and fifty thousand Kalashnikov rifles to the Croatian government in 1990 (a revelation that unleashed a parliamentary scandal in Budapest).[2]

Seasoned diplomats like the U.S. Ambassador to Yugoslavia, Warren Zimmermann, recognized the danger when extreme nationalists became winners in the 1990 elections. In a later speech to the Washington Center for Strategic and International Studies,[3] Zimmermann referred to the elections as a "double-edged sword," for American policy had to support democratic elections, but in all cases they brought "intolerant leaders to power" and "polarized nationalism." The judgment of most Western observers, including members of the U.S. Congress, however, was still under the influence of Cold War anti-Communism: anyone who opposed the Communist Party and Communist leaders was, by definition, to be supported. The revolutionary transition in Eastern Europe during 1990–91 was being driven by alliances of longtime Western and relatively new Eastern anti-Communist crusaders who created an atmosphere of revenge and retribution against anyone with connections to the former regimes. On the basis of the stated objective of ridding Eastern Europe of the last remnants of Soviet influence, they in fact displayed a cavalier attitude toward human rights and due process. In the Yugoslav case, this was manifest in a tendency to judge events as described by the new Slovene and Croatian governments, whose ex-Communist leaders skillfully portrayed their election results as a victory for democrats in reaction to Communist dictators in Belgrade (whether federal officials or officials of the Serbian republic—the distinction was lost), and to ignore or downplay the abuses of human rights and the signs of political repression by elected governments, as in Croatia (in contrast to their frequent denunciations of the Belgrade government for repression in Kosovo).

Both Western Europe and the United States were far more focused during the summer and fall of 1990 on events in Hungary, Poland, and the German Democratic Republic, and with the fate of Gorbachev's reforms and possible instability in the Soviet Union. When, in August 1990, Serb irregulars in the Dalmatian hinterland around the town of Knin disrupted traffic and blockaded the railroad along the main north-south Zagreb-Split route for commerce, the United States and its allies had their attention on the Iraqi invasion of Kuwait.

Preoccupied with Moscow and the Middle East, U.S. foreign policy also reflected the belief held in European circles that if the Yugoslavs could not resolve their own quarrels, there was little the United States could do. Moreover, the great hope being attached to the CSCE for early conflict resolution did not yet translate into institutional capacity. The CSCE Conflict Prevention Center had only been created in Paris in November 1990.[4] It opened its doors on March 18, 1991, and had no military capacity.

By the time of the Slovene referendum on independence in December 1990, the external environment was helping to create and reinforce the political divisions within the country between federalists and supporters of the prime minister, Ante Marković, and the confederalists in Slovenia, Croatia, and Kosovo. On the one hand, this led Slovenia and Croatia to expect political (and most likely economic) support for independence from their neighbors and Germany, and encouraged their belief that they could "join" Europe quickly. On the other hand, it gave Serbia and the YPA general staff further evidence for their suspicions that there was a revival of the World War II Axis alliance and German revanchism against them. This exacerbated fears, strengthening the very bases of Milošević's appeal to the Serbian population as the nation's protector—and encouraging those who already were inclined to reach for arms and to rely on themselves against a hostile environment.

The West's position to the federal government was increasingly inconsistent. While the West's verbal support for the country's reforms and its territorial integrity remained strong, leading pro-Yugoslav forces throughout the country to assume that the West was siding politically with Marković, financial support was, in fact, dwindling rapidly.

Meanwhile, the army's troop movements in Croatia during January brought a warning from the United States that it would not accept the use of force to hold Yugoslavia together. A little more than a week after the attack on Baghdad, on January 25, 1991, Ambassador Zimmermann made this warning public, reinforcing statements of concern made the day before in Washington by members of the U.S. Congress who had just returned from Yugoslavia.[5] The United States was in effect telling the Yugoslav army that it would consider illegitimate the army's definition of its constitutional obligation to defend the borders of the state from internal threats.

Slovenia and Croatia's drives for independence gained a substantial boost on March 13, 1991, when the European Parliament passed a resolution declaring "that the constituent republics and autonomous provinces of Yugoslavia must have the right freely to determine their own future in a peaceful and democratic manner and on the basis of recognizing international and internal borders."[6] While most European governments continued to support the federal government and to insist that the Yugoslavs stay together, the apparently uncontroversial nature of this declaration demonstrates how far Slovenia and Croatia had influenced European opinion and how little chance there was that alternatives to republican sovereignty would be heard.

It was by then well known that Germany had already joined the ranks of Austria, Hungary, and Denmark in at least covert support and encouragement of Slovene and Croatian independence. A week after the declaration, on March 20, Slovene president Milan Kučan was in Bonn having talks with German foreign minister Hans Dietrich-Genscher. Austrian support for a breakup became more assertive during the spring. Italy, by contrast, remained in an ambivalent position. The flight of almost twenty thousand Albanians to Italy in early March 1991 had the Italians, as well as other Europeans, sensitized to the prospects of more refugees. The Italian foreign minister, Gianni De Michelis, was particularly active in promoting EC involvement to manage the crisis. As Foreign Minister Lončar and Prime Minister Marković had hoped, EC president Delors and the prime minister of Luxembourg, Jacques Santer, did visit Belgrade on

May 29–30 and made a commitment to the territorial integrity and international borders of Yugoslavia.

The week before, and the very day after Croatians voted for a referendum on sovereignty and independence, the EC had made the Yugoslav-EC association agreement contingent on the country remaining united. Delors also promised to request $4.5 billion in aid from the EC (the sum needed to service the Yugoslav debt during 1991), in support of the Yugoslav commitment to political reform.[7] This carrot, however, was to reward the Yugoslavs only on certain conditions: if they implemented the very reforms that were at the heart of their quarrels—a market economy (and its financially centralizing reforms), democratization (at so rapid a pace that it favored nationalists), a peaceful dialogue on a constitutional solution (while cutting the budgets for defense, government programs, and welfare), a respect for minority rights (which was now largely outside federal competence), and the seating of Stipe Mesić (the representative of Croatia who declared his goal as president of Yugoslavia was to achieve Croatian independence) as presiding chair of the collective presidency. Without regard for the consequences of these demands on the internal political conflict, the offer repeated the added condition that Yugoslavia remain united.

These escalating efforts to address the impending crisis even caught the momentary attention of the U.S. secretary of state, James Baker. Stopping in Belgrade en route to Tiranë, Baker declared the United States ready to aid Yugoslavia if domestic conditions became normalized. He also declared the United States unwilling to recognize an independent Slovenia and Croatia, calling any "unilateral secession" both "illegal and illegitimate."[8] Although Baker extracted a promise (so he thought) from the Slovene and Croatian leaders not to act unilaterally, he also told Serbian president Milošević that if there came a choice between "democracy and unity," the United States would choose democracy. He then declared his open support for the compromise constitutional formula on confederation within a federation put forth June 6 by the republican presidents of Bosnia and Herzegovina and Macedonia, Alija Izetbegović and Kiro Gligorov, at the sixth Summit of Six (republic leaderships) meeting outside Sarajevo.

Four days after Baker's visit, and twenty-four hours before they had originally announced it, Croatia and Slovenia followed through on their intent to declare independence. The Slovene government sent military forces and civilian officials to take over control of eight border controls and customs, replacing signposts for Yugoslavia with ones that read "Republic of Slovenia." The Austrian and Swiss consul generals and several Austrian provincial governors attended the Slovene independence celebrations on June 26. The federal government had warned that it would use all means necessary to protect the territorial integrity of the state. On June 25 the parliament and the cabinet ordered army units based in Slovenia and Croatia to assert Yugoslav sovereignty over its borders with Austria and Italy.

The unilateral action by Slovenia presented Western powers with a serious dilemma. There were, in fact, two polar positions. The Austrian position, presented by Foreign Minister Alosius Mock, was that Yugoslavia was—and always had been—an artificial state, and that denial of the Slovene right to secede threatened war. But this argument patently appeared to be one of national interest, based on Austria's assessment that its border was more secure with an independent Slovenia and with the Yugoslav army at a distance (a position that many read as the continuation of Austria's century-old rivalry with Serbia and policy to keep Serbia from becoming a regional power). The fact that Germany now openly began to call for immediate recognition, however, gave the Austrian position greater weight. The other pole was represented by the United States. Secretary of State Baker and Ambassador Zimmermann argued that the breakup of Yugoslavia would be highly destabilizing and could not occur without war and horrendous carnage. This position also had strong French and British support. Although many acknowledged Slovene, Croatian, and Albanian aspirations, preoccupations with stability in the Soviet Union and the risks of its disintegration if a precedent were set in Yugoslavia dictated the hope of many that Yugoslavia would remain united.

Given the lack of international definition of the practical meaning of self-determination in the complex example of multinational Yugoslavia, the introduction of the criterion of force (prohibited by CSCE norms to change borders) and the distinction between its defensive and aggressive use appeared to give those intent on separation, as an expression of the right to self-determination, a winning strategy. If they could provoke the Yugoslav army into violent resistance of their moves toward independence and appear to be using force only in self-defense, they could trigger EC and U.S. support for their goal. Indeed, within hours of the army's move, British foreign secretary Douglas Hurd announced a change in policy, saying that the United Kingdom was obliged to qualify an earlier statement supporting the integrity of Yugoslavia by adding that this should not include the use of force. On June 30, U.S. deputy secretary of state Lawrence Eagleburger said that the United States supported "sovereign republics" and the idea of a Yugoslav confederation.[9]

Slovene minister of defense Janez Janša had made extensive preparations for the possible confrontation, including the illegal purchase abroad of sophisticated weapons and the formation of a network of pro-Slovene military officers and conscripts within the YPA. The Slovene government continued to express its appreciation of the importance of a combined political and military strategy, striving to shape international opinion in favor of Slovenia and the "naturalness" of its actions.

In the aftermath of the ten-day Slovenian war, the Brioni Agreement of July 7 (named for the island where the EC troika met with representatives of the Yugoslav federal government and the republics to sign a cease-fire and a return to barracks by the YPA) in effect recognized the Slovene victory. The European Community thus accepted that republics were states and their borders were sacrosanct. The source of their sovereignty was the right of a nation to self-determination. This also made Slovenia and Croatia the subject, de facto, of international law and cleared the way for the eventual recognition of their statehood.[10] Although foreign journalists at the Brioni meeting challenged Dutch foreign minister Hans van den Broek (head of the troika as of July 1) to explain how the EC could treat Slovenia in isolation from the rest of the country, the EC troika assumed that the only issue left to the negotiated cease-fire was its monitoring. With a mandate from the CSCE to deploy thirty to fifty observers, the European Community Monitoring Mission (ECMM), called "ice-cream men" by Yugoslavs for the white uniforms they chose, began its first-ever effort at peacekeeping.

The prospects for a military test of Croatian sovereignty were thus dramatically enhanced. By small steps made in rapid succession, the EC and the CSCE were helping to complete the demise of the federal government: withdrawing support from Marković's government, accusing the army of aggression, and taking over the presidency's role as interlocutor among the republics. Despite the tendency in the Western press and among some diplomats to equate Serbia with the federal government, the Brioni Agreement also accomplished the first step of Serbian nationalists' goals: to remove Slovenia and make it possible to redraw internal borders.

Perhaps most decisive of all, the Brioni Agreement struck a serious blow against the authority of the faction within the army leadership that was fighting to hold Yugoslavia together, and of those (called the Titoists by their critics on all sides) who still hoped to play a mediating, pacifying role in the nationalist quarrels. Forced to choose between loyalty to Yugoslavia or to the new national armies, army leaders at the highest levels began to rethink their role in this political quarrel, and the balance of opinion began to shift toward those who could only see a military solution to border conflicts.

Moreover, the loud support for Slovenia and Croatia from Austria, Hungary, Denmark, Germany, the Vatican, and eventually Italy, on the one hand, and the great reticence about an interpretation of self-determination that would dissolve an existing state on the part of France, Britain, Spain, and Greece, on the other, had the appearance of geopolitical alignments affecting the Balkans at several points in the preceding century. Thus the EC division was likely to add to the revival of historical memories by nationalists aiming to mobilize support for their goals within Yugoslav politics and to undermine the credibility of EC or CSCE efforts at moral suasion.

Even more important at the time was the implication of this split within the EC for adoption of the Maastricht treaty at the end of the year; its commitment, in Title 5, to a common foreign and security policy; and its primary purpose for Britain and France, to constrain German economic (and potentially foreign) power. As fighting escalated in Croatia during July and August, the opposing positions on self-determination became opposing policy positions on what to do. The Group of Seven called for a UN peacekeeping force and the foreign ministers of Luxembourg, the Netherlands, and France proposed to send in European interposition troops, while the German parliament voted to recognize Croatia and Slovenia immediately. But the EC had no troops to send, and Britain opposed the use of military force; as for the alternative, the United States, the Soviet Union, and the Yugoslav government rejected UN involvement in what they still considered an internal affair.

As the Maastricht summit loomed closer and the failed Moscow putsch of August and rapid dissolution of the Soviet Union improved prospects for involving the UN (where France and Britain could influence events without direct confrontation with Germany), France became less concerned about maintaining Yugoslav unity and more concerned about EC unity on security matters. This made the Austrian and German positions even bolder. On August 24, Foreign Minister Genscher informed the Yugoslav ambassador that Germany would recognize Slovenia and Croatia if the army did not cease its violence. The Austrian vice-chancellor, Erhard Busek, declared that "the collapse of communism in the USSR modifies the situation in Yugoslavia and there is no reason not to recognize the independence of Slovenia and Croatia."[11] And Hungary lodged a diplomatic protest charging Yugoslav forces with violating its air space.

Three days later, on August 27, the EC abandoned its fiction of a commitment to Yugoslavia. The EC declared the use of force by the Yugoslav federal army "illegal" and stated that Serbs who opposed their new minority position in the Croatian constitution could not "lawfully receive assistance from the YPA."[12] The EC declaration demanded that Serbia permit EC observers in Croatia, requested a third emergency meeting of the CSCE's Committee of Senior Officials, set up an arbitration commission of international jurists headed by French constitutional lawyer Robert Badinter to arbitrate issues of succession among the republics, and proposed a peace conference. It then threatened further action if there was no cease-fire by September 1.

Even before the peace conference opened in The Hague on September 7, Milošević had rejected its good offices and made it clear that he, along with many citizens in Yugoslavia, did not consider the EC neutral. Even the conference's mandate was decided by the EC rather than the parties to the conflict, and the uncompromising diatribes from both Tudjman and Milošević in their opening remarks cast a pall over European hopes for a rapid agreement. Tudjman called the Serbs war criminals who were engaged in a "dirty, undeclared war," and Milošević accused the Croatians of a "policy of genocide."[13]

On October 2, Slovene president Kućan announced in Paris that French president François Mitterrand had agreed to recognize Slovene independence. In Belgrade—in the name of a Yugoslavia without Slovenia, Croatia, and Macedonia—the Serbian bloc of four within the rump federal presidency declared a state of emergency and assumed the extra powers allowable under the constitution in the case of imminent danger of civil war.

The next day an emergency meeting at The Hague among the Yugoslav minister of defense, General Kadijević, presidents Tudjman and Milošević, and EC representatives van den Broek and Lord Carrington accepted in principle a peace plan that took as its starting point confederation and presumed the eventual independence of all republics that desired it. The basis for a new settlement was a legal opinion requested from the Badinter Commission: that since October 8, Yugoslavia had been a "state in the process of dissolution."

This legal hedge on the principles in conflict had no standing in international law. By opting against the alternative definition of the conflict — that it was a case of secession — and then recognizing the continuation of a smaller Yugoslavia, the EC took yet another step in support of recognizing Slovenia and Croatia.[14] It also opened the door to independence for the other republics — Macedonia and Bosnia-Hercegovina — that had so declared in the meantime.

In a letter to van den Broek on December 2, 1991, Lord Carrington warned that premature recognition of Slovenia and Croatia by the EC "would undoubtedly mean the break-up of the conference" and "might well be the spark that sets Bosnia-Hercegovina alight." Even President Izetbegović made an emotional appeal to Genscher in early December not to recognize Croatia prematurely, for it would mean war in his republic.

Despite all this, at the twelfth hour, all-night EPC meeting of foreign ministers in Brussels on December 15–16, Chancellor Kohl (responding to domestic public opinion and party pressures, the leanings of mass media, an active Croatian émigré community, and the Vatican-led campaign beginning several years earlier) refused to budge. He obtained the agreement of the remaining holdouts — Britain, France, and Spain — by making two concessions. The first was a set of compromises on the EC monetary union that Britain had been seeking. The second was to concede to the demand that all six republics of Yugoslavia be treated equally and thus be equally eligible for recognition as independent states. The conditions required that the republics request recognition formally by December 23 and meet the criteria to be established by the Badinter Commission. In the meantime, the republics were required to continue working toward an overall settlement by January 15, 1992, and to satisfy UN, EC, and CSCE criteria on the rule of law, democracy, human rights, disarmament, nuclear nonproliferation, regional security, the inviolability of frontiers, and guarantees for the rights of ethnic and national groups and minorities. At 2 A.M. during the quarrel in Brussels, Greece inserted an additional requirement: that any state requesting recognition have no territorial claims against a neighboring EC state and not use a name that implied such claims — a blatant reference to Macedonia.

Without waiting for the decision of the Badinter Commission, Germany recognized Slovenia and Croatia on December 23. Ukraine had preceded Germany on December 12, and the Vatican made its recognition formal on January 13.

Germany's success in its campaign for recognition of Croatia and Slovenia was, as Carrington warned in his letter to van dan Broek, the death knell to the peace negotiations.[15] The EC decision in December to recognize Croatia addressed neither the status of Serbs in Croatia nor the fate of the population in the remaining four republics. Although seen as an alternative policy to interpositioning troops, particularly to UN involvement, this European policy of "internationalizing" the conflict—by recognizing Croatian sovereignty and declaring Serbia (in fact, rump Yugoslavia) guilty of cross-border aggression and deserving of economic sanctions— had been running parallel, after October 8, 1991, to a UN diplomatic mission, led by former U.S. secretary of state Cyrus Vance, as special envoy for UN Secretary General Perez de Cuéllar, to negotiate a cease-fire in Croatia. Signed on November 23, 1991, and ratified by military leaders at a signing in Sarajevo on January 2, 1992, the cease-fire agreement enabled the United Nations to reverse its position regarding noninterference and send peacekeeping troops to Croatia. The two policies that had been in opposition throughout the summer and fall of 1991 were now being implemented simultaneously. But the terms of the Vance plan, that the presence of UN troops would be "without prejudice to the final political settlement," presumed the continuation of The Hague negotiations for a comprehensive settlement for all of Yugoslavia, whereas international recognition of Croatian sovereignty within its republican borders now defined the question of Serbian rights and the territory Serbs held as an internal affair. The presence of fourteen thousand UN Protection Forces, who began to arrive on March 8, 1992, did keep the cease-fire holding for the most part (with momentary, though significant, breakdowns during 1992 and 1993 and the necessity of a new cease-fire agreement signed March 29, 1994) until May 1995, when the Croatian army overran one of the four UN protected areas and expelled its Serbs. The contradiction between the two international policies was resolved with a second military action in August 1995, when the Croatian army "reintegrated" the territory of the two protected areas of Krajina, more than one hundred thousand Serbs fled to neighboring Bosnia or Serbia, and the UN operation dissolved.

Contrary to the reasoning of the German policy of recognition, the EC's unwillingness to address the problem of Serbian rights alongside those of Slovenes and Croats left substantial ambiguity over territorial rights to self-determination while recognizing a state that was not in control of one-fourth of its territory—and refusing to send troops except under the auspices of UN peacekeeping troops to monitor a cease-fire. The German haste to use the issue for domestic political gain exacerbated the unsettled character of both the principle and the reality.[16] Kohl had accepted the condition that each republic submit to certification by the Badinter Commission before it was recognized. However, Germany recognized Slovenia and Croatia before the commission could meet. According to the commission's ruling in January 1992, only Slovenia and Macedonia satisfied its conditions on specific democratic standards and rights of minorities. Yet the EC refused to recognize Macedonian sovereignty so as to keep the government of Greek prime minister Constantine Mitsotakis in power and buy its affirmative vote on the Maastricht treaty. As for Croatia, the commission ruled that it did not meet the minimal conditions for recognition because it was lacking in its commitment to human rights—including protections for the rights of Serbs and other minorities.

Genscher did press the Croatian government to respond to the Badinter Commission ruling on this matter of specifying the rights of minorities (Serbs included) and of instituting a human rights court. But the government refused to amend the constitution, adopting instead a "constitutional law" months later, in May 1992, in which no affected domestic groups (including the Serbs of Krajina) had any say. The Croatian government never set up the required human rights court. In September 1995, a month after the Croatian army operations to end the UN deployment and retake control of the Krajina, the Croatian parliament revoked the constitutional law that had guaranteed, at least formally, Serbian human rights.

Moreover, Germany followed its diplomatic blitzkrieg with a rapid retreat from engagement in the issue, including any attempt to conduct oversight to ensure that Croatia was actually implementing the new provisions it had adopted to justify German recognition. This did little to reassure Krajina Serbs that they were now secure and could therefore reduce their resistance to the Croatian state, or their allegiance to local politicians who became intent on creating a separate state of Serbian Krajina that would one day be joined with Serbia proper. Despite the terms of the UN cease-fire, the Serbs continued to believe that they could not safely disarm. There was also nothing in European or international diplomacy to undermine the alliance that had formed between Serbian communities on either side of the republican border linking Serbs in the Croatian Krajina and Bosnian Krajina. Each group perceived itself in the minority in its respective republic and preferred to remain within a new Yugoslavia.

Viewed from its denouement in 1995, the war of Croatian independence came to be seen as a simple conflict between a legitimate state and a rebel population. Only the methods by which it would be resolved were uncertain; the outcome was a given. This view was reinforced by the received wisdom, as it developed during 1991 and 1992, that any international intervention was too late after August 1990, when Serbs around Knin first resorted to violence after they were deprived by the republican parliament in Croatia, elected in the first multiparty elections in April 1990, of rights that had been constitutionally guaranteed since 1945 — or certainly too late after March 1991, when the federal presidency and army proved unable to stem the crisis over Slovene and Croatian intentions, Serbian opposition, and mass demonstrations against president Milošević in Belgrade.

In fact, European foreign ministers had a number of alternatives still to be tried during 1991, had they been willing to look beyond the nationalist rhetoric of the republican politicians. Neither the commission nor the EC ministers, for example, gave consideration to holding a referendum of the entire Yugoslav population as an expression of the right of self-determination more in line with international practice. Nor did they raise questions about the legitimacy of the Slovene and Croatian nationalist claims that their "mandate" for independence was constitutional when the Slovene government refused to participate in the federal elections that had been planned to follow the republican elections, in December 1990, and upon which Yugoslav prime minister Marković and liberals in his reform alliance in all parts of the country had counted. Although invisible to the West, moderate mayors in Serb-majority towns within Croatia late into 1992 and the far larger number of urban Serbs living dispersed in Croatia proper (who constituted two-thirds of the 12 percent of Croatian population of Serbian identity and who had accepted the fait accompli of Croatian independence) viewed themselves as citizens of the new Croatian state and sought to find their accommodation with it despite antagonism from both Croatian nationalists and Serbian radicals. Also invisible with the nationalist spectacles worn by the West were members of the army and local police forces throughout the country still trying to keep peace throughout 1991. World opinion, in fact, delegitimized (and thereby eventually helped to eliminate) army professionals and senior staff who did not support nationalist agendas. Denied support, sanctuary, publicity, or representation to counteract the process of radicalization, all these groups had insufficient resources to counteract the process. Instead, world opinion accepted the geopolitical and cultural prejudices of the west Europeans—that there was a difference in civilizations between West and East, which ran between Croatia and Serbia; that the Serbs throughout what was no longer a country were indeed aggressors; and that Macedonians and Bosnians were irrelevant.

All of this demonstrated to Serbian nationalists, moreover, that Milošević had been right all along about German and fascist revanchism, foreign victimization of Serbs, the Serbs' need to protect each other because no one would come to their aid, and their ability to survive as they have historically, by standing alone, against overwhelming odds.

The European Community's willingness to break up multinational Yugoslavia on the principle of national sovereignty showed little regard for the consequences for the multinational republic of Bosnia-Hercegovina. This mistake was compounded by U.S. insistence on recognizing Bosnia's sovereignty before its ties with other parts of the former country (particularly its neighbors, Croatia and Serbia) were clarified and before some negotiated arrangement had been reached among the three ethno-national political parties (each claiming the status and rights of "constituent peoples" or "nations") governing the republic in coalition as a result of the November 1990 elections in the republic. The result was an artificial dilemma over the cause of the war—was it a civil war or external aggression from Serbia?—and appropriate actions to end it. This problem, never resolved, prevented Western powers from addressing the actual nature of the conflict and formulating an appropriate policy toward it. Instead, having recognized Bosnian statehood (on April 6–7, 1992) and membership in the UN (on May 22, 1992), the international community had to behave as if Bosnia was a state besieged by both rebel forces and external aggressors. In practice the international community treated the war as a civil war. The goal of international negotiations was to contain the war that erupted in March 1992 within Bosnian borders, by obtaining a political settlement among the three former coalition partners. The parties' aim, however, was to create separate national states on contested territory.

Bosnia's fate was a consequence of its interior location at the geopoliti-

Sarajevo, former front line, one streetcar stop before the suburb of Ilidza: February 1996. Photo by Maja Munk. Courtesy of the photographer.

cal and cultural heart of the former Yugoslavia—cordoned off from Europe by the republics of Croatia and Serbia, with no external border except a tiny outlet to the Adriatic Sea at the cluster of fishing huts, tourist inns, and villas for Sarajevo politicians called Neum. Its war could not spill over Western borders. Thus, Bosnia-Hercegovina had no strategic significance.

The absence of vital interest for major powers meant they would not become engaged militarily in the war, but as the violence, atrocities, and violations of international conventions on war and humanitarian law invaded television screens throughout the world, pressure from the media and the public acted as a moral campaign, reminding the world that international conventions and moral law were being violated and demanding that the major powers take decisive military action. This dilemma made concrete the proverbial identification of Yugoslavia—and particularly Bosnia-Hercegovina—as a crossroads. It was, but it also was not, a part of Europe.

In fact, the pressure to act did not lead the powers to reflect on ways to improve policy or existing institutions, after their disagreements and mixed results in the case of Croatia. The approach of Western governments to Bosnia-Hercegovina was nearly identical to the failed approach toward Croatia, and that approach reflected a continuity in thinking from the Cold War period. The decision to recognize Croatia without a previous political settlement on the "Serbian question" and on guarantees for Serbian rights within the republic not only created a stalemate in Croatia but also provided no precedent for the place of Serbs (and Croats) in Bosnia-Hercegovina. Although the EC decision on immediate diplomatic recognition for Slovenia and Croatia in December had abrogated the principle of The Hague conference (that a comprehensive political settlement covering all of the former country was necessary), the conference was kept as a framework for separate talks for Bosnia. Those began in early February 1992, under the auspices of the EC troika and its negotiator, Cutileiro from Portugal, and repeated the earlier pattern. The leaders of the three ethnic political parties that had won the most votes in the 1990 elections were treated as legitimate interlocutors for all citizens of Bosnia-Hercegovina (to invite others was apparently seen as interference in internal affairs). Presumably because the objective was to find a political settlement upon which the three party leaderships could agree, the EC negotiators accepted that the conflict was ethnic.

The EC had done nothing on Bosnia during January and February 1992—except to wait for a referendum on sovereignty on February 28 to March 1 that was required by the Badinter Commission but that Serbs had already made clear they opposed. They thus lost an invaluable opportunity for political negotiations before the referendum, uncertainty, violent incidents, and emerging U.S. policy diminished the possibilities for any compromise. And just as Germany ignored the Badinter Commission's advice that Croatia did not meet its conditions for recognition, so the EC ignored a crucial ruling by the commission on Bosnia-Hercegovina—that a vote on the required independence referendum would be valid only if respectable numbers from all three communities of the republic approved. As it turned out, one-third of the population—the overwhelming majority of the Serbs—boycotted the referendum.

The Lisbon talks had foreclosed options in one direction by assuming the conflict in Bosnia-Hercegovina to be ethnic and by mediating on proposals made by the leaders of the three nationalist parties. The referendum closed options in the other direction by assuming Bosnia to be an independent state. Because the nonethnically based Bosnian parties were not represented in the talks, there also was no discussion of rights and identities that could exist independently of territorial administration. Moreover, no attention was apparently paid to the fact that this concept provided no defense against those, such as Croatian and Serbian nationalists, who viewed Bosnia as either Croatian or Serbian territory.[17] The Lisbon agreement (on principles, including tripartite ethnic cantonization of the republic, but not on the map this would entail) was signed on March 18, 1992. Whether emboldened by the growing U.S. pressure on Europe for immediate recognition of Bosnian sovereignty, as many argue, by promises of support from Middle Eastern leaders, or by the negative implications of the accord for Bosnia and the Muslim nation, President Izetbegović reneged on his commitment to the document within a week. He was followed by the Bosnian Croatian leader Mate Boban, who saw the opportunity to gain more territory in a new round of negotiations.

The collapse of these talks did not, however, create an opportunity to reconceptualize a political settlement for Bosnia-Hercegovina. Appeals from several corners to send UN peacekeeping troops to Bosnia were also rejected when the UN envoys, Cyrus Vance and Marrack Goulding, declared that conditions were not ripe. And then, continuing the direct parallel with European actions toward Croatia, the United States insisted on extending the German policy of preventive recognition to Bosnia-Hercegovina, ending all efforts at negotiating a settlement on April 6–7, 1992, as localized clashes and ethnic terror erupted into full-scale war.

Since 1991, knowledgeable Yugoslavs and some Western diplomats and scholars had warned publicly, and made proposals to the responsible authorities, that in case of Yugoslavia's breakup there would have to be an interim international protectorate for Bosnia-Hercegovina. Adherents of the idea became more numerous once the war in Bosnia began. They were convinced that only a UN protectorate that would place a bell jar over the republic could save Bosnia's sovereignty, hundreds of thousands of innocent civilians, and Muslim rights of national self-determination. Nonetheless, a new UN secretary general in January 1992, Boutros Boutros-Ghali, accepted the advice of his deputy, Goulding, that conditions were not appropriate for UN involvement in Bosnia. In line with the policy of the Bush administration at the time, Boutros-Ghali added that responsibility for conflict management in the post–Cold War period should belong primarily to regional organizations.

Instead, the international choice that followed was like that made by Europeans at Brioni when they sent unarmed monitors to Croatia as an act of prevention. The United Nations briefly set up headquarters for its peacekeeping operation (UNPROFOR) in Croatia and in Sarajevo, as a symbolic act of deterrence. As fighting worsened and refugees flooded Europe, France, Britain, and the United States began to talk about a humanitarian operation under UN auspices. At the same time that such action presumed the fighting to be a civil war, however, the United States and the EC simultaneously resumed their position (as they did the previous July toward Croatia) that this war was the result of external aggression from Serbia. Economic sanctions on the new Federal Republic of Yugoslavia (Serbia and Montenegro), declared after Bosnia was recognized, became the main international policy toward the Bosnian war after May 1992.

In the summer of 1992, televised pictures and firsthand accounts of concentration camps, mass rape, columns of Muslims expelled from their homes, and other atrocities of the Bosnian-Serb campaign to control territory in eastern Bosnia sought to shock international public opinion into taking a principled stand against the reappearance of genocide in Europe. Unwilling to alter its rock-bottom policy against sending soldiers, the United States began to push through resolutions of the UN Security Council to strengthen enforcement of the sanctions on Serbia and Montenegro and to supplement this by helping to defend the Bosnian government indirectly by reducing the military imbalance on the ground that favored the Bosnian Serbs. The United States thus argued for a naval blockade in the Adriatic Sea to be enforced by NATO and West European Union (WEU) ships and for a no-fly zone against military flights over Bosnian airspace. It also began to argue for a policy of "lift and strike" to defeat the Bosnian Serbs: lifting the arms embargo on the Bosnian government on the basis of Article 51 of the UN charter—that a member had a right to self-defense—and threatening NATO air strikes against Bosnian Serb heavy weapons and supply routes.

Economic sanctions against Serbia were the obvious solution to the dilemma of moral pressure without strategic interest—between the major powers' refusal to become militarily involved and the growing pressure for action from domestic publics outraged by their countries' apparent indifference to the particular immorality and injustice of the war. Sanctions gave the appearance that governments were taking appropriate action. Sanctions particularly suited the Bush administration's concept of the war—that Serbian president Milošević was responsible and that the appropriate regional security organization for dealing with the Yugoslav crisis was the CSCE. But sanctions also suited the view most often associated with Britain—that this was instead a civil war, and that although little could be done to prevent or stop it, its end could be hastened, by analogy to a wildfire, by depriving it of fuel and ammunition from the outside. In this sense, the sanctions could be seen as a continuation of the policy that had motivated the UN Security Council to impose a generalized arms embargo on all of then Yugoslavia the previous September.

This capacity of economic sanctions to serve many masters, providing not only an alternative to decisive military action but also the lowest common denominator among competing views of the war, meant that the sanctions also protected major powers from having to formulate a policy for the war's conclusion. But they also merely worsened the dilemma regarding national sovereignty by identifying the problem with Serbia and Serbs and by handing its resolution to Milošević. Their identification of the Serbian nation as a political entity rather than as a people living in different states with different political allegiances was the goal of Serbian nationalists who insisted on material support to the Bosnian Serbs, the very behavior that the sanctions intended to punish and reverse. By imposing sanctions on all Serbs, they seemed to concede the very point for which Milošević was most criticized—his claim that it was in the national interest of Serbia to protect Serbs wherever they lived. By imposing economic hardship, the sanctions aimed to create an angry public opinion that would turn against Milošević and demand a change in policy toward Bosnia or, if necessary, overthrow his rule altogether. But economic hardship had nurtured nationalist sentiments and feelings of being endangered in the first place, and negotiators became increasingly dependent on keeping Milošević in power as the primary interlocutor and the primary lever of pressure with the Bosnian Serbs. And their differential treatment of the Croats—such as ignoring the Croatian role in Bosnia and the links between Bosnian Croats and Zagreb—not only undermined the effectiveness of the sanctions on Serbs but also dramatically reduced external leverage on the Croats when they, too, threatened the integrity of a Bosnian state.

Instead of undermining the sitting regime, the sanctions undercut the prospects of democratic and antiwar pressures, and they increased the ability of the ruling party and nationalist militants to Milošević's right (those with police connections or the kind of wealth that only criminal networks and sanctions runners could amass) to control the mass media and to interpret the meaning of the sanctions. The sanctions regime made newspapers prohibitively expensive, reduced the sources of information from outside the country, and cut the funds of opposition forces. Even if they did lead the government to reduce support for the Bosnian Serbs over time, their effect would move too slowly to make much difference in the course of the war in Bosnia-Hercegovina.

Europeans felt the direct effect of the war through the flow of refugees. Germany, the primary foreign host, began to demand after mid-July 1992 that European countries set quotas for the number of refugees they were willing to accept. This called forth a containment response: to beef up the work of the United Nations High Commissioner for Refugees (UNHCR) and humanitarian relief to keep those displaced by war from becoming refugees. As one of the prime targets of German criticism for not accepting a fair share of refugees, Britain proposed that safe havens for civilians be established instead within Bosnia-Hercegovina. The result was to extend the area of operation of the United Nations Protection Forces (UNPROFOR) into Bosnia, from its peacekeeping mission in Croatia to a mandate, under chapter VII of the charter, to protect the delivery of humanitarian relief to the population and other actions to aid civilians caught in the war.

Soon UNPROFOR II became the largest, most complex, and most expensive operation ever undertaken by United Nations peacekeeping troops.[18] But it was not designed or suited to end the war that outraged world opinion. As a result, the United Nations came increasingly under attack for sending peacekeeping troops (lightly armed and acting under rules of engagement defined by consent, impartiality, and the use of force only in self-defense) into a war.[19] But the mission reflected the criteria chosen by the European powers and the United States from the beginning: that the norms of sovereignty govern (and limit) international intervention, that the sovereign units were the republics of former Yugoslavia, and that because the area no longer affected the vital, strategic interests of any of the major powers in Europe in general, they would not send troops into combat. United Nations forces suited the major-power interests of the Security Council in that they neutralized domestic critics by sending humanitarian assistance while containing the fighting and refugee exodus within Bosnia-Hercegovina, so that it did not spread to areas that were of strategic concern.

This was a false humanitarianism. Channeling moral concerns into humanitarian relief while refusing to confront the political causes of the conflict (both within the country and among foreign powers) was creating more war, more casualties, and more need for humanitarian assistance. The humanitarian approach was only a way for the EC and the United States to avoid defending the choices they had made and defining a political objective in intervening. The cost to the United States alone of military operations to enforce the no-fly zone and economic embargo and to drop aid packages from the air during 1993 was far in excess of $300 million, and this did not forestall sending troops in the end, when it finally acted diplomatically to end the war in 1995 and sent nearly twenty thousand troops to a new peacekeeping mission.

Despite the failure of The Hague Conference, European official opinion still held that the only solution lay with a negotiated end to the conflict. Thus, under the British presidency in the summer of 1992, the EC called a new conference at London in August 1992 that established a permanent peace conference at Geneva, the International Conference on Former Yugoslavia (ICFY), to negotiate all aspects of the succession crisis. Insisting that it would be illegitimate interference to "impose a political solution," however, the conference handed the task back to those who could not generate one before the wars. The great public attention to presidents Tudjman and Milošević as if the HDZ and SDS leaders in Bosnia-Hercegovina were under their tutelage, seemed to contradict the firm declaration of Bosnian independence.

The cochairmen of ICFY, Lord David Owen for the EC and Cyrus Vance for the UN, soon became consumed by the task of only one of its six commissions, the attempt to negotiate an end to the Bosnian war. Like The Hague conference and its subsequent negotiations at Lisbon in February– March 1992, the ICFY drew up a set of political principles on sovereignty, a constitution, and a map allocating territorial governance among the three warring parties. In place of the three-canton proposals made at Lisbon, the Vance-Owen Peace Plan of January 1993 divided Bosnia into ten provinces and aimed to protect, by means of a weak central government, a multinational and multiethnic Bosnia. It was rejected by the Bosnian Serbs, in May 1993. Owen and Vance's successor, Thorvald Stoltenberg, then drew up a new peace plan in August 1993 (revised as the Invincible plan in September, with subsequent revisions in late fall by the European Union) that partitioned Bosnia again into three areas but that retained the extensive international monitoring of human rights from the Vance-Owen plan. This in turn was rejected by the Bosnian Muslims, and ICFY negotiators fell back on trying to keep communication open among all the parties and quietly proposing that there could be no solution to the Bosnian war without returning to the comprehensive approach recognizing Bosnia's link to the rest of Yugoslavia. This implied finding a more global solution to Croatia and Bosnia, proposing small adjustments in the republic borders to satisfy the strategic interests (such as access to the sea) of independent states, and negotiating with the leaders seen to determine events, the presidents of Serbia (Milošević) and Croatia (Tudjman).[20]

The failure of ICFY negotiations in 1993 led to increasing impatience with the Bosnian war on the part of major powers contributing troops to the UN Protection Forces (above all, Britain and France). It also revealed that the larger problem remained conflicts among the major powers and their continuing inability to work in concert toward an agreed objective, in effect working often at cross purposes and sending mixed messages to the parties that encouraged each to hold onto its maximal goals.

By the end of 1993, there were three competing approaches in play at the same time. The UN forces sought to improve conditions for peace on the ground by classic peacekeeping principles: negotiating cease-fires, if necessary in one village at a time, and using the lull in hostilities to restore daily life and open communication across battle lines—such as through family visits, trade, and restored utilities—that would rebuild the confidence and trust necessary to a political settlement in the long run: a "piecemeal peace," in the words of UNPROFOR civilian head Yasushi Akashi, from the bottom up. The ICFY negotiators shuttled tirelessly among the political capitals of Belgrade, Zagreb, Sarajevo, Knin, and Pale, and gathered leaders of the warring parties and neighboring states in Geneva to negotiate a peace plan, with endless hours poring over detailed maps. And the United States talked incessantly of creating a military balance through arms and training of Croats and Bosnians, air strikes against Serbs, and a military alliance between Bosnian Croats and Bosnian Muslims directed against the Bosnian Serbs.

By early 1994, under the pressure from the European Community and particularly an impatient France, the United States became reengaged diplomatically in the issue and began a series of maneuvers with the opposite tactic from that of the ICFY: not to treat the Yugoslav succession crisis as a set of interrelated conflicts but to break each conflict into ever smaller pieces and dyadic relations. It thus insisted on separating the Croatian and Bosnian conflicts on the principle of their recognized sovereignty and then, in the Washington Agreement of March 1994, negotiated (together with Germany) a cease-fire for half of Bosnia between two of its three parties, Bosnian Muslims and Bosnian Croats.

By April 1994, the ICFY process was being replaced by a third diplomatic mechanism—a Contact Group of the five major powers (the United States, Germany, Russia, Britain, and France). Their peace plan, presented in July 1994, reduced previous plans to little more than a map dividing the territory of Bosnia-Hercegovina, 51 and 49 percent, between two entities, a Muslim-Croat federation and the Bosnian Serbs. But when Bosnian Serbs demanded adjustments before they would sign, the long-standing division between the U.S. and Germany, which opposed any concessions to the Bosnian Serbs, on the one hand, and Britain, France, and Russia, which saw no reason not to grab at any chance to end the war, on the other, came into the open. And once again, their mutual disagreements led to diplomatic impasse, episodic attention from Washington, and growing impatience with the costs of the humanitarian mission and with the increasing risks to soldiers' lives as the war intensified.

The turnaround began in mid-1995, when the two competing policies to end the war in Bosnia began to converge: the U.S. policy to create a military balance to defeat the Serbs in Croatia and in Bosnia, and the European policy to negotiate a settlement recognizing the new Balkan reality of nation-states and thus the ethnic partition as well of Bosnia-Hercegovina. Beginning with the Croatian military destruction of the Krajina Serb enclaves protected by UN troops, in May (for Sector West) and August (for Sectors North and South), well-trained, well-equipped, and well-informed Croatian troops effected a fundamental change in the strategic situation on the battlefield that continued in Bosnia in offensives overrunning much of western Bosnia, expelling Serbs, and joining up occasionally in selected parallel operations with Bosnian government forces in northwestern Bosnia.

By July 1995, two months after Bosnian Serbs had reacted to NATO bombing by holding UNPROFOR soldiers hostage and the crisis led Britain and France to send in rapid reaction forces in preparation for total withdrawal of their troops, the Clinton administration persuaded its allies that NATO bombing of Bosnian Serbs would complete the strategic reversal. Facing realization of its commitment, made in late 1994, to assist in withdrawing UN troops, the Clinton administration came around to the European view that the Bosnian war could only end through a negotiated solution. Between August and November 1995, American negotiators ran a marathon of shuttle diplomacy in Balkan capitals and a new peace conference (called proximity talks) in Dayton, Ohio, to get signatures on a political settlement and enable a NATO-led, peace implementation force (IFOR) under American command to replace UNPROFOR.

The Dayton Accord, signed in Paris on December 14, was a victory for the realists but came wrapped in the idealism of the moralists supporting the Bosnian government. To get signatures among warring parties, it accepted a Republika Srpska for Bosnian Serbs, retained the federation giving equal rights to Bosnian Croats and Bosnian Muslims, repeated international recognition of a sovereign Bosnia-Hercegovina, and committed American resources to equip and train a Bosnian army that could defend an integral Bosnian state when international peacekeeping forces left after twelve months.

But the constitution written at Dayton created a political system with all the flaws of the former Yugoslavia: extensive regional autonomy legitimized by national rights and a weak central government with no functions that could bind the loyalty of all its citizens. To enable international military forces to leave within twelve months (a commitment made by President Clinton to a U.S. Congress reluctant to deploy any American soldiers), the Dayton Accord set out rapid deadlines for implementation, including a political process that would yield electoral results in September 1996, giving democratic legitimation to the three nationalist parties and producing a parliament stalemated by block voting and countervailing vetoes. A program of economic assistance led by the International Monetary Fund, World Bank, and European Union—on which the possibility of a stable peace and the survival of Bosnia-Hercegovina depend—repeated the same conditionality that led to the disintegration of Yugoslavia in the 1980s: that there be economic and political reform policies to ensure that debt is repaid and to transform a socialist system rapidly into a market economy, without attention to the fiscal consequences of inevitable defense interests and raising all the political-legal conflicts over economic assets and jurisdictions between the regional governments and a central government that Yugoslavia could not resolve. The international peace implementation operation, combining military and civilian tasks and administrations, continued to talk to representatives of the three official parties who had gone to war and controlled armies, not to those who had opposed the war, nationalist propaganda, and ethnic partition. The American policy of equipping and training a Bosnian army is in sharp conflict with the European policy for long-term regional stability based on an arms control regime (as defined by the Organization for Security and Cooperation in Europe (OSCE). And if the three units of Bosnia-Hercegovina choose to go their own way—to dissolve as did former Yugoslavia—the international community will be faced again with a fait accompli it cannot recognize.

Western governments failed in the case of Yugoslavia, but not only that: they also revealed little capacity for learning. Their actions over the period 1991–96 repeated over and over the same approach, same thinking, and same mistakes. NATO's credibility on the other hand, was being tested not by war but by peacekeeping in Bosnia-Hercegovina, its very survival tied to the uncertain outcome of a peace implementation process in which NATO commanders insisted on the narrowest mandate so as to avoid the fate of UNPROFOR. Instead of the original role of NATO and the EU to contain Germany, Germany was acting unilaterally to secure its eastern and southern flanks with a ring of friendly, prosperous, stable states from Poland to the Czech Republic, Hungary, Croatia, and Slovenia, and without regard for the destabilizing potential of this new, if invisible, border in eastern and southeastern Europe. As a result of the Yugoslav crisis, a new forum for resolving major issues of European security is replacing existing institutions: an informal gathering of five major powers, apparently returning to balance-of-power and balance-of-interest principles, based on the Contact Group set up in March 1994 to negotiate a Bosnian peace.

The priority given to national over collective interests characterized all major players in the Yugoslav drama. It was not only Austria, the Vatican, Germany, and the EC Europeanists who saw the Yugoslav crisis as an opportunity in changing times. France saw an opportunity to enhance its declining resources and prestige in Europe with its power in the UN Security Council and as a potential military guarantor of Europe. Britain used the case to remain a major power, balancing its own position to keep

A Serbian refugee from Kninska Krajina (Croatia) arrives on his tractor to the out-skirts of Belgrade: August 1995. Photo by Duško Gagović. Courtesy of *Vreme* news agency.

center stage. Russia used it to gain acceptance at major economic forums (such as the G-7) and to gain financial assistance for its reforms. Turkey has found a new foothold in the Balkans, with its support of the Bosnian Muslims and the role delegated to it by the United States in equipping and training the Bosnian army. And the United States, while acting for the most part as a conservative power and reluctant leader, managed to protect NATO's centrality to European security and America's position of dominance in Europe and the Middle East.

However, Europeans have not yet addressed the conflict among Helsinki principles that wreaked such havoc in Croatia and Bosnia-Hercegovina. They, therefore, have no solution for the issue of Kosovo that might prevent the competing claims of sovereignty over the province between Serbia (of which it is legally a part, making this an "internal affair") and Albanians (who formed the vast majority and had voted in a popular referendum for independence) from being resolved through war. Who has a right to a state, and what procedures exist to guide the process peacefully? The Croatian "solution" of encouraging the mass exodus of Serbs who held the same position and the de facto partition of Bosnia into three areas of ethnically pure population are surely not acceptable models for the future. Despite some growing public expressions of unease over the methods used by Croatia against the Serbs, Europe and the United States continued to support Croatia, economically, diplomatically, and militarily, and to accept the priority of sovereignty norms by which human and minority rights were internal affairs of states. While they did oppose the population transfers, both voluntary and violent, in Bosnia-Hercegovina, they did little to prevent them other than to declare, at Dayton, the right of all displaced persons and refugees to return to their prewar homes, and they continued to insist that the recognized borders of the republic were inviolable.

For all the loud insistence in 1991 that "this is not 1914," when great-power conflicts could be ignited by events in Belgrade or Sarajevo, the Balkans retain the capacity to lure the major powers into their local conflicts and to create conflict among them over national interests and over principles of European and global governance. And just as in 1914 and 1947–49, this capacity is not a reflection of some cultural predisposition of Balkan peoples but of the state of relations among the major powers.

NOTES

This chapter is based on excerpts from Susan L. Woodward, *Balkan Tragedy: Chaos and Dissolution after the Cold War* (Washington, D.C.: Brookings Institution, 1995) and related articles.

1   On the leaked 1990 report of the Central Intelligence Agency see John Zametica, "The Yugoslav Conflict," Adelphi Paper, no. 270 (London: Institute for International and Strategic Studies, 1992), p. 58.

2   Donald Forbes, "Hungary: Pressure Grows for the Dismissal of Hungarian Ministers," Reuter Newswire, 8 February 1991.

3   Zimmermann delivered the speech in Washington, D.C., on June 9, 1992.

4   The center was to be housed in Vienna, with a staff of nine and an emergency mechanism for "unusual military activities."

5   On March 13, 1991, Zimmermann also warned of a cutoff in U.S. aid if the military "enforced a crackdown" (*Washington Post*, 15 March 1991, p. A33).

6   Cited in James Gow, "Deconstructing Yugoslavia," *Survival* 33 (July/August 1991): 308.

7   *Financial Times*, 23 May 1991, p. 2.

8   See David Gompert, "How to Defeat Serbia," *Foreign Policy* 73 (July/August 1994): 30–42.

9   See Gow, p. 309.

10   Marc Weller, "The International Response to the Dissolution of the Socialist Federal Republic of Yugoslavia," *American Journal of International Law*, vol. 86 (July 1992).

11   *Calendrier de la Crise Yougoslave*, prepared by staff of the European Commission in Brussels, fall 1991, p. 15.

12   Weller, pp. 575–76. But see Weller's discussion, pp. 576–77, on the continuing ambiguity in EC declarations about whether Yugoslavia did or did not exist.

13   Paul L. Montgomery, "Yugoslavs Joust at Peace Meeting," *New York Times*, 8 September 1991, p. A8.

14   See Vojin Dimitrijević, "The Yugoslav Precedent: Keep What You Have," in *Breakdown: War and Reconstruction in Yugoslavia*, ed. Anthony Borden et al. (London: Institute for War and Peace Reporting, 1992), pp. 62–64.

15   For a detailed discussion of the role of Germany in the recognition of Croatia and Slovenia and for my account of the motives for the recognition see Woodward, pp. 183–89, 468–70 nn. 110–23.

16   Ibid.

17   One of Croatian president Tudjman's advisers, political scientist Zvonko Lerotić, argued in January 1992, three months before full-scale war in Bosnia, that "war is not necessary to finish off the republic, because that process is already complete," adding that "war would only be necessary if one wanted Bosnia and Herzegovina to become a united and sovereign republic" (cited by Milan Andrejevich, "Bosnia and Herzegovina: A Precarious Peace," Radio Free Europe/Radio Liberty [RFE/RL] *Report on Eastern Europe*, 28 February 1992, p. 14).

18   Its annual budget of $1.6–1.9 billion was almost half the entire peacekeeping bud-

get of the UN (Information Notes: Update: May 1994, United Nations Peacekeeping, PS/DPI/14/Rev.5 [May 1994]).

19 Two representative examples are Jane M. O. Sharp, *Bankrupt in the Balkans: British Policy in Bosnia* (London: Institute for Public Policy Research, 1992), and, particularly caustic, David Rieff, *Slaughterhouse* (New York: Macmillan, 1995).

20 An excellent survey of all of the Bosnian peace plans by the lawyer most involved in drafting each is in Paul C. Szasz, "The Quest for a Bosnian Constitution: Legal Aspects of Constitutional Proposals Relating to Bosnia," *Fordham International Law Journal* 19, no. 2 (December 1995): 363–407.

The Resistance in Serbia
Ivan Torov

That independent media exist in Serbia and that a number of groups have organized a sustained resistance to the war will come to many readers as a surprise. Abroad there has been little media coverage of either, and, more important, neither has succeeded in mobilizing a massive grass-roots challenge to the regime of Slobodan Milošević. Yet the independent media and the antiwar groups did something else: they offered a voice of conscience and reason in the times when none other was heard. The electronic and the print media supplied and most continue to supply to this day highly reliable, well-researched information about the war, often sought after by foreign agencies and journalists, among others, and used by academics as a source for analysis.

Journalists in Serbia found themselves divided roughly into two groups as the war was approaching. Many were swept into the service of the official propaganda machine. Some, however, recognized early on that their only resort was to sever themselves from the regime by starting privately owned, independent, alternative media. Those journalists succeeded at great personal risk. Between 1989 and 1990 one major daily (*Borba*), one weekly (*Vreme*), and one biweekly journal (*Republika*) were launched in Belgrade as independent print media.[1] Two broadcast media, Independent TV Studio B and Radio B-92, started their broadcasts in 1989.

From the beginning the opposition media faced two kinds of obstacles: political and economic. Troubles with financing turned out to be the harder ones to surmount. International sanctions imposed on Serbia in 1992 caused a drastic and rapid decline in the standard of living, and consequently a precipitous drop in the circulation of the press. In 1991, and particularly in 1992, as salaries and pensions turned insufficient even for bread and vegetables, most Yugoslavs, who have always been avid readers of newspapers, found themselves buying the papers—independent and official alike—only every other day. Soon, if they hadn't given up the daily press altogether, most could afford just the Sunday editions.

The official press was, and is, much less affected by this trend because it is state-subsidized and does not depend on the income from circulation. The independent press faced from the beginning difficulties in paying for paper and printing ink, supplies, and, last but not least, salaries. *Borba*, *Vreme*, and *Republika* have barely been able to finance the costs of investigative reporting, their raison d'être.

The three publications have different backgrounds and different editorial policies. *Republika* and *Vreme* date back to 1989 and 1990. *Borba* is one of the two oldest dailies in the country, launched as an opposition paper in 1922 in Zagreb, to serve as the mouthpiece of the then illegal Yugoslav Communist Party.[2] Until World War II, the paper appeared sporadically, but during the war it was published with remarkable regularity at the front, among the Partisans, as the paper of the National Liberation Movement. In 1945 *Borba* entered the least exciting chapter of its history by becoming the establishment daily of the ruling Communist Party, its top management and editors being people close to Tito. In 1948 especially, at the time of Tito's break with Stalin, *Borba*—required reading for party members—reached the enviable daily circulation of eight hundred thousand. People carried it in jacket or coat pockets folded so that its logo was clearly visible: to read *Borba* was a demonstration of party loyalty. Later, in the 1950s, 1960s, and beyond, circulation was kept high by free subscriptions, especially to higher-echelon party members.

When Stanislav (Saša) Marinković, a prestigious Belgrade journalist and *Borba*'s new editor in chief, decided in the summer of 1986 to turn *Borba* into a professional, objective, vigorous paper, the first problem he faced was expanding the readership. He first had to rid the daily of its party connection. It worked in his favor that by then Yugoslavia had become a rather weak federation and that the republics had little interest in a federal paper such as *Borba*. The enthusiasm of Marinković's staff was tremendous, and *Borba* changed day by day, tackling sensitive problems with ever greater analytic focus and courage. As other media in Serbia began to succumb to narrow nationalism, *Borba* was developing a liberal, critical, unshrinking voice. It opened itself to the politically most sensitive issues: the effects of the 1974 constitution, the mounting crisis in Kosovo, the declining economy, political cover-ups. In 1987, its new image was consolidated through its objective reporting from the Serbian

Eighth Party Session, when Slobodan Milošević made his grab for power, replacing Serbian president Ivan Stambolić and taking the office himself. *Slobodna Dalmacija*, a Croatian paper with a similar orientation, voted *Borba* the "Newspaper of the Year" for 1987.

Milošević immediately realized the threat *Borba* posed to his regime. The paper repeatedly and loudly warned of the danger of rising nationalism and demagoguery of the regime. By the end of 1989 Saša Marinković died, and in 1990 Milošević tried in various ways to choke off the paper. But at the time, the republic of Serbia had no power over it: *Borba* was still nominally a "federal" publication. In September 1990, new pressure was added, and this time *Borba*'s printers—whose director was an important figure at the founding congress of Milošević's Socialist Party— surrendered, refusing to run the presses, allegedly because of some late payments.

The new policies and image of *Borba* attracted many top journalists and caused them to transfer from other Belgrade media (Belgrade TV, *Politika*, and most of the evening papers), to *Borba*.[3] It was not an easy decision for any of them; the official pressures on *Borba* had been mounting since 1987. The paper had been accused by official television of being on the payrolls of the Vatican, Germany, and the CIA; it was called a destroyer of Yugoslavia, a reviver of capitalism. When propaganda did not work, Milošević imposed higher taxes and created artificial shortages of newsprint and other supplies, hoping to break the paper financially. When that failed, an attempt was made to annul the already completed privatization and confiscate the paper's property.

In March 1991, during the week of student uprisings, however, the readers waited in line to get hold of an issue of *Borba*, the paper that supported their demonstrations and the antiwar movement. *Borba*'s circulation rose to 150,000. Shortly afterward, the daily was able to put its shares up for public bidding and sell all but 17 percent of property rights to 3,200 shareholders, including a number of banks, insurance agencies, tourist organizations, and sponsors of sports events. Seventeen percent of the shares remained in the hands of the state.[4] *Borba* continued its policy of serving as an uncomfortable witness, and the regime tried again to sabotage it in September 1992. Its printing press, as before, refused to print the paper for two days. The same happened again in 1993.

At the time of the Croatian war *Borba* had resident correspondents in Zagreb, Sarajevo, Split, Osijek, and many other important towns throughout Yugoslavia. But when the telephone connections and postal services between Serbia and Croatia were cut off in 1991, the headquarters was severed from its network of correspondents. The international sanctions made automobile fuel all but impossible to buy, making it increasingly difficult to send staff members out on special assignments. The services of the international news agencies remained beyond reach because the paper had no foreign currency to pay for them.

To sustain its level of reporting, *Borba* turned for help to the ham radio network. Cautious selections from the Serbian news-agency dispatches were also made, and, whenever finances permitted, correspondents were sent by public transportation on longer assignments to war areas. With time, *Borba* was able to establish a few resident correspondents in Herce-govina, Knin, and even Sarajevo.

Their unbiased reporting made these reporters targets of all three war-ring sides. In 1992 the Serbian side in Sarajevo kidnapped two young *Borba* journalists, a man and a woman: Željko Vuković and Natka Butu-rović. These correspondents were unknown before being sent to Sarajevo, but they quickly gained great respect in Belgrade for their eyewitness re-ports.[5] Despite repeated protests from *Borba*, nothing could be learned about Vuković and Buturović for months. Finally they were released in 1993, and Vuković received a special prize for journalism for the year 1992. In August 1992 the Bosnian-Serb side captured another correspon-dent from Sarajevo, Vladimir Srebrov, sentencing him to five years for "anti-Serb reporting." Srebrov was not freed until October 1995.

The pressures escalated in 1994, when the public prosecutor requested that the privatization of *Borba* be annulled. By that time Milošević had been accepted in the West as a cooperative partner in peace talks and wanted to sustain the same image at home.[6] After much sound and fury, in November 1994 his government installed the federal secretary of infor-mation, Dragutin Brčin, as the main editor of *Borba*. Brčin insisted that this was not an attempt to meddle in the editorial politics but a way to straighten out "property relations."[7] The printing press was instructed to refuse to print the next issue, to prevent the information about the take-over from being made public. Official radio and TV informed the public only about the appointment of Brčin. Only Studio B, Radio B-92, and for-eign agencies reported on the wholesale assault on *Borba*.

On December 15 the European Parliament issued a resolution insist-ing that independent media, and *Borba* in particular, serve the interest of the European democracy and must be allowed to continue unhindered. The American Committee for the Defense of Journalists sent a letter of protest to president Milošević.

Out of 120 *Borba* journalists only 5 joined Brčin, despite the threats that all those who refused to work with him would receive prison sentences. The original editorial board managed to print ten thousand copies at the ABC Printing Press. The entire edition was sold on the streets by the reporters themselves and their friends. That wildcat edition, later to evolve into "*Naša Borba*" (Our Borba), became known affectionately as a "tramp." Meanwhile, Brčin presided over his own *Borba,* a pathetic caricature of its former namesake.

The regime tried to undermine the editorial board of *Naša Borba* by withdrawing printing paper. The irregular edition that came out three days after the takeover was printed only in one thousand copies. The first regular issue of the new daily appeared on February 1, 1995. Three days later, the journalists were forcefully prevented from entering the facilities. Despite all obstacles, however, *Naša Borba* has been coming out ever since and becoming an ever better paper.

The weekly *Vreme* was founded in October 1990 with limited initial capital it received from a well-known Belgrade liberal lawyer, Srdja Popović. The idea of starting a weekly newsmagazine came from a group of his journalist friends who wanted to have an independent weekly to represent a liberal, pro-Yugoslav viewpoint at a time when the collapse of Yugoslavia appeared all but imminent. The idea attracted some of the best journalists still working for the official media. They took a risk with a magazine that at the outset could not even be registered in Serbia.[8] *Vreme* was registered in Croatia instead and moved to Serbia only six months later, when the law allowing the registration of privately owned media was finally passed. By abandoning the official media for a private, independent weekly, journalists who joined *Vreme* were gambling their entire careers. Nevertheless, the original staff grew to twenty-three full-time journalists and forty additional staff, an overwhelming number of whom are non-Serbs.

At the outset *Vreme* was conceived of as a newsweekly, but it has evolved into a news and opinion magazine covering in depth all aspects of the Croatian and the Bosnian war, as well as the political, economic, and cultural life in Serbia. The point has been to lay bare the realities behind

Journalists and staff of the Belgrade independent weekly *Vreme:* March 1992.
Photo by Goranka Matić. Courtesy of the *Vreme* news agency.

the scenes and at the front, and to openly discuss the war crimes, the role
played by the Yugoslav army in the war, and the human and material cost
of the war to the civilian populations on all sides. The magazine also features critical coverage and analysis of the economy—hard to find in any
other domestic source. Its tone is deliberately restrained, in contrast to
the often hysterical tone of the official media. Its graphic design is modeled on some prominent world weeklies, such as *Newsweek* and *Time,*
but simplified and bolder.[9] *Vreme* considers even its design to be a form
of active opposition to the regime.

High school and college students wearing *Vreme* T-shirts used to sell
the magazine on Saturdays and Sundays at open markets, in front of super-
markets, at bus and tram stops, and right next to the newsstands. For
these young people, selling *Vreme,* and more recently, *Borba,* is a way of
earning some money, but it is also a statement of personal protest against
the regime. In Zagreb, where Tudjman banned its sales, *Vreme* is distributed clandestinely, in doorways, or hand-delivered directly to the home
addresses of secret subscribers. Slovenia, Macedonia, and Banja Luka receive *Vreme* regularly. Whole issues, or photocopies of particular articles,

used to crop up even at the front lines in Bosnia. The total circulation of the weekly is twenty-three thousand copies.

Despite its small circulation, *Vreme* has become a major source of independent and unbiased information, not only internally but also internationally. Foreign news agencies, including such giants as the BBC, for example, often request interviews and analyses from *Vreme* journalists. The magazine used to be housed in downtown Belgrade, in a space the size of a large private apartment, but in 1994 moved to better facilities. At the beginning, its journalists had only ten computers, forcing many to work on old manual typewriters. In 1993 the cost of producing each issue exceeded its newsstand price. The sanctions depleted circulation, reducing earnings to a fraction of what they were when the weekly was founded in 1990.[10]

The regime has never attempted a direct uprooting of the magazine, but the official slanderous propaganda has succeeded in making many common people suspicious. Like many other antiwar organizations and groups in Serbia, *Vreme* has received help from the George Soros Foundation, a private organization working for the advancement of open societies in Eastern Europe. Soros bailed the magazine out, offering it financial assistance at its most difficult moment, in 1993. Yet *Vreme* is regularly attacked by state television, in government statements, and in the parliament, and is subject to harassment by tax inspectors. Members of its editorial staff have been taken to court and acquitted. Its journalists occasionally receive anonymous letters and phone calls, which frequently allude to information about their families or themselves that is private and would be hard to obtain by regularly available channels. Even though *Vreme* has no proof of the government's involvement in this kind of harassment, it seems clear that some of the threatening information used against its journalists cannot be obtained without official cooperation.

Despite all this, in July 1996 *Vreme* celebrated its three hundredth issue. In regard to both its professionalism and its political integrity, it is a journal unlike any other that has ever existed in the Balkans.

Republika, the first periodical of civil opposition in Yugoslavia, was founded in March 1989, eighteen months before *Vreme*. From the first issue to spring 1993, this small-circulation journal received most of its funds from Rudi Supek, one of the most distinguished Croatian philosophers. Three years before his death in spring 1993, Supek donated his whole pension—paid by the French government for having participated in the French Resistance and having been a Buchenwald concentration camp prisoner—to *Republika*. Since Supek's death, the journal has depended on the voluntary contributions of its supporters and, for paper costs, on the Soros Foundation. Its financial survival, however, is continuously in jeopardy.

Republika is devoted to political commentary and analysis, not news, and to the active support of the individuals and movements resisting the war. In the first half of 1990 it published as a separate book the only comprehensive study of the Kosovo crisis available in Serbia, covering all relevant dimensions of the issue—legal, political, and cultural. Publication of the study was financed by its main editor, Nebojša Popov, with money from the sale of his parents' house. In the spring of 1991, four months before the outbreak of war in Croatia, *Republika* was the first journal to warn of the dangers of fascism in Serbia and Croatia. It was the first, also, to feature criticism of the Serbian authoritarian regime and to promote antiwar ideas, groups, and movements. From the start of the war, the journal encouraged and supported draft resisters and war deserters. It also paid for lawyers willing to offer resisters legal counsel and emigration advice. In a special 1992 issue it published valuable documentation on antiwar activity in Belgrade. It has continuously worked to bring together the various antiwar groups, organizing round tables and publishing several special studies on acute problems related to political issues and the war. *Republika* was the first to report in 1992 on the expulsions of Croats from the Vojvodina village of Hrtkovci, and the first, in 1993, to write on the disappearance of a group of twenty-one Muslims, most likely killed, from a Belgrade-Bar train. To this day *Republika* runs a support group for the families of the disappeared and pays for their lawyers.

In 1995 *Republika* addressed academics and cultural and political commentators with the idea of starting the Ogledi (analyses) Edition, in-depth studies relevant for the current crisis. The critical monographs published are of tremendous documentary and analytic value and represent the most serious efforts thus far at understanding the causes and the complexities of the war and a variety of aspects of the present reality.[11]

Because of its limited financial resources, the journal publishes only between five thousand and fifteen thousand copies per issue, depending on its finances. It has subscribers in all countries of Western Europe, in the United States, and in Japan. Issues are often photocopied and sent on to friends. Because of the limited circulation, in Belgrade and abroad, each issue is circulated from hand to hand. The old *Borba*, in its daily column "What Others Write," used to regularly carry lead articles from *Republika*.

Independent TV Studio B (NTV Studio B) began broadcasting in November 1990 with only one direct transmitter and four relays, reaching no more than 3.5 million viewers in the radius of about sixty miles. To broadcast across Serbia, three or four additional relays were necessary, since satellite transmission was financially beyond reach. Because of its independent policies and its determination to offer objective coverage, the station was labeled the enemy channel from the very outset. In March 1991, at the time of antiwar demonstrations that drew 100,000 people and left 2 dead, 203 wounded, and 158 thrown in jail, its studios were raided by the police and its broadcasting interrupted.[12] The tapes of the demonstrations were confiscated.

Between 1990 and 1993 Studio B provided reliable information, named war criminals, provided coverage for the protests of antiwar groups, and exposed the machinations of the regime. In one of its most popular programs "Viewers' Interview," a well-known person directly answered called-in questions. This program was the first to bring Milošević's party members face to face with the members of the opposition. Studio B also featured daily reruns of the news and information reports carried by the international television networks, most often the BBC. On a few occasions World Net linked Studio B journalists over satellite with analysts and reporters in Washington, Philadelphia, Paris, and London for a live broadcast.

With a great deal of effort, in late 1991 Studio B was able to collect the funds for the equipment necessary to slightly upgrade its broadcasting range. But even though the equipment had already been paid for in London, it could not be imported because economic sanctions had been imposed before the shipment was made. Appeals to the UN Security Council, urging the obvious—that without an independent TV channel Serbia was doomed—were to no avail.[13]

The equipment was allowed to cross the border into Serbia only ten days before the 1992 Serbian elections were to take place. By then it was too late to reverse the impact state-controlled television had on the voters. In any case, immediately after the truck carrying the equipment entered

Serbia, it was kidnapped on the open road by a band of masked, armed men. The Studio B staff assumes that the operation was most likely run by the Serbian police.

As with all the other independent media, maintaining sources of information has been the most serious professional problem for Studio B. Direct communication with the correspondents in Croatia and Bosnia-Hercegovina was impossible after telephone connections were cut off and all communication had to go through Hungary. Lack of automobile fuel presented another serious obstacle. Gasoline and diesel fuel was rationed under the sanctions, and Studio B had to service all its needs on only thirteen gallons a month.

In the summer of 1993, the station was forced to drastically reduce its programming because of financial difficulties. Inflation was rampant at the time (the rate of exchange of foreign currency changed drastically from the morning to afternoon), and all independent media were extremely hard hit. The government took advantage of the situation by providing abundant financing for its own spin-off channel, TV Politika. This channel was able to obtain some recent U.S. films despite the sanctions and to produce a quantity of new entertainment programs. As a result, its viewer ratings jumped whereas ratings for Studio B dropped.

In 1993 Studio B lost many of its advertising clients, and the financial crunch affected its programming. Large enterprises were ordered to stop using the station as advertising agent, which just about finished off the station.[14] The management decided that rather than go broke, it would sell airtime to the political parties involved in the upcoming 1993 elections. This caused a bitter conflict between Dragan Kojadinović, the director and main editor of Studio B, and the editor of the newsroom, Lila Radonjić, who left Studio B immediately with a group of its strongest reporters.[15] A new crew of young and semitrained staff without the same commitment, ambitions, and ideals was hired. When on February 15, 1996, the Supreme Court ordered nationalization of the exhausted, internally torn, and dispirited Studio B, there weren't enough people at the station to support a strike. The politicians insisted that the programming of Studio B would not change, and that money would be given for it to become a modern, efficient, informative station. The news that Studio B was nationalized attracted only about one hundred persons who came to demonstrate in front of the downtown skyscraper housing Studio B offices.

Radio B-92 is still going strong, even though the station, which broadcasts without a license, has an insufficient supply of tapes, cassettes, and parts to repair technical equipment. The station is run by young people, whose motto is "Believe no one, not even us."[16] Their programming is a mixture of information, sharp satire, entertainment, and, above all, good music. The news analysis is unsparing and in-depth, intentionally rendered in an enfant terrible style. The reporters rely on humor and surprise as their method of delivery, even though their investigative and analytical work is extremely serious. At one point in 1993 the station announced that the regular team had gone on vacation and was temporarily replaced by a new team that had changed the name of the station. "From now on," the announcer said, "we are the SPS Radio" (the radio of Milošević's Socialist Party). Listeners called immediately in disbelief. Meanwhile sympathetic things were said about the government and criticism directed at antiwar groups. More and more phone calls came in. In all, there were about six hundred the first day. The main message of the listeners was "What on earth do you think you are doing!? Don't think we'll let you get away with this. Shape up or get off the air." B-92 taped every call and broadcast the gems the next day to protest the government's repeated denials of the station's requests for a frequency license. The listeners of B-92 are mainly the young and middle-aged. Without B-92, many say, life in Serbia would be nothing but an exercise in self-degradation.[17]

The independent media have given coverage to all the manifestations of the civil opposition: the Civil Resistance Movement, the Center for Antiwar Action, the student movement, Women against War, the Women's Antiwar Caucus, Women in Black, the Women's Parliament, the Belgrade Circle, the Belgrade branch of the Helsinki Civil Parliament, and other peace groups outside of Belgrade—in Novi Sad, Priština, Bečej, Pančevo, and Ada, as well as in Zagreb, Ljubljana, and Skopje. Without the wide and up-to-date coverage provided by the Belgrade independent media, the antiwar movement would be the best-kept secret even in Serbia.

Some antiwar demonstrations have brought out large crowds, others only small groups of fifty to one hundred people. In former Yugoslavia there was no tradition of independent public protest and civil disobedience, which turned out to be a major handicap. The absence of experience in organizing public protest has had a toll whose significance cannot be underestimated: the antiwar movement remained quite isolated and proved unable to inspire the support of a wider stratum of the population.

On July 15, 1991, immediately following the start of the war in Slovenia, the Center for Antiwar Action, founded earlier that month, called a press conference to set out its position of "negotiations instead of war and violence" and to call for desertion from the army. To help deserters, the center organized assistance by a small number of Belgrade's best lawyers. The call for desertion spread throughout Serbia, and the center opened branches even in the out-of-the-way villages.

The Civil Resistance Movement joined the call for desertion and in late 1991 launched the Civil Campaign against War, with the goal of collecting the hundred thousand signatures necessary to force the government to hold a referendum on the draft. In the very tense atmosphere, a few months after the fighting began in Croatia, *Borba* published on ten separate days the call of the Civil Resistance Movement for signatures. Studio B aired several special spots with the message that in a fratricidal war one may not be drafted against one's personal will. Every individual, the message read, had the right to make a decision according to his or her own conscience.

In many towns, people went out on their own initiative to collect signatures requesting that a referendum be held. In Belgrade, a number of public personalities joined in the street campaign to collect signatures. But instead of the required one hundred thousand signatures, only seventy thousand were collected. The referendum was not held, but this first mass campaign with its message "We demand to be asked!" found a wide reception in the Serbian public and encouraged over one hundred thousand men in Serbia and Montenegro to avoid the draft by escaping across the border or by going into hiding with friends or relatives.

From October 1, 1991, to February 1, 1992, every evening, the Civil Resistance Movement and Center for Antiwar Action organized the lighting of candles in front of the presidency building in the heart of Belgrade. The candles were lit in memory of all, regardless of nationality, who had died and would still die in the war, and in solidarity with Serbia's growing number of war deserters. Among others, Cyrus Vance lit a candle on New Year's Eve 1991. *Borba* daily covered the campaign in pictures and words throughout the four months of its nightly duration.

At the end of the candlelighting campaign, in February 1992, two months before the fighting began in Bosnia-Hercegovina, *Borba* allowed the main person behind the Civil Resistance Movement, Nataša Kandić, to prepare a daily column under the heading "The Civil Antiwar Campaign." She invited prominent people in public life and many others to write for the column. Not one of the persons she asked refused, and the column appeared daily for two and a half months.

On April 22, 1992, a huge rock concert organized by the Center for Antiwar Action was held in Belgrade. "Don't Count On Us!" was the message sent to the draft and recruitment centers. On May 4, the Civil Resistance Movement organized a public "black ribbon" demonstration in support of and solidarity with the people of Sarajevo. A column of 150,000 people carried a black paper ribbon 1,400 yards long (cloth was unavailable in the empty stores) in total silence through the downtown center of Belgrade. The ribbon arrived intact at its final destination after many hours of marching.

In May 1992, Belgrade composers and actors protested the distortions of nationalism in the culture by kneeling in silence in the park across the street from the Yugoslav parliament building. On June 30, the "Tolling Bells" protest was held, organized by the Civil Resistance Movement together with other antiwar groups and demanding an immediate end to the regime's politics of war and Milošević's immediate resignation. Bell towers were built on trucks borrowed from the town's theaters, and the intention was to drive through the center of downtown with the bells ringing. However, at the start of the demonstration, police blocked the passage, claiming that trucks as theatrical equipment required special transit permits. Having anticipated that the police would find a way to sabotage the demonstration, its organizers had asked ahead of time that participants bring bells as well as pots and pans of their own. The marchers circled through the city, ringing their small hand-held noisemakers all the way up to the steps of the presidency building.

In July 1992, a long student protest began that included a series of partial strikes and ended with a peace march of several thousand students through the city. That summer also, the Center for Antiwar Action held a number of open panel discussions and talks.[18] The practice of open discussions had been established by the Belgrade Circle, founded in January 1992 by a group of writers, university professors, artists, architects, journalists, and actors. The discussions originally were held every Saturday morning in a centrally located small theater at the Youth Center but then moved to the theater Rex, an abandoned hall outside of the center of town. Some of the discussion topics have been "Life with the Monstrosity," "Is Another Serbia Possible?" "Manufacturers of National Hate,"

The Black Ribbon March in solidarity with the people of Sarajevo, Belgrade:
May 1992. Photo by Goranka Matić. Courtesy of the *Vreme* news agency.

"The Murderers of Cities," and "How Far Have We Fallen." A guest from one or another European country was occasionally the speaker. At the end of 1992, with the financial assistance of *Borba*, the Belgrade Circle published *The Other Serbia*, a collection of articles reflecting the existence in Serbia of many different antiregime voices favoring the end to the war and an affirmation of an antinationalist, pluralist society. The book was translated into English, German, and French. During 1993, the Belgrade Circle spread its activities to other towns in Serbia and also to Skopje in Macedonia and Ljubljana in Slovenia.

The Belgrade Circle followed the initiative in 1992 of the Civil Resistance Movement and the Center for Antiwar Action of protesting against the ongoing harassment and expulsion of the non-Serbian population in Vojvodina. The Civil Resistance Movement also brought to the attention of *Borba*, *Vreme*, and Studio B details of the pressures and outright persecution of some old Croatian families in the village of Hrtkovci, which was aimed at forcing them to leave the village. A loud campaign followed in the independent media. In July 1992, a "yellow ribbon" protest took place in front of the parliament building, drawing a crowd of some two thousand, all wearing yellow ribbons around their upper arms. The reference was to the Star of David that Jews were forced to wear during World War II. At the end of the protest, the yellow ribbons were tied to the ropes of the flagpoles in front of the parliament, raised, and left fluttering in the wind. Protesters also wore cardboard signs around their necks with a bull's-eye over the heart. Written on one sign was "I am Orthodox, and Catholic, and Muslim, and Jewish, and Buddhist, and atheist."

In the second half of 1993, the Center for Antiwar Action, which by that time had received important funding from the Soros Foundation, UNICEF, and the UN High Commission for Refugees, undertook a series of interrelated projects aimed at reinforcing the traditional spirit of tolerance in Serbia's multinational communities. It sent teams of about ten specialists into towns and villages of Vojvodina to hold three-week conflict-resolution meetings with the local populations. The center ran a similar program in Belgrade and outlying schools, especially in those where enrollment included a large proportion of children of mixed ethnic origin. Center specialists instructed teachers, school counselors, and psychologists in the principles of conflict resolution to be applied in the classroom and with children individually. The center also sent teams, reinforced with clinical psychologists and social workers, to refugee camps for mothers and children in Serbia and Montenegro, to help the refugees adjust to their new circumstances.

Women's groups sent a number of organizations of their own, among others the sos hotline for battered women and children and an aid center for war victims of rape. One group, Women in Black, had held a regular weekly antiwar protest since 1991 in Belgrade. Independent women's groups work with other antiwar groups in Belgrade, Novi Sad, Priština, Bečej, Ada, and Pančevo, as well as in Skoplje, Zagreb, and Ljubljana.

In late 1992, with the help of the Soros Foundation, a collection center for documentation of war crimes and violations of human rights throughout the territory of former Yugoslavia, called Humanitarian Law Center, was founded in Belgrade. The center, whose executive director is Nataša Kandić, conducts field investigations by tracing and interviewing witnesses to crimes. The purpose is to corroborate every story with at least three or four independent sources. The fund issues regular "Spotlight Reports" on specific instances of war crimes, expulsions of local populations, massacres, and rape, as well as every other category of human rights violations. The fund has gained high regard among the international organizations and agencies working in this field. Its reports are prepared in Serbo-Croatian and English and sent to a long mailing list of organizations and individuals within Yugoslavia and abroad. The purpose is to keep the public at home and abroad informed and to maintain constant pressure on the governments throughout former Yugoslavia to act against violations of human rights. An important goal of the fund is to identify the criminals and crimes and thus work against the tendency in former Yugoslavia and abroad to attach collective guilt to entire populations.

The philanthropic Soros Foundation, which supports many antiwar groups and independent media, was always officially considered the principal "anti-Yugoslav" organization to be avoided by patriots. Yet, in addition to its aid to the antiwar groups and media, the Soros Foundation also aided the refugees, child-care institutions, schools for handicapped children, and medical centers across former Yugoslavia. In 1993 alone, it sent $9.3 million worth of medicines and medical supplies to Serbia alone.[19] In spring 1995 the Soros Foundation came under sustained and vicious attack on the part of many government agencies, including the somewhat unlikely office of the president of Belgrade University, who said one should stop George Soros in his tracks and prevent him from "infiltrating the schools and the university." The director of the Clinical Center of Serbia boasted that he had refused this organization's help and had thus prevented Soros from infiltrating the Serbian health care system.[20] The government tried to ban the foundation but encountered resistance and in June 1996 reestablished the organization under the title "Foundation for Open Society."

In 1996 the antiwar groups the foundation supported seemed threatened by exhaustion and haunted by the awareness that results over five years of protest had been slim.[21] True, the movement and the independent press have kept the principles of human rights and democracy alive in an extremely hostile political environment, but they have failed to significantly affect the course of events. The measure of their failure is also a tragic measure of the incalculable importance of traditions of grassroots activism in times of populist totalitarianism. The absence of the spirit of protest in the culture as a whole meant also the absence of political context for efforts of this kind to take strong root and become a force of consequence.

Nobody expected that the winter of 1996–97 would bring about the most massive and the longest-lasting anti-regime demonstrations Belgrade had ever seen. In November 1996, however, three movements came together: the student movement, continuing its unfinished business from 1991 and 1992, when it was suppressed in blood; the movement in support of the Zajedno Coalition (comprising the Serbian Renewal Movement, the Civic Association, and the Democratic Party); and the movement of private citizens without any party loyalties, the proverbial silent majority. The catalyst for the deluge was the victory of Zajedno at the November 1996 municipal elections, which Milošević had not expected and tried to annul, using all means at his disposal. In response, all major cities in Serbia were brought to a standstill, and the republic rocked day after day from November 17 to February 24.

The protests remained peaceful until the very end. Massive turnout on the streets of Belgrade, varying from eighty thousand to four hundred thousand people from all walks of life, revealed the depth of pent-up discontent with "The Family," as Slobodan Milošević and his wife Mira Marković had come to be known in the independent press. In the temperatures reaching 0 degrees Fahrenheit, under snow and sleet, marched students, high-school teachers, university professors, musicians, actors, writers, church dignitaries, housewives, retired clerks, children of all ages, even some army officers. Famous actors canceled their theater performances in support of the protesters, who were brutally beaten twice in late January and once in early February (one person was killed, another badly injured). Many judges voiced their support of the students. Old academicians gave speeches to huge exuberant crowds. The spirit was that of a carnival, of a collective high where new forms of peaceful, irreverent challenge to the regime were being invented day after day. The unfolding street burlesque, nutty, loud, and brilliant, showed, among other things, how starved people have become in the years since the war had started for a chance to let go and plain play.

The protesters wanted the daily protest to gradually bleed out the power of Slobodan Milošević—and in the end, it did. Above all, they wanted the election victories of the opposition reinstated, and television freed of government control. Milošević, who had been silent for a year, failed to address the demonstrators even once. He tried to use the electoral commissions and the courts in every way possible to prevent the opposition from claiming its victory. But in the end, on February 24, 1997, he had to give in, conceding fourteen of the most important cities in Serbia to the opposition.

The protest has aroused tremendous collective energy and enormous hopes. After five years, a popular movement has finally proved itself able to significantly affect the course of events. Slobodan Milošević is still in power, but the experience of a sustained, peaceful and determined collective action, the first of its kind in the Balkans, represents tremendous political capital for the future.

NOTES

1 Smaller papers, such as *Svetlost* (Kragujevac), *Novi Pančevac* (Pančevo), and *Košava* (Vršac), were launched across Serbia.

2 Only *Politika*, founded in 1904 as a liberal paper, has a longer tradition. (Since 1987, however, *Politika* has acted as a mouthpiece of the Socialist Party of Slobodan Milošević.)

3 The best names of Yugoslav journalism seemed to have gathered around *Borba*: Grujica Spasović, Djuro Bilbija, Gordana Logar, Radivoj Cvijetićanin, Miša Brkić, Mirko Klarin, Bojana Jager, Manojlo Vukotić, and others.

4 Tanja Jakobi, "Vlasništvo, stvarni i prividni uzrok sukoba," *Republika* (February 1995), p. ix.

5 In November 1992, when official media failed to offer a single scrap of reliable information about the situation in Sarajevo, Željko Vuković was dispatching to *Borba*

a series of fascinating lengthy reports under the title "The Killing of Sarajevo" ("Ubijanje Sarajeva"). Under the series title "Sarajevo's collapse" ("Sarajevski Suno-vrat"), Natka Buturović reported on the problems of everyday life in the city where the bread-baking factory was under assault (see, for example, "Najednom je banula glad," *Borba*, 4–5 December 1992, p. ix).

6   A critical discussion of the strengths and weaknesses of *Borba* can be found in Oli-vija Rusovac, "Gradjanske ideje u pozadini," *Republika* (February 1995): xv.

7   Velimir Ilić, "Hronika najavljene smrti," *Republika* (February 1995): iii. The court resorted to a legal trick in December 1994 and proclaimed that the *Borba* holding company actually never existed (see Bojana Oprijan-Inić, "Pravne akrobacije," *Re-publika* [February 1995]: vii).

8   Serbia still had no legislation in the area of private-sector news companies.

9   The boldness of the *Vreme* graphic design is in part the effect of turning necessity into virtue: *Vreme* simply cannot afford design extravagance. At times it is forced to print on the lowest-quality paper, which had not been used in this country since the early 1950s.

10   Interview with *Vreme* journalist Zoran Jeličić.

11   The following themes have been covered: Drinka Gojković, The Writers Asso-ciation and the war; Rade Veljanovski, Radio and television: From socialism to nationalism; Olivera Milosavljević, The role of the Academy of Sciences in the war; Radmila Radić, The Church and the "Serbian question"; Aleksandar Nenadović, The daily *Politika* and nationalism; Latinka Perović, The escape from moderniza-tion in Serbia; Olga Zirojević, Kosovo in the historical memory; Dubravka Stoja-nović, Serbian parliamentary opposition; Olivera Milosavljević, Yugoslavia as a fic-tion; Vojin Dimitrijević, The international community and the crisis in Yugoslavia; Miroslav Hadžić, The army and the war; Ljubomir Madžar, The economic condition of Serbia and Yugoslavia; Ivan Čolović, Football, hooligans, and the war; Nebojša Popov, The trauma of a party state; Milan Podunavac, Caesarism and democracy; Sreten Vujović, The city in the war; Marina Blagojević, The emigration of Serbs from Kosovo: A trauma or a catharsis?

12   The demonstrations are discussed at some length by Milan Milošević, "Dan koji je potresao Beograd," *Vreme*, 7 March 1994, pp. 32–35.

13   Interview with the Studio B staff (summer 1992).

14   In order to survive, Studio B accepted early on the sponsorship of two private banks (Jugoskandik and Dafiment) that eventually collapsed after having robbed their patrons royally. At the peak of their business, these banks helped Studio B to obtain the equipment it otherwise would have been unable to purchase on its own and to regularly receive spare parts.

15   Rade Veljanovski, "Na ivici ponora," *Republika* (January 1996).

16   Julie Flint, "B-92," *Republika* (September 1993): 15.

17   In his 20 June 1994 column in *Nation*, "Watching Rights," Aryeh Neier argues that *Vreme*, Radio B92, and the Croatian satirical weekly *Feral Tribune* "are in urgent need of protection" (p. 862). International recognition of these media, which was withheld, would have made a great difference.

18   Topics included "Bosnia Today," "Fascism at the End of the Twentieth Century,"

"A Peaceful Bosnia," "Bosnian Vukovars," and "Open Society Parties in Serbia and Montenegro."

19   "Šoroš za izbeglice," *Vreme*, 25 April 1994, p. 33.

20   Stojan Cerović, "Čuvari Tvrdjave," *Vreme*, 13 March 1995. Cerović comments ironically: "They won't let Soros school their children and save their ill. He had signed the appeal for the removal of Karadžić's tanks even before Milošević had discovered Sarajevo was being bombarded and before he decided he himself had always advocated peace. Does Soros think he can help the people and at the same time oppose the regime? Doesn't he know that Serbs make no such distinctions? Until he has learned that basic lesson, Soros himself should worry where to place his money."

21   In 1992 Milan Milošević wrote: "To work for peace in Serbia in the last year implied many risks, from immediate exposure to repression, to getting used to all manner of insult, to accusations of 'treason' and of being a 'bad Serb,' to the despair over humble successes" ("Rizik mirnog puta," *Vreme*, 5 October 1992, p. 14). The same is true to this day.

The Opposition in Croatia
Sven Balas

In the spring of 1984, I was sitting with a friend in a Dubrovnik bar. On the wall over the bar hung a picture of Marshal Tito—four years dead, yet immortal—in a snow-white uniform, playing the piano. Looking at Tito through his beer glass, my friend cried out, "Sam, please, don't play it again."

The icon remained silent, but Croatia today must suffer through an endless, unentertaining spectacle, provided by the aspiring new Tito, the self-appointed Arch-Croat, Franjo Tudjman. Like Tito, Tudjman travels in a private jet, rides in a bullet-proof limousine, resides in a variety of castles, enjoys handmade suits and shoes, sails a yacht, and maintains his own personal vacation miniparadise in the islands of Brioni off the northern Adriatic coast—where Tito also disported himself.

Every year, Tudjman picks, with his own hands, a basket of tangerines from an orchard that was Tito's, on the isle of Vanga at Brioni. The fruit is then mailed to selected orphans. Tito cultivated the same habit. In both cases, the gift of tangerines suggested to the public that the wise Father of the Nation cared for his children.

In some ways Tudjman also resembles Slobodan Milošević, his Serbian counterpart in extremist nationalism. Although a generation older than Milošević, Tudjman is a product of the Yugoslav Communist apparatus, too. He was born in 1922, joined the Partisan movement during World War II as a convinced Marxist and rose to become the youngest general in Tito's armed forces. Like Milošević, who studied business, Tudjman, who became a historian, was trained in the Tito state's system.

Today he exercises near-dictatorial power in Croatia and plays a determining role in the fate of Bosnia-Hercegovina.[1] And while the blame for the war rests squarely on Slobodan Milošević and his partners in ideology, Radovan Karadžić, Ratko Mladić, Vojislav Šešelj, and others, the fate of Croatian people, and of many Muslims, is shaped now by Tudjman. His six years in power already have made Tito look good to many and have made others wonder if a Pinochet or some other Third World dictator would not have wished, after all, to have been more like Tudjman.

The election of Tudjman and his party, the Croatian Democratic Union (HDZ) in 1990 was fair. The HDZ was mainly opposed by the crumbling remnants of the Croatian Communist bureaucracy, which did not lack talented personalities but which was profoundly discredited among the mass of Croats, and by a coalition of small social democratic and liberal parties headed by intellectuals who were widely respected and admired but whom few Croats thought could lead the country through the difficult transition from Yugoslav socialism. Most important, neither the Croatian Communists nor the opposition coalition projected an image of martial strength in the face of the Milošević threat. Tudjman, by contrast, could point to his military background. In addition, he had been imprisoned during the Tito regime for Croatian nationalism and thus enjoyed somewhat the halo of a martyr. The HDZ won handily.

But doubts about Tudjman were also expressed, from the beginning, by Croatian liberals, raised by Tudjman's revisionist views of Croatian history, as well as his apparent authoritarian leanings, which many saw as a continuation of his Communist past. Nevertheless, like other post-Communist states, Croatia in 1990 basked in the celebration of what all took for granted would be a new regime of democratic rights.

One such right applied to free press. Croatia enjoyed broad literacy and a profound commitment by its intelligentsia to literary excellence as well as to the protection of the Croatian language. In addition, its media were proud of their professionalism, rare enough in Tito's Yugoslavia but offering a staggering contrast to the press even in such literate socialist countries as the former Czechoslovakia. Nearly all Croatian intellectuals and journalists believed the fall of the Communist regime would bring about an enormous expansion of free media. But it was not to be.

Tudjman—who had promised when he came to power to privatize the media—turned television into an HDZ fiefdom from the very beginning. One by one, print journals and reporting teams known for their objectivity and independence fell under his control. Tudjman attempted to justify his restrictions on the media by citing the management difficulties in the transfer of former Communist media properties to new owners. In addition, he asserted that virtually the whole Croatian media class were nothing but the hirelings of the former regime.

But these pretexts did not address certain other, interrelated questions. Why should issues of management or, for that matter, ideology impinge on editorial and reportorial professionalism? Why was it nearly impossible for liberal Croatian intellectuals, who had never been associated with the regime, to set up new, serious organs of opinion? And why, by contrast, was it so easy for Ustashe-nostalgics to suddenly flood the country with their printed propaganda?

The cases of the Zagreb weekly *Danas* (Today) and the Split daily *Slobodna Dalmacija* (Free Dalmatia)—considered among the highest-quality news media in former Yugoslavia—are illustrative. "Liberated" from Communist supervision, they came under attack from the HDZ, whose hard-line wing, based on a layer of ultranationalists from Hercegovina, interpreted any variation from the new party line as treason to the Croatian cause. Once the 1991 war began in earnest, the HDZ became annoyed with journalists who had not surrendered to Tudjman's "coordination" and charged them with betrayal in wartime. Experienced, professionally capable reporters and editors were denounced as Chetniks, Yugoslavists, Communists.

Danas attempted to resist the onslaught. However, its publisher was the Zagreb daily *Vjesnik* (Courier), which became the mouthpiece of Tudjman's regime and which was pressured into refusing to print *Danas*. Its team turned to Slovenia instead, but Tudjman then outlawed the magazine's distribution. That meant that newsstands and individuals selling *Danas* ran the risk of court action. *Danas* expired.

The history of *Slobodna Dalmacija* was more complex. Published in the port of Split, this daily, open to all sides, had a circulation of one hundred thousand in the 1980s and was read all over Croatia as well as in the diaspora. In 1991, it denounced Croatian violations of the human rights of Serbs—the issue no other Croatian media would touch. But Tudjman's government decided to privatize the paper through issuance of stock, while barring the journalists—who were labeled, along with their former managers, as holdovers from the Communist era—from becoming majority stockholders. The best editors and reporters quit in protest, and *Slobodna Dalmacija* came under direct government supervision, through bank control of the stock majority. Its editorial policies were redefined and it became yet another nationalist organ.

Still, through the transition and war, some opposition voices established themselves. They include the daily *Novi List* (New journal), published in the northern Adriatic port city of Rijeka, which also issues the political-satirical weekly *Feral Tribune* as a supplement edited by former *Slobodna Dalmacija* journalists. Other independent mass media include Omladinska Televizija (Youth television) and Radio 101 in Zagreb. The popular radio, which the regime declared to be the agent of Voice of America, had its air rights denied in November 1996—the event that provoked an unexpectedly massive public outcry, drawing one hundred thousand people to the streets of Zagreb. That protest ignited another one a day later, when ten thousand retirees protested against the government because of poverty-level pensions.

The most consistent and forceful expression of opposition to Tudjman's Croatia has come from two intellectual journals issued in Zagreb, *Erasmus* and *Vijenac* (The Wreath). *Feral Tribune*, however, represents the loudest and most spirited protest.

Erasmus and *Vijenac* are serious, highbrow journals, handsomely designed and printed, profoundly opposed to the regime. Their audience, however, is limited to the educated classes in both Croatia and the diaspora. The editor in chief of *Erasmus* is Slavko Goldstein—who is also a columnist for *Feral*. Goldstein is one of the most remarkable figures in the history of postwar Croatia. Born in the old Hapsburg garrison town of Karlovac, and among a group of fifty-five Jews protected during the early period of the Holocaust by a village of Croatian peasants, Goldstein had served as president of the Zagreb Jewish community in the last decades of the Tito regime but was better known as a publisher and a prominent defender of Croatian culture. In this context, he became something of an idol for the pre-1990 Croatian public and even cooperated with Tudjman during his dissident period. In the 1990 election Goldstein became the architect of the liberal coalition that presented itself as an alternative both to the old Communist bureaucracy and to the HDZ.

The contributors to *Erasmus* include poets, politicians, philosophers, artists, authors, and professors, as well as the acclaimed intellectual leaders of the Croatian diaspora. *Vijenac* is published by *Matica Hrvatska* (The Croatian mother bee), one of the most noble and significant institutions in Croatian cultural history. Established in 1842 to advance Croatian culture and paralleled by *Matica Srpska* (The Serbian mother bee) and other Slav entities of the same character, in 1972 *Matica Hrvatska* was suppressed, its branches throughout Croatia shut down, for its defense of what was alleged to be Croatian nationalism. *Matica Hrvatska* is viewed as above reproach by many Croats, and its values have always been rational and liberal. Like *Erasmus, Vijenac* publishes the outstanding Croatian intellectuals of the present time.

The leading group of opposition intellectuals includes Ivan Supek, physicist, essayist, philosopher, dramatist, historian, and rector of Zagreb University, a true Renaissance man with a long and valiant career defending the freedom of the mind against Hitlerism, Stalinism, and Titoism as well as Tudjmanism. Supek is perhaps the most representative Croatian intellectual of this century, like his late brother, Rudi Supek, who financed, until his death, the antiwar monthly *Republika* in Belgrade. As a scientist, Ivan Supek studied under Werner Heisenberg at the University of Leipzig, where, upon receipt of his degree, he was arrested by the Gestapo and deported from Nazi Germany as a Communist. A Communist he was, but of the remarkable, now forgotten kind once so common in central Europe, equating revolution with a challenge to human limits, and as much at home in a discussion of modern art or psychoanalysis as of physics or Croatian history. His lightly fictionalized treatment of Tito's repression of Croatian Communists directly after World War II, *Krunski Svjedok Protiv Hebranga* (Crown witness against Hebrang), is a central document of contemporary Croatian history.

While Supek resides in Zagreb, another member of this group whose talents, achievements, and high principles are widely admired, Ivo Banac, is a professor of history at Yale University. The youngest of the group, Banac is the author of two major historical works, *The National Question in Yugoslavia: Origin, History, Politics* and *With Stalin against Tito.* Both works have established him as a leading Slavic scholar in the United States. A brilliant stylist in English scholarly prose as well as a superb researcher, a popular lecturer, and mentor to students, Banac is a considerable thorn in Tudjman's side, all the way from New Haven.

Another leading figure in this group is the poet Vlado Gotovac, the guiding spirit behind the post-1990 resurrection of *Matica Hrvatska*, a writer of great literary gifts and a man of unbreakable honesty and morality who was imprisoned and nearly murdered in Tito's prisons after the 1972 purge of Croatian intellectuals. His book *Moj Slučaj* (My case) is a genuine classic of the antitotalitarian dissident experience; it is no surprise, therefore, that Gotovac is an exceptionally articulate critic of Tudjman's authoritarian pretensions. The saddest aspect of Croatian life today is that men like Supek, Gotovac, and Goldstein, once so highly esteemed for their activity in defense of Croatian liberty, are freely subjected to the cheap attacks of Tudjman's government, while Croats who should know better remain silent.

Vijenac and *Erasmus* share this group of contributors, although *Vijenac* is perhaps more reader-friendly than the rigorous *Erasmus*. Both, however, are mainly aimed at a specialized, intellectual audience.

The intellectuals who write for the two journals have been the most prominent Croatian critics not only of Tudjman's abuses of power but also of his clear propensity to strike a rotten deal with Milošević, mainly to the disadvantage of the independent Bosnia-Hercegovina. Tudjman has indicated he would favor a carving up of Bosnia-Hercegovina that would grant Milošević much of the Greater Serbia for which he launched his wars, so long as Croatian ambitions in western Hercegovina were satisfied. For Banac and other opposition figures, any such deal with Milošević represented a moral disaster and a real possibility of national suicide.

Novi List, published in Rijeka, draws on different resources in its pursuit of an independent democratic line. It is by no means so aggressively critical as the intellectual organs, although it issues *Feral Tribune* in a print run of fifty thousand weekly copies, distributed throughout Croatia. *Novi List* reflects long-established suspicions on the part of the communities living on the northern Adriatic coast, including Istria, the communities closer to the real West in Italy, cosmopolitan and relatively well off, toward the centralizing powers in Zagreb, the Croatian capital. Istria has a small Italian minority and also has its own dialect of Croatian, known as čakavica, which has largely fallen into neglect. *Novi List*'s columns regularly express Istrian regional concerns in undiluted language. One of its most prominent and entertaining contributors is the author and journalist Roman Latkovic, whose comments on the latest manifestations of insanity in Croatian national economic and political life are discussed for days in cafés, on the streets and in the parks, at work or in class, with friends and around the family dinner table.

Feral Tribune, purposefully projecting a graphic image of a tabloid, is in a class by itself. Its masthead says that it is "the property of those who write and read it." Its basic message during the war, embedded in its satirical and its analytic journalism, proclaimed that not all Croats are the same, out to massacre Serbs and Muslims, and not all Serbs want to cut the throats of Croats; they all are victims of a madness fostered by the army and the police, a madness nourished by fear. This message, simple enough on its face but in Croatia as elsewhere in former Yugoslavia now extremely complicated, is conveyed through native wacky irony. *Feral* seeks not only to point out the individuals and events that brought Croatia to its present nightmare but also to be funny. Its spirit reflects the Mediterranean mentality of Dalmatia, like Istria suspicious of Croatian centralists and also known for the prevalence of unsparing quick wit, cultivated in the streets of cities like Šibenik, Zadar, Split, and Dubrovnik, where an inability to take a joke is considered a major character flaw.

Feral applies that wit, ingrained in the local culture, to the analysis of public policy. Early every Monday, after *Feral* arrives on the newsstands, people are seen giggling on the street as they turn the journal's large pages with sophisticated graphics. After years of shameless propaganda and lies from the "coordinated" media, it is quite remarkable that *Feral* can still make people want to read newspapers. It accomplishes that goal by giving the average person the satisfaction of seeing the regime they hate torn to shreds, if only verbally.

The paper's title and nameplate are a modified version of the *International Herald Tribune* logo, thus poking fun at the paper's limited, local interest but also hinting at ambitions transcending regional concerns. In the Dalmatian dialect of Croatian, *feral* means "street lamp" or simply a light. Between the words *Feral* and *Tribune* in the logo appears an old miniature engraving of a goddess surrounded by butterflies, rising from a floating banner that reads, in Italian, "Pazzia, Regina di Mondo" (Madness, the queen of the world)—a takeoff on "Pax, Regina Mundi" (Peace, the queen of the world). Peace is indeed the main concern of *Feral Tribune*. Beneath the logo the paper defines itself as a "weekly magazine of Croatian anarchists, Protestants, and heretics, dear to God but not unpopular with the Devil either."

Feral's editors are Viktor Ivančić, Predrag Lučić, and Boris Dežulović. The first syllables of their names have been merged to form the paper's slogan: Viva Ludež. Ludež is *Feral*'s term for insanity, a word absent from the Croatian dictionary but easily recognized not only in Croatia to mean screwball goofiness.

Yet *Feral Tribune* is not only a satyricon. It is also a serious political journal that interprets the Yugoslav tragedy. In the front lampoon section, computer graphics are used to create collages bringing together absurd composites in a single image. The favorite subject is, of course, Franjo Tudjman, who, like the British politicians seen in *Private Eye* or the French ones featured in *Canard Enchaine* (The bound duck), has appeared naked in *Feral* many times. The cover of a still remembered winter 1993 issue shows a composite photograph of the fat, naked Tudjman enjoying a post-sex pillow chat with an equally nude Milošević. The text reads: "Is this what we fought for?" On another issue's cover, a naked Milošević, posing as the proud father, shows off an infant with the head of Radovan Karadžić. Two pages further, the Croatian prime minister Nikica Valentić is shown sitting on the toilet.

Tudjman's government has sought to exploit *Feral*'s use of sexual or other scandalous graphics. On June 18, 1994, a "pornography" tax was slapped on the paper. This measure, in effect a tax on images, aimed at destroying *Feral Tribune* while disguising what was, in truth, an act of brutal censorship. Tudjman has always wanted his government to appear Western and democratic along German or Austrian lines. But the voice of the opposition irritates him; it irritates him intolerably. A tax on "pornographic" publishing, he hoped, would allow him to avoid the accusation of censorship while wiping out *Feral Tribune*.

It is, of course, more than a matter of personal irritation on the part of Tudjman at a media source beyond his control. *Feral Tribune* calls things by their real names; it denounces Croatian racism and anti-Semitism as well as the intrigues and mutual back scratching within the new establishment. It addresses the greatest of taboos: Croatian war crimes. It even publishes Serbian opposition journalists, such as Petar Luković or Stojan Cerović of *Vreme*, the independent Belgrade weekly. Worst of all from the perspective of the HDZ hard-liners, *Feral* is in high demand in Belgrade, where its articles are reprinted both in *Vreme* and in the daily *Borba* (now *Naša Borba*). *Feral* must therefore be part of a Chetnik-Communist conspiracy against Croatia. Many impressionable folk are swayed by such arguments; many suits have been filed against *Feral* over the years, demanding astronomical sums for damages.[2]

In the summer of 1994, Tudjman ordered the name of the Croatian currency changed from the dinar to the kuna. The kuna takes its name from skins of animals, weasel or mink, used in the distant past for barter. But the kuna was also the name of the Croatian currency under the so-called Independent State of Croatia—the pro-Nazi puppet regime of the Ustashe, the party of Ante Pavelić during World War II. Instead of doing everything he could to distance himself from Pavelić, Tudjman reinstated the currency used in Pavelić's state. Slavko Goldstein accurately described

Tudjman's triumphalism after the proclamation of the kuna as that of a politician who did not know how to be a statesman, an autistic, self-deceptive autocrat who has ruined all life in Croatia, except for the military.[3] Ivo Banac wrote on the occasion: "We who have dedicated our lives to struggling for the defense of Croatia from kunaism, as it were, may now thank political commissar Tudjman for his gesture of historical reconciliation."[4]

Under the Ustashe regime, fewer than 10 percent of the Croatian populace supported Pavelić. Liberal and democratic Croats, as well as those who felt pride at Tito's partial Croatian heritage, have oscillated between outrage and depression about the post–World War II suggestions that all Croats were genocidal neo-Nazis. But such unfair and prejudiced judgment is not easily alleviated today when the press accurately reports that some high officials in Tudjman's Croatia declare themselves to be the followers of Pavelić and his regime.[5]

Tudjman's decision to turn the memorial site of the World War II Jasenovac concentration camp, Yugoslavia's Auschwitz, into the burial ground for both the victims of fascism and the "victims of Communism" (Croatian fascists fighting under Ante Pavelić), has provoked a series of scathing articles in *Feral Tribune*. Tudjman first mentioned the idea of Jasenovac's conversion in 1990, then in 1991, 1993, 1995, and finally, in early summer 1996. As Marinko Čulić, one of the leading *Feral* commentators, has written, Tudjman thereby announced his intention to "reconceptualize and in fact destroy the memorial's principal message."[6]

Bogdan Bogdanović, the Serbian architect of the extraordinary Jasenovac memorial, intended it to symbolize "forgiveness, the flux of life being renewed, even reconciliation—but reconciliation in spirit and never, I repeat, never, political reconciliation."[7] Jasenovac was the major memorial Bogdanović built after World War II. Since the early 1990s it has lingered in utter neglect and disrepair.[8] Most other monuments Bogdanović designed—the antithesis in their abstract sophistication and aesthetic vision to the exalted monuments of wounded or fallen soldiers across eastern Europe—have been vandalized, some of them totally destroyed after 1991. This pained Bogdanović, but he has said a number of times that in the larger scale of things the ruin of his lifework was far from the worst thing that had happened to Yugoslavia. Tudjman's intended desecration of Jasenovac, however, was too much. "No one in Europe today would dare change the character of an antifascist memorial," Bogdanović said in March 1996 to the *Feral* reporter, vowing to prevent Tudjman by all the means he could employ.[9]

Commenting on Tudjman's Jasenovac idea, Viktor Ivančić, *Feral*'s editor in chief, wrote that Tudjman urged "a reconciliation" by mixing in a mass grave the bones of victims and of criminals. If Tudjman got his way, claimed Ivančić, we would have the "United Colors of Jasenovac." He charged that regarding Jasenovac, Tudjman acted as a declared follower of the Spanish general Francisco Franco.[10]

His charge did not go unnoticed. In early summer 1996 Ivančić was accused of slander and brought to court. His defense was as hilarious as it was brilliant. He reminded the court that in July 1990, in an interview with the German journal *Tageszeitung*, Tudjman himself insisted that creating a common grave for the victims of fascism and communism was nothing new. Tudjman mentioned that Franco—who had a chapel built in Toledo to commemorate the victims of the Spanish Civil War—argued that both Falangists and Communists had fought for Spain, each soldier under his own flag. They ought to be buried together, said Franco, and Tudjman agreed.[11]

In April 1991, Ivančić said, Tudjman gave an interview to the Croatian weekly *Start*, in which he said that "in the figure of Franco, Spain found someone who had the courage and wisdom to say that Spanish Communists and Spanish Falangists equally fought for Spain, but under separate flags. The same was happening in Croatia."[12] And so, asked Ivančić, "what does the accusation that *Feral* had portrayed Tudjman as Franco's follower actually mean? . . . Regarding the morbid idea of the reconciliation of the dead, Tudjman is clearly Franco's follower. That much is not debatable. Furthermore, Tudjman sees nothing wrong in the idea of such reconciliation. Why then is he offended to be identified with the idea? And how does the prosecutor's conclusion follow—that Tudjman has been offended and slandered—if Tudjman himself sees Franco as his model? . . . I, of course, think that Tudjman has 'the courage' and 'the wisdom' to follow Franco's idiocies, but president Tudjman does not think those are idiocies. He considers them to be great ideas. The prosecutor and I, however, think the opposite—that those are idiocies. And that is the core of the misunderstanding at this trial."[13] The judge found no way to indict and postponed the process.

The trial coincided roughly with the passing of the new media law that made the criticism of high government officials an offense. Under that law, Tudjman's office charged Zagreb Radio 101—the station that gave him his political start in 1989 and 1990—for defamation. Radio 101 reported on the local and parliamentary elections in October 1995, which ended with the victory of the coalition of the opposition parties. Tudjman first vetoed all four candidates the opposition suggested for the mayoral post, citing the threat to "national security." He then appointed his own candidate, but the council gave her a vote of no confidence. Following that, Tudjman simply reinstated his candidate in open defiance of the law and, in May 1996, dissolved the whole city council. The reporting of the events on Radio 101, suggesting that Tudjman's actions were motivated by the sale of state-owned businesses to his own close associates, made Tudjman very nervous, and he threatened to close the station at about the same time he launched a defamation suit against *Feral Tribune*.

In 1993, *Feral* was the first journal to break the story of the Croatian war against the Bosnians. The official media meanwhile claimed Muslims were getting help from Shia and Islamic groups and importing terrorism and fundamentalism. In April 1996 *Feral* raised the issue again, having obtained information about a university professor, Fahrudin Rizvanbegović, captured in Stolac, taken to the Dretelj concentration camp, later to be transferred to another camp in Ljubuški. Between April 1993 and April 1994, along with Rizvanbegović, about twenty thousand other Muslims found themselves incarcerated in the so-called concentration centers in Gabela, Dretelj, Ljubuški, Helidrom near Mostar, Otoka, Kočerin, Posušje, Duvno, Sujica, Bijelo Polje, and Široki Brijeg. *Feral* underscored the fact that none of those overseeing the "centers" or torturing prisoners have been brought to trial. Yet some of the camps housed children of thirteen and old men and women above seventy years of age.[14] In the Dretelj camp 450 to 700 people were packed into a space of six hundred square feet.[15] During summer months the temperature in the tunnels soared to 115 degrees Fahrenheit, but the metal doors remained permanently shut. *Feral* wrote that prisoners were starved and denied water, and that well-known Herceg-Bosna figures under the command of Mate Boban and Tuta Naletić—the current mafia boss of Mostar—frequently visited the camps, selecting at random prisoners to be viciously beaten up or tortured and sometimes shooting into the crowd packed indoors.

Feral is also the only journal in Croatia that reported on the existence of ten mass graves of Serbian civilians, scattered between the towns of

Glina in northern Croatia and Dvor, the town on the Una River bordering on Bosnia. The reporters quoted a local civilian, Djordje Lazic, who
testified that the dead were being buried during seven nights in the summer 1995.[16] Other interviewees asked to remain anonymous, saying that
the army told them those who talked would be killed.[17]

The abuses of human rights in the deserted Krajina region of Croatia
would have remained entirely hidden from the public were it not for the
Feral reporting. Most Serbs, about two hundred thousand, fled the region
in the summer of 1995, trying to escape the Operation Storm. Between
the summers of 1995 and 1996, HVO troops burned property, assaulted the
few old dwellers who had stayed, and killed at random. *Feral* wrote that
on the average, six people were murdered each day.[18] In the small village
of Čakići a bomb was thrown into the house of a handicapped man, Sava
Šolaja. When his head appeared in the window, he was mowed down by
gunfire.[19] In its June 3, 1996 issue, *Feral* featured three remaining elderly
Serbs from an entirely burned-down village. All three were attacked and
brutally abused by the soldiers one afternoon in May 1996. Milan Tribu-
lin, one of the villagers, told the *Feral* reporter how the soldiers piled logs
up on his outstretched arms until he could take it no longer. He was then
told to sit down, and the soldiers urinated on him. Afterward, he was
ordered to dig his own grave. His friend who stayed in the house—wrote
Feral reporter Boris Rašeta—was threatened with having his arm cut off
with an ax unless, without protest, he allowed the soldier to break his finger on the edge of the kitchen table. The old man chose to have his finger
broken.[20]

In 1996 *Feral Tribune* received from the International Press Directory
the annual award for freedom of reporting. Tudjman's HDZ party, however, considers this kind of reporting a part of the psychological war
waged against the regime not only by the independent media but also
by everything that does not belong to the HDZ itself: the trade unions,
the opposition, even individual workers who protest against low salaries. Along with the *Feral* reporters all protesters are labeled "orthodox Yugo-communists," "paranoics inspired in Belgrade," "communist
lumpen revolutionaries," and are charged with intending to obstruct the
Croatian state. According to Tudjman, they are all enemies who would
rather that the independent Croatia didn't exist.[21]

This claim is harder to advance against such people as Ivo Banac, who
considers the high esteem in which he is held to hinge not only on his

scholarly work but also on his readiness to fight for a democratic Croatia.[22] In a recent issue of *Feral*, Banac identified Tudjman as the main source of the country's instability.[23] Viktor Ivančić and the rest of the *Feral* staff share that opinion. Their spirit, not Tudjman's, is the true expression of what is best about the Croatian nation.

NOTES

1   See Slavko Goldstein, "Država to sam ja," *Feral Tribune*, 22 April 1996, pp. 20–21.
2   Viktor Ivančić, "Porijeklo bijesnila," *Feral Tribune*, 8 July 1996, pp. 17–18.
     In addition to suits against *Feral*, the government also tried to undermine the journal by drafting Viktor Ivančić into the Croatian army in the spring of 1994. He was the only editor in chief of a Croatian journal to whom this happened. His conscription represented a violation of law in that, as defined constitutionally, the role of journalists in wartime is to remain with their publication and keep its editorial board together. It was only because of reaction abroad, especially from Italy and France, that Ivančić was released from military service.
3   Goldstein, pp. 21, 22.
4   Cited in Gojko Marinković, "Od hrdanja do hrkanja," *Vreme*, 6 June 1994, p. 26.
5   Drago Hedl, "U sjeni vrbe," *Feral Tribune*," 1 July 1996, p. 24.
6   Marinko Čulić, "Čuvar državnog miksera," *Feral Tribune*, 24 June 1996, p. 12.
7   Cited in Vesna Knežević, "Ustajem protiv Tudjmanova kulturocida," *Feral Tribune*, 25 March 1996, p. 30.
8   Milivoj Djilas, "Kosti u mikseru II," *Feral Tribune*, 20 May 1996, pp. 12–13.
9   Knežević, p. 30.
10 Drago Hedl, "Jasenovac pred sudom," *Feral Tribune*, 17 June 1996, p. 3.
11 See transcript of the defense of Victor Ivančić, "United Colors of Jasenovac," *Feral Tribune*, 17 June 1996, p. 4.
12 "United Colors of Jasenovac," 5.
13 Ibid. Before the trial, Viktor Ivančić wrote a stinging open letter to Tudjman, titled "To the dearest reader, with love" (see "Jasenovac pred sudom," *Feral Tribune*, 6 May 1996, pp. 6–7).
14 Goran Malić, "Herceg lager," *Feral Tribune*, 29 April 1996, p. 19.
15 Malić, p. 21.
16 Joan Ballast and Abe de Vries, "Smrt iz vedra neba," *Feral Tribune*, 1 July 1996, p. 10. The article was reprinted from the Dutch journal *Trouw*.
17 Ibid.
18 Toni Gabrić, "Misli globalno, ubij lokalno," *Feral Tribune*, 22 July 1996, p. 8.
19 On the ethnic cleansing of the Serbian population of Imotsko see Petar Dorić, "Eksplozija suživota," *Feral Tribune*, 11 March 1996, pp. 24–25.
20 Boris Rašeta, "Molio sam da me ubiju," *Feral Tribune*, 3 June 1996, p. 10.
21 *Feral*'s reports on forced evictions from private homes of unwanted families and

individuals. Even those who are old or quadriplegic are dismissed by the regime as *feralovstina,* or "Feralism" (see Goran Flauder, "Marš u Srbiju," *Feral Tribune,* 19 February 1996, p. 23; Petar Dorić, "Bez milosti," 25 March 1996, p. 13; Franjo Tot, "Useljenje nasilja," *Feral Tribune,* 1 April 1996, p. 24).

22 Heni Erceg, "Tudjman je sinteza naših nedaća," *Feral Tribune,* 8 July 1996, p. 6.

23 Erceg, p. 4.

Conclusion
Jasminka Udovički

◆

Having lived through the war, can Bosnia—can the states of what was Yugoslavia—survive peace?

As the Dayton talks were drawing to a close at the end of 1995, the staff of the Sarajevo independent journal *Free Bosnia* answered this question, by focusing on the natural resources. Lead, zinc, and three-quarters of the coal deposits, argued the journalists, are located in the territory belonging to the federation, but almost all deposits of fuel necessary to operate the power plants are in Republika Srpska. Republika Srpska sits on two-thirds of all the iron deposits, but the entire iron-production industrial plant is situated in the region owned by the federation. Three-quarters of the bauxite deposits are in the mines of Republika Srpska, but the center for the industrial processing of bauxite is in Mostar. Banja Luka, the self-proclaimed capital of Republika Srpska, is potentially a strong industrial, cultural, and educational center but is completely cut off from the sources of electrical energy, which are under the control of Bosnian Croats. The forests, finally, are divided roughly fifty-fifty. Most of the lumber industries, however, are in the federation.[1]

The federation was slated to receive $1.23 billion from the World Bank and European Union in 1996, and a total of $3.7 billion over the next three to four years, to jump-start the industrial production, now at 5 to 10 percent of the prewar level.[2] The funds were intended to help rebuild roads, bridges, water supply, sewer systems, and heating networks, and to prod small business and provide employment to 250,000 demobilized soldiers. However, by spring 1997, the World Bank had spent only one-third of the originally intended sum, because the political framework created by the Dayton Accord stood in the way of any viable economic reform.

Today, with financial help uncertain, the Bosnian part of the federation, small and landlocked, faces a precarious future. Even if the federation

A Muslim woman selling milk and *kajmak* (a milk product), in Tuzla, Bosnia: September 1995. Photo by Maja Munk. Courtesy of the photographer.

boosted industrial production in the foreseeable future, Muslim—that is, Bošnjak—Bosnia remains dependent on its neighbors for transport and trade of virtually everything, including food resources. Under the current division, almost all agricultural land belongs to Republika Srpska. Should the federation fall apart, with NATO gone and the world looking elsewhere for the news, Bošnjaks would starve.

The specter of interdependence haunts all other parts of the former Yugoslavia as well. Even the westernmost state of Slovenia has yet to reach its production level of 1989. Its market has shrunk tenfold: from a territory encompassing twenty-three million Yugoslavs to one consisting of merely two million Slovenes. Despite its relative success in comparison with other Eastern European countries, Slovenia's industrial production is still falling, and the core of its current economic policy is not so much growth as control of inflation. Its leading economist, Aleksandar Bajt, who was, with the Croat Branko Horvat, a leading economist of the former Yugoslavia, predicts a good future for Slovenia but warns that it is a long way off from having recovered from the collapse of the Yugoslav market.[3] In order for the regions of the former Yugoslavia to stabilize again, political relations among the new states must heal. Slovenia, says Bajt, owes its good prospects to its prewar comparative advantage over the other Yugoslav republics, not to its progress since 1990:

> We should never forget that what Slovenia has achieved, earning the top place among postsocialist countries, is the result of Slovenia's achievements within the system of self-management of the former Yugoslavia. The fact that today our social product tops seven thousand dollars per capita is the consequence of its level in the former Yugoslavia that amounted to nine thousand per capita. We still have not reached the level we had in that "unsuccessful" self-management system.[4]

In neighboring Croatia, the average income barely amounts to one-sixth of that in Slovenia. Croatian industrial production in 1994 fell 2.7 percent since 1993, reaching roughly one-half the production level of 1987.[5] In 1996 it was still 40 percent of its 1990 level.[6] Before the war, Croatian nationalists had claimed that a disproportionate part of Croatia's national product was absorbed by the Serb-dominated federation. Today they blame the falling standard of living on the war.[7] Yet, again, at the heart of Croatia's decline is the loss of its economic partners, gross economic mismanagement, and corruption. "Croatia can look forward to the future of a tourist country, meaning a country of waiters and farmers, something like a Caribbean colony, not a modern European state," said Branko Horvat in an interview.[8]

In the former Yugoslavia, the northwestern Croatian town of Varaždin used to produce car brakes for automobiles assembled in Zastava, a large plant located in Kragujevac, an industrial town in central Serbia. In 1989 Zastava produced 223,750 Yugos and had plans to expand production and enter foreign markets.[9] By 1992, however, Zastava's output fell to twenty-four thousand vehicles.[10] At the heart of the crisis that broke the giant were parts. Zastava relied on a network of more than one hundred cooperatives.[11] The dashboards and plastic interior fittings used to come from Split in Croatia, electrical parts from Nova Gorica in Slovenia, locks and seat belts from Ohrid, Macedonia. Management tried to substitute those parts with products from Serbia-based industries, such as Elektronska Industrija and Petrohemija, both large, expensive, and thriving enterprises before the war. Only six months later, in June 1993, however, production at Zastava came to a standstill. A total of two thousand cars was produced, but owing to the lack of motor parts, plastic fittings, and tires, they ended up stored on platforms for uncompleted vehicles. At the end of 1992 Zastava laid off sixteen thousand of its eighteen thousand workers. Unemployment in the town of Kragujevac soared to 50 percent.[12] Workers in Kragujevac, as well as those subject to mass layoffs across Serbia, were sent on "mandatory vacations" paid by the state through uncontrolled minting of fresh dinars. The resulting inflation—an indicator of Serbia's economic, political, and civic nosedive—reached 1 million percent in December 1993.[13]

In the last five years, Serbia and Montenegro—the republic which remained with Serbia in rump Yugoslavia—have closed most of the existing industrial plant, lost one-half their former social product, and fallen to 159th place on the list of 198 investment-worthy countries issued by the *International Banker*.[14] This caused an almost total disappearance of the middle class. Seventy percent of the population in Serbia has fallen to the poverty level, while in 1990 less than 8 percent were poor.[15] The economic sanctions imposed on rump Yugoslavia—typically presented in official media as being unjust and vindictive toward the Serbs—served the regime as the explanation for the intolerable drop in the standard of living and the extreme hardships endured particularly by industrial workers, urban families with children, and elderly people.[16] Some of the best economic commentators, however, insisted that the precipitous decline preceded the sanctions and was caused by military overextension, disastrous economic policies, and disintegration of the common market, for which Serbia itself was the most responsible.[17]

Montenegro, which could not risk a confrontation with Serbia by disentangling itself, has little say in the economic or political affairs of the federation, which are fully controlled by Slobodan Milošević. This represents an anomaly in the practice of federalism, not only because federalism implies democratic equality of constituent units, but also because Milošević is not the president of the federation but only of Serbia, one of the two units of the federation. To give the system the appearance of normality, Zoran Lilić, whose name is barely known outside Serbia and Montenegro and who takes no part in political life, has been given the position of president of the federation. Both long-term and short-term decisions are made by Slobodan Milošević, whose party does not have the majority either in the federal or in the Serbian parliament but holds all administrative posts. Yet the policies of Belgrade apply equally to Montenegro and Serbia, which, as Srdjan Darmanović, a Montenegrin lawyer, has argued, is a "state within a state or, rather, the only real and sovereign state in the territory of the Federal Republic of Yugoslavia."[18]

Recovery of the entire former Yugoslavia is likely to be a slow and deeply troubled process. It hinges on political rapprochement, itself contingent on genuine democratization and on foreign financial help. Neither can be counted on. The end of the Bosnian war, and the establishment of political and economic relations between the newly formed states, would be a first step and the precondition for healing overall. But have we seen the end of the war yet?

According to the Dayton Accord, the mid-September 1996 Bosnian elections should have established a joint three-member presidency, opened the way for the normalization of life, and made possible the withdrawal of the twenty thousand U.S. troops by the end of the year. In spring 1996, the Organization for Security and Cooperation in Europe (OSCE), in charge of making a recommendation for or against elections by June 14, 1996, found itself split between Flavio Cotti, the Swiss foreign minister and OSCE chairman, and Robert Frowick, head of the OSCE Bosnian mission.

The OSCE internal human rights report for May painted a dismal picture of the electoral scene, noting that Bosnian Serbs have obstructed the establishment of institutions to monitor free elections, blocked freedom of movement, and continued to threaten the Muslim population. Consequently, Flavio Cotti was ill inclined to consent to elections.[19] Robert Frowick nevertheless prevailed. On June 14, 1996, in Florence, the agreement was reached to go ahead as planned.[20]

The wanton preelection violence perpetrated on the Bošnjaks who had endured the war in the few Serb-held enclaves where they had been protected and supported by their neighbors made preelection conditions worse. Anticipating the elections, local police and a handful of thugs, encouraged by high-level Bosnian-Serb leaders, tried to make life intolerable and drive the remaining Bošnjaks out from such enclaves. Hand grenades were thrown at their houses and people on the streets were beaten at random. Six months after the signing of the Dayton Accord, in the last week of May 1996, scores of Bošnjaks who had stayed undisturbed throughout the war in the small town of Teslić in north central Bosnia had to flee across the border to the government territory. The Serbs of Teslić, who maintained good relations with their Bošnjak neighbors throughout the war, hoped that the Dayton Accord would bring a chance for reconciliation throughout Bosnia. Instead, they themselves were threatened by the thugs and intimidated into silence. Rade Pavlović, general manager of the Teslić chemical industry, who had retained 120 of his Bošnjak workers on the job despite the war, found himself at a loss after Dayton, when every Bošnjak house became a target for the thugs' hand grenades.[21] The Dayton Accord made no provisions for either NATO or the UN to assist people like Rade Pavlović. Under the eyes of the two world organizations, enjoying police protection and the protection of Bosnian-Serb authorities at the highest level, swaggering local mafias were free to carry out their designs.

The lack of NATO and UN protection and the absence of any viable lever with which to unseat the existing power structures enabled nationalist leaderships on all three sides to create conditions favorable to winning votes in September. Expelling members of the "wrong" ethnic group and bringing in refugees embittered by the war and supportive of the nationalist option had been a tested strategy among the Serbs. In spring 1996, the Bosnian government applied the same strategy.

The crisis in the Bosnian presidency between its Muslim Party for Democratic Action (SDA) wing and the non-SDA members had been simmering for some time. Ever since the summer of 1994, the Croatian, Serbian, and even some Bošnjak presidency members, such as Nijazs Duraković, repeatedly accused Alija Izetbegović and Ejup Ganić of ultranationalism. The first overt signals of the turnabout in the government's ideology of multiculturalism were the calls in the government-financed press, during the summer and fall of 1994, to ban mixed marriages. This was followed by the decree of the culture minister, Enes Karić, forbidding the broadcasting of Serbian and Croatian songs on Sarajevo radio. In February 1995 Sejfudin Tokić, vice president of the Union of Bosnia-Hercegovina Social democrats, accused the SDA of having identified the party with the state, and of purging people assumed to be disloyal to Alija Izetbegović from all leading positions in the field of economics, the police, and the army.[22] The Bosnian army that used to be 18 percent

Croatian and 12 percent Serbian, retained only 1 percent of each ethnic group in its officer corps by the end of 1995. All other officers had been placed on extended leave or made to retire. A particularly striking demotion was dealt Brigadier General Jovan Divjak, the most highly educated general of the Bosnian army and a Bosnian Serb devoted to Bosnia. Among common people, including Sarajevo children, Divjak enjoys enormous popularity for his wisdom and bravery in defending their city, and for the many instances of care for the common soldier in the trenches, for which he became legendary. Yet, in summer 1994, Divjak's duties were reduced to the formalities of representing the army at official occasions. In 1995, President Izetbegović tried to force him to retire but had to abandon the attempt under pressure of the presidency's non-SDA members. Despite protests, however, Izetbegović signed Divjak's retirement on December 31, 1996.[23]

It should come as no surprise then that in spring 1996 Izetbegović was less than lukewarm in issuing assurances of safe stay to the Serbs on the outskirts of Sarajevo. By May 1996, the seven thousand Serbs who had remained in their homes despite the threats and harangues organized by the Bosnian Serb authorities, fell victim to Bošnjak refugees that the Bosnian government itself bused into the areas. Just like their Serbian counterparts, the Muslim refugees harassed, beat, and threatened local inhabitants. The police as well as NATO observers, remained uninvolved.

Originally conceived as guaranteeing freedom of movement, the press, and association, and thus a mechanism for paving the way for the September elections, NATO's mission gradually mutated to that of being an observer, like the United Nations.[24] U.S. Navy admiral Leighton W. Smith signaled this transformation when, instead of taking measures to assure a peaceful transfer of the Sarajevo suburbs to the Bosnian government, he offered Serbian hard-liners buses and trucks with which to evacuate the Serbian population. At that point the Serbs understood that NATO was no greater obstacle to their designs than the UN has been. "We realized that we could treat NATO much like we treated the UN. It was obvious after Sarajevo that they would not get in the way of the work we needed to do and that they are not going to stop us from forming our own state," said a senior Serbian official.[25]

Equally important, NATO did little to advance the reunification of Mostar, universally seen as a precondition for the survival of the Bošnjak-Croatian federation. President Tudjman, who himself proclaimed the partition of Bosnia on more than one occasion, had given promises after Dayton that he would use his authority to promote Mostar's reunification. Yet just like the Herceg-Bosna hard-liners, he, too, saw the federation as an inconvenience.[26] Hans Koschnik, Mostar's EU administrator who planned to create a reunited central zone in the city, faced a Croatian riot on February 7, 1996, and decided to leave his post after his car was sprayed with gunshots. By threatening to arrest the investigators of this incident, local police prevented the collecting of evidence on the attack. Local Herceg-Bosna authorities also made a mockery of the very notion of a Bošnjak-Croatian federation by rejecting the attempt of Bošnjak refugees from Stolac (the town some twenty kilometers south of Mostar, which Bosnian Croats had destroyed and then captured) to visit their homes. When they did agree to allow fifteen families to go back to Stolac and rebuild their homes, the action was sabotaged by constant harassment of the Bošnjaks and by the authorities' failure to prevent the arson of one nearly finished home. Croatian hard-liners continued to dynamite the houses in Stolac in 1996 and 1997.

In west Mostar, far from allowing reintegration, Croatian authorities tolerated continued evictions of Muslims and of remaining Serbs from their apartments. No legal system existed for filing a complaint. People were stopped on the street for identity checks that often were followed by "information talks" at the police station. Cars and buses were halted at checkpoints, where sizable amounts of money were extorted for passage. In April 1996, rather than calling to task the Croatian police and requesting that it curb this flagrant violation of the Dayton Accord, Superintendent Leif Bjorken, chief of the International Police Task Force, sought from the Croatian police permission for passage of a convoy of buses carrying Bošnjak refugees.[27]

On February 10, 1997, another major setback occurred as a peaceful group of Bošnjaks tried to visit the cemetery in west Mostar on the holiday of Bajram. Croatian police, working on the orders of the Croatian Democratic Union (HDZ) in Zagreb and some Herceg-Bosna high-ranking officials closely linked with organized crime gangs, fired on the visitors and beat many of them with iron bars. One person was killed and thirty wounded. International peacekeeping troops took pictures of police shooting women in the back, but did nothing to intervene.

The absence of any strategy to hold local police accountable and to promote reintegration has contributed to a further weakening of the federation—and to further degradation of the West's role in the region. At the urging of the United States in particular, the three nationalist parties (the Muslim-led Party of Democratic Action, the Serb Democratic Party, and the Croatian Democratic Union) won the elections, which, as predicted, were blatantly unfree, unfair, and undemocratic.[28]

There are also flash points outside Bosnia. Istria, Croatia's northern peninsula on the Adriatic, with about 250,000 inhabitants, was the only part of Croatia where Tudjman was booed and Croatian Democratic Union (HDZ) overwhelmingly rejected in 1990. The region used to have a large Italian population before the end of World War II. After the war, however, three hundred thousand Italians were ordered to leave—a process paralleling the expulsion of the Volksdeutsch population (of German origin) from Vojvodina. Still, both Italian and Croatian are spoken in Istria today.[29] It represents one of the most developed parts of Croatia, having enjoyed the most rapid growth between 1972 and 1988. Istrians are often called the "Croatian Japanese" because of their dedication to work and the reserve of their demeanor. From the very beginning, they quietly but stubbornly rejected the forced "Croatiazation" of the peninsula, insisting they wanted to be a "Euro-region." In February 1993, the Istrian Democratic Sabor (Diet) won an overwhelming 72 percent of the vote in local elections. The Sabor was accused by Zagreb of "regional egotism" and its four representatives were regularly hushed in the Zagreb Sabor. What Tudjman found unacceptable was Istria's determination to gain autonomy, its nonnationalism, and its open criticism of his policies. The HDZ has tried to place its own cadre in economic enterprises and in political positions but has not been able to change the political climate in Istria. It remains in every sense insular, and its Italian minority of about thirty thousand, together with most other Istrians, is pushing for the Croatian part of the peninsula and its Slovenian part, reaching to the city of Trieste, to be unified into a single, open region. A great irritant to Tudjman, Istria is too important for him to risk a sharper confrontation. Instead, he has tried to fragment the peninsula by dividing it into thirty-six municipalities and using the town of Pazin—where the HDZ has a slightly higher following—as the party's headquarters.

Tudjman faces a much tougher problem in regard to the so-called Sector East, or eastern Slavonia, separated from Istria by the entire width of Croatia across the vast Slavonian plain, and bordering the Vojvodina

province along the Danube. The region, surrounding the town of Vukovar, was captured by the Serbs in 1991. The Serbian-Croatian agreement
of 1995, however, had provided for the return of Sector East to Croatia in
two years. In the interim period Jacques Paul Klein, commander of the
UN Transitional Administration for Eastern Slavonia (UNTAES), was appointed to oversee the gradual reintegration into Croatia of Serbs now
living in the region, and the return of Croatian refugees to their homes.
With the eventual reintegration of eastern Slavonia, Franjo Tudjman will
have fully realized his objective of turning Croatia into one of the most
ethnically pure countries in Europe.[30]

What will be the price of this operation, which implies the return to
their homes of about seventy-five thousand Croats, who had abandoned
the area in 1991–92? Of roughly 160,000 inhabitants of eastern Slavonia
today, 95,000 are Serbian refugees from other areas of Croatia.[31] Belgrade
has left them to themselves, offering only scant assistance or none at all.
The gross national product in the region has fallen to 12 percent of what
it had been before the war.[32] Vukovar, the town shelled into submission
by the YPA in November 1991, used to be the largest river transport har-
bor in the Yugoslav section of the Danube. Abandoned, rusted cranes still
sit on the riverbank. Only the hotel, hospital, police station, town hall,
and a few coffeehouses have been repaired. None of the former industries
are working. The open market sells smuggled goods. Before the arrival of
Jacques Paul Klein, the region was controlled by war profiteers associated
with Željko Ražnjatović-Arkan, as well as the private militias, Jumping
Snakes and Scorpions. Klein has managed to drive them underground.

"Here, we are 200 percent uncertain," said Boško Binkulac, a farmer
from the eastern Slavonian village of Negoslavci in the spring of 1996.[33]
Hostile radio messages originating in Osijek, home of the displaced
Croats, pledge Croats will take back what once was theirs. In anticipation
of that moment, some refugee dwellers in Vukovar and the surrounding
towns have already started preparations for a speedy departure. At night,
they truck their belongings across the border and store them with friends
in Serbia.

Operation Lightning, launched in western Slavonia on May 1, 1995, and
Operation Storm in western and southern Krajina, launched on August 4,
1995, have all but emptied Croatia of its Serbs.[34] In late fall 1995, many
old people among the thirty-five hundred remaining Krajina Serbs were
found with a bullet in the back of their heads or with their throats slashed.

A Serbian woman, one of the few who stayed, in front of her house in Krajina (Croatia): March 1996. Photo by Maja Munk. Courtesy of the photographer.

The systematic campaign of arson, murder, and looting across the Krajina that continued unabated for months after Operation Storm led UN officials to conclude that Zagreb was bent on driving away every remaining Serb and preventing those who had fled from returning.[35] This policy casts doubt that Croatian authorities will be better inclined toward the Serbs in Sector East, in and around Vukovar, when the time comes in 1997 for the Croatian takeover of that region. Judging by the two precedents set in 1995, Serbia may receive another large wave of Slavonian refugees in 1997.

Devastated by the collapse of its industry and trade, plagued by the influx of seven hundred thousand refugees and staggering unemployment, and undermined by a large-scale brain drain, Serbia may become an incomparably more volatile region in the next few years. The possible influx of Sector East refugees will be preceded by the return of 100,000 to 150,000 Albanians currently living in Germany and the Scandinavian countries. Germany is eager to repatriate most of the refugees it has hosted in the past three years, and Albanian exiles, most of whom emigrated in 1989 and 1990, are likely to be the first to be told to go back. During his May 1996 visit to Belgrade, German foreign minister Klaus Kinkel insisted before anything else that Slobodan Milošević consent to an immediate return of Albanian émigrés, and Milošević gave his consent. Yet in Kosovo an odd standoff between Serbian authorities and Albanians poised for independence has maintained a state of limbo in Serb-Albanian relations. Mass emigration of Albanians in search of work in the West has served to ease somewhat the economic crisis and prevent the standoff from becoming a large-scale armed conflagration.[36]

The brutality of martial law imposed by the Belgrade government on Kosovo in 1989 and 1990 strengthened the already firm determination of Kosovo's leaders and common citizens to seek total independence.[37] Defining the imposition of martial law as an issue of aggression perpetrated by an anachronistic Communist regime against democratic forces in Kosovo and placing the crisis in the context of human rights violations, Albanian leaders effectively internationalized the conflict. Kosovo's geopolitical location assured that Serbia's future in world affairs would depend as much on finding a solution to the Kosovo crisis as on ending the war in Bosnia.[38]

Albanian politicians and leading intellectuals refused to take part in the work of Serb-imposed institutions in Kosovo or in Serbian elections. They completely removed themselves from the political process to avoid becoming part of the system of open repression that had driven the social, political, and cultural life of the Albanians underground.[39] The economic life in Kosovo, the most underdeveloped region of former Yugoslavia, took a plunge. The industrial park of Kosovo, which absorbed close to $10 billion in investment money between 1965 and 1990, closed down. The famous Trepča mine, which had once produced one hundred thousand tons of lead, forty thousand tons of electrolytic zinc, about a hundred thousand tons of silver, and thirty thousand tons of bismuth and cadmium a year, sat idle until the summer of 1995.[40] In 1992, Albanian sources cited the desperate economic situation as the reason that three hundred thousand young Albanians emigrated to Western Europe.[41]

The economic collapse was followed by a rise in lawlessness. Evictions from homes and various forms of arbitrary harassment and intimidation became common.⁴² Members of the leading Democratic League of Kosovo (LDK), schoolteachers, journalists, human rights activists, and many ordinary citizens—amounting to more than fifteen thousand people during 1994 alone—were summoned for "informational talks," meaning police interrogation.⁴³ Those taken into police custody for alleged possession of illegal weapons or for starting an illegal political organization were subjected to brutal beatings and, in some cases, to electroshocks.⁴⁴

The Albanians have responded by cutting off all contact with Serbian authorities and by establishing their own political, legal, cultural, and educational institutions.⁴⁵ On September 30, 1991, following a referendum of Kosovo Albanians, the Republic of Kosovo was proclaimed. The Serbian government issued a warrant for the arrest of the republic's founding members—Jusfo Zejnulahu, Agim Malja, and Bujar Budjola, who fled the country and formed a government in exile. On May 24, 1992, Ibrahim Rugova, the leader of the LDK, was elected president of the self-proclaimed republic.

Albanians also have opened exclusively Albanian shops, theaters, and health-care centers, and, as noted above, they have formed their own educational system: kindergartens, schools, and thirteen departments at Priština University. The only places in towns and villages where Serbs (numbering about 200,000) and Albanians (numbering 2 million) come face to face are the generally lush, plentiful green markets. Although Albanian and Serbian children sometimes attend the same schools, they use separate entrances, play separately in the school yards, and study under two different educational programs. Many Albanian children attend private schools held in private apartments and houses.⁴⁶ These schools lack practically everything—sufficient space, desks, educational props, proper illumination, even fresh air. From the official standpoint, they are illegal. Students nevertheless attend them openly. For lack of space, children often sit on the floor, holding notebooks on their knees.⁴⁷ Even in this rudimentary form, the educational system is the most expensive segment of the entire parallel structure of Albanian life, costing up to $20 million a year.⁴⁸ Albanian language, literature, history, and geography have been changed to reflect the Albanian point of view.

Serbian authorities insist they will not allow Albanian education at regular schools as long as Albanians refuse to adopt the educational programs that apply to the entire state. In February 1996 the Serbian government indicated it would recognize six years of Albanian parallel education if Albanians consented to passing additional exams in history, biology, sociology, music, art, and Serbian as a foreign language.[49] Albanians insist their children must be allowed to attend regular schools but maintain they are educating their own cadre, not the citizens of Serbia; they thus view Serbian recognition of their degrees as irrelevant. Abduj Rama, who is in charge of educational issues, has commented that the minimum requirement for opening a dialogue with Belgrade would be the reestablishment of Albanian scientific institutions, such as the Institute for Albanology, and cultural institutions, such as Kosovo Film and *Rilindija*.[50]

Serbian and Albanian authorities see the Kosovo crisis within two irreconcilable frameworks. For the Serbian government, the framework is the Republic of Serbia, Kosovo being an integral part of Serbia and thus its internal problem. For the Albanian leaders, the framework is Albanian national identity, independence being the precondition for the realization of this identity. For the international community trying to arbitrate the crisis, the greatest challenge is, on the one hand, securing the legitimate right of the Kosovo Albanians to autonomy and, on the other, forestalling their secessionist ambitions.[51] Yet even the doves among the Albanian leadership who stand for a peaceful resolution (such as Fehmi Agani, the vice president of the LDK, or Azem Vlasi, the last president of the League of Communists in Kosovo) insist on the right of the Albanian nation in Kosovo to self-determination and are willing to consider autonomy only as a transitional mechanism. Albanian hard-liners, such as Mahmud Bakali, one of the leading Kosovo politicians of the Tito period, and the academic Rexep Quosja, reject the idea of autonomy altogether, accusing Bill Clinton of betraying the Albanian cause. They request the unification of all Albanians in a single state. Ibrahim Rugova favors a neutral Kosovo, independent from and maintaining "soft" boundaries with Albania; alternatively, he has entertained the idea of a Kosovo/Serbia confederation.[52] Rugova also had considered working out an arrangement with the large population of ethnic Albanians living in the Republic of Macedonia, particularly its western part, bordering Kosovo itself and Albania.

Milošević hoped he would be able to correct the ethnic balance in Kosovo by sending to the region in the summer 1995 Serbian refugees from the Krajina. This backfired as the original Serbian residents continued to emigrate, and the newcomers, numbering about fifteen thousand, found themselves trapped in a land that bore little resemblance to the one they knew. The return of the 120,000 Albanians from Germany will tip the balance even more in favor of Albanians. In five to ten years, the region's demographics may determine the politics in Kosovo.

The proportion of Albanians in Macedonia's population is a subject of considerable debate. A 1991 census, in which Albanians refused to participate, recorded a total population of two million, with 20 percent, or 425,000, of Albanian origin. The Albanians themselves claimed that their numbers in Macedonia ran closer to 40 percent of the total, or 800,000. The same census listed forty-two thousand Serbs, who also insisted their number was four to ten times greater. A similar tendency to exaggerate characterized the claims of the Turks and Romanies.[53] The Council of Europe and the European Union attempted to conduct a new census in June 1994, despite the threats of Albanians that they would refuse to be a part of it. Under pressure from the international community, the Albanians participated in the census but disputed its results of only 23 percent Albanians.

The 1990 elections—which polarized Croatia, Slovenia, and Serbia by bringing ultranationalists to the fore—ended in Macedonia with the victory of Kiro Gligorov, a person many consider the only true statesman among Balkan politicians.[54] A committed nonnationalist and a man of stamina and tolerance, Gligorov was able to negotiate a peaceful exit from former Yugoslavia, despite the shrill calls of Serbian radicals, such as Vojislav Šešelj, for Serbia to either annex "its southern part," Macedonia, or to divide it up with Greece, Albania, and Bulgaria.[55] Gligorov also successfully steered another difficult course, between the nationalist factions in Macedonia itself, the radical VMRO-DPMNE (Internal Macedonian Revolutionary Organization-Democratic Party for Macedonian Unity), whose radicalism fueled Albanian nationalism, and the Party of Democratic Prosperity (PDP), representing Albanians.[56] The PDP splintered into a moderate wing that entered Gligorov's coalition government and a radical wing that remained opposed to any collaboration with the government, including participation in the legislature, unless Albanians were guaranteed a higher number of parliamentary posts and representatives in the state bureaucracy. In October 1992, the new prime minister of Macedonia, the thirty-year-old Branko Crvenkovski, formed a multiethnic coalition government, including five representatives of the PDP, the Democratic

Union of Turks, the Socialist Party, and the Party for the Emancipation of Romany. His purpose, like Gligorov's, was to build a new Macedonia as a civil state, not a state of any one ethnic group.[57] This inclusiveness, however, failed to avert Albanians' loud demands for territorial autonomy—a demand the Macedonian government refused, fearing that the autonomous territory would eventually merge with Kosovo and Albania.

The militancy of Albanian claims provoked anti-Albanian and even a certain pro-Serbian sentiment in the general population.[58] Tensions were further exacerbated by the international community's focus on the human rights of Albanians in Macedonia and Kosovo, paralleled by the relative indifference toward the human and constitutional rights of the remaining twenty-five ethnic groups also living in Macedonia.[59] Albanian nationalists used the expression of international interest as a token of self-legitimation—a tendency with a strong destabilizing potential in a country that was fighting for economic survival and international recognition.

Macedonia's economic survival was radically threatened by sanctions imposed against Serbia, traditionally Macedonia's major trading partner. In the summer of 1992, the effect of the sanctions was not yet fully evident, and people from Belgrade who visited the legendary Lake Ohrid reported that, in comparison with Serbia beset by sanctions, Macedonia—colorful, lush, and abundant, its stores full and prices reasonable—looked "like California."[60] To defuse the impact of sanctions, Macedonia had successfully redirected much of its commerce through the Greek port of Thessaloníki.

Macedonia's next-door neighbor, Greece, however, obstructed international recognition of Macedonia, which the Arbitration (Badinter) Commission approved in 1992. Claiming that the name *Macedonia* was originally Greek and could not be used by another state, Greece conducted a secret economic boycott of Macedonia in 1992–93. On February 17, 1994, it declared its own economic blockade against Skopje—as it chose to call Macedonia—cutting the Thessaloníki-Skopje lifeline. The blockade cost Macedonia $60 million per month.[61] President Kiro Gligorov tried to reason with the Greek prime minister, Andreas Papandreou, who had been elected in October 1993, by offering assurances that Macedonia had no aspirations to any part of Greek territory.[62] The Papandreou government, however, continued the policies of the previous conservative government of Constantine Mitsotakis.

Because of the Greek blockade, Macedonia had to redirect its trade through Bulgaria and Albania, abandoning the traditional north-south route from Belgrade to Athens via Skopje. The state of disrepair of the transportation and commerce infrastructure along the alternative, long-neglected west-to-east route caused a fourfold increase in the cost of Macedonian exports and imports, and the closing of businesses. Factories were forced to suspend two-thirds or more of their production and to lay off workers; farmers were forced to stop raising crops for export. The economic crisis deeply destabilized Macedonian currency and financial institutions, feeding the discontent of both Macedonian and Albanian nationalists.

The international community failed to acknowledge a link between the rising Albanian discontent and the overall economic situation in Macedonia. Instead, it chose to treat the Albanian issue in Macedonia as a human rights issue isolated from its context. Consequently, it made no attempt to give economic support to the nonnationalist government of Kiro Gligorov even though economic improvement would have been a better guarantee than any other one for the improvement of interethnic relations. The lack of international pressure on Greece to lift its embargo exacerbated the precarious situation and contributed to Gligorov's decision to offer the Albanians some special guarantees of their status. When the promises failed to materialize, however, there was an even louder outcry from Albanian radicals, causing an ever deeper rift with the remaining Macedonian community.[63]

Instead of fostering an overall economic revival to enhance the chances of the democratic forces in Macedonia, the Clinton administration, until October 1995, avoided establishing full diplomatic relations with Gligorov owing to the Greek-Macedonian dispute. This made it impossible for the Macedonian economy to obtain credit from international monetary institutions.[64] The more farseeing strategy of buttressing Gligorov's regime—the only one in former Yugoslavia that remained genuinely committed to multiculturalism, and therefore also to cooperation with its Albanian minority—never crystallized in the international community.

On September 13, 1995, Greece and Macedonia signed an interim accord in Washington, leaving the dispute over the name Macedonia for future negotiations. Macedonia agreed to change its flag, which featured the sun of Vergina, a cultural symbol Greece claimed as its own, and Greece agreed to take steps to lift its nineteen-month embargo.

Exactly six months later, on April 13, 1996, Macedonia and rump Yugoslavia signed a document of mutual recognition. This was a significant event, indicating that Serbia had no designs to spread south—a possibility worrisome not only for Macedonia but also for the international community. The agreement concerning recognition had in fact been reached in Belgrade on October 2, 1995, a day before the assassination attempt on Kiro Gligorov in Skopje. Earlier, Milošević had mentioned to Gligorov the idea of a loose Belgrade-Athens-Skopje confederation. Gligorov, who favors opening the Balkans to Europe rather than a local enclosure, remained unimpressed.[65]

Meanwhile, owing to the unresolved conflict regarding the autonomy of the Macedonian Albanians, the relations between the two main communities have sharply deteriorated. In 1996, the Albanian Party of Democratic Progress (APDP)—the radical wing, and now the stronger wing of PDP—won the municipal elections in most towns with an Albanian majority. In Tetovo, one of the larger urban centers, demonstrations were held in March 1997 with the slogan "This is Albania, Macedonians go home." This had a profound effect on the non-Albanian community, convinced that any compromises on Albanian autonomy serve to bring the Albanians closer to demanding outright secession.

The early 1997 massive uprising in Albania itself has made the Macedonian situation even more dangerous. Scores of weapons captured from Albanian depots during the uprising may find their way across the Albanian-Macedonian border, and with tensions in Macedonia growing, may serve to detonate a crisis with far-reaching consequences for Kosovo, Serbia, Greece, and the Balkans as a whole.

If on behalf of the Albanians in Kosovo and in Macedonia, the international community showed some interest and applied intermittent pressure, none was forthcoming regarding 250,000 Muslims of Serbia and Montenegro.[66] Yet, for the past five years, they had been subject to brutal searches, arrests, beatings, and torture by the police and various paramilitary groups from Serbia and Bosnia. Systematic assaults on people and property, amounting to a campaign of ethnic cleansing, had compelled thousands to leave their homes and resettle elsewhere in Serbia, or to emigrate to Macedonia, Turkey, or Western European countries.

The crisis escalated in June 1990 with the formation of the Sandžak branch of the Party of Democratic Action (SDA), an offshoot of the Bosnian

SDA, under the leadership of a Muslim hard-liner, Sulejman Ugljanin. In the hot 1990–91 climate in Serbia, Ugljanin argued that the Muslims of Sandžak must be granted the same rights and autonomy sought by the Serbs in Croatia and Bosnia. This first provoked the notorious paramilitaries of Šešelj supporter Milika Dačević-Čeko to bomb and shell twenty-five Muslim shops and religious monuments in the Montenegrin municipality of Pljevlja in the summer of 1992. The police failed to act even when the owners of the shops took down the perpetrators' license plate numbers.[67] Simultaneously, in the border town of Priboj, about thirty kilometers to the north, Tavolino, a small coffeehouse was blown up. Shortly afterward, in the village of Sjeverin, the paramilitary group of Momir Savić killed an old Muslim, Ramo Bero, and the next day, in the village of Sočice near Priboj, three Muslim houses were set on fire. The Muslims accused the authorities and the police of acting in cahoots with private armies. Meanwhile, Dačević-Čeko's paramilitaries halted buses, beat up Muslim passengers, and ordered the Serbs to stay away from the Muslims. In the mountain region of Bukovica, bordering the Bosnian municipalities of Foča, Čajniče and Goražde, several people were beaten up. House searches, often accompanied by theft of cash and jewelry, and confiscations of arms even from owners who had licenses, forced another six hundred persons to abandon their homes by the end of 1992.

In the winter of 1993, Bosnian-Serb army members were allowed to cross from Bosnia into Serbia and kidnap whole families, including children. The houses of old people were raided, dwellers beaten, and their money and horses taken away. Bosnian-Serb intruders became particularly bold in the aftermath of the statement by Vojislav Šešelj that a thirty-kilometers-deep border belt between Serbia and Bosnia must be cleared of all Muslims.[68]

Two cases of kidnapping and disappearance, one in the village of Mioče on November 23, 1992, and the other in the village of Štrpci on March 1, 1993, profoundly shook up the Muslim community, causing about 60 percent of Muslims to leave the Pljevlja and Priboj regions by the spring of 1993. Mioče is situated on the Bosnian side of the border, along the local bus route Priboj-Rudo, traveled daily by many people living on one side of the border and working or shopping on the other.[69] The bus route crosses the winding Serbian-Bosnian border four times. At dawn on November 23, a group of men stopped the bus and ordered all Muslims to step out. Eighteen people were taken away and have not been seen since. Despite repeated requests by their families, the Belgrade government has offered no explanation to date and has named no perpetrators. The route was closed for "security" reasons, cutting people off from their jobs, children from their schools, and making it impossible for humanitarian organizations and medical personnel to reach Sjeverin in more than three years. Shortly after the kidnapping most of the five hundred Sjeverin Muslims took a ten-hour night trek across the mountain, to Priboj. Today only ten Muslim inhabitants remain. In other villages along the Serbian-Bosnian border, fifteen hundred have left; only a few hundred remain.[70]

The second incident occurred in the same area, on March 1, 1993, when a group of about forty armed men forced the Belgrade-Bar 671 train to stop in the village of Štrpci, on the Bosnian side of the border. The train made a twenty-minute stop, allowing the armed group to check passengers' identity cards and force twenty Muslims from the towns of Prijepolje, Bijelo Polje, and Bar to leave the train. The men were loaded on a truck and taken away and the train continued on. As in the previous case, the missing men remain unaccounted for to this day. A parliamentary committee to gather information was formed, but the authorities have prevented it from examining the documentation.[71] No relevant witnesses—such as the train operator, train conductor, or the police present in the train at the time of the kidnapping—were contacted. The authorities have done nothing to find the disappeared or to convey to the public any information about the case, despite the promises to the contrary by Slobodan Milošević. Meanwhile, the Muslim population has continued to withdraw from the area.

On June 6, 1993, in a heated atmosphere, the Muslim national assembly of Sandžak adopted a Memorandum on the Institutionalization of the Special Status for Sandžak, which envisioned the establishment of a parliament, constitution, autonomous police, and independent courts. The government of Sandžak would control the customs, education, banks, energy, and economy, and Serbia would handle ecological matters, transportation, and the postal system.

The Užice municipal court banned the distribution of the memorandum as soon as it was printed. The general secretary of the SDA, Rasim Ljajić, who floundered and finally emerged as a moderate, has since tried to open a dialogue with Serbian authorities. He has not given up on the idea of Sandžak autonomy, but his immediate aim is halting the repression. In 1993–94, many persons interrogated for arms possession were tortured in police custody: clubbed on the soles of the feet and palms;

tied to the furniture and beaten for hours; repeatedly kicked in the head and stomach; subjected to electroshocks; and deprived of sleep, food, and water.[72]

Ljajić's wish to bring the situation back to normal through dialogue brought him into open conflict with Sulejman Ugljanin, who fled to Ankara on July 6, 1993, but remained SDA's president in exile. He was charged with inciting Sandžak Muslims to arm and organize, with the ultimate objective of effecting the secession of Sandžak from Serbia. Ugljanin and his Coordination Body maintained that no bilateral talks were possible unless Serbia recognized Bosnia, and that the basis for eventual talks remained the memorandum. Ljajić, by contrast, advocated negotiations as necessary to curb police brutality and improve the political situation, economic life, and the dismal state of the Sandžak educational system and cultural institutions.[73]

Sandžak Muslims have adopted the name Bošnjak, used by the Muslims of Bosnia. To secure a modicum of normal life, many have withdrawn from politics and focused on starting small businesses and on day to day survival. In Sandžak municipalities, Serbs control all state institutions; Muslims have a hold on private businesses and the black market.

The Muslim electoral body in Serbia has been fragmented into two, and in Montenegro into four, electoral units.[74] Muslims represent the majority in only one of those units, which makes it impossible for them to get adequate representation in the parliament. With no international pressure regarding its Sandžak policy, Belgrade is likely to maintain the status quo as long as possible. This implies continued Muslim emigration and growing instability.[75]

Maintaining the status quo has also been the strategy of the Serbian regime in the northern province of Vojvodina, which, like Kosovo, used to enjoy a republic-like autonomy, until 1989.[76] Dimitrije Boarov, the leading analyst of Vojvodina, observes that today Novi Sad, Vojvodina's capital, makes no decisions about anything. "The streets of Novi Sad are named in Belgrade, as are directors of a few hundred of Vojvodina's elementary schools. . . . Vojvodina has melted into Serbia," wrote Boarov.[77] Over the last four war years, three hundred thousand refugees from Croatia and Bosnia have settled in Vojvodina, whose population was roughly two million in 1991.[78] The massive influx of a disenfranchised, radicalized, suddenly impoverished, and desperate populace completed Vojvodina's transformation, forced on this region in 1989 by the dismissal of all its political, economic, and cultural institutions, and the choking off of all its free media. Novi Sad does not have a single local TV channel and depends exclusively on Belgrade's official TV stations. During the war in Croatia, TV Novi Sad, purged of all "disloyal elements," functioned as the foremost war-propaganda squad.[79]

The first wave of about 150,000 refugees in the winter of 1991 engendered its own sort of ethnic cleansing, causing the departure of about 80,000 Hungarians and Croats from Vojvodina. Some refugees who have left behind, in the rich region of Slavonia's Sector West, comfortable houses, prosperous farms, and expensive farming equipment became easy targets of Šešelj's ultranationalist Serbian Radical Party and were almost immediately recruited for a quiet, unpublicized war against Hungarians and Croats, the region's two most numerous minority groups. Bombs went off in the backyards; "announcements" urging Hungarians and Croats to leave before it was too late were nailed to the doors of their homes.[80] In the village of Hrtkovci, the home of about three thousand people of seventeen different nationalities, the Serbian Radical Party rally was held in May 1992. Vojislav Šešelj read seventeen family names of those "disloyal to Serbia," people "whose place was not in the village" because they allegedly helped Croatia financially or supplied the Croatian army with arms.

Afterward, a group of about a dozen hard-line refugees installed themselves in the Hrtkovci local government. Armed men barged unhindered into private homes and tried to force household heads to sign statements authorizing the exchange of their homes for others in Croatia. Their families would have to leave everything behind: cash, tractors, furniture, television sets, appliances. On the night of June 28, 1992, Marika Štefanac, a forty-five-year-old Croat, was killed. Police took no action. By August, 70 percent of Croatian and Hungarian families, whose ancestors had lived there for generations, had left.[81]

Other towns and villages, such as Kanjiža, Novi Žednik, Kupusina, Ruski Krstur, Novo Selo, Nikinci, Golubinci, Beška, Gibarac, Šot, Sarvaš, Novi Slankamen, and Ruma, all came under attack.[82] The authorities used refugees to do the job of ethnic cleansing. The decision in August 1995 — following Operation Storm — to settle Serbs from the Croatian Krajina in Vojvodina caused a bitter reaction from the Democratic Association of Vojvodina Hungarians (DZVM). This exacerbated ethnic tensions in the region and, in turn, worsened the position of indigenous minority groups.

Belgrade authorities perceive Vojvodina as a far smaller problem than Kosovo or Sandžak. Vojvodina has a much more solid tradition of civic institutions than do the other two regions, and though Vojvodina's body politic would now favor autonomy, it is not inclined to risk an armed conflict over the issue. Belgrade chooses to interpret the willingness of Vojvodina citizens to take part in the elections and join Serbian governing bodies as the loyalty of ethnic minorities to rump Yugoslavia.[83]

Serbian minister for human rights, Margit Savović, who alleged that behind the DZVM concept of autonomy was the prodding of Hungary, declared the demands for autonomy unconstitutional. In an attempt to strike some kind of deal with Belgrade and to avoid open conflict, DZVM has been trying to work out the concept of Vojvodina autonomy within the larger framework of rump Yugoslavia. Legally and politically, however, this task is made excessively difficult, owing to the absence of any coherent policy regarding the protection of minorities that would apply across the board to the entire territory of former Yugoslavia.

The international community is committed to secure the existing borders within former Yugoslavia. The protection of the minorities within those borders is seen as desirable, but clear and firm universal principles of minority rights, applying equally to all minorities in the former Yugoslavia, do not exist. A charter of minority rights would not only provide a standard with which to assess the state of minority rights in Bosnia today and in the future; such a charter would also make it harder for Belgrade to treat—as it typically does—every claim for minority rights as a claim for autonomy, and every claim for autonomy as a claim for ultimate secession. Finally, a charter of minority rights would be binding on Zagreb to abandon its violations of minority rights—its practice of requesting a Domovnica (the form certifying proof of Croatian origin) as a precondition for guaranteeing its citizens access to services and protection under the law; its treatment of the Serbs remaining in Krajina; and its policies regarding the return of Serbian refugees.

The international community, however, took a twofold approach regarding minority rights. On the face of it, it appealed to the need for the states to guarantee minority rights; in practice, it focused on a single minority—the Kosovo Albanians. All other minorities—Serbs in Croatia, Croats in Serbia, Hungarians, Sandžak Muslims, Romanies—found their appeals for the international community's support futile.[84] The majority-minority conflict—lying at the root of the war in Croatia and Bosnia, and

A Serbian man from Krajina (Croatia), who went mad when a bomb hit his neighbor's house: May 1996. Photo by Maja Munk. Courtesy of the photographer.

of the crippling economic crisis in Serbia, Macedonia, and Montenegro—remained unaddressed in international peace negotiations. Groups and individuals who at great risk to themselves worked for minority rights and tried to find forms of multicultural existence amid the chaos of war, received precious little international attention, and were domestically sidelined and perceived as traitors.

The Dayton talks offered a chance for the international community to lend visibility to these groups and individuals.[85] Had some or all of them been invited to Dayton as participants, or at least as observers, their chances in the upcoming elections would have been increased. Instead, from the beginning in 1991 in The Hague to the end in 1995 in Dayton, the international community took seriously only the ultranationalists.

Consequently, in Bosnia, Serbia, and Croatia alike, a widespread perception took root that no real political alternatives existed. That perception was largely shaped by the political reality constructed through the internationally sponsored diplomatic process, which buttressed the view that only people like Milošević, Tudjman, or Izetbegović were legitimate representatives of their ethnic constituencies—or at least that they alone were the "real" players.[86]

The widespread conviction, however paradoxical, that the same nationalist parties that brought about the war (and control all relevant media) represented the only political option, was key in the Bosnian elections. Today, those elected in 1996, relying on three hostile armies confronting each other on a tiny territory, render the commitment to peace inherent to the Dayton Accord an oxymoron, as it were, in four major ways. First, this arrangement precludes the creation of common central institutions that Muslims, Serbs, and Croats alike would support; without such institutions the functioning of Bosnia as a unified state is fiction. Second, the arrangement forecloses the possibility that refugees would return and millions of people would resume normal life. Third, the apartheid-style framework of the Bosnian-Croatian Federation, the still existing Herceg-Bosna, and the Republika Srpska, all three resting on military and police support, undermines the revival of economic life and the effective use of international aid. Fourth, the armies and the para-entities they represent prevent the emergence of a civic, nonethnic Bosnian identity, without which genuine reconstruction, and reintegration into Europe, remains an illusion.[87]

Meanwhile, unresolved regional tensions having to do with the Kosovo Albanians, Sandžak Muslims, Vojvodina Hungarians, and Krajina Serbs, along with all other smaller minorities, beset Serbia and Croatia. These unresolved tensions cannot be uncoupled from what in some yet unforeseeable future must become a comprehensive Balkan solution. At its heart rest respect and explicit guarantees of minority rights, now nonexistent in Serbia or Croatia, but in reality the preconditions for their economic recovery and democratization.

The chances for the states of former Yugoslavia to regain stability depend also on the commitment, good will, and foresight of the international community. Following World War I, concern was lacking, which also meant that the prewar trade ties with this region were hardly renewed, and that foreign loans were scarce. Sluggish economy came at a high political cost, as many in the kingdom drew the conclusion that a common household was not the answer after all. The situation was radically different after World War II. Owing to its significance in the geopolitics of the Cold War era, Yugoslavia received considerable Western help, allowing its economy to surpass by far all other Balkan and East European countries. Economic growth was paralleled by the widespread sense of loyalty to Yugoslavia as a common home—the loyalty this last war was waged in order to destroy.

After the deaths of 145,000 Muslims, 95,000 Serbs, and 23,000 Croats in the Bosnian war, stability in former Yugoslavia is contingent above all on the removal of old leaderships from power; on the prosecution of war criminals; on the establishment of free media; and on economic growth. This will be an arduous process.[88] Nonetheless, now as in the past, Balkan stability remains the condition for stability of Europe.

Even if peace holds in Bosnia, and a revival takes place in the former Yugoslavia, moral catharsis is unlikely in the short run. The war has impoverished the moral life of the former country too deeply. Yet in the long run, some form of cooperation, economic above all, will be restored between the former Yugoslav republics. Without such cooperation, the successor states will face insurmountable obstacles to development. Not morality or mutual affinity, but economic reality, will eventually render ethnically pure fiefdoms obsolete. The bonds broken for the sake of territorial division will tend to form anew, not because anyone has forgotten the horrors of war, but because interconnection will prove to be the least costly and economically most rational outcome—indeed the only one viable. Everyday life will compel the populations to intermix once again. Perhaps by the time that happens, the regions of former Yugoslavia will have produced leaders able and keen to foster moral rebirth. Such leaders will understand that the stability and sovereignty of the newly formed states hinges above all on each of them earning the full, heartfelt support of their *minority* populations.

NOTES

1 Quoted in Aleksandar Ćirić, "Sirotinja i sirovine," *Vreme*, 27 January 1996, pp. 24–25.

2   Craig R. Whitney, "$1.23 Billion Is Pledged in New Aid for Bosnia," *New York Times*, 14 April 1996, p. 9. Hasan Muratović, the Bosnian prime minister, estimated the total cost of remedying the physical damage to Bosnia at $80 billion.

3   Cited in Svetlana Vasović-Mekina, "Slovenija je osudjena na uspeh," *Vreme*, 27 January 1996, p. 27. Branko Horvat expressed a view similar to Bajt's when interviewed by *Vreme* in the same month: "Of great significance is the factor of the disintegration of the Yugoslav market. Yugoslavia was not entirely integrated, centrifugal tendencies were strong, particularly in the ten years [preceding the war], yet a market existed, with a level of integration higher than that thus far achieved in the European Union" (Boris Rašeta, "Povratak u Kraljevinu Jugoslaviju," *Vreme*, 6 January 1996, p. 30).

4   Aleksandar Bajt, in Vasović-Mekina, p. 26.

5   Gojko Marinković, "Kraj ekonomskog čuda," *Vreme*, 6 March 1995, p. 30.

6   Boris Rašeta, "Povratak u Kraljevinu Jugoslaviju," p. 30.

7   In an interview conducted by *Feral Tribune* and reprinted in *Naša Borba*, Branko Horvat adamantly refutes this claim, charging the authorities with having destroyed the moral and material basis of the Croatian society (Milan Gavrilović, "Hrvatska preživljava ekonomsku katastrofu," *Naša Borba*, 17 June 1996, p. 12).

8   Branko Horvat made this statement in 1993, but today he maintains that the state of the Croatian economy is even worse than it was three years ago (see Zmago Herman, "Hrvatska, karipska kolonija" interview with Branko Horvat, *Vreme*, 14 June 1993, p. 45).

9   Zoran Radovanović, "Premijeri obećavaju, fabrika propada," *Borba*, 23 July 1993, p. 14. Despite its very low prices, to succeed long-term in international competition, Zastava—employing eighteen thousand workers—would have had to greatly improve the quality of its cars. But instead of improvement and growth, it was facing total collapse.

10 Dimitrije Boarov, "Pismo iz pomrčine," *Vreme*, 3 May 1993, p. 24.

11 In Serbia alone forty-seven enterprises worked for Zastava; in Croatia, fourteen; in Slovenia, fifteen; in Bosnia, nine; in Macedonia, two; in Montenegro, two; in Vojvodina, eleven; in Kosovo, four (see Milan Milošević, "Fićina deca," *Vreme*, 3 April 1996, p. 50).

12 See Perica Vučinić and Zoran Radovanović, "Sezona prinudnog šverca," *Borba*, 9 November 1992, p. 11. The same fate befell other Kragujevac industries, as well as the large factories employing a total of twenty thousand workers (i.e., 21 Maj, Industrija Motora Rakovica, Jugostroj, Tehnogas, Napred, Rudnik), located on the outskirts of Belgrade, in Rakovica. Most of these enterprises laid off 80 percent of their workers, sending them, like Kragujevac workers, on "mandatory vacations" paid, again, by uncontrolled emissions of cash (see Slavko Ćuruvija, Gradiša Katić, and Željko Kristić, "Mastodont na infuziji," *Borba*, 16 November 1992, p. 9).

13 The state bought social peace and prevented large-scale strikes at the last minute by providing back pay requested by the workers (see Zoran Radovanović, "Stigle pare, nema bunta," *Borba*, 23 October 1992, p. 21). On the inflation in Serbia, one of the

worst in history, see Ljubomir Madžar, "Pogubne odluke gospodara rata," *Borba*, 14–15 August 1993, p. vi; and Jasna Kesić and Zmago Herman, "Stručnjake nije imao ko da slusa," *Borba*, 10 January 1994, p. 11.

Indicating the scale of the economic collapse were the titles of articles on the economic pages of *Borba* in 1992–93: "There Is No Tomorrow," 9 September 1992; "Serbia Faces an Epidemic: Hospitals Can Afford Medication Only for Extreme Cases," 14 September 1992, p. 4; "Life in Disgrace," 15 October 1992, p. 30; "Not Even Nobel-Prize Economists Could Save Us," 21–22 November 1992, p. v; "2.5 Thousand Enterprises Facing Bankruptcy," 22 October 1992, p. 5; "Bread, a Scarce Commodity," 29 January 1993, p. 21; "Life below the Line," 4 March 1993, 11; "Will the Sanctions Drown the Fleet?" 26 April 1993, p. 6; "A Desperate Attempt at the Resuscitation of the State," 12 April 1993, p. 6.

14 Branko Milanović, "O iluzijama i novcu," *Vreme*, 18 September 1995, p. 64. Milanović notes that only Sudan, Zaire, and North Korea were placed behind Serbia.

15 Dimitrije Boarov, "Tek ćemo izgubiti 100 milijardi dolara," *Vreme*, 5 June 1995, p. 19; Aleksandra Pošarac, "Urbana agonija," *Vreme*, 30 December 1995, p. 22. *Borba* reported in 1992 that at least ten thousand people, many of whom received pensions, sustained themselves by collecting scraps of food from the large garbage containers used on the city streets (Branko Čečen, "Alisa u zemlji djubreta," *Borba*, 5–6 December 1992, p. iii). A survey of the condition of families with children, conducted by the Economics Institute in Belgrade, showed that out of 1,095 families only 26.6 percent thought they were able to cover their basic expenses (Nenad Lj. Stefanović, "Bez igračke i pomorandže," *Vreme*, 6 January 1996, p. 23).

16 Many analysts have tried to account for the fact that the hardest-hit strata of the population failed to stage a sustained mass strike. Aleksandra Pošarac presents a convincing set of reasons for the passivity: (1) The trade union used to be an integral institution of the party state — thus the absence of the tradition of grassroots organizing and of the impulse to protect one's own vital interests through sustained strikes; (2) poor grasp of the rights of the workers' movement; (3) lack of understanding of the potential strength of mass action; (4) the inability to distinguish personal from collective interest and to link personal to collective interest; (5) fear of loss of the little support still received from the state; (6) skillful manipulation of the workers on the part of the regime (see "Trpljenje bez bunta," *Republika* [March 1996]: 4).

On punitive measures undertaken against strikers and worker organizers see Bojana Ljubinović-Andrejić and Božidar Andrejić, "Kažnjivo sindikalno organizovanje," *Republika*, 3 March 1996, 1–8.

17 A rigorous, clear, and detailed economic analysis of the way in which the Serbian economy was destroyed after 1990 is offered in Mladjan Dinkić, *Ekonomija Destrukcije*, (Beograd: VIN, 1995). For shorter analyses see Dimitrije Boarov, "Pola veka unazad," *Vreme*, 6 July 1992, pp. 6–8; Bojana Jager, "Politički konsenzus, ubiti privredu," *Borba*, 19 July 1993, p. 14; Ljubomir Madžar, "Deset optužbi na račun države," *Borba*, 13, 14–15 August 1993, p. vi; Dejan Anastasijević, "Kratak pregled propadanja," *Vreme*, 7 November 1994, pp. 46–48.

18 Srdjan Darmanović, *SRJ — četiri godine posle*, Ogledi Edition, *Republika* (June 1996),

p. vi. Darmanović points out that according to legal theory a two-member federation is problematic. The generally accepted view is that federated states made of two units only are the most unstable ones, because of the difficulty of settling conflicting claims in such states (p. viii).

19   Chris Hedges reports that in the first week of June in Geneva the Americans pressed Cotti to announce the holding of elections against his own better judgment. At that meeting, according to a diplomat, Cotti crossed his arms and glared silently at the Americans in disbelief (see "Swiss Diplomat Resists U.S. on Certifying Bosnian Vote," *New York Times*, 8 June 1996, p. A4).

20   In the beginning of June, Robert Frowick acknowledged to the *New York Times* that he had instructed his staff to foreground the developments favorable to holding of the elections and downplay the obstacles. Frowick's chief of staff, William Staubner, had resigned in the last week of May in protest over the decision of the U.S. government to press for the elections despite the flagrant evidence of impediments (Chris Hedges, "U.S. Envoy Told Staff in Bosnia to Take Optimistic Line on Vote," *New York Times*, 5 June 1996, p. A1).

In Florence a consensus was reached that key human rights provisions for the elections had not been fulfilled. The United States indicated clearly, however, that it would not give ground. The Florence summit reached the conclusion that its decision regarding the elections would not be based on what was happening in Bosnia, that is, that the elections should go as planned (Daniel Williams, "Bosnian Rivals Agree on Arms Balance," *New York Times*, 15 June 1996, p. A22). This was an exercise in illusionism. Even before the Dayton Accord was signed, outlining the free and fair elections in the fall of 1996, Professor Ivo Banac called Richard Holbrooke "President Clinton's chief Balkan illusionist" ("Shotgun Wedding in the Balkans," *Nation*, 23 October 1995, p. 466).

21   The story of the Teslić Muslims is told by Mike O'Connor, "Along an Ethnic Fault-Line, Bosnians Fear Hard-Liners," *New York Times*, 1 June 1996, p. A4.

22   Rusmir Spahić, "Ovde se pravi SDA država," *Vreme*, 13 February 1995, p. 24; and Zlatko Dizdarević, "Tokić: Interview," *Svijet*, 11 July 1996, pp. 16–21.

23   In an interview in August 1992, Divjak said: "I stayed in Bosnia and Hercegovina on the side of its defenders because the YPA shifted to one side, serving the extremists with its entire military might. I have lived for twenty-six years in Sarajevo and Mostar, in very close and wonderful relations with the citizens of all nationalities. I have never been hurt in any way. I stayed also because one of my daughters-in-law is Croatian and the other Muslim. . . . Which other side should a citizen of Bosnia-Hercegovina, and by accident a Serb, have taken?" (Ejub Štitkovac, "Beogradski Sarajlija," *Borba*, 4 August 1992, p. 11).

In February 1996, the Sarajevo weekly *Svijet* featured an interview with Divjak, in which he revealed that he had spent twenty-seven days under house arrest, imposed by his own Bosnian army, after being accused of collaborating with the Chetniks. Divjak spoke openly of the disappointment at being excluded by the Bosnian General Rasim Delić from partaking in any strategic and military decisions (Rajko Živković, "Nepoželjni miljenik raje," *Svijet*, 2 February 1996, pp. 35, 36).

General Divjak had not been informed personally about his sudden retirement at the end of 1996 in any way. He found out he had been retired a few hours before midnight on New Year's Eve, from a friend who called him up, having watched TV news that night (Jasminka Udovički, interview with General Divjak, March 1997).

24 On NATO's reluctance to get involved in any substantial way (e.g., capturing Radovan Karadžić and Ratko Mladić; protecting civilians returning to their homes in Stolac; giving sanctuary to seven Srebrenica men hiding from the Serbs; preventing Serbian gangs from burning and looting the suburbs of Sarajevo; helping to remove from office ultranationalist hard-liners, such as the Muslim mayor of Bugojno, Dževad Mlaco, or the Croatian warlords in Mostar), see John Pomfret, "U.S.-Led Bosnian Mission at Crossroads," *Washington Post*, 19 June 1996, pp. A21–22.

25 Pomfret, p. A22.

26 Franjo Tudjman frequently expressed his opinion on Muslims. He made one of the most striking of these statements when he was interviewed by *Le Figaro* on September 25, 1995: "Europe and the Western countries did not want an Islamic state, even a tiny one, in Bosnia and Hercegovina. They did not want to give the Serbs an opportunity to support Muslim fundamentalist activists in Europe. So through the efforts of Western countries, a Croatian-Muslim federation was proposed. For strategic reasons, Croatia agreed. We therefore accepted this task given to us by Europe, namely: to Europeanize the Bosnian Muslims" (cited in Christopher Hitchens, "Minority Report," *Nation*, 18 December 1995, p. 776).

27 John Pomfret, "Muslim-Croat Federation Falling Apart," *Manchester Guardian Weekly*, 7 April 1996. On the destruction of Stolac in 1996–97 see Mehmed Dizdar, "Kome teče Bregava," *Svijet*, 23 January 1997, pp. 60–63.

28 Increasing polarization of ethnic sentiment favoring nationalists at the elections was the overall effect of unimpeded nationalistic excesses, coupled with the lack of will among NATO officials to use their authority to control the situation on the ground.

29 "Istra želi samostalnost," *Borba*, 30 July 1993, p. 19; and Jovo Paripović, "Odlazi li Istra," *Borba*, 30 September 1993, p. 11.

30 The percentage of Serbs living in Croatia has dropped from 12 percent to about 3 to 4.5 percent (see Miloš Vasić and Tatjana Tagirov, "Zagrebački ping-pong," *Vreme*, 30 March 1996, p. 21).

31 Perica Vučinić, "Beg u suton," *Vreme*, 13 April 1996, p. 10.

32 The estimate is Jacques Paul Klein's (cited in Chris Hedges, "Serb Gangs Rule in Last-Chance Fief of the U.N.," *New York Times*, 22 June 1996, p. A5). See also Damir Pilić, "Ujedinjeni protiv KOMARACA," *Feral Tribune*, 3 May 1996, pp. 14–16.

33 Vučinić, 10.

34 In November and December 1991, after a secret agreement between Croatia and Serbia, the YPA gave an order to evacuate 180 predominantly Serbian villages in western Slavonia. The population—nonextremist, well integrated, and well off—was transferred to eastern Slavonia, Baranja, and Serbia. The villages were burned by the Croatian troops in the next six months. In February 1992 the region (Sector West) came under UNPROFOR protection. Of more than 20,000 Serbs, 9,500 (including the refu-

gees from the surrounding villages) remained in the old baroque town of Pakrac. Attempts of the Serbian leader Veljko Džakula, who stayed with the people in Pakrac trying to normalize life, were sabotaged by both Serbian and Croatian authorities. Džakula was placed first in prison in Glina and, after his release, kidnapped in Belgrade and taken to Knin. In April 1994 the Belgrade volunteer group called The Bridge, which specialized in nonviolent crisis resolution, started its successful work in Pakrac of trying to bring together its Serbian and Croatian population.

On May 1, 1995, at 2:30 A.M., the Sector West UN commander received a letter from the commander of the Croatian army, requesting that he shelter his troops. The next morning Croatian forces overwhelmed the entire region, encountering little resistance. Dodging the aircraft artillery, civilians tried to escape across the Sava River. After thirty-six hours of bombardment and infantry attack, Croatia took control of the entire region from Okućani to Pakrac. Veljko Džakula and three other Serbian leaders stayed to protect the remaining population as best they could. Refugees who fled to Bosnia were immediately conscripted into Karadžić's army; those who fled to Serbia found its borders closed and, once let in, were on their own, without any help from any side (see Jelena Šantić, "Pakrac—juče, danas, sutra," *Republika* [July 1995]: 11–12; Miloš Vasić, "Pad zapadne Slavonije," *Vreme*, 8 May 1995, pp. 8–14; Drago Hedl, "Krava žvaće zavesu," *Vreme*, 15 May 1995, pp. 14–15; Uroš Komlenović, "Ničji ljudi," *Vreme*, 12 June 1995, pp. 22–25).

In a similar pattern, encountering no resistance, Operation Storm cleansed the remaining part of Krajina of the Serbian population. (See earlier chapter "Croatia: The First War.")

35 The statement was made by Allan R. Roberts, the UN press officer of Knin (quoted in Chris Hedges, "Arson and Death Plague Serbian Region of Croatia," *New York Times*, 1 October 1995, p. A6). See also Petar Dorić, "Odlučan da ubije," *Feral Tribune*, 27 January 1997, pp. 12–13.

36 One of the leading Albanian intellectuals, Skeljzen Malici, sees the escape to the West as a key social and political vent for Kosovo that has averted an explosion in the aftermath of the layoffs of a hundred-fifty thousand Albanian workers in 1989 and 1990 ("Kinkelova lista," *Vreme*, 25 May 1996, p. 11).

37 For the events of 1989 and 1990 in Kosovo see the earlier chapter in this volume titled "The Interlude: 1890–1990." In his report of 1994 Aryeh Neier writes that none of the Albanians he met—party leaders, journalists, doctors, former professors, relief workers—would accept Kosovo becoming an integral part of Serbia, even under the conditions of autonomy. Autonomy meant one thing in federal Yugoslavia and was seen as quite another in the context of rump Yugoslavia ("Kosovo Survives!" *New York Review of Books*, 3 February 1994, 27).

38 In 1993 Lord David Owen underscored the importance of Kosovo, together with Sandžak and Macedonia, for stability in the Balkans: "The main concern was the fuse line from Sarajevo to the Sandžak Muslims and to the Albanians in Kosovo, both in Serbia, to the Albanians in Macedonia, to Albania itself, and then to Turkey and perhaps beyond. It is hard to pretend that this powder keg could not ignite. . . . There is a real risk of the Turks and the Greeks being on opposite sides in any Serb

confrontation with the Albanian people and such a war would certainly affect the vital interests of the European Union as well as NATO" ("Yugoslavia," the 1993 Churchill Lecture (transcript), delivered on November 25, 1993, Guildhall, London, p. 5).

39 Following the July 2, 1990, Constitutional Declaration on Kosovo, issued in Belgrade, the parliament and the executive council of Kosovo were suspended. Soon after, the Albanian media, notably the daily *Rilindija* and Priština television, were closed down with the help of the police. All intellectual and academic activity was driven underground. For an account of these developments, see "The Interlude: 1890–1990."

Because of the Albanian boycott of the Serbian parliamentary elections of December 1992, the war criminal Željko Ražnjatović-Arkan, who ran for a seat as a representative of Kosovo portraying himself as a protector of Kosovo Serbs, was elected and remained in the post until the new elections of 1993, when he lost.

40 Perica Vučinić. "Kosovska akademija gluvih," *Vreme*, 7 March 1994, p. 27. During 1992, Janjevo, the richest village in Kosovo, numbering three thousand residents, saw the emigration of its majority Croats. They made their decision to leave their comfortable houses following the visit of Vojislav Šešelj to the village. The hard economic situation caused the local water supply to dry out, the medical center to close for two months, and 450 out of the former 500 private enterprises to close down (Bahri Cani, "Vojvoda došao, Hrvati krenuli," *Borba*, 14 February 1994, p. 11).

41 Milan Antić, "Od turizma do politike," *Borba*, 22 December 1992, p. 27.

42 The Humanitarian Law Fund reports, for example, the case of a Trepča miner, Sejdi Rahmani, who in 1986 received legal occupancy rights to his apartment from his place of employment. On December 7, 1992, a Serb accompanied by four other men, two of whom were in police uniform, broke into Rahmani's home and threatened to kill him if he did not clear out within an hour. The Secretariat of Urban Affairs in Pristina and the municipal court remained deaf to the charge of forced eviction filed by Ljirei Osmani, Rahmani's lawyer (*Spotlight Report No. 16: Kosovo Albanians II* [Belgrade: Humanitarian Law Center, February 1995], p. 10).

43 *Spotlight Report No. 16*, p. 28.

44 *Spotlight Report No. 16*, pp. 14–17.

45 In 1918, when Belgrade also tried to control Albanian education, Albanians opened underground centers of learning that worked successfully (see Ivo Banac, *The National Question in Yugoslavia: Origin, History, Politics* [Ithaca, NY: Columbia University Press, 1984], pp. 298–99). The current system continues that tradition.

46 The Albanian parallel educational system is composed of 418 elementary schools and 65 high schools, serving 312,000 children aged 7–10, close to 57,000 children of high school age, and a little over 12,000 students in their twenties. Twenty thousand teachers and professors work in the system (Perica Vučinić, "Novi Zakon fizike," *Vreme*, 17 February 1996, p. 20; see also *Spotlight Report No. 16*, p. 3). On the earlier period of the Albanian parallel school system, beginning in 1990, see Nataša Kandić, "Država u Plavom," *Vreme*, 9 August 1993, pp. 34–37.

Aryeh Neier describes a clinic run by a Catholic Mother Teresa organization, situated in a three-story house a family donated for the purpose and operated by exclusively Albanian women doctors assisted by interns in training (Neier, p. 27).

47 See Ivan Radovanović, "Kolevka se ljulja," *Vreme*, 5 April 1993, pp. 26–28; and Vuči-
    nić, "Novi Zakon fizike," pp. 20–21.

48 Vučinić, "Novi zakoni fizike," p. 21.

49 This was expressed in a statement by the federal minister Margit Savović on TV
    Politika, but it was not an official offer. Thus far, thirteen unsuccessful negotiation
    sessions regarding the Kosovo educational system have been held in Geneva, under
    the auspices of the Geneva Conference on Yugoslavia. The first to make a genuine
    attempt to discuss a peaceful integration of Albanians in the political, educational,
    and cultural life of Kosovo was the then prime minister of rump Yugoslavia, Milan
    Panić, in October 1992 (see V. Oroši and S. Dzezeiri, "Šal za Dvoje," *Vreme*, 19 Octo-
    ber 1992). Work groups to discuss the existing problems in the legislature, the court
    system, education, media, and health care, were founded. Panić pledged to return
    to work the Albanians who had been laid off and offered Rugova three seats in the
    government. The talks were met with resentment in Serbia and contributed to the
    ouster of Panić from the government.

50 Vučinić, "Novi Zakoni fizike," p. 21.

51 Lord David Owen is quoted by *Koha*, the Albanian weekly edited by Venton Suroi,
    as saying that "secessionists want the kind of autonomy that would lead to separa-
    tion [from Serbia], while unionists offer an amount of autonomy so small as to guar-
    antee the endurance of Serbia as an integral state." He further comments that the
    international community has to steer a course between the two (quoted in Perica
    Vučinić and Violeta Oroši, "Odgovori Beogradu," *Vreme*, 17 April 1995, p. 13).

    The international community vacillated in its stand toward Kosovo from the be-
    ginning. In the early stage, in 1991, the Conference on Security and Cooperation
    in Europe (CSCE) took the position that all former federal units, which included
    Kosovo, were entitled to statehood. Later on, however, this position was modified
    to a view that statehood could be guaranteed only to former republics and that
    Kosovo had the right of comprehensive autonomy within Serbia. Susan Woodward
    argues that the U.S. position in 1993 "left open the ambiguity over the status of
    Kosovo's borders and over the grounds for Albanian political rights." She sees this
    as a trap, analogous to the one faced in the peace negotiations in Bosnia: on the one
    hand Serbia received support for its territorial integrity, and on the other Kosovo
    Albanians received "encouragement and even legitimation for Albanian national
    aspirations" (*Balkan Tragedy: Chaos and Dissolution after the Cold War* (Washing-
    ton, D.C.: Brookings Institution, 1995), p. 343).

    In May 1993 in Washington, the agreement was reached that Kosovo should be
    given a high degree of autonomy (including political self-rule and elements of state-
    hood) within the framework of Serbia (Skeljzen Malici, "Albanski realizam," *Vreme*,
    6 June 1994, p. 19).

52 On Agani and Vlasi see *Vreme*, 14 March 1994, p. 26; *Vreme*, 31 October 1994, p. 15;
    Vreme, 13 February 1995, p. 28; and *Vreme*, 17 April 1995, p. 13. On Bakali and Quosja
    see *Vreme*, 13 February 1993, p. 28; and *Vreme*, 17 April 1995, p. 13. On Rugova see
    Vreme, 14 March 1994, p. 26. On the emergence of the new terrorist organization
    (Oslobodilačka Armija Kosova, or OAK) on the otherwise Ghandian political scene in
    Kosovo, see Milan Bečejić, "Olovo i Metohia," *Feral Tribune*, 27 January 1997, p. 29.

The author suggests the possibility that behind OAK, which has planted bombs and carried out unexplained assassinations in 1996–97, may stand the Belgrade regime.

53   Miloš Vasić and Dragoslav Grujić, "Tačka dodira na koti Čupino," *Vreme*, 27 June 1994, p. 24.

54   Gligorov was a member of the federal presidency in the early 1970s, and from 1974 to 1978 he was the president of the federal assembly. Thereafter he withdrew from politics until the late 1980s, when he was invited by the prime minister Ante Marković to be one of the team of experts requested to develop the draft of the new market reform. An interview indicative of Gligorov's political position and strategy was published in 1993 (see Dragan Nikolić, "Nismo zaljubljenici zabluda i mitova," *Borba*, 26–27 June 1993, pp. x–xi).

55   Nenad Lj. Stefanović, "Beograd-Skoplje, preko Atine," *Vreme*, 6 February 1995, p. 25.

56   The VMRO-DPMNE insist on preserving the national character of the state and thus require that the criteria for citizenship take into consideration the national composition of Macedonia.

57   Cited in Nenad Lj. Stefanović, "Malo balkansko čudo," *Vreme*, 19 October 1992, p. 33. The framers of the draft of Macedonian constitution originally defined citizenship in terms of residence, not ethnic origin. They encountered stiff resistance on the part of the VMRO, which held a little over one-third of the parliamentary seats and insisted that Macedonia be defined as a state of the Macedonian people. In the end a compromise was reached by saying that Macedonia provides "peace and a common home for both the Macedonian people and other nationalities living in [it]." This, however, angered both the VMRO and the Albanians (see Julie Mostov, "Democracy and the Politics of National Identity," in *Yugoslavia: Collapse, War, Crimes*, ed. Sonja Biserko [Belgrade: Centre for Anti-War Action, Belgrade Circle, 1993], pp. 24–25).

58   President Gligorov tried very hard to maintain neighborly relations with Serbia, despite Milošević's stubborn refusal to recognize Macedonia. Gligorov's position was based on two factors: his belief that the only effective and non-self-defeating tool in the Balkans was dialogue and Macedonia's economic dependence on the illegal trade with Serbia despite the UN-imposed sanctions. From the beginning, Gligorov's strategy in regard to Serbia had been much shrewder than the strategies of Slovenia or Croatia. In contrast with Croatia, Macedonian army units never blockaded YPA barracks (which triggered the war in Slovenia and Croatia), and Gligorov ensured that the army evacuated from Macedonia without incident (Dragan Nikolić, *Borba*, 26–27 June 1993, p. x).

59   Susan Woodward suggests that this ignited a struggle for national identity among other ethnic constituencies in Macedonia, with the Romanies, Turks, and Macedonian Muslims being the most worrisome for the Macedonian government (*Balkan Tragedy*, p. 508 n. 18).

On the political claims of the Turkish and the Romany minority in Macedonia see Nenad Lj. Stefanović, "Zraci Sunca iz Vergine," *Vreme*, 19 April 1993, p. 31.

60   Author's interview (July 1992) with Vesna Pešic, the chairperson of the Civic Alliance in Belgrade and a member of Zajedno coalition, and Nebojša Popov, the editor of *Republika*.

61 Julian Borger and Helena Smith, "Caught on the Edge of a Balkan Abyss," *Manchester Guardian Weekly*, 24 July 1994, p. 6; and Nenad Lj. Stefanović, "Blokade i cehovi," *Vreme*, 12 September 1994, p. 28. Greece introduced the boycott despite the partial international recognition of Macedonia in April 1993, and its admission into the UN, under the name Former Yugoslav Republic of Macedonia.

62 The motivation for Greece's refusal to recognize Macedonia, however, was domestic in nature, not international. Had it recognized Macedonia, Greece would have made itself vulnerable to claims for recognition by Greek Macedonians and Turks. In May 1994 Hristos Sideropoulos was prosecuted in Greece for statements he made in 1990 at a press conference in Copenhagen, in which he alleged that he had been denied the right to declare his Macedonian origin (see Aryeh Neier, "Watching Rights," *Nation*, 7 November 1994, p. 519).

63 Stojan Andov, the president of the Macedonian assembly, had insisted as early as 1993 that only an internationally supported plan of economic revival for the Balkans would fend off nationalist tensions and open the way to the democratic forces that had been silenced and marginalized (see Dragan Nikolić, "Sigurnost pod američkim kišobranom" [interview with Stojan Andov], *Borba*, 18–19 September 1993, pp. iv–v).

64 The international community helped Macedonia primarily by looking the other way as the trade between Macedonia and Serbia flourished at the height of the time when sanctions were being imposed against Serbia. Macedonia was considered one of the biggest violators of the sanctions (Raymond Bonner, "Balkan Conflict's Spread to Macedonia Is Feared," *New York Times*, 9 April 1995, pp. 12–13).

65 Nenad Lj. Stefanović, "Beograd-Skoplje, preko Atine," *Vreme*, 6 February 1995, p. 24.

66 The Muslims are concentrated in the southeastern Serbian region of Sandžak and Kosovo, in the underdeveloped southeastern municipalities of Tutin, Sjenica, Novi Pazar, Prijepolje, the central Serbian municipality of Priboj, the Kosovo municipalities of Leposavić, Dragoš, and Prizren, and the Montenegrin municipalities of Bijelo Polje, Pljevlja, and Berane. In all these regions the Serbian and Muslim settlements are intermixed.

67 Dačević-Čeko's paramilitaries took over all the strategic points in Pljevlja. Looting, shooting, and calls for the extermination of all Muslims were daily events. From Pljevlja Dačević-Čeko's paratroops crossed the border to the Goražde front in Bosnia, where they terrorized women and old people. Dačević-Čeko is also suspected of involvement in the later killings of the Muslims in Bukovica, and for the kidnappings of eighteen men from Sjeverin. Even though he was arrested a few times, he was released each time, most likely because of his connections with the leading politicians and the role of his paramilitaries in aiding the regular army forces (Velizar Brajović, "Pljevlja na buretu baruta," *Vreme*, 3 August 1992, pp. 29–31; Velizar Brajović, "Prst na okidaču," *Vreme*, 24 August 1992, pp. 30–31; Uroš Komlenović, "Čeko, jedna karijera," *Vreme*, 27 January 1996, pp. 12–13).

68 Nataša Kandić, "Stradanja Muslimana," *Vreme*, 17 May 1993, pp. 35–37.

69 Nine factories belonging to different firms that used to employ three thousand people were located on both sides of the border, between fifty and five hundred meters apart. Before the war, about fifteen hundred workers from the Rudo municipality in Bosnia worked in Priboj (see Zvonko Prijović and Zoran Šaponjić, "Puto-

vanje preko šesnaest graničnih prelaza," *Borba*, 11 March 1993, p. 11; and Zvonko Prijović, "Rat je u komšiluku," *Borba*, 3 September 1993, p. 26).

70 Dragan Todorović was the first journalist allowed to enter Sjeverin since the disappearance of the men ("Ni u Priboj, ni u Rudo—nidje," *Vreme*, 2 March 1996, p. 11).

71 This was confirmed by the president of the committee (see Velizar Brajović, "Istraga prekinuta," *Vreme*, 2 March 1996, p. 9; Filip Švarm and Velizar Brajović, "Zakopana istina," *Vreme*, 6 March 1995, pp. 18–21). Milan Lukić—the leader of the group Osvetnik, who participated on June 18, 1992, in the killing of twenty-one Muslims on the bridge in the Bosnian town of Višegrad—was considered a possible participant in the Štrpci kidnapping and was extradited to the authorities in Republika Srpska in May 1994, allegedly for trial. He was released immediately upon extradition.

72 *Spotlight Report No. 11: Policijska represija u Sandžaku* (Belgrade: Humanitarian Law Center, 23 March 1994), pp. 1–16. The report notes that in November and December 1993 alone, in Sjenica, Tutin, and Novi Pazar, three hundred persons were subjected to police violence during arms searches and interrogations, and it conveys the interesting perception among Muslims that those who after the first interrogation surrendered the arms to the police were treated less brutally and released more easily than those who did not. People thus began purchasing automatic rifles just so they could turn them over if they were searched. A sixty-eight-year-old villager said: "One can no longer find a gun to buy. Everyone is holding on to theirs to have when the police asks" (p. 7). Another person testified: "They requested that I turn in the M-48 and 3,000 bullets. I did not have either and did not want to say I did. That's why my son was beaten to a bloody pulp. He was in the next room and I heard them beating him. He confessed he had arms and two hundred bullets. Then they released us to give us time to bring in the arms by next Friday. I paid 1,900 German marks for an M-48, an automatic rifle, and two hundred bullets. Then they left us alone. Whoever has arms will surrender them and will be left alone. And whoever does not have it, that one's dead" (p. 8).

The authorities had apparently found a way to force the Muslims to finance the arming of the Serbian forces.

73 In an interview in 1995, Ljajić said that a social science textbook for the fourth grade did not mention Muslims as being among the minorities of rump Yugoslavia and a geography textbook remarked that "inventing new nations, such as Muslims, turned out to be a disruptive factor" (cited in Perica Vučinić, "Oprezan iskorak," *Vreme*, 8 May 1995, p. 20).

74 S. Biševac, "Izmedju izlaska i bojkota," *Naša Borba*, 28 May 1996, p. 5.

75 Ljajić was quoted in *Naša Borba* as saying at the Naša Borba Round Table on Sandžak, that Milošević counted on the likelihood that by maintaining the status quo, time would work for him, since Muslims would be leaving the region in increasing numbers (*Naša Borba*, "Round table, Izaći na izbore ili ne," 23 April 1996, p. 13).

76 Vojvodina belonged to southern Hungary from 1683–1918. Under the Turks it was a vacant marshland. To repopulate it and turn it into a reliable frontier, Maria Theresa

encouraged peasants of many nationalities—Serbs, Croats, Magyars, Ruthenians, Slovaks, Germans, Romanians—to settle in the fertile plains along the Danube and defend them. In the eighteenth century, however, Vojvodina also became a cultural center. Its capital, Novi Sad, became the home of the major Serbian cultural society Matica Srpska. Located on the fringes of the great empire, Vojvodina towns developed a specific sophisticated culture and nurtured a polyglot population of about twenty-five larger and smaller ethnic groups that lived in harmony and prosperity until the 1990s. The only ethnic group ever expelled from the region before the terror of 1991 were the 360,000 Volksdeutsch Germans (Germans who had lived for generations in former Yugoslavia), forced to leave after World War II even though many among them had been anti-Nazi. (Some, however, participated in the notorious Prince Eugen ss division.)

77 Dimitrije Boarov, "Vojvodina na zalasku stoleća," *Vreme,* 13 January 1996, pp. 23–25. On the economic collapse of Novi Sad see Boarov, "Kako zaustaviti opadanje," Glasnik Edition No. 6/97, *Republika,* February 1997, p. iii.

78 The census of 1991 recorded 1,151,353 Serbs; 340,946 Hungarians; 97,644 Croatians; 63,941 Slovaks; 44,721 Montenegrins; 38,831 Romanians; 16,641 Macedonians; 17,887 Ruthenians; 168,859 Yugoslavs, and 71,703 others (Dimitrije Boarov, "Umor od Seoba," *Vreme,* September 1992, p. 33. See also Dušan Breznik, *Stanovništvo Jugoslavije* [Titograd: Chronos, 1991], p. 169).

79 On the gradual transformation (1988–91) of TV Novi Sad from an independent station to an outpost of the Serbian regime see the study written by the investigative team of the Independent Association of Vojvodina Journalists, "Sukobi i raspleti na TV Novi Sad, *Republika* (May 1993): 19–30.

80 On the methods of ethnic cleansing in Vojvodina and the resistance of Hungarians and Croats and the Serbs who supported them, see James Ridgeway and Jasminka Udovički, "War without End," *Village Voice,* 10 November 1995, pp. 30–36.

81 Both Croats and Hungarians genuinely felt that Vojvodina was where they belonged. Slavica Rakoš from Hrtkovci, a Croatian by origin, said to the author in the fall of 1992: "Croatia is a foreign country to me. We've been living here for three hundred years. We have nowhere to go. The only place they can take us is the cemetery."

82 In March 1993 the minister for human rights, Margit Savović, who visited Hrtkovci, said there was no ethnic cleansing in the region (S. Džakula, "Savović: Nema etničkog čišćenja," *Borba,* 23 March 1993, p. 9).

83 For the Belgrade authorities the troubling groups are the Democratic Association of Vojvodina Hungarians (DZVM) and its spin-off, the Association of Vojvodina Hungarians (SVM); the Reform Party of Vojvodina (RPV); the League of Vojvodina Social Democrats (LSV); and the Vojvodina Club—all organizations that espouse one form or another of limited autonomism. The DZVM submitted to the Belgrade authorities a "concept of three-tier autonomy"—that is, personal autonomy (implying guarantees of the cultural and ethnic identity of minorities); territorial autonomy (implying self-government of Hungarian municipalities through a separate legislature, schooling system, police, and the creation of an association of municipalities); and local rule (implying that Hungarians in other parts of former Yugoslavia would en-

joy home rule). Pal Šandor, a member of DZVM, formulated some basic principles that would advance a solution for the minority status in Serbia: (1) minorities must be granted collective rights in the realm of education, culture, the media, and the use of native language; (2) minorities must be granted political rights ("political subjectivity") allowing them to elect their representatives for assembly bodies in the state; (3) the request for autonomy must not be identified with the intention to secede; on the contrary, the request for autonomy implies recognition of the state granting the autonomy; (4) in the territory of former Yugoslavia the same standard should be applied to all minorities: whatever Serbia demands for its minority in Croatia, Serbia must grant its own minorities (Pal Šandor, "Teze za rešavanje pitanja nacionalnih majina u Srbiji" *Republika*, 16–31 December 1995).

84   Laslo Joza, a Hungarian lawyer from the Vojvodina town of Subotica, noted in 1995 that most European governments were restrained in their responses to the pleas of the Vojvodina minority groups for support for their rights and autonomy (Laslo Joza, "Vlast i manjine," *Vreme*, 15 May 1995, p. 23).

85   I have in mind people of whom some are party leaders, and other members of various civic groups: Selim Bešlagić, Sejfudin Tokić, Zlatko Lagumdžija, Bogić Bogiće-vić, Mirko Pejanović, Milorad Dodik, Mica Carević, Milorad Pupovac, Veljko Dža-kula, Branko Horvat, Ivan Zvonimir Čičak, Vesna Pešic, Nebojša Popov, and others.

86   Sejfudin Tokić, a Bosnian parliament member, commented on this paradox at the November 1994 international conference titled "Is Europe Possible without Multi-culturalism?" held in Tuzla, the town universally perceived as heroic for having preserved its multicultural spirit. Tokić thanked the guests for thinking so highly of Tuzla but said: "Tuzla is not a rare oasis of multinational life in the vortex of this war. Many Bosnians, hostages of their national oligarchies, are simply unable to behave like Tuzlans—in part because of the support great powers have given to those oligarchies" (quoted in Stojan Obradović, "Kad se i Musliman krsti," *Vreme*, 21 November 1994, p. 24).

87   Of the three armies, that of the Republika Srpska, no longer supported by Belgrade, is the weakest. It has been reduced to less than one-third its original size, and for lack of funds has allowed a good deal of its military equipment to fall into disrepair. Owing to noncompliance with the Dayton Accord, Republika Srpska has been vir-tually cut off from international aid, receiving only 3 percent of what goes to the Federation (Susan Woodward, Roundtable discussion, National Convention of the American Association for the Advancement of Slavic Studies, November 14–17, 1996). The unemployment rate among the Bosnian Serbs is 90 percent (see Chris Hedges, "Bosnian Serb Area Destitute and Vulnerable," *New York Times*, 11 March 1997, p. A4). When NATO peacekeepers leave Bosnia, the American-trained and freshly equipped Bosnian army will find it difficult to resist attacking the destitute Serbian entity in order to regain more territory.

88   The figures on the war casualties stem from the author's March 1997 interview with Jovan Divjak, the Bosnian general whom president Izetbegović retired in 1997.

BIBLIOGRAPHY

In addition to the sources listed, the authors made extensive use of the daily *Borba*, the weeklies *Vreme, Feral Tribune*, and *Svijet*, the monthly *Republika*, and *Spotlight Reports* of the Humanitarian Law Center in Belgrade. These and other such publications are cited in the notes following each chapter.

Babić, Anto, et al., eds. *Istorija naroda Jugoslavije*. Vols. 1 and 2. Beograd: Prosveta, 1953.

Banac, Ivo. *The National Question in Yugoslavia: Origin, History, Politics*. Ithaca, N.Y.: Columbia University Press, 1984.

Banac, Ivo, John G. Ackerman, and Roman Szporluk, eds. *Nation and Ideology: Essays in Honor of Wayne S. Vucinich*. Boulder, Colo.: East European Monographs; distributed by Columbia University Press, 1981.

Berberoglu, Berch, ed. *The National Question: Nationalism, Ethnic Conflict, and Self-Determination in the Twentieth Century*. Philadelphia: Temple University Press, 1995.

Bigelow, Bruce. "Centralization versus Decentralization in Interwar Yugoslavia." *Southern Europe* 1, no. 2 (1974).

Biserko, Sonja, ed. *Yugoslavia: Collapse, War, Crimes*. Belgrade: Centre for Anti-War Action, Belgrade Circle, 1993.

Blagojević, Marina. *Iseljavanje Srba sa Kosova: Trauma i/ili katarza*. Ogledi Edition, *Republika*, November 1995.

Bogdanović, Bogdan. *Mrtvouzice*. Zagreb: August Cesarec, 1988.

Bogosavljević, Srdjan. *Drugi svetski rat—žrtve u Jugoslaviji*. Ogledi Edition, *Republika*, June 1995.

Borden, Anthony, et al., eds. *Breakdown: War and Reconstruction in Yugoslavia*. London: Institute for War and Peace Reporting, 1992.

Bugarski, Ranko, *Govor skrivenih namera*. Ogledi Edition, *Republika*, June 1995.

———. *Jezik od rata do mira*. Beograd: Beogradski krug, 1994.

Ćerić, Salim. *Muslimani srpskohrvatskog jezika*. Sarajevo: Svijetlost, 1968.

Cerović, Stojan. *Bahanalije*. Beograd: Vreme, 1993.

Ćirković, Sima. *O kosovskom boju 1389*. Prizren-Beograd-Ljubljana, 1987.

Clissold, Stephen, ed. *A Short History of Yugoslavia from Early Times to 1966*. London: Cambridge University Press, 1966.

Cohen, Leonard. *Broken Bonds: The Disintegration of Yugoslavia.* Boulder, Colo.: Westview Press, 1993.

Čolović, Ivan. *Fudbal, huligani i rat.* Ogledi Edition, *Republika,* June 1995.

———. *Bordel ratnika.* Beograd: Biblioteka XX vek, 1993.

Čolović, Ivan, and Aljoša Mimica, eds. *Druga Srbija.* Beograd: Plato Beogradski Krug, Borba, 1992.

Čubrilović, Vasa. "Poreklo muslimanskog plemstva u Bosni i Hercegovini." *Jugoslovenski Istorijski Časopis* 1 (1935): pp. 368–403.

Čuvalo, Ante. *The Croatian National Movement, 1966-1972.* Boulder, Colo.: East European Monographs; distributed by Columbia University Press, 1990.

Cvijić, Jovan. *Aneksija Bosne i Hercegovine.* Beograd: Državna štamparija, 1908.

Dedijer, Vladimir. *Tito.* Rijeka: Liburnija, 1981.

———. *Novi prilozi za biografiju Josipa Broza Tita.* Zagreb: Mladost, 1980.

———. *Sarajevo, 1914.* Beograd: Prosveta, 1966.

———. *Tito Speaks: His Self-Portrait and Struggle with Stalin.* London: Weidenfeld and Nicolson, 1953.

Dedijer, Vladimir, Ivan Božic, Sima Ćirković, and Milorad Ekmečić, eds. *History of Yugoslavia.* New York: McGraw-Hill, 1974.

Dimitrijević, Vojin. "Medjunarodno zaštićena ljudska prava u Jugoslaviji." *Anali pravnog fakulteta u Beogradu* (1987): 715–27.

———. "The Yugoslav Precedent: Keep What You Have." In *Breakdown: War and Reconstruction in Yugoslavia,* ed. Anthony Borden, et al. London: Institute for War and Peace Reporting, 1992.

Djilas, Aleksa. *The Contested Country: Yugoslav Unity and Communist Revolution, 1919-1953.* Cambridge: Harvard University Press, 1991.

Djilas, Milovan. *Conversations with Stalin.* New York: Harcourt Brace and World, 1962.

———. "Novi Tok Istorije." *Socijalizam* 1 (1990).

———. *Tito.* New York: Harcourt Brace Jovanovich, 1980.

———. *Wartime.* New York: Harcourt Brace Jovanovich, 1977.

Djordjević, Dimitrije. *The Creation of Yugoslavia 1914-1918.* Santa Barbara, Calif.: Clio Press, 1980.

Djukić, Slavoljub. *Izmedju slave i anateme.* Beograd: Filip Višnjić, 1994.

———. *Kako se dogodio vodja.* Beograd: Filip Višnjić, 1992.

Doder, Dusko. *The Yugoslavs.* New York: Random House, 1978.

Donia, Robert J., and John V. A. Fine. *Bosnia and Hercegovina: A Tradition Betrayed.* New York: Columbia University Press, 1994.

Ekmečić, Milorad. *Stvaranje Jugoslavije 1790-1918.* Vols. 1 and 2. Beograd: Prosveta, 1989.

Fine, John V. A. *The Early Medieval Balkans.* Ann Arbor: University of Michigan Press, 1991.

———. *The Late Medieval Balkans: A Critical Survey from the Late Twelfth Century to the Ottoman Conquest.* Ann Arbor: University of Michigan Press, 1987.

———. *The Bosnian Church: A New Interpretation: A Study of the Bosnian Church and*

Its Place in State and Society from the Thirteenth to the Fifteenth Centuries. Boulder: Colo.: East European Quarterly; distributed by Columbia University Press, 1975.

Gagnon, V. P. "Serbia's Road to War." *Journal of Democracy* 5, no. 2 (April 1994).

Gayim, E. *The Principle of Self-Determination: A Study of Its Historical and Legal Evolution.* Oslo: Norwegian Institute of Human Rights, 1990.

Glenny, Misha. *The Fall of Yugoslavia.* New York: Penguin, 1992.

Gojković, Drinka. *Trauma bez katarze.* Ogledi Edition, *Republika*, June 1995.

Gompert, David. "How to Defeat Serbia." *Foreign Policy* 73 (July/August 1994).

Gross, Mirjana. "Croatian National Integrationist Ideologies from the End of Illyrianism to the Creation of Yugoslavia." *Austrian History Notebook* 15–16 (1979–80).

Gow, James, "Deconstructing Yugoslavia." *Survival* 33 (July–August 1991).

Habermas, Jürgen. *Strukturwandel der Öffentlichkeit.* Darmstadt und Neuwied: Herman Luchterhand Verlag GmbH, 1978.

Horvat, Branko, *Kosovsko pitanje,* Zagreb: Globus, 1988.

———. *Jugoslavensko društvo u krizi: Kritički ogledi i prijedlozi reformi.* Zagreb: Globus, 1985.

Hudelist, Darko. *Kosovo, Bitka bez iluzija.* Zagreb: Centar za informacije i publicitet, 1989.

Janjić, Dušan, and Paul Shoup, eds. *Bosna i Hercegovina izmedju rata i mira.* Beograd: Dom omladine, 1992.

Jelavich, Barbara. *History of the Balkans.* Vols. 1 and 2. New York: Cambridge University Press, 1983.

Jelavich, Charles. "Serbian Nationalism and the Question of Union with Croatia in the Nineteenth Century." *Balkan Studies* 3 (1962).

Jović, Borisav. *Poslednji Dani SFRJ.* Beograd: Politika, 1995.

Kadijević, Veljko. *Moje Vidjenje raspada: Vojske bez države.* Belgrade: Politika, 1993.

Kann, Robert, Bela Kiraly, and Paula S. Fichtner. *The Hapsburg Empire in the First World War.* New York: Columbia University Press, 1977.

Lampe, John R. *Yugoslavia: Twice There Was a Country.* Cambridge: Cambridge University Press, 1966.

Lapidoh, Ruth. "Sovereignty in Transition." *Journal of International Affairs* 45, no. 2 (winter 1992).

Lederer, Ivo. *Yugoslavia at the Paris Peace Conference.* New Haven: Yale University Press, 1963.

Letica, Slaven, and Mario Nobilo. *JNA—Rat protiv Hrvatske.* Zagreb: Globus, 1994.

Lydall, Harold. *Yugoslavia in Crisis.* Oxford: Clarendon Press, 1989.

MacKenzie, David. *Ilya Garašanin: Balkan Bismarck.* Boulder, Colo.: East European Monographs; distributed by Columbia University Press, 1985.

Madžar, Ljubomir. *Ko koga eksploatiše.* Ogledi Edition, *Republika*, September 1995.

Malcolm, Noel. *Bosnia: A Short History.* New York: New York University Press, 1994.

McClellan, Woodford. *Svetozar Marković and the Origins of Balkan Socialism.* Princeton: Princeton University Press, 1964.

Milosavljević, Olivera. *Upotreba autoriteta nauke.* Ogledi Edition, *Republika*, July 1995.

Milošević, Slobodan. *Godine Raspleta.* Beograd: BIGZ, 1989.

Nakarada, Radmila, Lidija Basta-Posavec, and Slobodan Samardžic, eds. *Raspad Jugoslavije, produžetak ili kraj agonije.* Beograd: Institut za Evropske studije, 1991.

Nenadović, Aleksandar. *Politika u nacionalistickoj oluji.* Ogledi Edition, *Republika,* April 1995.

Pavlinić Vlado, ed. *Okovana Bosna: Razgovor/Adil Zulfikarpašić, Vlado Gotovac, Mika Tripalo, Ivo Banac.* Zurich: Bošnjački Institut, 1995.

Pavlowitch, Stevan K. "Who Is Balkanizing Whom? The Misunderstanding between the Debris of Yugoslavia and an Unprepared West." *Daedalus* 123, no. 2 (spring 1994).

Petranović, Branko. *Istorija Jugoslavije 1918–1978.* Beograd: Nolit, 1978.

Popov, Nebojša. *Srpski populizam.* Special monograph edition, *Vreme,* 24 May 1993.

Popov, Nebojša, ed. *Srpska Strana Rata: Trauma i katarza u istorijskom pamćenju.* Beograd: Republika, 1996.

Popović, Srdja, Janča Dejan, and Tanja Petovar. *Kosovski čvor, drešiti ili seci?* Beograd: Republika, 1990.

Pribićević, Svetozar. *Diktatura kralja Aleksandra.* Beograd: Prosveta, 1952.

Ramet, Sabrina. *Balkan Babel: The Disintegration of Yugoslavia from the Death of Tito to Ethnic War.* Boulder, Colo.: Westview Press, 1996.

———. "Western Peace-Making in the Balkans: A Skeptic's View." *South Slav Journal* 17, nos. 1–2 (spring–summer 1996).

———. *Nationalism and Federalism in Yugoslavia, 1962–1991.* Bloomington: Indiana University Press, 1992.

Rašković, Jovan. *Luda Zemlja.* Beograd: Akvarijus, 1990.

Roberts, Walter A. *Tito, Mihailovich, and the Allies, 1941–1945.* New Brunswick: Rutgers University Press, 1973.

Roksandić, Drago. *Srbi u Hrvatskoj od 15. stoljeca do naših dana.* Zagreb: Vijesnik, 1991.

Rothenberg, Gunther. *The Military Border in Croatia, 1740–1881.* Chicago: University of Chicago Press, 1966.

———. *The Austrian Military Border in Croatia, 1522–1747.* Chicago: University of Chicago Press, 1960.

Rusinow, Dennison. *Yugoslavia: A Fractured Federalism.* Washington, D.C.: Wilson Center Press, 1988.

———. *The Yugoslav Experiment, 1948–1974.* Berkeley: University of California Press, 1977.

Seton-Watson, R. W. *The Southern Slav Question and the Habsburg Monarchy.* London: Constable, 1911.

Seton-Watson, R. W. and R. G. D. Laffan. "Yugoslavia between the Wars." In *A Short History of Yugoslavia,* ed. Stephen Clossold. London: Cambridge University Press, 1966.

Sharp, Jane M. O. *Bankrupt in the Balkans: British Policy in Bosnia.* London: Institute for Public Policy Research, 1992.

Shoup, Paul. *Communism and the Yugoslav National Question.* New York: Columbia University Press, 1960.

Singleton, Frederick Bernard. *A Short History of the Yugoslav Peoples.* Cambridge: Cambridge University Press, 1985.

———. *Twentieth Century Yugoslavia.* New York: Columbia University Press, 1976.

Stambolić, Ivan. *Put u bespuće.* Beograd: Radio B-92, 1995.

Stavrionos, L. S. *The Balkans since 1453.* New York: Rinehart, 1958.

Stiglmayer, Alexandra. *Mass Rape.* Lincoln: University of Nebraska Press, 1944.

Sugar, Peter F. *Southeastern Europe under Ottoman Rule, 1354-1804.* Seattle: University of Washington Press, 1977.

Sumner, Benedict Humphrey. *Russia and the Balkans, 1870-1880.* Oxford: Clarendon Press, 1937.

Szasz, Paul C. "The Quest for a Bosnian Constitution: Legal Aspects of Constitutional Proposals Relating to Bosnia." *Fordham International Law Journal* 19, no. 2 (December 1995).

Tomasevic, Jozo. *The Chetniks.* Stanford: Stanford University Press, 1975.

Trotsky, Leon. *The Balkan Wars, 1912-13: The War Correspondence of Leon Trotsky.* New York: Monad Press, 1980.

Tucović, Dimitrije. *Srbija i Albanija.* Beograd-Zagreb: Kultura, 1946.

Udovički, Jasminka. "Nationalism, Ethnic Conflict, and Self-Determination in Former Yugoslavia." In *The National Question,* ed. Berch Berberoglu. Philadelphia: Temple University Press, 1995.

Udovički, Jasminka, and James Ridgeway, eds. *Yugoslavia's Ethnic Nightmare: The Inside Story of Europe's Unfolding Ordeal.* New York: Lawrence Hill Books, 1995.

Vlasto, A. P. *The Entry of the Slavs into Christendom: An Introduction to the Medieval History of the Slavs.* Cambridge: Cambridge University Press, 1970.

Vucinich, Wayne C. "Mlada Bosna and the First World War." In *The Hapsburg Empire in the First World War,* ed. Robert A. Kann, Bela Kiraly, and Paula S. Fichtner. New York: Columbia University Press, East European Quarterly, 1977.

———. *Serbia between East and West.* Stanford: Stanford University Press, 1954.

Weller, Marc. "The International Response to the Dissolution of the Socialist Federal Republic of Yugoslavia." *American Journal of International Law* 86 (1992).

West, Richard. *Tito and the Rise and Fall of Yugoslavia.* London: Sinclair-Stevenson, 1995.

Wilson, Duncan. *The Life and Times of Vuk Stefanovic Karadžić.* Oxford: Clarendon Press, 1970.

Woodward, Susan L. *Balkan Tragedy: Chaos and Dissolution after the Cold War.* Washington, D.C.: Brookings Institution, 1995.

Zametica, John. "The Yugoslav Conflict," Adelphi Paper, no. 270. London: Institute for International and Strategic Studies, 1992.

Zirojević, Olga. *Kosovo u istorijskom pamćenju.* Ogledi Edition, *Republika,* March 1995.

Zulfikarpašić, Adil, Vlado Gotovac, Mika Tripalo, and Ivo Banac. *Okovana Bosna: razgovor.* Zurich: Bošnjački Institut, 1995.

Županov, Josip. *Marginalije o Društvenoj Krizi.* Zagreb: Globus, 1983.

CONTRIBUTORS

Sven Balas is the pseudonym of a young Croatian writer and broadcaster who wishes to remain anonymous.

Branka Prpa-Jovanović (Croatian) is a historian who works at the Institute of the History of Modern Serbia in Belgrade.

Milan Milošević (Serbian) is one of the founders of *Vreme* and its political commentator. He is a member of the Honor Court of the Independent Association of Serbian Journalists. From 1972 to 1990 he was a journalist and an editor at the Belgrade weekly *NIN.*

James Ridgeway, the Washington political correspondent for the *Village Voice,* is the author of more than a dozen books on domestic and international politics, including *Blood in the Face, The Rise of a New White Culture, The March to War,* and *Red Light.*

Stipe Sikavica (Croatian) was a journalist for *The People's Army* and *Front,* two principal army periodicals in the former Yugoslavia. He was forced to retire in 1991 after publishing an article on the role of the military establishment in helping Milošević consolidate his power. He has been a freelance writer since 1989 for *Borba* (now *Naša Borba*), the Belgrade independent daily, and *Republika,* the independent monthly.

Ejub Štitkovac (Muslim) graduated from Gazi Husrevbeg, Sarajevo's Islamic theological school, and worked as an imam for two years near Mostar. He is currently a commentator on the Islamic and Arab world for the independent daily *Naša Borba* and the author of a book of poems and a novel about his Bosnian hometown of Žepa.

Mirko Tepavac (mixed Serbian and Croatian origin) was the minister of foreign affairs in the former Yugoslavia from the 1960s until he resigned in protest in 1972. He is now the main contributor to *Republika,* the independent opposition monthly in Belgrade.

Ivan Torov (Macedonian) is a political commentator for the independent Belgrade daily *Naša Borba* and the recipient of *Borba*'s annual award for journalism for 1987. Before the war he also wrote for *Danas* (published in Zagreb) and *Oslobodjenje* (published in Sarajevo).

Jasminka Udovički (Serbian) is Professor of Social Science, Department of Critical Studies, at the Massachusetts College of Art in Boston. She is a coauthor of *The National*

Question, with Berch Berberoglu. Her reports on the wars in former Yugoslavia have appeared in the *Village Voice, Radical America,* and *In These Times.*

Susan L. Woodward is a Senior Fellow at the Brookings Institution and the author of *Balkan Tragedy: Chaos and Dissolution after the Cold War* and *Socialist Unemployment: The Political Economy of Yugoslavia, 1945-1990.*

INDEX

Library of Congress Cataloging-in-Publication Data
Burn this house : the making and unmaking of Yugoslavia /
Jasminka Udovički and James Ridgeway, editors.
Includes bibliographical references and index.
ISBN 0-8223-2001-0 (cloth : alk. paper). —
ISBN 0-8223-1997-7 (pbk. : alk. paper)
1. Yugoslavia—History.   2. Yugoslav War, 1991–   —Causes.
3. Yugoslav War, 1991–   —Protest movements.
I. Udovički, Jasminka, 1945–   .   II. Ridgeway, James, 1936–   .
DR1246.B87 1997   949.703—dc21   97-21606 CIP